Letters and Photographs from the Battle Country

The World War I Memoir of Margaret Hall

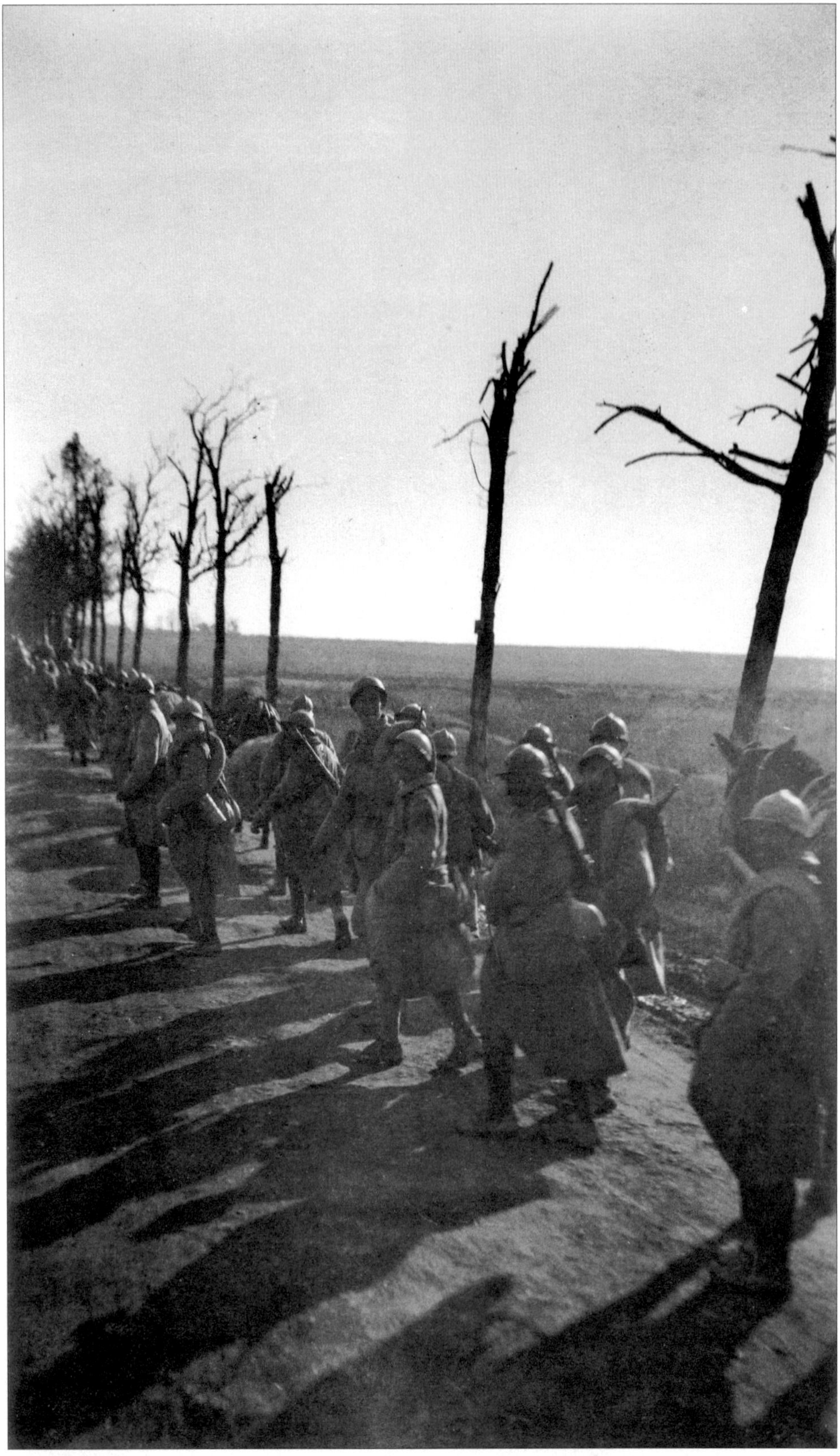

Letters and Photographs from the Battle Country

The World War I Memoir of Margaret Hall

Edited by Margaret R. Higonnet
with Susan Solomon

Massachusetts Historical Society
Boston, 2014

Distributed by the University of Virginia Press, Charlottesville

© 2014 Massachusetts Historical Society
All Rights Reserved

Library of Congress Cataloging-in-Publication Data

Hall, Margaret, 1876-1963.
  Letters and photographs from the Battle Country : the World War I memoir of Margaret Hall / edited by Margaret R. Higonnet with Susan Solomon.
    pages cm
  Includes bibliographical references and index.
  ISBN 978-1-936520-07-7
  1. Hall, Margaret, 1876-1963. 2. Hall, Margaret, 1876-1963–Correspondence. 3. World War, 1914-1918–War work–France. 4. War relief–France–History–20th century. 5. Canteens (Establishments)–France–History–20th century. 6. American Red Cross–History–20th century. 7. Women volunteers–United States–Biography. 8. World War, 1914-1918–Personal narratives, American. 9. United States. Army. American Expeditionary Forces–History. 10. World War, 1914-1918–France–Pictorial works. I. Higonnet, Margaret R. II. Solomon, Susan, Ph.D. III. Title.
  D638.U5H36 2014
  940.4'771092–dc23
  [B]
                                2014010547

Book design by James T. Connolly and Ondine E. Le Blanc.

Contents

Illustrations	vi
Acknowledgments	xi
Introduction	xv
American Relief Organizations in France	1
Wartime Paris	11
The Canteen at Châlons-sur-Marne	27
The American Expeditionary Force	43
Armistice	67
Refugees and the Repatriated	77
Battlefield Tourism, Souvenirs, and a Sacred Land	91
Destruction and Reconstruction	105
The Allied Occupation of the Rhineland	123
Cemeteries and Commemoration	135
Versailles Treaty	157
Appendices	
Biographical Key	171
Selected Chronology of World War I	180
Places and Monuments: The Geography of War	189
Period Terms	199
Foreign Terms	200
Notes	202
Index	221

Illustrations

All photographs by Margaret Hall unless otherwise indicated. The images in this book are reproduced from the typescript at the Massachusetts Historical Society except where otherwise indicated. Each title reproduced below reflects the caption that Hall wrote into the typescript. To see reproductions of all 271 photographs that Hall pasted into the MHS copy of the typescript, visit www.masshist.org/photographs/hall.

Poilus.	ii
MHS seq. no. 1. Printed from Cohasset Historical Society (CHS) copy.	
M. H. ready to sail.	xiv
Courtesy of Suzanne Diefenbach.	
Canteen garden.	xvii
From entry September 25 to October 12, 1918. MHS seq. no. 48a. CHS.	
Cigarettes	xix
From entry September 25 to October 12, 1918. MHS seq. no. 52a. CHS.	
106th Regiment—(Châlons) home from the war.	xxiv
From entry February 11th. MHS seq. no. 217. CHS.	
M. P. B. was at the station	xxvi
From entry Treaty of Versailles. MHS seq. no. 306a. CHS.	
Entrance to Fort Douaumont.	xxviii
From entry Memorial Day, 1919. MHS seq. no. 243a. CHS.	
Margaret at Bryn-Mawr College	xxx
Courtesy of Suzanne Diefenbach.	
M. H. at Ecury Oct. 13. 1918. French Ambulance No. 5.	1, 53
From entry October 13th. MHS seq. no. 93b.	
Photographer unidentified (Margaret Hall is in the photo). CHS.	
Cenotaph. July 13th 1919	11
From entry Notes from Diary. MHS seq. no. 330a. CHS.	
—"three long ones"—	26
From entry September 25 to October 12, 1918. MHS seq. no. 60a. CHS.	
Where I sat.	27
From entry November 29th to December 11th. MHS seq. no. 156. This is a commercial photograph; the canteen worker pictured is not Margaret Hall. CHS.	
Outside Canteen.	29
From entry September 25 to October 12, 1918. MHS seq. no. 46e. CHS.	
"Military procession underneath—"	33
From entry September 25 to October 12, 1918. MHS seq. no. 60.	
Châlons "Caves."	36
From entry September 25 to October 12, 1918. MHS seq. no. 56. CHS.	

Abri in the garden.	38
From entry September 25 to October 12, 1918. MHS seq. no. 71. CHS.	
Americans.	43
From entry Thanksgiving, November 28th. MHS seq. no. 154b. CHS.	
On their way to the "caves"—for the night.	49
From entry September 25 to October 12, 1918. MHS seq. no. 74d. CHS.	
Ambulance— Ecury.	58
From entry October 13th. MHS seq. no. 105b. CHS.	
Canteen Kitchen. Cook and her helpers.	61
From entry October 20th to 26th. MHS seq. no. 110b. Photographer unidentified (postcard). CHS.	
[No caption].	67
From entry November 11th. MHS seq. no. 127. CHS.	
"Little villages"—	73
From entry November 11th. MHS seq. no. 140b. CHS.	
"Enormous holes"	74
From entry November 11th. MHS seq. no. 136a. CHS.	
"75s"	76
From entry February 11th. MHS seq. no. 215a. CHS.	
[No caption].	77
From entry Notes from Diary. MHS seq. no. 328b. CHS.	
Later surrounded by barbed wire as protection against American souvenir hunters	91
From entry Memorial Day, 1919. MHS seq. no. 282c. CHS.	
Dug-outs: Pinon— (Elsa Bowman)	93
From entry Notes from Diary. MHS seq. no. 345. CHS.	
Battle-field Cemetery	98
From entry December 18th. MHS seq. no. 171a. CHS.	
German trench and barbed wire.	101
From entry December 18th. MHS seq. no. 174c. CHS.	
Monfaucon.	104
From entry June 23rd. MHS seq. no. 295a.	
Verdun.	105
From entry June 23rd. MHS seq. no. 290a. CHS.	
Verdun.	110
From entry June 23rd. MHS seq. no. 292c. CHS.	
Top of Fort Douaumont.	114
From entry January 11th. MHS seq. no. 201a. CHS.	

German trenches as seen from Fort. 114
French barbed wire in foreground.
From entry January 11th. MHS seq. no. 201b. CHS.

[No caption]. 123
From entry March 13th. MHS seq. no. 223a. CHS.

Anywhere in France, in the "Zone des Armeés". 135
From entry September 25 to October 12, 1918. MHS seq. no. 40.

The Cromwells. 140
From entry April 1st–July 1st. MHS seq. no. 239.

Mort Homme— 142
From entry Verdun and The Argonne. MHS seq. no. 249. CHS.

American graves decorated by the French. 150
From entry Memorial Day, 1919. MHS seq. no. 268b. CHS.

Croix-de-Guerre— Châlons canteen. 155
From entry June 23rd. MHS seq. no. 300. CHS.

General Pétain 157
From entry Notes from Diary. MHS seq. no. 335b. CHS.

Belgium. 161
From entry Notes from Diary. MHS seq. no. 360. CHS.

Last day of Canteen— 162
From entry Treaty of Versailles. MHS seq. no. 312b.

Cloth Hall—1919— Tommies 164
Notes from Diary. MHS seq. no. 323b. CHS.

German Gun Emplacement. Coucy-le-Château. 167
From entry Notes from Diary. MHS seq. no. 343c. CHS.

German coast protection—Seebrugge. 169
From entry Notes from Diary. MHS seq. no. 351b. CHS.

Figures 1-25 appear in the insert following 66.

Fig. 1   In the garden.
From entry September 25 to October 12, 1918. MHS seq. no. 46b. CHS.

Fig. 2   Six Nationalities
From entry September 25 to October 12, 1918. MHS seq. no. 46c. CHS.

Fig. 3   Outside Canteen.
From entry September 25 to October 12, 1918. MHS seq. no. 46d. CHS.

Fig. 4   Algerian graves.
From entry October 27th to November 1st, 1918. MHS seq. no. 119b. CHS.

Fig. 5   Châlons ruins.
From entry September 25 to October 12, 1918. MHS seq. no. 52b. CHS.

Illustrations ix

Fig. 6   "Châlons hard suffering"
From entry September 25 to October 12, 1918. MHS seq. no. 74b.

Fig. 7   Station platform.
From entry October 4th. MHS seq. no. 87a. CHS.

Fig. 8   Camouflage. (Road to Douaumont)
From entry October 6th. MHS seq. no. 87f. CHS.

Fig. 9   Coffee.
From entry October 13th. MHS seq. no. 98b.

Fig. 10   [No caption].
From entry October 13th. MHS seq. no. 98a.

Fig. 11   Écury—
From entry October 13th. MHS seq. no. 100b.

Fig. 12   Champagne forest.
From entry December 22nd. MHS seq. no. 174a.

Fig. 13   Train of prisoners— Germans— Turks— Bulgarians.
From entry Châlons, January. MHS seq. no. 209.

Fig. 14   "France triumphant rising out of her ruins"
From entry November 11th. MHS seq. no. 134.

Fig. 15   Camouflaged trench—Douaumont.
From entry January 11th. MHS seq. no. 197b.

Fig. 16   Road to Rheims.
From entry February 11th. MHS seq. no. 215b.

Fig. 17   American Army.
From entry April 1st-July 1st. MHS seq. no. 237a.

Fig. 18   Landscape near Vaux—
From entry Verdun and The Argonne. MHS seq. no. 262b. CHS.

Fig. 19   Death Valley—between the two Forts—
From entry Verdun and The Argonne. MHS seq. no. 245b. CHS.

Fig. 20   Varennes ruins. (Mme Oblin)
From entry February 11th. MHS seq. no. 219b. CHS.

Fig. 21   Our Abri.
From entry September 25 to October 12, 1918. MHS seq. no. 54. CHS. Pictured: Marjorie Coryn and Frances King.

Fig. 22   Ypres.
From entry Notes from Diary. MHS seq. no. 324c. CHS.

Fig. 23   Living over a Railroad Station.
From entry June 23rd. MHS seq. no. 302c. CHS.

Fig. 24   German.
From entry Memorial Day, 1919. MHS seq. no. 275b. CHS.

Fig. 25 German tank.
From entry Memorial Day, 1919. MHS seq. no. 277b.
The image shows an English tank that was captured by Germans and decorated with German crosses.

Figures 26-36 appear in the insert following 146.

Fig. 26 Long Wy.
From entry Memorial Day, 1919. MHS seq. no. 287a. CHS.

Fig. 27 Long Wy.
From entry Memorial Day, 1919. MHS seq. no. 287b. CHS.

Fig. 28 Verdun.
From entry June 23rd. MHS seq. no. 292a. CHS.

Fig. 29 Argonne.
From entry June 23rd. MHS seq. no. 294c.

Fig. 30 Monfaucon—
From entry June 23rd. MHS seq. no. 295b.

Fig. 31 German Prisoners—Romagne.
From entry June 23rd. MHS seq. no. 296a. CHS.

Fig. 32 U.S.A. National Cemetery. Romagne— Argonne. June 1919.
From entry June 23rd. MHS seq. no. 296b.

Fig. 33 Plank road near Tahure—
From entry Treaty of Versailles. MHS seq. no. 309b.

Fig. 34 Lens.
From entry Notes from Diary. MHS seq. no. 318a.

Fig. 35 Armentières. (narrow gauge r.r. in street)
From entry Notes from Diary. MHS seq. no. 328a. CHS.
The town pictured is actually Arras, not Armentières.

Fig. 36 Forest d'Houlhulst. Belgium.
From entry Notes from Diary. MHS seq. no. 327a.

Acknowledgments

The pleasure of reading Margaret Hall's memoir and learning more about her life has been afforded us through the kindness, encouragement, and direction of her family, the Massachusetts Historical Society, and the Cohasset Historical Society. Hall's nephew Philip Hall, Jr., and his daughter, Suzanne Diefenbach, shared papers and photographs as well as stories about Margaret Hall and her relationships to other members of the family. Since her father's death, Suzanne has been particularly generous with her time. Our search began when Elizabeth Swayze introduced me to the series of autobiographical publications at the Massachusetts Historical Society and to Ondine Le Blanc, who has enthusiastically promoted the publication of Hall's typescript, with its beautiful photographs, for as broad an audience as possible. She and all the members of her multi-talented supporting team—Judith Graham, Jim Connolly, Peter Drummey, Suzanne Carroll, Nancy Heywood, Laura Wulf, and Jeanine Rees—each brought special skills and knowledge to bear on the manuscript, which is much better than it could have been otherwise.

The initial breakthrough in our research was achieved by Susan Solomon, whose detective work tracked Hall down to her residences in New York City, Boston, and Cohasset. Susan's evidence led her to the Cohasset Historical Society, where we discovered Margaret Hall's own three-volume version of the memoir. There Lynne DeGiacomo's knowledge of Cohasset enabled us to reach the Hall family. She organized an exhibit in 2005 of Hall's enlargements, with posters and memorabilia that Hall had collected during her year in France. The richly documented Cohasset album was an invaluable resource for Hall's instructions from the Red Cross, her travel documents, and the occasional musical and theatrical entertainments she attended during her year in France.

Other archives have also given us repeated help. One of the four albums Hall had made was purchased by Bryn Mawr College. At Bryn Mawr, Lorett Treese, College Archivist, and Marianne Hansen, Special Collections Librarian, tracked down a copy of Hall's initial report on her work, published in January 1919, as well as a body of related material in the papers of Anna V. S. Mitchell, co-director of the Cantine des Deux Drapeaux. Carol A. Leadenham at the Hoover Institution Archives also searched the Mitchell papers that are held at Stanford University for us. Catherine Healey, a specialist in Smith College war workers, shared her information drawn from her archival work. Tab Lewis at the National Archives and Records Administration of the American Red Cross, in College Park, Maryland, searched for records concerning the canteen, as did Pascaline Chamarac-Watier, curator of documentation in the Archives municipales of Châlons-en-Champagne (the modern name of Châlons-sur-Marne). David Bosse, librarian at the Historic Deerfield Library, shared documents from the Emma Lewis Coleman Papers at Pocumtuck Valley Memorial Association Library. Julian Bullitt, Hilary Roberts at the Imperial War Museum, London, and Marie-Pascale Prévost-Bault at the Historial de la Grande Guerre,

Péronne, gave advice about the technical production and interpretation of Hall's photographs. Arnaud Dubois, a specialist on Châlons-sur-Marne, shared images of the station, maps, and leads about other resources.

Susan Solomon undertook the primary research for the appendices concerning people whom Hall met, her family, historical references, and specialized vocabulary. Since she carefully weighed the section breaks, the selection of photographs, and questions to be asked, much of her work also has nourished the headnotes and the introduction, although Margaret Higonnet had primary responsibility for writing those parts of this edition.

Many hands and eyes have helped us over the course of the years. Julia Kete at Harvard and Mara Reisman at the University of Connecticut gave long hours to pursue and check needed information; Giuliana Vetrano shared her Harvard thesis on Radcliffe women in France; and Carol Strauss Sotiropoulos, Elizabeth Swayze, Margaret Buchholz, and Kate Capshaw read sections with thoughtful care. Janis L. Solomon held copy, and Nick Toscano gave encouragement throughout. For a decade, Patrice Higonnet has admitted Margaret Hall to our family circle for conversation at all times of day and night.

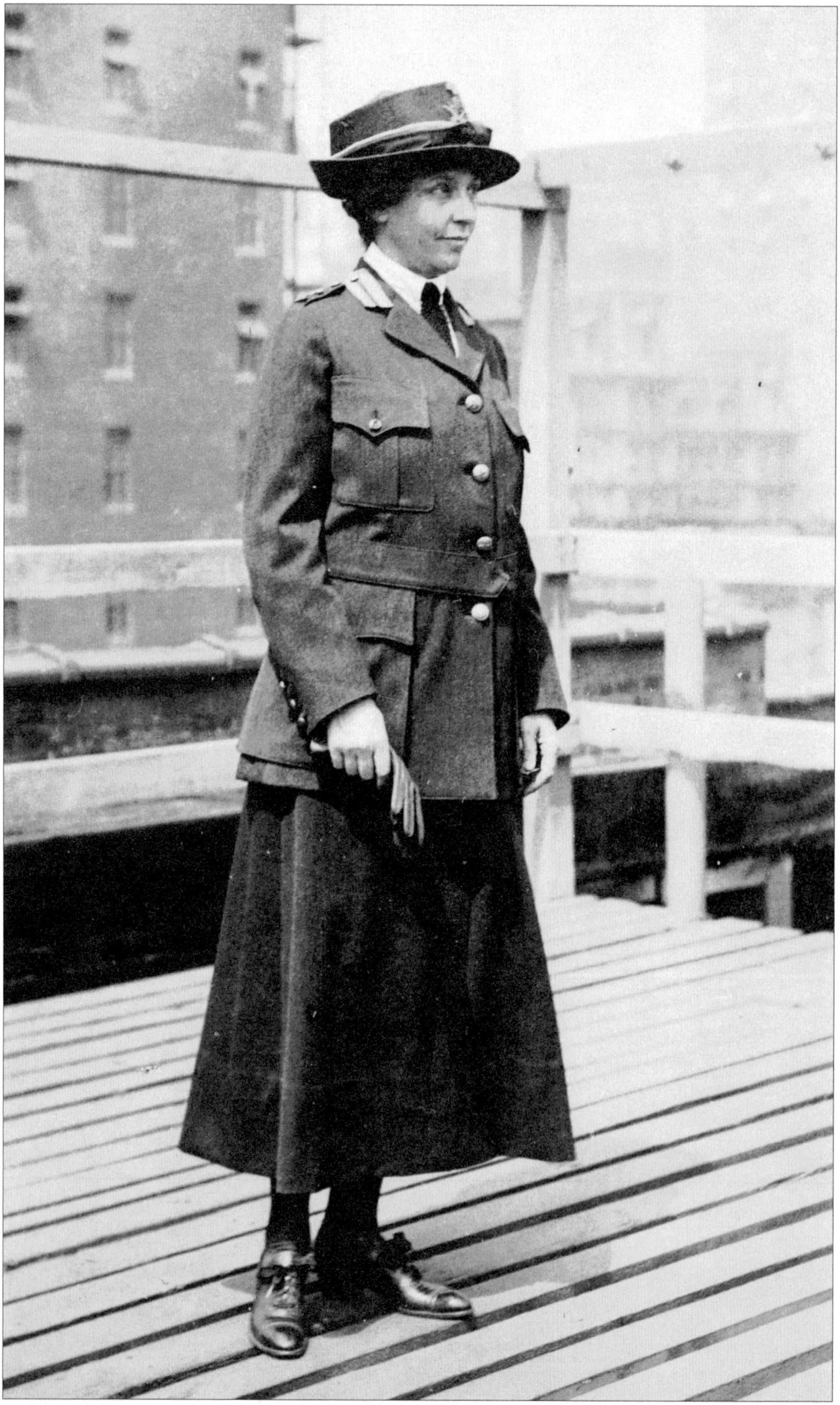

Introduction

> "In my day you could not get married and see the world. I chose to see the world."
> —Margaret Hall

A handsome family portrait of Margaret Hall (1876-1963) shows her in her American Red Cross uniform from Abercrombie and Fitch, on a pier in New York before she boarded the SS *Chicago* for France on August 23, 1918.[1] She is restraining a smile and looking away.[2] Seen from a three-quarter view, as if she were about to leave, the resolute angle of her gaze prepares us for the forceful but wry memoir of her canteen service during the last year of the Great War. Titled "Letters and Photographs from the Battle Country, 1918-1919," a typescript of that memoir is now preserved by the Massachusetts Historical Society.[3]

Hall tells a boldly modern story, in which she ironically observes her own performance as a canteen worker, while she keeps her eye on the progress of the war and its aftermath. Critic Paul Fussell famously argued that the industrial slaughter of at least nine and a half million soldiers in World War I broke up myths of chivalry, class privilege, and a natural political order, thereby shaping the ironic voices of great soldier-poets such as Wilfred Owen; he believed, however, that women—who could not experience the war in the same way—were too sentimental to achieve significant irony.[4] Margaret Hall explodes this long-standing assumption about women who narrated the Great War they had known. Her unpublished memoir combines brisk anecdotes with a stunning series of battlefield photographs, and it demonstrates that a "New Woman's" determined engagement with this historic moment could encompass reflective questions, impulsively daring use of her camera, and a sense of humor about the new roles that war called upon women to perform.[5]

A progressive Republican, patriot, and lover of things French, Hall was certainly proud to be wearing a uniform and to be following the thousand soldiers who had just marched onto the

SS *Chicago*.[6] Her father, George F. Hall (1844–1915), an active supporter of Civil War veterans and honorary brigadier general, would also have been proud of her.[7] Although his daughter was a graduate of a Quaker college (Bryn Mawr, class of 1899), Margaret was not a pacifist. She had kept herself informed both about the war and about American relief efforts in France, which had started already in 1914, three years before America declared war on Germany. In August 1918, even before her departure on the 23rd, she would have been keenly aware of the growing involvement of American forces in the fighting. The "Hundred Days" of the American and Allied advance leading to the defeat of the German army in France, at enormous cost of life, began in August, when some 250,000 American soldiers were arriving in France each month.[8] The dramatic German offensives under Gen. Erich Ludendorff that had started the previous March, striking on multiple fronts along the Somme, in the Aisne, and in Champagne, had threatened Paris in May and were halted only at the Marne River in July, with the Second Battle of the Marne; it seemed like a terrible return to the first months of the war in August and September of 1914. Thrown into combat under French command to thwart the German advances, inexperienced American troops played key roles over the summer of 1918 in attacks at Cantigny in the Somme and at Belleau Wood and Château-Thierry on the Marne. August 8 marked a turning point for the Allies, when Ludendorff realized that his massive offensive had failed. Even while his effort nearly exhausted his forces and supplies, American troops were arriving in large numbers.[9] By the beginning of September, when Hall arrived in Paris, Gen. John J. Pershing was about to launch the first major offensive consigned to the American Expeditionary Force (AEF) in his own command: a quick and successful pincer attack on September 12 against the exposed German position at Saint-Mihiel on the Meuse River, southeast of Verdun.

August marked a turning point not only in the war but in Margaret Hall's life. As Hall's erect stance suggests, this forty-two-year-old woman was mature and self-confident. Her well-to-do Boston family had provided her with an excellent education as a historian, practical experience in accounting, instruction in photography, an interest in women's rights, and a cosmopolitan admiration for European culture. Hall's wealth and business acumen gave her independence. Already in 1908, she had moved out of the family home in Boston and settled in an apartment in Manhattan.[10] During the critical summer of 1918, she signed up to join the two million American men who reached France between Pres. Woodrow Wilson's declaration of war on Germany on April 6, 1917, and December 1918, after the signing of the Armistice.[11] The death in 1915 of her father, a lawyer who owned a woolen mill in Nonantum and real estate on the Fenway in Boston, not only passed on to her the management of these properties on behalf of her mother and two brothers, but also freed her from paternal constraints.[12] Hall chose to leave behind a life of comfort and the responsibilities that her father had confided to her, in order to work actively for the war effort. When Hall boarded the ship, she had already opened a bank account in Paris with $1,500 to cover her expenses while in France, since she was required to pay for her own food and lodging, as well as all other incidentals.[13] She was ready to step out

Introduction   xvii

of her chauffeured Cadillac and begin hitchhiking in the back of a truck.[14] She had a number of reasons to volunteer, and she studied her options among the kinds of relief work available to the thousands of women who crossed the Atlantic.[15] Aboard ship and in Paris, she continued to observe the types of social organizations that were reaching out to help both the French and the flood of soldiers in the AEF. Above all, she was eager to become part of history and to fulfill her vocation as a historian.

One manifestation of Hall's determined spirit was her persistence in requesting frontline service once she got to Paris. To grasp the facts of the war, Hall felt she had to share the civilian hardships in the damaged regions, not in the relative safety of Paris. A great many women suffered from "frontline fever," but Hall was driven by her sense of history as well as by her spirit of adventure.[16] While she assisted in Paris hospitals, refugee centers, offices tracking soldiers and their families, and train stations where wounded were arriving at all hours of the night, Hall was also watching at the local American Red Cross (ARC) office until the right assignment became available. She wanted to go straight to the front with the soldiers, requesting placement in the French war zone of Champagne, which was close to the AEF led by Pershing and very close to the German lines.[17]

Hall's desire coincided with the demand arising from the mid September American offensive at Saint-Mihiel and the imminent September 26 offensive in the Meuse-Argonne, which would deploy three hundred thousand troops. Throughout that month, the women working at the Cantine des Deux Drapeaux at Châlons-sur-Marne, a railroad junction in Champagne

Soldiers heading into Cantine des Deux Drapeaux in Châlons-sur-Marne.

at a critical position between Reims and Verdun, were besieged by "tremendous" crowds.[18] Marjorie Nott, one of the canteen's two founders and directors, went to Paris to secure new workers, but came back the next day without anyone, for lack of volunteers with the necessary official papers.[19] When Hall learned in mid September that there was an urgent call from this canteen, dedicated to serving the "two flags" of the French and American armies, she wrote home, "I am so delighted to get it that I am almost like a Cheshire cat" (17). Located right at the train station, the canteen had been celebrated in American papers, so Hall knew it was one of the largest, best outfitted, and busiest ARC centers. A woman who had arrived in 1917, even before the building had been completed, described it for the *New York Times* as "a most elaborate affair" with a large dining room, a reading room, a dozen showers, and a dormitory with stretcher-bunks for eight hundred men. The *Times* published corresponding photographs.[20] By September 25, despite Hall's inexperience, the ARC office had rushed through her paperwork, and she took the train to Châlons. The train passed through the fresh battlefield of the Marne, whose landscape made a powerful impact on travelers, including Anna Mitchell, who commented in a letter that same week on its "broken bridges, or temporary pontoon ones; the discarded helmets and equipment; the whitening bones of animals; the fields full of shell holes; and the new made graves."[21] As Hall would learn on the night of her arrival, when the battle of Meuse-Argonne was launched with French artillery at 11:30 p.m. and American artillery at 2:30 a.m., Châlons was so close to the front that she could hear the cannon and see the flashes.[22] With its proximity to the tracks, the Red Cross canteen protected the station but was also endangered by it.[23] Evenings were punctuated by frequent air strikes that interrupted her sleep and forced her to hurry from her room to the converted wine cellars or from the canteen to a bomb shelter in the canteen garden. "Each day brings some phase of war new to me," she noted (62). An October 10 report in the *New York Sun* praised the canteen for the good food and service offered to "soldiers of all the allied nations" and mentioned Margaret Hall among the group drawn from "the best known women in America."[24] Nonetheless, even while the work kept her intensely busy in October, she wrote home that she yearned to move yet closer to the front: "I often feel like jumping into one of the trucks going by + smuggling myself up there."[25] She wanted to experience the battlefield firsthand.

With her departure for France, Hall had to set aside momentarily the cultural and political world of her friends in Manhattan, whom she was accustomed to meet at the Bryn Mawr Club.[26] Her new work, however, was firmly rooted in her political commitments over the previous decade. Hall had worked in New York on the cause of suffrage with Elsa Bowman, a friend from Bryn Mawr College who was also her frequent travel companion. Hall's politics were well to the left of her parents' views: she had been a picket in an International Ladies' Garment Workers' Union strike in New York, as she reported to the *Bryn Mawr Alumnæ Quarterly*.[27] She and Bowman had marched together for women's right to vote in 1912 and 1913 in New York, and they had participated in the dramatic suffrage parade in Washington, D.C., on March 3, 1913, just before Wilson's first inauguration.[28] She may have anticipated that women's wartime service would be rewarded by the vote.[29] Just one month after Hall arrived in France, in fact, on September 30, 1918, Wilson addressed the Senate on behalf of female suffrage, stating, "We have made partners of the women in this war. . . . Shall we admit them only to a partnership of suffering and sacrifice and toil and not to a partnership of privilege and right?"[30] Women like Hall were confident that their sacrifices would be recognized.

Hall was ready to plunge into the harsh conditions of life close to the battlefront, in a town where houses had been sliced in half, food supplies were limited, and heat and hot water were rare luxuries. She had signed the printed American Red Cross contract, which states,

> I agree to give my entire time to the service of the American Red Cross for six months. . . . I understand that I am to work in France, which is a country under martial law, and that I may be called on to work full seven days a week, full time on all working days, on either day or night duty. I agree to accept whatever work is assigned to me, to be ready to go wherever sent, and to adapt myself to whatever conditions of living that may be necessary, and to abide by all rules, regulations, and orders of the service.[31]

Her basic job was routine: she offered coffee and hot chocolate along with cigarettes to the men passing through on trains, and inside the canteen she served meals to soldiers on relief, some of whom stayed in the dormitory overnight. The work was heavy, as she was asked to "do a thousand things at once" (61); in mid October, she directed the kitchen for a week: cutting and weighing sausages, washing and boiling vegetables, pouring out soup, locking the storeroom, and kicking the cat out of the food (60). Visitors to the canteen included not only French and American troops but also other Allied soldiers, labor battalions, and occasional prisoners of war; from November on, increasing numbers of returning refugees also streamed in. From the time she arrived in Paris on September 4, she requested no leave until the middle of December, when she took a few days to see Woodrow Wilson arrive in Paris. Aside from several trips away, she continued to work at the canteen until it was transferred to French control on July 1, 1919.

"Cigarettes"

Once the Armistice was signed on November 11, the gradual reduction in demand at the canteen and looser military controls over civilian movements allowed Hall to take occasional daytrips, and she always brought a camera, hoping to record the impact of war on northeastern France.[32] Hall's French "Ordre de Mission Z 1404" documents her intermittent travel. It lists her train travel in December to Paris and to Sedan, to Strasbourg (and the Rhineland) in March, and to Luxemburg in May.[33] Several of those trips reflected her interest in the movement of the AEF to occupy the German Rhineland with the other Allies, in accord with the

Armistice. Quick train rides to Paris allowed her to see the celebration of the Treaty of Versailles on June 28, and the French Bastille Day parade on July 14, 1919. From November on, Hall hitchhiked her way around the countryside, catching rides with empty ambulances (the Sanitary Section Unit of the American Ambulance Field Service), in the back of an American undertaker's truck, and in French officers' limousines, among other vehicles. She preserved but did not follow a mimeographed sheet of "General Orders" for Red Cross canteen workers that instructed her: "Make no appointments to walk with, dine with, or accompany an officer or soldier of any nationality anywhere alone, except with the permission of your directrice. No one is permitted to ride in military motors except on business."[34] While she usually found another worker to accompany her, she had talents that aided her travel: she was a nonconformist who charmed those who stopped her, and sometimes she slipped quickly past guards. She had an air of command when she wore her uniform on trains, and she probably profited from the fact that she was twice as old as most military policemen. Once she reached her destination, she explored for hours on foot, often alone, to fulfill her passion as a war photographer. With luck (which included good light) she managed to record nearby battle sites and still return to Châlons in time to fulfill her nighttime obligations. When the end of her year rolled around in August 1919, the Cantine des Deux Drapeaux had been transferred to French control, several of her coworkers had been decorated with the Croix de Guerre, the peace treaty had been signed, and the two million American soldiers who had arrived by December were being shipped home steadily.

The contract tells us Hall was just the kind of woman the Red Cross sought to attract for service abroad. Single, financially secure, and able to speak French and German, at forty-two Hall was unlikely to cause any sexual scandal.[35] She was also a modern woman who had a college degree with a double major in history and political science as well as a background in accounting. She wore a luminescent wristwatch (which she used to light her path at night), performed military exercises during the transatlantic passage, and cherished freedom to travel at a historic moment when travel was very strictly regulated. An avid traveler, Hall explained to her great-niece, "In my day you could not get married and see the world. I chose to see the world."[36] Hall was accustomed to camping as well as to more luxurious lodging; she first went to Europe for a year in 1903 with her mother and returned again in 1911, when she sailed to Naples. In 1914 she took trips to Bermuda, the Southwest, California, Montana, and Alaska, and in 1916 she reported to the *Bryn Mawr Alumnæ Quarterly* that she had visited Cuba.[37] Travel to a war zone was an entirely new experience, however. In a teasing letter to her younger brother Philip, who had stayed in Scarsdale and volunteered as a firefighter, Hall wrote in mock rivalry about the intensity of her life in Châlons, located as it was at a main intersection of army traffic: "You'd certainly enjoy being where I am—getting up and rushing to fires in the middle of the night is nothing compared to what I do now—In fact I never undress at all any more."[38] When a truckload of defective hand grenades exploded in an accident at Châlons in mid-October, the blast killed several people and damaged yet more houses; it also shattered the panes in her window and her skylight. Châlons was not safe, as she had learned already on October 2, when a bomb landed on Evacuation Hospital No. 2 and killed over sixty people.[39]

While Hall took her tasks seriously, she was also an astute negotiator, who could arrange to trade her assigned hours of work with others, in order to achieve her own goals while fulfilling her contractual obligations. Not only did she wish to serve the nation at what Wilson called "the very skirts and edges of the battle itself," but as a trained historian, she wanted to photograph the world that was being reshaped by the war.[40] Hall combined seriousness with ironic resistance; she was scrupulously dedicated to her tasks but also playfully defiant of the rules. That startling mix constitutes a lively attraction of her memoir, and it becomes directly evident in the story of her cameras. One of the cards that she inserted into her copy of the memoir is a list of military prohibitions addressed "To the American Soldier in France." It warns that the Red Cross worker, as a member of the AEF, is "militarized" and subject to censorship. "Don't talk too much": She should not carry

> Maps, documents, or private papers of a military nature nor a diary or note book containing military hints of value to the enemy except when it is your official duty to do so.
>
> All members of the American Expeditionary Forces are forbidden to take photographs, unless photography is a part of their official duties.

These were rules that many soldiers and auxiliary workers honored in the breach. Hall brought with her a large National Geographic map (32.75 by 26.87 inches) on which she could closely follow combat reports: as the Allied forces pushed back the Germans, she marked up the map showing each advance. She kept a diary, although it contained no clues to forthcoming military operations. And she apparently carried two cameras, even though she knew it was forbidden.[41] She gloats in her memoir that, when the ship docked at Bordeaux, the police and customs inspectors "forgot to ask if I had a camera, so I was lucky!" (10) We are not surprised later to read that she violated the posted rules in the shattered cathedral of Reims, when she found the crabby guardian was not looking, and slipped up the unstable stairs of the tower in order to capture a picture of the flying buttresses. "Why not?" she asks (120).

Hall stands out among the men and women who wrote memoirs about their work during the war through a combination of three features. Her droll, even Chaplinesque touch in describing herself reminds us of the changes she faces in this topsy-turvy world; she is attuned to echoes of war in all aspects of daily life; and the photographs she pasted into her album construct a visual narrative, a sequence that carefully tells her story.[42] Initially, for the benefit of her family, she tells comic anecdotes about her sudden change in status. Mocking her confusion at night as she sought her deck chair on the *Chicago*, she recounts her adventures as if they were happening just now: "I lose my balance, and either my pillow or life preserver lands on top of them. After I have reached the end of the passage, my real trouble begins. . . . I plunge on, however, stumbling against the people on the outside row, and on the rebound onto those on the inside.

I never escape putting my hand on someone's face; oftener than not it lands in their mouths" (7). Her first injury is a skinned nose, a casualty due to a collision on the deck. Her first battle will be engaged once she arrives at Châlons, when she is sent to filthy lodgings, where a bed crawling with vermin provokes her mock-heroic description of a "slaughter" of bedbugs (31). Throughout, she refers tongue in cheek to herself in the third person as "M.H." or "Mlle." in response to questions or orders from others. The most obviously ironic passages about her new role as an apprentice canteen worker involve something she was particularly good at: accounting. While assembling and handing out meals, she had to calculate the collective cost of the items including deposits for cutlery, and give out small change in French francs, centimes, and sous. Unaccustomed to menial work and to "mental arithmetic," Hall humorously details the frantic pace of either feeding thousands of impatient men at the canteen or serving hot drinks directly on the platform of the railway station next door. Since she does not stand on her own dignity, she quickly warms to the good humor of the soldiers she encounters.

Part of Hall's story concerns the social-economic side of daily life in France, such as the lack of heat and hot water. For her letters home, Hall singled out observations that were related to the war. As the ship left Manhattan, for example, she noticed the observation balloons used to protect the harbor and shipping; to her family, she recounted how the boat zigzagged in a convoy of crazily camouflaged transports, in order to avoid U-boats; and she described the black-out conditions on deck, where she and most passengers slept because of the oppressive August heat. From the time of her arrival in Paris, Hall gleaned evidence of the changes wrought by war, in part by talking to refugees, wounded soldiers in hospitals, and local Parisians. One refugee tells Hall that "her husband had gone crazy from shell shock," the first of several allusions to trauma among the soldiers and canteen workers that Hall recorded in the memoir (17). She closely followed current events such as the American attack on Saint-Mihiel on September 12. And from a sailor who had survived the September 5 torpedo attack on the transport ship SS *Mount Vernon*, she learned that the ship was able to limp into port. In Hall's walks around Paris, she found sandbags piled up around monuments, paper pasted onto windows, and restricted hours for serving food. She visited the street where her mother had lived decades earlier, when studying in Paris, only to discover that the place had been "shattered" by "the big gun," a long-range German cannon that targeted Paris from March to August. She visited the church of Saint-Gervais that the "Paris gun" had hit on Good Friday. On September 15 she witnessed a major air raid, which appeared like "fireworks on all sides" (22).

Hall's temporary hospital work in Paris for the American Red Cross enabled her to describe different kinds of war injuries: facial mutilations, deeply infected wounds treated by irrigation with "Carrel-Dakin's" solution of sodium hypochlorite, and burns both internal and external from a German gas attack at Soissons in mid July. The patients, one of whom was a professional singer, had throats "so burned that they can scarcely speak" (19). Once she reached Châlons, she saw soldiers passing through with diseases such as typhoid, tuberculosis, and trench mouth. In October, she spent a week at a tent hospital in nearby Écury, feeding influenza and pneumonia patients who were racked with coughs. Highly aware of the risk of infection, Hall worried about hygiene and carried her own wash basin with her (89). Marjorie Nott was away part of the fall due to a severe case of skin anthrax.[43] Through a gradual compilation of these details of human suffering, which frame her work in the canteen, Hall creates a pointilliste picture of the way war medicine evolved in response to the "devilish" innovations of military technology.

Hall observed social changes such as the mixing up of classes; in fact, one of the first things she noticed when she boarded the *Chicago* was the elimination of such distinctions: "First class, second class and steerage all together, as the rest of the ship is given over to troops" (5). Of course, she also noted which jobs were newly performed by women in the absence of men. The memoir includes a photograph of women working on a train that is carrying military equipment. Hall's letters point to the abandonment of many Victorian taboos during the war period. She records the entrance of women (smoking!) into the public sphere, the promiscuity of a younger worker eager to "pet" with a soldier she has just met, and her own shocked contact with the profoundly wounded male body. Obliquely she refers to matters such as abortions among the women with whom she works, or the suicide of two coworkers, the Cromwell twins, who had been traumatized by the intense strain of their relief work.

The topics of sexuality and gender roles figure extensively in her discussion of entertainment by a vaudeville group of the 106th Infantry, who perform at the canteen. One comedian modeled on "Charlot," or Charlie Chaplin, makes comic use of a "wiggly" umbrella, another tells risqué stories, and the favorite, the "prima donna" soprano who plays the "soldier in a skirt," performs on and off stage with "a ladylike switch to the tail of his horizon blue overcoat" (140-141).[44] His sudden death in the spring sheds gloom over the whole canteen. As for her own place in this world, Hall retains her sense of surprise at being allowed to participate as a woman in this moment of history: "I can't believe it is I who am here," she remarks, "hearing the guns from the front as I am at this moment, seeing flashes in the sky, and being so near to this terrible but fascinating horror."[45] The guns banging away interrupt her letter and remind her that she is not the same person she had been at home in America. Hall seems to have found what canteen co-director Anna Mitchell called "the luxury of a life that someway seems simplified; of having what corresponds to a man's business; and of companionship that is in no way connected with clothes, or social effort."[46]

Hall's history of a year in the "battle country" locates heroism in the French people's everyday struggle to carry on. The most poignant moment in the memoir may be February 11, 1919, the day when the Châlons regiment, the 106th, returned and were honored by the general of the Sixth Army. "As they marched into Châlons with their band playing, they were met with a deadly silence; not a cheer, no clapping of hands,—nothing. Some had big bunches of flowers and some little bunches, but that was all. Twenty-eight men, all who were left of the original regiment, marched alone behind the music, and the only sounds heard in the streets were sobs" (121). She admires French stoicism, she ponders people's attitudes toward the meaning of the war, and she assesses their feelings about their allies, in what a historian today might call a study of mentalities.

The poilus of the 106th Infantry returning to Châlons-sur-Marne in February 1919.

Hall's depiction of Americans in France conveys a more complicated view. When she first arrived, she was impressed by how grateful the French were to the youthful and even reckless American soldiers; she commented on the French care for American graves and enthusiasm for the American flag. As time wore on, she concluded that the Americans did not recognize the magnitude of the French people's own sacrifices over four years. President Wilson in particular seemed indifferent, refusing to visit battle sites in order not to be "prejudiced" by witnessing the devastation (103).[47] When the American army occupied the German Rhineland after the Armistice on November 11, a number of canteen workers returning from the Occupied zone commented on American soldiers' naïve attitudes toward the Germans and French they met—especially the belief that the French had not fought as fiercely as they themselves had.[48] Hall likewise pondered that the warm billets and adequate food in Germany certainly contrasted with poor supplies and combat conditions American soldiers had endured in France, and she worried that these inevitable difficulties had undermined their understanding of French heroism and generosity.[49]

When Hall chatted with the people she met, she sought to elicit a larger picture of the war and its military management. Listening to disgruntled American soldiers led Hall to observe problems of organization in the American military—problems that historians have since confirmed. When she visited Château-Thierry, "where our boys had fought so hard," she "tried to picture how it looked down in the valley of the Marne and across on the other hills those summer days when they were rushed there from all quarters, almost pushed off the trains, told to place their cannon and fire, where or in what direction they didn't know, and no one else seemed to know, so I've been told over and over again" (98). Poor training, the absence of maps, and unclear commands when officers were knocked out of line all repeatedly hampered American units, causing high casualty rates.[50] She noted that the American drive in the Argonne led to "terrific fighting and terrific mortality" (62). Soldiers separated from their units straggled into the canteen, hungry and homesick, complaining sometimes about their officers (146). In mid September, Prime Minister Georges Clemenceau himself had observed "hopeless congestion" and a breakdown in the American supply lines, and again when he visited the Argonne on September 29, American drivers told him their traffic jam had already lasted two nights.[51] Even in October, Hall found, "Lots of boys say they have not been paid for months" (51). Hall's attention to economic factors underpins her analysis of the soldiers' attitudes: she points out the presence of profiteers in all countries at war and contrasts the local economy with an economy oriented to strangers (145-146). Here and elsewhere, we can observe how she capitalizes on her training to understand wartime circumstances, and to temper her enthusiasm for the AEF by examining different kinds of information. She discounts the rumors that soldiers and others spread. "I've tried to give you a perfectly true, unexaggerated view of the life here," she explains to her family (42).

Hall took a particular interest in the involvement of Americans in the battles of the final three months of the war: the 42nd and 77th Divisions had fought together with French forces in Champagne and in the Argonne. She comments on the racial diversity of the American force, which included Native American and African American soldiers, many of whom worked with labor crews cleaning up the battlefields (25, 102) after the Armistice.[52] She also notes the mingling of white and "colored" soldiers at the canteen.[53] Gen. Henri Gouraud, whose headquarters were at Châlons, had under his command African American troops including the 369th Infantry, called the Harlem Hellfighters, whom Hall occasionally saw.[54] Her comments but especially her snapshots emphasize the cultural diversity of the European and colonial soldiers who passed through her canteen, and her letters refer to distinctive details of conduct or costume that testify to the global reach of the war.

Throughout we find Hall discussing events of the war with men she meets. Perhaps because she had grown up with three brothers, she seems to have readily entered into conversation with soldiers about their experiences. She grasped empathetically the situation of some of the men she met, such as a Tommy caring for his Irish friend, who was ill following long imprisonment in a prisoner of war camp. In the course of her battlefield excursions, Hall developed a friendship with a man she called "M. P. Baker," a sergeant and military policeman in the 77th Division, stationed at Fort Douaumont, whom she met in the spring of 1919 while hiking across the rough contours between forts near Verdun. Together they toured sites in the Argonne where his division had fought, and one night when she could not find a hotel, she shared his lodging in Verdun. Her photographs from that trip suggest he guided her to the positions he thought were important. She was creating a visual map of memory that could show, in Anna

Mitchell's words, "bits of ground whose names ha[d] become familiar" in news accounts over the long months past.⁵⁵

The strangeness of these experiences for a wealthy Bostonian made them sometimes seem elusive: "There never has been anything real about my life over here. I can't believe that it is I who am seeing it with my eyes, living in something that is a reality and not a dream. It worries me sometimes for I am afraid it will disappear out of my memory like a dream, and I don't know just what to do to hold on to it" (62). Through photography, of course, she could try to capture what she saw.

"M. P. B. was at the station"

Hall's photographs are exceptional in more than one way. Her interest in photography as an instrument for recording history had been nurtured by her aunt, Emma Lewis Coleman, who gave her a camera when she was a small child.⁵⁶ In turn, Hall handcrafted for Emma one of the four photographically illustrated typescripts of her memoir.⁵⁷ Coleman was a published historian, whose 1925 history of captivity narratives centered on Deerfield, the place where she lived for many years with her older friend Alice Baker. Coleman photographed many of the houses of Deerfield and created a photographic essay on sharecroppers in the South.⁵⁸ We can see Coleman's influence in her niece's decision to attend Bryn Mawr College, with her double major in history and what we today would call economics. Both aunt and niece understood photography as another tool with which to pursue their interests as historians and students of social economy.

For Hall, this kind of history meant documenting the war's impact on everyday life. She shows us children playing in the rubble of a house broken up by an air raid (fig. 35), as well as townspeople who push a wheelbarrow filled with bedding and other possessions, so they can spend the night in an old wine "cave" used as a shelter (p. 49). She pastes into her memoir a postcard of these neighbors in their bomb shelter at night (p. 36); exposed by the light of a magnesium flare, they look tired and somber. Hall's own snapshots show war oddly domesticated, with a "sausage" observation balloon tethered next to a grazing horse. Inevitably, the train station right next to the canteen is filled with stretchers laid out on the platform (fig. 7). Sets of small prints gather different instruments of war she shot as they passed through on flat-bed trains, including small Renault "baby tanks" and machine guns (p. 33).[59] When she photographed the canteen, she was less interested in collecting portraits of her colleagues than in capturing the urgency of the men hurrying to grab a moment of relief. Such scenes allow us to see why the work of the canteen was important and how periods away from the front fit into the larger system of the army as an institution.

When Hall began to photograph the battle zone, she also commented on the technical nature of her task. In February, the weather frustrated her attempts: "The country was covered with snow, and I tried to take some pictures, but my rubber bulb was so frozen that it wouldn't squeeze, and my hands so cold that they wouldn't work, and my feet so cold that they wouldn't take me where I wanted to go, so I'm afraid I didn't get much" (121). She wandered through abandoned trenches and down shafts, observing the remains of dead soldiers still strewn everywhere in the bitter winter cold. She was intrepid in her quest for the right image: she mounted the German Crown Prince's observation tower to survey the countryside and explored deep into a dugout where gassed German soldiers remained seated around their card table, turning her camera to the light in the doorway from the darkness below. At a larger scale, she trained her camera on the destroyed fabric of cities and towns and especially on the sacred space of churches.[60] Her message is clear: she memorializes the damaged, historic cathedral of Reims, by titling it "France triumphant rising out of her ruins" (fig. 14).

Hall's observant camera captures the kind of ironic disparities that we relish in anti-pastoral poetry by writers like Wilfred Owen, who hears the war music of "shrill demented choirs of wailing shells" and who asks "What passing bells for these who die as cattle?"[61] A creased and cratered chalkland as white as snow, with splintered tree-trunks, is captioned "Champagne forest" (fig. 12). On her return in April 1919 to Verdun, walking between the forts of Douaumont and Vaux, Hall observed, "The battlefield was covered with violets, great, big, wonderful ones, and the larks were singing high up in the sky, but the dead were everywhere in our path. At one place there seemed to be a skeleton in every shell hole" (141). She photographed flowers in bloom next to a single gauge rail line, and a few pages later placed the image of a German skeleton in her album (fig. 24). Hall's images of the dead have a starkly realist dignity. Just as soldier-poet Isaac Rosenberg juxtaposed intensely red poppies with the blood of death, Hall on a trip in June juxtaposed her contradictory perceptions: "This time the battlefields are garden spots, covered with lovely yellow flowers, and the grass has grown higher, so much of the desolate effect is gone, but the weather is hot, and the battlefield odor is almost unendurable" (206). She transforms the artifacts and architecture of war into images of death; the way in which she has panned her camera over slits in the horizontal blank face of Fort Douaumont, for example, reinforces its deadliness.

Sometimes Hall has laid out a sequence of photographs on a page as a visual narrative, echoing the words on the facing page. Unlike the mistily romantic and painterly effects of her aunt's antiquarian photographs, Hall's photographs generally foreground sharp details of context such as barbed wire or rubble, the detritus of war, together with depth of field. Her centered, framed focus can lead the eye through a ruin onto miles of white lines that we slowly realize are trenches. Her experiments with perspective transform many battlefront images into works of art. In pictures of monumentally devastated yet elegant ruins, her striking aesthetic reminds us that for soldier-poets, World War I rewrote the Trojan War in a new key. Margaret Hall's memoir becomes the diary of a photographer in the making, who struggles to understand the history that is falling into decay and rust before her eyes. She seeks to be "alone with the dead" at Fort Douaumont (113), in order to gather meaning before the traces vanish. Even after the chaos of the canteen amid the rumble of cannon fire has waned, she confesses months later that "The greatest luxury in life I have is to sit down all alone and think" (156).

"Entrance to Fort Douaumont."

Editorial Principles

Transcription

The text presented in this edition of Hall's memoir reflects the copy held at the Massachusetts Historical Society. Historical spellings have not been modernized. Typographical errors, usually transposed letters, have been silently corrected. These were checked against the typescript at the Cohasset Historical Society to determine that they were keying errors rather than nonstandard spellings. Inconsistent spellings have also been silently corrected; that is, if Hall spelled one word one way in almost every instance but once or twice veered off into a different spelling, the latter instances have been made consistent with her internal standard.

Hall's punctuation, including peculiarities, remains intact. Where we would use an em-dash today, she uses hyphens. Due to the limitations of the typewriter, Hall's secretary represented dashes with a hyphen surrounded by a space on either side; this edition employs standard typography to communicate Hall's meaning clearly. She often uses a dash in place of, or in conjunction with, the period at the end of a sentence, as well as following commas and surrounding appositives and nonbinding modifiers. All of those have been retained.

The text is full of foreign words and phrases. Diacritical marks over letters (e.g. Châlons, Pétain) are handwritten in the typescript due, as before, to technological limitations. French contractions in which the typist inserted a space after the apostrophe have been closed in this edition.

There are very few deletions in the typescript, and none of them offers valuable insight into Hall's composition process—that process took place before typing began. They have therefore been silently omitted. Similarly, instances in which Hall indicated by hand an addition to the typed text—usually to fix spelling or punctuation errors—have also been silently incorporated.

Annotation

Context for Hall's narrative is provided in the chapter headnotes and five appendices: glossaries of personal names, places, foreign terms, and period terms, and a chronology of selected events from World War I. In special cases, such as the potentially unclear abbreviation of a name, a brief note appears in the margin of the historical text to direct the reader to the appropriate entry in the appendices.

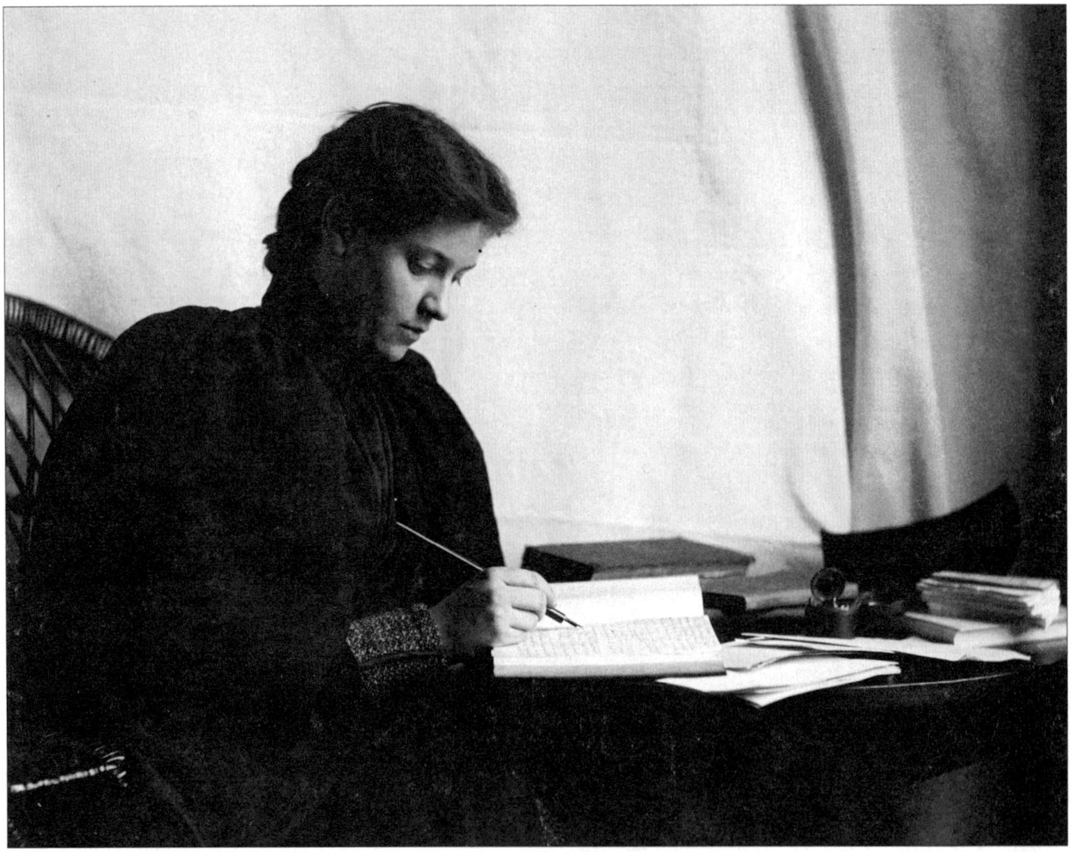

American Relief Organizations in France

Margaret Hall describes her fellow passengers on the SS *Chicago* in August 1918 as a representative sample of the American relief organizations that rushed to Europe during the war. She highlights the welfare societies associated with the American Expeditionary Force (AEF): the American Red Cross (ARC), the Young Men's Christian Association (YMCA), the Knights of Columbus, and the Salvation Army. In addition, she tells us about Quakers and Christian Scientists, and she mentions "White nuns" in a neighboring cabin who came from Canada.[1] As the names of the groups indicate, many of these volunteers were motivated by religion, and it was not unusual for the organizations to minister separately to soldiers from each faith.[2] The clubhouses of the Knights of Columbus, a Catholic fraternal service organization, for example, encouraged attendance at religious services and sports. But they also served free food and cigarettes to soldiers regardless of race or religion.[3] In addition to the largest relief organizations, American men and women volunteered with a wide range of smaller organizations set up by Europeans and Americans.[4] With passage of the Selective Service Act in May 1917, most men aged twenty-one to thirty resigned from volunteer organizations in order to join the military. Women, however, signed on in swelling numbers. After the declaration of war in April 1917, the AEF drew an estimated 16,500 women overseas, to serve as nurses, drivers, librarians, clerks, telephone operators, and canteen workers.[5]

In September 1914, the first ARC ship, called "the Mercy Ship," carried 170 surgeons and nurses bringing humanitarian aid to countries on both sides of the war. As a neutral country until 1917, the United States sought to provide nonpartisan assistance. On April 6, 1917, the same day as the declaration of war, President Wilson published a Statement on the Coordination of Relief, by which the main American associations offering welfare and relief services were brought together by Wilson under the ARC, in order to coordinate their work for the AEF. Wilson himself became president of the Red Cross and militarized the organization under the direction of the ARC War Council, headed by Henry P. Davison. From Hall's perspective, the relief organizations were mutually supportive. She notes that when Wilson arrived in Paris in December 1918, "All our organizations lined up" in symbolic unity.[6]

Between 1914 and 1919, at least ten thousand American women nurses and doctors served abroad. Thousands of other women served in Europe, the Middle East, and Russia to perform relief and refugee work, for an estimated total of twenty-five thousand women.[7] The most familiar poster images of women's war work might represent nurses or relatively unskilled workers in hospitals and canteens. At the same time, French, English, German, and American posters from the period called upon women to perform a broad array of new tasks in agriculture, industry, and government jobs. Wartime work outside the home gained women recognition for their significant roles in this world-historical event. While women's personal experiences varied enormously, the social perceptions of their roles generally followed boundaries set by existing gender norms. Thus a poster design for the ARC represented a nurse cradling a miniature soldier on a stretcher as the "Greatest Mother in the World."

The ARC served not only in hospitals but in about 130 hospitality huts and canteens in France alone, both of which offered respite and recreation for soldiers.[8] Many of these women were eager to taste the risks of war in zones close to the battlefront.[9] At first they found that French Army regulations governing the Service de Santé (medical service) barred female volunteers from the war zone, but beginning in 1916, the indispensable support supplied by women's organizations gradually won the recognition of the French government and military, and the restriction was lifted.[10]

The ARC, for which Hall worked, was the most prominent among the numerous American relief organizations that collaborated during the first years of the war in serving the needs of France, England, Russia, and Germany, on neutral principles.[11] The ARC was perhaps best known for providing medical staff and setting up hospitals and mobile clinics. But it also provided canteen and hut services at hospitals and at transportation hubs ("lines of communication," or LOC). Canteens fed and sometimes offered a temporary bed to soldiers, prisoners of war, and civilian victims. Once the AEF began to arrive in Europe in 1917, many American relief organizations like the Red Cross shifted their attention to American soldiers. By the end of the war, the ARC had founded fifty-four hospitals overseas, most of them in France. Women in the canteens served food to roughly fifty million American and Allied soldiers, sometimes over a thousand per day in a single canteen. In their recreation huts they provided stationery, stamps, magazines, books, and occasional movies. With these distractions, canteens sought to protect men from hard liquor and prostitution.[12] The same goals were pursued in the French system of Foyers du Soldat and the YMCA.

Despite their different religious affiliations and assignments to specific sectors by the AEF, many of these organizations shared resources. Charles D. Norton, a member of the Red Cross War Council, reported to the *New York Times* that volunteer service organizations collaborated well: "The Y.M.C.A. and the Knights of Columbus are doing fine work in this respect, everywhere working hand-in-glove with our Red Cross."[13] While the Red Cross assumed responsibility for canteen work at railroad junctions like Châlons-sur-Marne and at hospitals and ports, the YMCA provided entertainment such as vaudeville or theatrical sketches in military camps, which Hall enjoyed on her trips to Verdun and to Germany. The YMCA made dormitory space available to visiting colleagues—hospitality from which Hall benefited several times during her travels. Collegiality enabled organizations to maximize their effectiveness.

Who were these volunteers? The American women Hall encountered in France often came from a cosmopolitan elite. They spoke French or other languages, could drive, and already had visited Europe.[14] Whether young or old, these women were often single. They signed a paper certifying that they had "no male relatives (husbands, sons, fathers or brothers) in the armed service of the Unites States, either here or abroad, or overseas in the service of any organizations such as the Red Cross."[15] Vast sums were needed to fund wartime relief operations, and many upper-class women devoted themselves to fundraising. The cost of overseas service restricted the numbers, since those who volunteered for relief work in France generally paid for their uniforms, their Atlantic crossing, and their housing. Some, like Gertrude Stein, even drove their own cars.[16]

Many of these women were highly educated, and relief units formed by women's colleges brought together a small number of exceptional volunteers, many of whom had supported suffrage or performed social work at home.[17] In April 1917, presidents of eight women's colleges (Barnard, Bryn Mawr, Goucher, Mt. Holyoke, Radcliffe, Smith, Vassar, and Wellesley) wrote to President Wilson offering the support of their institutions to the war effort. Their letter declared, "Although we believe that the settlement of international difficulties by war is fundamentally wrong, we recognize that in a world crisis such as this it may become our highest duty to defend by force the principles upon which Christian civilization is founded."[18] They therewith launched committees for fundraising activities and agricultural projects linked to the Woman's Land Army of America at home and war relief work abroad.[19]

Hall refers in her letters to women whom she had met earlier at Bryn Mawr College, in Boston, or in New York. Aboard the *Chicago*, she traveled with the widow of a Bryn Mawr professor, Ethel D. Earle, who spoke French, German, and Flemish, and was assigned hospitality hut social work at Digne, in the south. In Paris, Hall stayed at the same hotel as several women from Smith College whom she had met on the ship. She got to know Ruth Gaines, a Smith graduate who had earlier in 1918 published a book about the Smith College Relief Unit, an organization founded in 1917 to bring relief to war-scarred areas of France. Gaines wrote two further books about the efforts of twenty-seven Smith graduates at Grécourt in the Somme to restore villages in this region.[20] Inevitably, many of these women were eager to write about their wartime experiences.

Relief workers often shifted from one assignment to another, as Margaret Hall herself did, sampling different Red Cross activities in Paris, before she received her assignment to the Cantine des Deux Drapeaux (of two flags) at Châlons-sur-Marne. While waiting for her opportunity to move closer to the front, Hall visited patients in the American Hospital at Neuilly; read casualty lists and reports in the Search office, in order to notify parents about the deaths of their sons; met wounded soldiers arriving on hospital trains; and visited refugee centers as well as hospitals for gassed patients and for patients with pneumonia. Later in October, she was transferred temporarily from Châlons to a nearby tent hospital. Her friend Mrs. Earle would eventually move from Digne to Châlons-sur-Marne. Another canteen worker in Châlons, Florence Billings, first volunteered in 1914 at the American Ambulance Hospital in Paris, then in 1917 signed up with the ARC as a canteen and relief worker. Like Hall, Billings worked at a tent hospital in Écury when it was short of nurses as well as canteen assistants.[21]

The Smith College unit collaborated with the American Women's Hospital and with the Comité Américain pour les Régions Dévastées (CARD), founded by philanthropist Anne Morgan. One of Hall's fellow passengers on the SS *Chicago*, the pianist Ethel Colgate, would join the CARD unit as an ambulance mechanic, driving her own car. Another member of Morgan's unit, Hall's college friend Elsa Bowman, invited Hall to see the relief work that CARD was doing (168). CARD was a descendant of the American Fund for French Wounded (AFFW), which Morgan had set up in 1915 to provide medical supplies to French hospitals and send parcels to wounded soldiers; in 1916, with Dr. Ann Murray Dike she created a civilian division of the AFFW, later called CARD, whose ten women volunteers performed medical and social work for twenty-five wrecked villages, on the model of Jane Addams's Hull House. Ten days after the March 1918 German offensive swept through the reconstructed region, Morgan reorganized the group, which first responded to the large numbers of refugees, then relocated villagers; built orphanages, kindergartens, and clinics; and helped restock and re-equip farms.[22]

The volunteer war work available to women became a worldwide phenomenon, as it opened up a wide range of occupations in the public arena.[23] Japanese nurses served in Paris at a hospital on the Champs Elysées.[24] Women from Ireland, Canada, Australia, and New Zealand served with the British both in Europe and in the Middle East; and the Danish author Isak Dinesen organized food transport in Kenya. In large numbers, women were encouraged to leave their homes to fill jobs previously held by men. On the home front some entered factories, others entered "land armies" or became policewomen, and yet others drove trains. Malawi women even worked as military porters.[25] Hall joined thousands of determined and highly intelligent women who volunteered to perform such tasks with the Red Cross and other associations in countries around the globe.

S.S. Chicago,
August 23–September 3, 1918.

It is rather discouraging to begin a letter, for I probably can't tell you the things of greatest interest. I think Mrs. Earle and I were about the last on board. She had forgotten her address book, and I grew nervous waiting for Pierce to go back and get it for her. One man after another told me it was time to go on. However, Pierce flew back at the last moment, and we walked down the pier past a row of officials, each of whom wanted to see one after another of our prized possessions; war zone cards, baggage checks, passports, and finally all our money. I told the money man I had no silver, and no gold banknotes, so he wasn't too fussy.

Ethel Deodata Earle
Pierce Butler

I am fortunate in my stateroom—a big cabin, so to speak—and my companions, three very quiet Red Cross nurses, who were all anxious to see whom they had drawn for a fourth.

The gang planks were pulled up in about an hour—the thousand soldiers having been marched down the pier before we were ordered on board—and we were all relieved to know we should not have to spend the night at the hot dock.

As we pulled out, the Hudson River boat pulled in. Such cheering and waving as they gave us! I couldn't and even now can't believe that I was on the boat which was being cheered, instead of being consumed with envy on the one giving the farewell wave. It was lovely going down the River. One of the nurses had her eyes glued on the New Jersey heights, and said to me, "There is my house up there. All my family are watching me now from the piazza." We passed many transports, loaded as we are, and then anchored for the night off Hoffman Island to wait for the rest of our convoy.

We are a varied crowd. First class, second class and steerage all together, as the rest of the ship is given over to troops. There are Y. M. C. A., Knights of Columbus, Red Cross and Salvation Army people on board, all in their different uniforms, and in the stateroom opposite ours are five White nuns from Quebec.

We watched the soldiers eat their dinner and wash their dishes in four great tanks of water. While we ate ours, with its delicious French sauces and salad, the boys, who were scattered about in groups all over the decks and in the rigging, began to sing popular songs, which they kept up all the evening. It was all unreal; a heavenly night with a full moon; Coney Island and Staten Island lights on the shore; two sausage balloons near Brooklyn; and eight or ten other transports lying near by.

The next morning there was a new excitement every few minutes. One by one other transports joined us, a battleship, some destroyers and a fleet of little submarine chasers. About ten o'clock we started, accompanied by a dirigible and a sausage balloon. There are twenty-three in our convoy.

Soon after we left the harbor, we were in war form. Guns pointed outward, lifeboats swung out, ladders ready. In two hours the zigzagging began which we are to keep up most of the way across.

At three o'clock we had our lifeboat drill. Having watched the soldiers we knew what to do, and did it as a matter of course. Our boat is discouraging; there are three children, the three nurses in my stateroom, some third class passengers, two officers, and five nuns, a rather helpless collection. We adjusted each other's life preservers, and noticed that those on the small people doubled over a good deal in front, and those on the large people wouldn't meet at all; but there was no joking about it.

At the bugle call at sunset, the port holes are closed and although they are painted black, wooden covers are put over them to make doubly sure that no light can escape. Every once in a while the first night, a soldier would forget and light a match, but it was instantly put out.

It has been hot and breathless in the Gulf Stream. The balloons, chasers and aeroplanes (which paid us occasional visits), left us one by one the first day, and now we are sailing along calmly in a safety zone. It is sociable to have so much company on the ocean. Wherever you look there are big transports camouflaged in crazy ways, one a perfect zebra, all going in different directions but all keeping together. A tanker passed us a little while ago and the battleship fired three shots over her bow. She was allowed to proceed, however, after giving a satisfactory account of herself.

Besides the large organizations, we have representatives of the Friends, and of Christian Scientists, some of the Smith Unit—Ruth Gaines, author of "A Village in Picardy," a Miss Colgate, who is to join the Anne Morgan unit, as a master mechanic in charge of ten trucks—they can be turned into ambulances if necessary—one of which was given by her family. She is little, slight and attractive, and plays the piano most charmingly. I hate to have her a mechanic for fear something will happen to her fingers. She has studied with Leschetizky, and has evidently been a mechanic for some time. I know less than anyone, almost, on board and feel I'd better ship for home right away.

We are thirty-five Red Cross workers, twenty nurses, not altogether preposessing all of them, and fifteen of our kind. Our leader, Dr. Bradley, is especially nice. She is taking over films to show the people how to take care of the young and coming generations. I have the nicest nurses of all in my stateroom. They are from Seattle, Minnesota, and Canada. The Salvation Army girls are most dignified. The one I have talked with joined the Army because she wanted hard work. One of the Knights of Columbus who speaks to Mrs. Earle and me turned out to be a New York ex-policeman, who has been at the East 35th Street Station a long time, and knows our locality like a book. He is a great big man of very liberal views. He tried to make the service in every way he could, but was too old, and finally accomplished his end in this way. His wife would have come if it had been allowed, a daughter has already gone, one son is in the Navy, another is an aviator, as are three nephews. He is living up to his conviction that if America is not good enough to fight for, she is not good enough to live in, and those who won't fight or work for her had better get out.

At ten o'clock a fine looking and finely developed young lieutenant gives us setting up exercises, and any woman who wants to take them can. I turn out, as I've always wanted a chance to do the military exercises. We furnish much amusement to the on-lookers. After dinner we are called to attention by the bugle and stand up for medical inspection. "We," the Red Cross, being semi-official, come under military control.

At 11 P.M. taps are sounded and we are supposed to keep quiet; some don't, though. It's impossible to stay below after the air is shut out, so almost everyone spends twenty-four hours on deck. I wish you could see me turning out for the night. I take off my uniform, put on my lavender kimono and bedroom slippers, and either a sweater or heavy coat; carry the big pillow off my bed, my little pillow and rug in one hand, and my life preserver, which we are ordered to keep within reach, in the other. I stumble up the stairs and have an awful time opening the door. Then my gropings begin, for the deck is pitchy black, and my chair is almost down at the other end of the ship. I have counted the lifeboats which I have to pass, for they can generally be seen against the sky. Then to find the passage into the back row where I am, I turn at right angles and walk forward until I bump something and am sent "a little farther down;" not knowing how much, I repeat the performance after a few steps, and another cheerful voice tells me to go still farther, and perhaps even the number of chairs to pass before reaching the passage; but that doesn't help a great deal, because I can see nothing. You can't imagine the relief when someone takes your arm and says, "Here it is, two steps this way," and politely shoves you towards your row. The marvel is that all the voices are so polite, for it is more than likely I have waked everyone up. Half the time, too, I lose my balance, and either my pillow or life preserver lands on top of them. After I have reached the end of the passage, my real trouble begins, for my chair is the seventh or eighth in, and the space between the rows is scarcely wide enough for one to walk in when unincumbered. I plunge on, however, stumbling against the people on the outside row, and on the rebound onto those on the inside. I never escape putting my hand on someone's face; oftener than not it lands in their mouths. When I finally reach the place where my chair ought to be, I begin to investigate each chair. If a rug is there already, it probably does not belong to me, but it may, so I have to examine to see if someone is under the rug. By this time I am in a state of hand-wringing, if I had any hands I could wring, and at the height of my despair, some unknown man becomes discouraged by the rumpus, gets up and settles me out of self-defense. One night it was too much even for him, so he told me to go out to a vacant chair in the front row, where he fixed me up with a second chair for my feet, so that I could lie down as flat as it is possible in a chair with a hump in it. One awful night I settled myself in the wrong chair, a long distance from mine. I was almost asleep when I noticed that my neighbors did not seem familiar. Fearing that the owner might turn up, I thought I'd better get out. I had made a terrible commotion getting in, and I felt like a fool bundling out again, but I sneaked off as quietly as possible with all my luggage, and finally found my own place.

I have been using the face of my wrist watch for a headlight on deck and it works quite well when I put my arm across my chest, but that is forbidden, I discovered one evening. A commanding voice from out of the blackness ordered "that light" out, so there will be more collisions for me. I already have a skinned nose; another girl has broken hers more or less.

When the wind is blowing and the water dashing up on the deck, you rather hope that if you have to get out in a hurry, it won't be that night. During the very hot weather in the Gulf Stream it would have been rather nice at times to have been nearer the water. No one seems in the least nervous. The Captain almost never appears. However, I think he feels pretty safe for the moment. Dusk and dawn are the favorite times for the submarine attacks, but most of us go below at dawn. Some mornings I have been caught in the deck-swabbing process and have to hop up on the nearest unoccupied chair, to escape the tidal wave which dashes down the deck.

The evenings have been rather dismal after the boys finished singing. Lights in the Salle de Conversation are so dim that we can neither read nor play cards there. Finally Mrs. Earle induced the Captain to open the dining saloon, where the light is better, between nine and eleven. He needed a good deal of persuasion, as on other trips people had insisted upon sleeping on the dining tables.

We have a daily dance. One of the lieutenants is a trombone player and he has collected all the men with instruments. For about an hour they play for dancing, which gives us a gay appearance. The music is delicious, it is so out of tune and queer, but it has a swing and I enjoy it a lot. A quartette from below sometimes sings between the dances, and one day two other boys came up. One played the piano and the other a violin, which had only one string left. He held it like a cello and could play anything provided his accompanist started in a low enough key.

The nuns have furnished me a little excitement by trying to catch glimpses of them unveiled and unrobed. Once I succeeded. Their curtain blew out just as one was climbing up into her berth, in a striped flannel nightgown and hair pugged tight down in the back.

All the Y. M. C. A. literature and library was put by mistake into the hold, so the days drag for some on board, and I've been tempted to send Leslie's magazines down to the boys. On Sunday the Y. M. C. A. and Salvation Army had a fifteen minute service. Songs—popular ones—were sung, "The Lord is My Shepherd" was read and explained; the Lord's Prayer, and we ended with "Onward Christian Soldiers." Not many boys took part. x x x x x x x

We have had the usual concert and entertainment, which took about two hours—everything of interest could have been done in fifteen minutes. Also a lecture on France, a mock trial, etc., nothing very sprightly. Some spicy gossip, but I suppose that is to be expected, conditions are so inviting.

We have to save electricity, water and ice. The water only runs in our basins at certain times, and ice water is next to impossible to get. At each meal we have only one piece of sour black bread and one lump of sugar, but everything else has the good French flavor.

There has been a rumor of possible quarantine—fourteen days—because of mumps on board. Rumors, too, that the other boats are annoyed with us because we go so slowly, and have signalled if we don't hurry up, they will leave us. We answered we didn't care if they did. They zigzag more than we and go back and forth across our bow in rather an impudent way. The officer in charge of our troops wonders why we were put in such a fast convoy. I hear that one of our boilers is broken.

Finally, on the fifth day, all the boats except the Lorraine did leave us for England.

Mrs. Earle has a pass which takes her all over the ship, as she teaches the soldiers French every day. There are both French and Italian lessons going at all hours in all parts of the boat.

On the second Sunday, the only service I heard was the little vesper singing from the nuns' cabin. It was very pretty and calming in the midst of the turmoil. No one is sensational, but the feeling of not knowing "what's doing" makes an undercurrent of suppressed excitement. Of course none of the boat's employees are allowed to say a word. If all the reports flying around were true, we should have been at the bottom of the Atlantic long ago. We always get daily war bulletins.

One night we were told that the Captain ordered the soldiers to keep their life preservers with them every instant. We had received an S.O.S. from a boat that was fighting a submarine not far from us, someone said; we could not find out where. We were all advised but not ordered to sleep out. For some reason I could not get excited, but I put Mother's little green bag under my pillow, with my brandy, malted milk tablets and flashlight in it, which added one more hump to my bed. That night, just as I reached my chair, three most awful flashes came from my bundle. Two or three exclaimed, "What is that!" Luckily no officer was near. I dropped everything in hopes the light would go out on the way down. Evidently a bottle had pushed the connection and lighted the bulb of my flashlight.

From the time of the S.O.S. scare we were in the danger zone again. The Lorraine was lost and we were alone, at the mercy of any old thing, in a terribly slow tub.

At five o'clock in the morning of the day before we landed, I saw two boats steaming straight for us. It didn't take them long to catch us, and I discovered that they were our convoy; two French torpedo boats. They certainly were sturdy and looked as if they had seen hard service. They zigzagged full speed around us and across our bow, until we reached the river. It seemed good to have company again, and the people on board were relieved. Our last night was supposed to be the most dangerous, and almost everyone slept out.

Some one called "Land!" on the morning of September 4th, and I saw the coastline quite distinctly, with its sand dunes and a tall white lighthouse in their midst. There were lots of little red-sailed fishing boats about, and an observation balloon attached to a boat which brought out our pilot. Then the torpedo boats left us.

After luncheon, the police, medical and customs inspectors came on board. I was the first to pass the police line, and they forgot to ask if I had a camera, so I was lucky! The customs inspector chalked my luggage and then asked if I had any sugar. I said "Yes," and he laughed and said it was forbidden, but he wouldn't say anything about a little. (The hospitals get what is taken away from people).

As we passed the American docks and buildings, the French kept saying, "America, all America!" There were miles of them. The first American locomotive we saw received a great cheer from the newcomers, and a Ford which hurried along right after it received a greater one. We were cheered and saluted constantly and asked where we came from, by many voices on the shore.

About fifteen minutes after we passed the American docks, we landed at Bordeaux, hoping they would not ship us up to Paris in the night train.

Wartime Paris

The Paris that Margaret Hall revisited in 1918 was a wartime capital, a wounded city. In September 1914 and again at the end of May 1918, advancing German troops threatened the city, in the first and second battles of the Marne. Paris taxis ferried troops to the battlefield in 1914 in order to save the city, symbolizing the heroism of the French and their spirit of national unity.[1] From early in the war, bombs hit the metropolis in nighttime raids by German zeppelins (rigid dirigibles) and "Taube" planes, so called for their dove-like shape. By 1917, waves of colossal "Gotha" bombers raided the city on moonlit nights, dropping bombs as heavy as six hundred pounds.[2] On March 23, 1918, the French capital was struck in daytime by mysterious shells from three long-range cannon called "Wilhelm Geschütz" or the "Paris Gun," hidden roughly seventy miles away in a forest near Coucy and firing intermittently without warning.[3] Although two of the "super cannon" were knocked out, by the time the third was withdrawn to Germany in August, the "unseen death" falling from the stratosphere had killed 256 in Paris.[4] While the use of planes and cannon against Paris had little military effect, their primary purpose of terrorizing civilians day and night had some success. Sirens sent everyone to cellars, disrupting sleep, even if one's windows and lodging remained intact. As refugees fled into Paris from German advances, government and other offices started to move further from the front. In a renewed exodus, up to eighty thousand fled in a day from Paris in June 1918.[5] On September 15, 1918, when Hall experienced the last fatal Gotha raid on Paris, she was dazzled by the fireworks but was shocked the next day by the sight of the destruction. She experienced another raid on September 20. Nonetheless, morale in the city remained surprisingly high, and Paris remained a magnet for soldiers on leave.

The working population of Paris had changed, as Hall discovered upon her arrival: her baggage was carried by a female porter. Another canteen worker, who had arrived in December 1917, commented lightly that "the train was manned by women."[6] Later in Hall's stay, a female chauffeur drove her to the battlefield of the Chemin des Dames. Eighty percent of eligible Parisian men enlisted. Their mortality rate was 14 percent, due to high losses in the bitter battles of 1918 and to the influenza pandemic.[7] By 1918, women had moved into many jobs formerly held by men. Roughly half of the workers in arms and munitions in the Department of the Seine were women. French feminists took note of this "female French army." Mme. Emile Borel gathered documents indicating perhaps two million women had been added to the seven million in the workforce in 1914. The importance of women to the war effort led Gen. Joseph Joffre to declare that if women in the factories stopped working for twenty minutes, the Allies would lose the war.[8] One expectation encouraged by this demographic shift was that women would earn the vote—a hope that would be disappointed in France.[9] The power of women workers became manifest in 1917, when the May 1917 mutiny of soldiers along the Chemin des Dames was followed by sympathetic strikes of Parisian "midinettes," women in the fashion industry. Interior Minister Louis-Jean Malvy estimated that 80 percent of the one hundred thousand strikers were women.[10] That imbalance reflected the fact that male strikers, even those in key munitions industries, could be sent to the front; women could not be punished in the same way. Strikers won wage increases that narrowed the gap between women and men. Feminists supported the strikers: the pacifist schoolteacher Hélène Brion and the couturière Jeanne Bouvier called for equal pay for equal work. Brion was tried for her pacifism (labeled "defeatist propaganda") and condemned to three years' suspended sentence of imprisonment and barred from employment as a teacher.[11]

The historian Jay Winter suggests that a French republican concept of citizenship fostered a more equitable distribution of necessary goods to civilians than was the case in Germany, whose economy was under military control that privileged the war and soldiers. Yet by the middle of 1917, the annual inflation rate was 100 percent on a basket of goods based on the price set in 1914.[12] In spite of the republican goal of fairness in distribution, manifest in rationing and price controls, women complained about shortages of coal, housing, and food. In January 1918, for example, a typical letter of complaint to the minister of public works protested the unjust allocation of almost four times as much coal to miners (called "draft-dodgers"!) as to war widows.[13]

One of the ways Hall measured the condition of wartime Paris was by noting how it differed from the city she had visited between 1902 and 1904. Shattered buildings in the city symbolized the loss of loved ones, just as they did in images of battlefields. The apartment where Hall's mother had lived had been destroyed. Nighttime blackouts and bombing raids, or "fireworks," were perhaps the most striking change. On the street, not only women workers but the black mourning garb of many women signaled four years of losses. Many other small details such as bread rationing and price controls showed that the war had changed everyday life.[14] Significant drops in protein consumption meant that people were thinner. When Hall walked with a loaf of bread under her arm, passersby wanted to touch it. Hall focused on the war injuries she saw in hospitals rather than the blind and armless or legless soldiers who mingled with civilians in Paris. Children in schools, however, drew pictures of the injured and war-mutilated that they saw on the streets.[15] In her own memoir of wartime France, the American novelist Edith Wharton described "the look" of Paris in February 1915 as darkened by curfew, its buildings "blind" at night, its "army" of refugees projecting a "look of concentrated horror," and wounded men carrying a "strangely purified" mask.[16]

By the time of Hall's arrival in September 1918, however, the rapidly growing influx of American soldiers had revived the hopes of Parisians. In June and July, American forces had helped to halt German advances at Belleau Wood and Soissons.[17] In mid September, Hall noted the arrival of wounded soldiers from the "big American offensive" at Saint-Mihiel. Their quick victory, in turn, was celebrated by the Parisians she met, who "adopted" the graves of American soldiers, decorating them with flowers. When Hall returned to Paris in the summer of 1919 to celebrate the signing of the Treaty of Versailles, the fourth of July, and Bastille Day, she found a city crowded with visitors and humming with activity. Her photographs show pedestrians strolling along the Champs Elysées, hung with gay bunting, or admiring war trophies. A long shot through the Arc de Triomphe captures the cenotaph that was set up to honor the dead.

Emma Lewis Coleman

Cenon

Paris, September 1918.

I have seen your French family. We landed at six o'clock, and were to take the ten o'clock train out. At the wharf we were piled into an army truck, balanced ourselves on the side rails and were rattled over the cobblestones to the centre of Bordeaux. There we were turned loose, with orders to be at the station at nine. It was then after seven, and Senon is on the other side of the river. At the pier I had asked a woman if we could go there, and she said it was too far, so I didn't talk much to her. I attacked a man next. He was much more encouraging and said we could do it in a taxicab. That was easier said than done. We flew around, talked to all the drivers of all the private cars we saw and to all the policemen. Finally a chauffeur pointed out a cab he thought was not taken. We rushed madly at it, found the driver in a café having a drink, but he decided to take us for twenty francs.

In Senon no one knew the street. We went to the post office, and found that it began with an S instead of an L, which made some difference. After we had driven for a while through the picturesquely curved little street, with low houses and gardens, we asked a woman where Mme. Olivier lived. She answered quickly, "Here, and there she is." We called her and asked her husband's name, to make sure we had made no mistake. She was somewhat overcome, but instantly asked us to her room, which was upstairs in what she called an old château. I guess anything not a peasant's house is a château here. She said at once, "These things do not belong to me; I have nothing." There were two beds, a little stove, three chairs, a table and cupboard, with a poor assortment of dishes. On the bed was a big pile of aprons which she was making for three cents apiece. She is a quick, bright woman, little and bent, probably from her hardships while she lived under German rule, (their home was in the Pas de Calais) and her escape under fire, with dead and wounded lying all about her; she wading through mud and water, sometimes almost up to her waist, carrying her little child to safety.

She put some shavings in her stove and said at least she could make good coffee. We had a cup apiece, but only one teaspoon for all of us! She had some sugar which she made us take. I hated to, but she said she could get a little once in a while—because she has a child, I imagine. It grew dark but she did not light a candle; perhaps she had none.

After coffee we went to see "le petit Florent," who was making a call on his grandmother, Olivier's mother. He was pale and much like the picture of his father. The grandmother was frail and nice; also Olivier's sister—she was writing to her brother when we went in—very pretty and polite. They, too, wanted to give us coffee, but finally brought out their good Bordeaux wine and we all had some, "le petit" even, in a little glass of his own. They talked much of the grandfather; how the Boches had forced him to work in the mud and rain and he had had pneumonia and died the next day, and "such a good husband, and a man who had never been sick before in his life." They all worked for the Germans, were paid a bit by the town, and were fed by the Americans. Your poilu is getting better. He was gassed and the Salonicá fever came back. I think they were glad to see us.

On the way back to Bordeaux we saw a big fire in a phosphate factory, but quite unlike America, no one seemed to pay much attention to it.

We had no time for dinner, and were packed, six of us, into a compartment and left for the night. No one slept a wink. A night like that, on top of twelve other wakeful nights on the boat was certainly a cap to the climax. When we reached Paris we were the worst looking, dirtiest crowd you ever saw, ever in your whole life. The Y.M.C.A. had fine accommodations in Bordeaux and came up on the day train, rested and ready for work. The Red Cross man (English in American Service) who met us acted as though he couldn't get rid of us fast enough and said there were no rooms in Bordeaux. Some of the girls tried to wash up and do their hair, but I was discouraged with the outlook and toilet accommodations, so made no attempt.

Going through Orleans we saw our first German prisoners—stolid fellows with set jaws, and W.P. on their caps and shirts. Mrs. Earle was dying to speak to them, but it seemed best not to take a chance. They were sweeping off the platform and stopped to watch the train.

At Paris I rushed down the platform and got a girl porter to go back with me to lug my heavy things; felt like a criminal; it was that or nothing, though. She staggered under the load but was nice about it when I offered to help and said it wasn't necessary. No one knew what to do; finally a Red Cross man came along and he didn't know much more, so I started ahead to the street with my porter, where we found a pleasant Miss Allen, who collected baggage checks, divided us into different living quarters, put us into army trucks and told us we were to register at Red Cross Headquarters at ten o'clock. It was then half past nine. She said she could not be cruel enough to ask us to get no breakfast, but requested us not to wash up, but to go as we were, for a hundred and twenty-five were expected the next hour from Italy.

We were taken miles up Avenue Victor Hugo and deposited in a pension where nothing was ready; not a room to go to, no water, no breakfast, but Madame, in a kimono, hurried up coffee, which we drank out of great bowls, ate a hunk of bread, and then flew back to the trucks, which landed us at the office a little after ten. We were enrolled, signed more papers, gave more references, etc. Finished at twelve, and were told we were to go to see someone at two o'clock, another at three and another at four.

We lunched down town and I engaged a room, bath and meals at Hotel de l'Arcade, where the Smith girls are, for twenty-two francs. We can have hot water only Saturday and Sunday, a law to save coal. I could not stay in that pension and room with another girl. After two weeks of discomfort I felt that I must have quiet, rest and privacy, at least, while I could.

Between two and three I rushed down to the U.S. Provost Marshall and registered there, which has to be done within the first twenty-four hours. Then at three there was a lecture by Mr. Gibson about Red Cross work and after that they tried to send us to the French police for our cards of identification, but could not get transportation for all of us. Two of us, Hospital Hut women, were turned over to somebody else, who was not in the office, so I went back to Avenue Victor Hugo for my luggage and settled at this hotel.

I have no hopes of getting anywhere near the front. The Red Cross does not send women near, they tell me. They may only say that because everybody wants to go, and the easiest way out of it for them is to say "Nothing doing!" Salvation Army is what I want and I wish to goodness I had tried for it. It's getting late and I ought to go to sleep. Paris is lovely. The valuable monuments are covered with concrete casings feet deep. Tell Mother it is lucky she wasn't spending the winter in her Paris room; it served as a target for one of the shells of the big gun and the place is shattered. I took a look at it today. It's a favorite locality for the Gothas, also. We are just back of the Madeleine. They all say the Germans are too busy now to think of raids or big guns. Lots of military people here, but there always have been in Paris. There are about as many Americans as French. Have not seen sugar of any kind. Horses all look thin. I have only seen one well fed; the others are pitiful. I mentioned it to a policeman and he said the people were the same, and he certainly did look white and thin. I think I feel too tired to have things penetrate very much yet.

I have met a good many Bryn Mawr girls, among them Emily Cross, who told me to try for the work I wanted and not to be in too much of a hurry, so I decided not to sign up with any department yet awhile. As I was supposed to do Search work and not Hut, I went to Mrs. Moore's office. Read casualty letters and reports, to see if I could do the work. They almost made me weep; in fact they did depress me the whole morning. I should have to write letters about the boys' last words; what they did and said, their funerals, etc., and collect all the information I could to send to their parents. I almost decided to take it, but just before the office closed I thought I'd make one more try for the front, and canteen work, which I really want, so went to see Mrs. Vanderbilt. She was out, but I saw Miss Burnett. I had heard somewhere that the only canteens the Red Cross have near the front are French ones, and as I like the idea of working with the French, I asked for a French canteen. Miss Burnett immediately said that they had just had a call for more workers for Châlons, and she thought I could go there, but told me to see Mrs. Vanderbilt on Monday, so my hopes are high. The Y.M.C.A. and Salvation Army have all the near front places.

Anne Harriman Sands Vanderbilt

If I get the Châlons work I shall have to stay here ten days longer. I am glad not to rush right away, for I am tired and have a cold. Everyone seems to have one. It is not warm, and rains part of every day already, so the bad weather has begun early.

We have had to search for our trunks, which were at a station far out of the way. While waiting to get them, we went to the American Red Cross canteen in the station, and were treated to rice and coffee; the rice, cooked with a little lemon peel and milk, was delicious.

This is a refugee canteen, and in it was a group of about twenty from Amiens; old men and women; one young woman with a baby which was pale and thin. She told me her husband had gone crazy from shell shock. One of the old women had been travelling all round the country, trying to find some of her family who would take her and no one could or would, so she had come back to Paris. They were all crying, some very hard; the old men and all. I almost added to the chorus by weeping too, and again had misgivings as to the value I'd be over here. The canteen workers told them they must be brave; that we were pushing the Germans back and soon they could go home, but they said they had been told they could not return for eight or nine months. A French woman, a lady, wife of a high official, was writing a letter to the mayor of a town, to ask him to let an old woman go home. She said she knew it would do no good, but it made the woman feel better. They had started up the phonograph and a little girl was playing the violin, to divert them, and after a while the weeping gradually stopped.

We had happened to meet the Smith girls, who were on a trunk hunt too, so we stayed together and all thought this our first hard taste of war.

Mrs. Earle found an agreeable Egyptian working at the canteen who persuaded the director of the station to send our luggage to the hotel in a refugee omnibus, so we all piled in and sat on top of the trunks.

Early Monday morning I saw Mrs. Vanderbilt and boldly asked for Châlons, which she gave to me, probably. I am not sure that she liked my asking for it, but I am so delighted to get it that I am almost like a Cheshire cat.

I don't write every day or two, because steamers don't go very often and I am generally too tired to write at night and too much occupied during the day trying to do all I can, to give up the time to letter writing. I feel it is my one great opportunity to see things. It is rather hard, even for me, for I did not know one thing when I came and everyone is so rushed with their own business that they don't have time to bother with anyone else. I hesitate to ask a question of anyone, so all the information I have I have acquired "by the way." No French person of authority likes to tell you anything in the way of facts, which adds to the difficulty. Then locomotion is difficult. There are taxicabs but they are expensive for Paris and hard to get in popular hours. The Metro.

is always filled with a pushing, elbowing mob, and anyway you have to walk about as far under ground as you would if you went all the way on foot over ground, so that is unsatisfactory, too. I can't seem to find any omnibus lines to go anywhere in now, so I go on my feet as much as I can and understand why they tell you to bring over a good supply of shoes.

I think the last time I wrote I was uncertain about landing Châlons. I have it, I think. It is in the French zone and it takes longer to get papers to go there than it does to the American, so I am here for a week longer, anyway, as the French papers could not be started until my Red Worker's card came. I know that I have to get my board and lodging off the town, and they say that the climate is so bad that you feel like cutting the fog with a knife in order to breathe. I also know that the people in the canteen are worn out, and the office here hopes that my temper is good. It is one of the best equipped canteens, I'm told,—a most desirable one, with an attractive staff of workers, and one that is given as a reward for work in less interesting places.

Some of the Smith unit have started for the near front today. They call themselves the "shock unit." There is a saying here—a little vicious, perhaps—that the only Americans in France are the Marines and the Smith Unit. (Perhaps the Smith Unit comes first, even). They have done wonderful work, anyway.

A big American offensive is on and the wounded and gassed are being rushed to Paris straight from the front. All the hospitals are over-crowded.

They say Paris has grown more cheerful within the last few months. Occasionally you see people sitting out at cafés, a thing they have not done for years, almost. The whole atmosphere has changed. They adore American soldiers, so they say. Not so American women workers, I take it.

Sandbags cover the monuments and are piled in front of the windows of the timid. Strips of paper are pasted on all the windows, many in fancy designs; to keep the vibrations from breaking the glass and if broken, from falling and injuring people. There are almost no private automobiles and only half as many taxicabs as usual, but they go twice as fast, so your chances are no better.

We went one day to the American Red Cross hospital at Neuilly, which is magnificiently managed. As we entered we saw bunches of flowers tied with red, white and blue ribbon, evidently for boys who would never go home. A chaplain offered to take us around. He stopped to speak to the very sick boys. I felt awkward about going up to the beds and talking; they looked too sick to be bothered. Those I did speak to were in chairs, wheeling themselves around. One boy from Detroit with half a leg gone was so cheerful that I wondered how it was possible to have so much courage. He had been two weeks in the hospital and expected to be out in another. Everything that money and skill can give the boys is there; the hospital is enormous. Practically all the patients are surgical cases. Some of the wards look almost like factories, arms and legs by the hundreds are suspended in such queer hanging apparatus, having the Dakin treatment. The chaplain wanted us to watch the doctors dress a typical shell wound. I hated to stare at the boy, but looked at them take off the dressing and saw the great deep hole in his thigh. We went through the ward for face wounds, but it was so shocking that I tried to see nothing. All the nurses look like ladies. We saw Mary Hoyt in her ward. A "searcher" was at work in another ward. Somehow I feel so stunned by it all that it doesn't seem to sink in. I have no feelings left. I am glad that I am not to be a "searcher," though.

Mary Fellows Hoyt

When we came out we tried to go for a little drive in the Bois, but no one would take us; it is not allowed, they must save gas. We walked round a little, saw loving couples, and came home for tea in our rooms. No food is served in France between meal hours.

A day or two later we went to the Red Cross hospital on a race course at Auteuil. This is all of big tents, not a single building. They say they are to keep it open all winter. I'm sorry for the nurses; one had just died of pneumonia. Perhaps the patients can keep warm under blankets. Their flag was at half mast and we were told there had just been a funeral. We saw the camions and a few soldiers forming behind to go to the cemetery with them. It was a pathetic little company, with no one who really cared, only soldiers whose business it was to go with them. We watched them start. On each coffin was a bunch of flowers and I suppose a little aluminum identification disk, to be nailed to his white cross.

The hospital was full of gassed patients. There are all sorts of villainous gasses, for external and internal torture, and sometimes they get the whole collection at once. They were a nice class of boys, many from Pennsylvania; you have probably read about them; they kept things busy around here for a while. They told us that fresh air was their only cure. Most of them wear colored glasses and their throats are so burned that they can scarcely speak. They had been trapped, they said; gone into dugouts near Soissons, left by the Germans, who had planted gas bombs with only stoppers in them, and when the boys walked on them the stoppers fell out and they were gassed—eighteen hundred of them!

Of course they tell us all sorts of interesting and remarkable tales, some almost incredible; such as German women, sixteen of them, fighting like men and fighting well. The Americans did not know it until they had shot four. The others were taken. The story is doubted, so take it for what it is worth. It was told me by a poor boy who could speak only in a very low whisper. The shell which killed his two companions and school chums had taken off his mask and knocked him unconscious. He had thought he never could kill a man, but found it simple when the time came. He showed us the scar the other fellow's bayonet had made first, and now he is crazy to get back to avenge his friends. He had seen Germans chained to their machine guns, and said the prisoners were half fed and glad to be taken, but treacherous always.

We went to the Hospital Hut, which was crowded with men able to walk. It was a beautiful day, and they were out all over the grounds in pajamas and bathrobes. I even saw them down at the gates of Paris in that costume, pushing each other in wheeled chairs. We were shown about the food storehouse. The man told us that morning it had been practically empty, but when we saw it, it was well stocked; great bottles of malted milk, sugar, flour, etc., and barrels of home made American preserves and jellies, made by our women, labeled in their own writing, and arrived at their destination in good condition. I was so glad to see them. I guess the boys will be gladder. They were having canned salmon hash for supper that night and good looking fresh beans. They all thought it a fine hospital, and appeared to like the way they were treated. In the Hut they were playing games and smoking, those who could; being served ice cream and fruit, both of which are good for their burned throats, and one, a musical genius, who had been a patient and had been begged off from going back for a while longer because of his gift for entertaining, was playing an accompaniment for another who was singing an original ditty about a cootie and her family which arrived a day after she did, and their families which came the next day. I imagine the cootie is a source of inspiration to many an impromptu poet. It was an interesting scene and I couldn't help thinking how many mothers would have given all they possessed to be where I was at that moment. The strong patients always help the weak ones to get about.

We sometimes go out to take a look at Paris in the dark; there are no lights. Street lamps are covered with black shades and bulbs are painted blue. All window shutters are closed and curtains drawn. The police came after us one night because we had not pulled ours low enough. Automobiles have only faint sidelights, painted blue. You almost walk into people on the street. Before I dare to go out I always study the map until I have a mental picture of where I am going, as it is impossible ever to <u>see</u> where you are.

I bought the first white bread I've had in months at the American Commissary yesterday. Had to carry it, a can of jam and bundle of matches under my arm unwrapped. Everyone carries bread in that way, so I was in the fashion. On the way home I went into a shop, and the people could not get over such "joli pain." They,—three women and a soldier,—patted it, caressed it, smelled it, exclaiming all the time, "quel joli pain, just like cake." I offered them some, but they would not take it. They were full of the big American victory at St. Mihiel.

Sunday I went alone to Notre Dame. On my way met a sailor from the Mount Vernon, who told me about the torpedoing. He said it was a marvel that they got her to port; that the captain considers it a perfect crew, and wants to keep them together on some boat. After Notre Dame went to St. Gervais to see the Good Friday ruin. The worst was all shut off, so no one could see it. A stone column fell and I think that did most of the damage. In the afternoon we went in search of the American soldiers' cemetery at Sûresnes. We had a hard time finding it, as no one seemed to know just what we wanted. Got into a taxicab driven by a Greek and finally after much inquiry and talk we found it, on the side of a clay hill, under Mt. Valerien. There is a beautiful view of Paris from there. It is just a small plot, surrounded by a white wooden fence, with very many, three or four hundred, little white crosses, as near together as possible, and places, some already dug, for more who are to come. They come every day, the French told us; in the morning the men to prepare and in the afternoon the little funeral processions, always at the same time. The French people in the neighborhood adopt the graves, put a metal plate with their own names on the crosses, and always see that the grass is kept green or fresh flowers put on every few days. Some take many graves. One man has taken a whole row, and comes each day to bring flowers. If he is prevented, he sends his maid. She was there on Sunday, and told us about it. The graves adopted by the well-to-do people have elaborate wreaths of bead flowers, grass borders and flowering plants on them. Those are often officers' graves. The ones adopted by the poorer women have fresh flowers also, but they are laid on top of the yellow clay. Whether adopted by rich or poor they are cared for with great tenderness and reverence, and when we thanked them, they always said, "Poor boys, they have won all we can give them, and they are so far from their homes and their mothers, we do for them what we should like to have done for us." It was quite full of French that day; we were the only Americans, and I was so glad that I had made the effort to go. It is hard to get to and perhaps that is why people don't do it. One woman came up to us before we left; she had adopted one of the graves made the day before, one of those boys whose funeral we saw start from the hospital, and she wanted to know how old the soldier was, for she had a boy of nineteen in the army and expected him home soon, and she wanted to tell him all about the Americans who had died for France. We said quickly, "Twenty-two," for we knew she wanted an answer. There were flowers on his grave and she couldn't understand it, as long as it was her grave. I told her probably a friend or soldier companion had put the flowers there, and that calmed and satisfied her. She was evidently jealous already, to think that someone else could touch her possession. As we came away a nice American boy stopped us and asked if he could show us the way to the train. He is in the search-light service of the defense of Paris on Mt. Valerien. He explained to us how the air raids took place, how they telephoned ahead when the Germans passed certain points, and we all decided that they had enough to do without annoying Paris again, so I was much surprised when I was waked that night (Sunday, September 15th) by Mrs. Earle's voice, saying, "Margaret, the sirens are blowing, get up!" I think if she hadn't called me I should have slept through the whole thing. You can just guess that Margaret did get up and in a hurry too. I didn't dare turn on the light, so fumbled round for my kimono and fur coat. Then I grabbed my money and flashlight and flew into Mrs. Earle's room, where we stayed hanging out the window for an hour and a half. She said her knees were shaking so with excitement that she could scarcely stand. I was crazy to go out to get a full view from Place de la Concorde, which was of course impossible. When I got to Mrs. Earle's room the "alerte" was in full blast. First three guns go off, before the sirens, which by the way are on top of all the churches (most peculiar looking megaphone affairs, pointing in all directions); then comes the "alerte"—the sirens. Everyone on the street is supposed to rush to the nearest shelter, but how they can see where they are, I don't see, as the streets are pitchy black. On almost all the houses there are signs saying, shelter for fifty, or any number their cellars will hold, and people all pile in. Mrs. Earle and I decided we would see one raid through. It was blood curdling to hear the sirens. They sounded like enormous creatures cornered, moaning and wailing for help. Finally they grew fainter and fainter, and at last seemed almost like echoes as we heard them from other parts of the city. In two or three minutes, we saw flashes of light in the sky and knew the defense of Paris must be at work. Then the searchlights began. They came up from all directions and searched the sky. Soon we heard the rumble of distant guns, which grew louder and louder and finally became an incessant roar. Shells began to burst near us and we heard the whirl of German aeroplanes approaching. They came nearer and nearer and the explosions became louder and louder, until finally they seem to be right over our heads, flying very low. No French planes go up, for they are caught in their own barrage if they do. The Germans kept going back and forth, and in a few moments we saw a red reflection in the sky and knew something had been set on fire. It was all so thrilling that I couldn't feel. I just stared until I thought my eyes would pop out. The bombs looked like little flashlights in the sky, and the exploding shrapnel like falling stars only brighter. We seemed surrounded by fireworks on all sides, and I couldn't realize that it was the real thing and not a Fourth of July celebration. Once in a while before the raid really started someone would turn on a light or light a match and then voices from out of the darkness would call, "Lumiére," dragging the "ére" and the light would disappear instantly. After the raid we all went to bed and at 3.30 were waked by another "alerte" and the whole performance was repeated, only it did not last so long, and the Boches did not break through the barrage that time. At the end the church bells ring and a bugler goes round the streets playing a cheerful little tune—the "berloque." After it was over I went to see the Smith girls. They had been hurried down into the cellar by the clerk and had spent the night there. In the middle of the affair the maid remarked that the ladies of 24 and 29 were not there, so the manager flew up to get us, but either was sidetracked or could not make us hear, for we never saw him at all. The girls said it was quite funny in the cellar; one woman fainted and had to be handed out; some of the women appeared in magnificent Parisian hats, and some with their hair in strings down their backs; some men in pajamas and others in swallow tails, shirtless and collarless. It was an amusing crowd, I imagine. The clerk would say every once in a while, "Here they come nearer; now they are flying over us," etc. There were slugs on the walls and floors and I am glad we were too ignorant to realize our danger, for if we had seen the destruction which we saw the next day, we should have hesitated that night about standing in such an exposed position. It takes quite a while to get details about a raid, and not much is ever told. About a dozen people were killed by flying shrapnel, mostly those in the streets, and the material damage was great. The next morning Mary Hoyt and I went to view the ruins. It was a big raid and a very long one. The Germans came in waves from all directions, the paper said, and dropped many bombs. Two German planes were brought down, one was found near Paris with three Germans killed beside it. We expected a raid the next night but had a thunder shower instead, and each night since it has rained. They had arranged to come every night for ten nights, up to the 25th, so papers found on a captured officer said. They say Paris was at its wits end the day the big gun began. The sirens kept blowing steadily for three hours and people almost lost their senses. No one knew what had struck them.

The only other interesting thing I've done, was to go to see the refugee quarters at St. Sulpice, where fifteen hundred refugees are kept all the time, and where during the German drive two or three thousand were kept over night often. They came, whole towns at a time, in camions and canal boats, and sometimes drawn by their own horses, bringing as many of their household belongings as they could get together, and as many of their animals and pets as they could manage. One woman refused to go to bed without her goat; she got it upstairs and into bed, and not until the police went after her did she give it up. Another woman arrived with ninety-three bundles; she took up a whole camion for herself and was checked in and out of St. Sulpice the next morning without losing one! Some days they give one or two hundred babies baths before they start off at eight in the morning. The babies are always washed and given new clothes before they are sent away. It is quite a wonderfully arranged place. A babies' hospital, a theatre, a garden for the children to play in, monks' cells for the residents to live in, and in the corridors countless cot beds for those passing through. There is also a part reserved for soldiers of the devastated country, who have no homes to go to during their "leave".

I'll let you know my new address as soon as possible. Of course I may not go to Châlons after all. You never can tell when they may switch you off or where. Where the need is greatest you go and it may be greater somewhere else just now. They want people for the aviation camps, I believe.

We were sent one night to the Gare de Vaugirard to help with the French hospital evacuation train. The freight station is used for the evacuations and the platform between the sanitary trains is full of tents with a little kitchen in between them. We talked to the boys—there were three hundered and ten of them—the convalescents, who seemed charmed to be amused, all except one boy, a professional singer, who had been gassed and lost his voice; he was so discouraged that nothing we could say had any effect—his life had been ruined and he might as well die now and have it over. Those on the stretchers in the train we did not see. A Red Cross lieutenant soon told those who were walking about to form a line, and cigarettes, coffee and sandwiches were passed by French women, who always said, "From the American Red Cross."

Capt. Georges Guynemer

On our way to Bellevue Hospital we stopped at the Invalides to see Guynemer's aeroplane and the captured Boches war relics. The plane is half under a shelter in a corner, and looks like a huge dragon fly just coming out. Wreaths and festoons of flowers decorate it. Long streamers of flowers hanging down from the front form perfect antennae. It did look so alive. He had brought down nineteen Boches in it. Then we went to see Napoleon's tomb, or rather the place where it is. It is covered with a pyramid of sandbags; thousands and thousands of them, some rotting and letting out the sand, which gives the place an untidy look.

When we arrived at the station for Bellevue, we found there was no funicular to take us to the top of the hill, but I enjoyed climbing up through the narrow street, with vine-covered walls, and peeping through the gates into lovely gardens.

The château on top, which is a gas hospital, is owned by Isadora Duncan, and she rents it to the U.S.A. for $1000 a month, I was told. The big mirror-lined hall, in which she and her pupils danced, is full of cots; the mirrors have been painted over. I asked if Isadora comes out to dance for the boys and the nurse said, "No." We talked to some of the patients, who looked well. They remarked that they might look well, but if they felt energetic and walked a step too far they were apt to fall dead at any moment. "They do it every day," one said.

Mrs. Earle and I were fortunate in having a chance to see a hospital train straight from the front come in at La Chapelle. Strangers are not made very welcome at that station. It is a French army post and they don't care to have Americans there. Some women have fainted and acted so foolishly that the Red Cross has been requested to bring only two each night as interpreters. It was a train of our boys coming down from Soissons and expected at eleven o'clock. We started from here about nine thirty, but heard when we arrived that the train would not get in until two. The French nurses were kind and invited us to sleep on hospital cots in their quarters and as there seemed to be some friction in the American Red Cross room and a very cross lieutenant in charge, we decided to keep away, and accepted their invitation. There were about a dozen steel helmets hanging up on the walls, which the nurses have to wear when they work during the raids. We were called in time to see the big U.S.A. train back slowly into the station. The suspense was frightful for me. It was my nearest approach to the battlefield, and no one knew whether we were to have one of those trains of agonized gassed boys or a simple wounded train. However, I felt reassured when I saw some of the boys lean out of the windows. First the walking cases came hobbling out, some in uniform and some in dressing gowns. They were sent off as quickly as possible. Then the stretcher cases were brought into the enormous hall and the stretchers placed on iron rails made to hold them. We had to get pillows for their heads, blankets for them if they were cold, and after the doctors had read the tags which were pinned on their clothes, and had given each a number card, which showed the hospital to which he was to be taken, we went round and gave chocolate or coffee to all except those who had Number 8. They were fever cases and could have no food. They had all been to first aid stations, but we were told to look out for fresh blood or for arms or legs in uncomfortable positions. Three hundred and forty came on that train, one real American Indian among them. At four o'clock everything was over and we were sent home in an ambulance.

The next afternoon Mrs. Earle, Ruth Gaines and I went to the hospital at Jointville-le-Pont, just beyond Vincennes. We thought it was a shell shock hospital, but found it was for pneumonia cases. The hospital hut worker took us about. While we were in the court we saw a little procession coming towards us. It was those who had just died being taken out. The chaplain came first, bareheaded, with an officer, and then four men carrying a pine coffin covered with our flag; then four more carrying another, and following them two or three privates. They went through an arch into another court, and came back in a moment to return again with two more coffins. After they had passed, we followed them, and saw the big camion standing there still waiting, and the little procession starting back once more. They returned immediately carrying others. As they were coming through the arch an officer signalled to some patients who were well enough to be sitting outside, to stand. We saw seven driven off. The hospital hut woman said that before she came two days ago, the boys well enough to be out had nothing to do but sit in the court and watch that procession go by all day long.

Plans were made and unmade at the office. I saw Châlons fading into the dim distance. I thought they had found someone better suited to go, and spent one bad night over it, waking at four to be sure to be at the office before it opened. There I was told they were going to try to rush us through without papers, as there was to be a great offensive on that front, and they needed immediate help. My spirits rose!

I have signed up for six months at Châlons-sur-Marne!

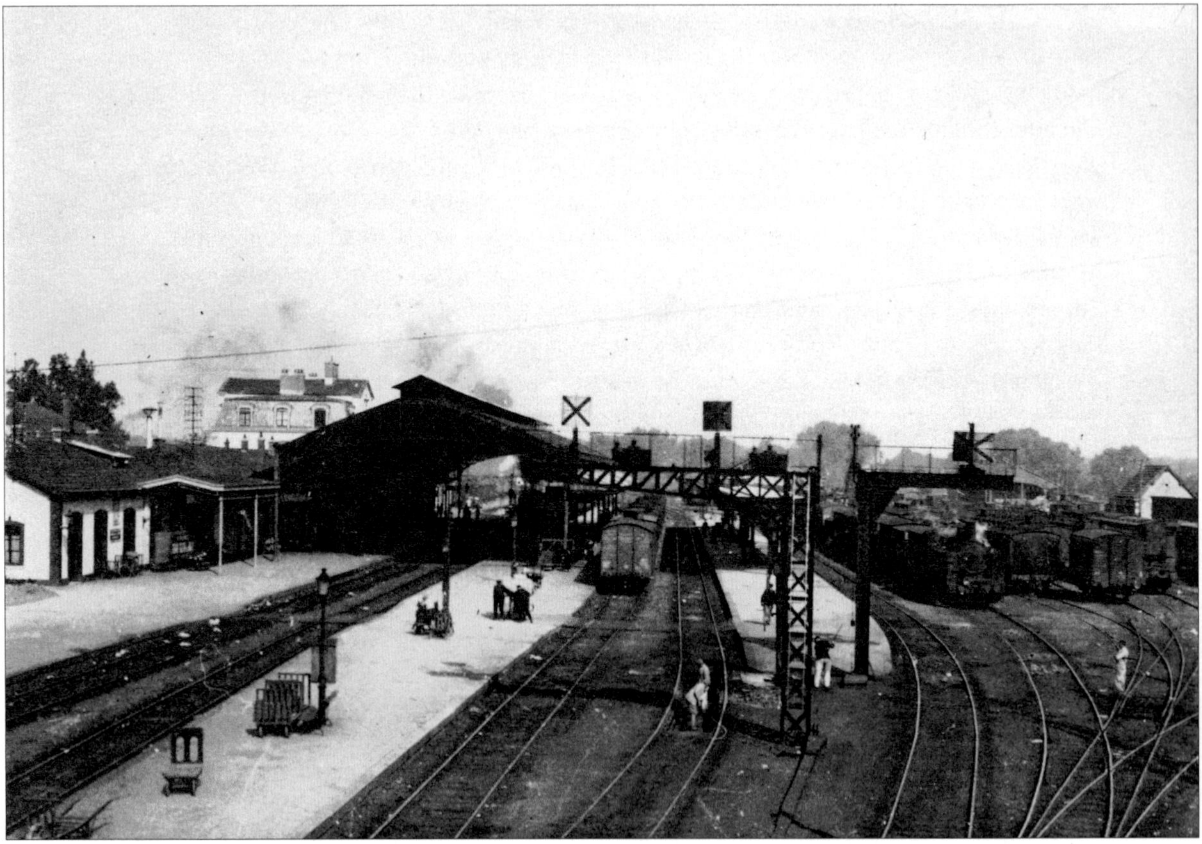

The Canteen at Châlons-sur-Marne

The Cantine des Deux Drapeaux at Châlons-sur-Marne was set up in the "French" war sector near Reims by Marjorie Nott and Anna V. S. Mitchell in June 1917 in order to serve French soldiers on their way to and from the besieged city of Verdun. In the fall, it was assimilated into the system of Red Cross canteens serving the American Expeditionary Force (AEF), whose sector lay further east.[1] When the canteen was formally opened in September, the *New York Times* spelled out the "special qualifications" by which the Woman's Bureau of the American Red Cross had selected one hundred women to take charge of canteen and rest stations in France. These women "between the ages of 30 and 50" were "willing to serve without pay and bear their own expenses abroad." The organization sought only "those of robust health who can speak French and who are willing to undergo hardships and discomforts" for canteen work, although in fact younger women also found jobs.[2] Hall may have read about this canteen in the *Times* before she was assigned to it by Anne Vanderbilt at the Paris office of the Red Cross. She considered it a plum assignment in the war zone for experienced workers. During a night raid at Châlons-sur-Marne, she wrote to her brother Philip how lucky she felt; yet she asked, "Can you think up any way or excuse for me to get up to the front[?] It is so near that I hate not to go."[3]

Hall notes that Châlons-sur-Marne was a railway crossing on the important route between Reims and Verdun, in the region of the Marne that had repeatedly been threatened by the Germans. During the First Battle of the Marne, forces commanded by Maj. Gen. Hugo von Seydewitz bombed the station on September 3, 1914, then occupied the town between September 4 and 12. He took three officials hostage and demanded a "deposit" of five hundred thousand gold and silver francs to guarantee the good behavior of the townspeople who had not fled.[4] In response to damages inflicted in 1914, foreign relief agencies coordinated assistance with the municipal government. The YMCA and British Quakers arrived in December 1914 to offer rural reconstruction work and relief work in town; the Friends set up a maternity hospital in Châlons. While most of Anne Morgan's CARD work was centered north of Soissons in the Aisne, the group also funded French hospitals and a maternity home in Châlons-sur-Marne, starting in 1917. In the course of her memoir Hall observes several times the efficacious work of English ambulance drivers in the region around Châlons and Reims. These might have been members of the British First Aid Nursing Yeomanry (FANY), or the Hackett-Lowther ambulance corps, a volunteer group attached to the French military, which was based near Cugny and then at Compiègne.[5]

Despite (or because of) the danger of this zone, visitors were drawn to Châlons on trips to the front. In February 1915, when Edith Wharton traveled on behalf of the Red Cross to inspect a fever hospital in Châlons, she found the town to be a beehive of activity:

> If one could think away the "éclopés" [lame] in the streets and the wounded in the hospitals, Châlons would be an invigorating spectacle. When we drove up to the hotel even the grey motors and the sober uniforms seemed to sparkle under the cold sky. The continual coming and going of alert and busy messengers, the riding up of officers (for some still ride!), the arrival of much-decorated military personages in luxurious motors, the hurrying to and fro of orderlies, the perpetual depleting and refilling of the long rows of grey vans across the square, the movements of Red Cross ambulances and the passing of detachments for the front, all these are sights that the pacific stranger could forever gape at.[6]

Anne Vanderbilt more soberly recorded a night at Châlons in August 1916, when she listened to anti-aircraft guns after traveling along roads lit up by the glimmer of flares.[7]

Intense military traffic created a need for a place where men could buy meals when on relief or in transit, and the canteens, like the French Foyers du Soldat, were designed to foster psychological recovery in common rooms that provided newspapers, cards, and writing paper. Canteens were established not only by the Red Cross but also by other groups such as the YMCA and the Salvation Army to provide inexpensive food and a safe place to rest. With their homey shelters and recreation centers, canteens offered an alternative to bars and were praised for "bringing together the classes and the masses."[8] On February 17, 1918, the *New York Times* published a set of six letters written between September and October 1917 by one of the half-dozen canteen workers assigned to Châlons-sur-Marne. She describes her trips to Verdun and Reims, as workmen completed the canteen's construction. Set next to the railroad tracks, this major center was composed of a huge dining room to serve meat and vegetables as well as hot drinks; a reading room "with papers, magazines and games"; a theater; a barber shop; showers; and a dormitory with stretchers for eight hundred placed on double-decker frames.[9] Three photographs in the *Times* show the canteen filled with men; they match postcards Hall pasted into her memoir. Hall's own photographs show the varied services, including a soldier receiving a haircut. On the back of one postcard of the kitchen that Hall numbered, she identified where fires were kept going all day long, where she slept when on night duty, and "where I spent hours this week cooking chocolate and having nightmares about it by night" (61).

Edith O'Shaughnessy, who volunteered in the canteen briefly in October 1917, drew a romantic image of the place, emphasizing the aesthetic effect of a building designed by former students at the National School of Fine Arts in Paris. She wrote that a lieutenant had "converted those old railway sheds into something most artistic. The walls are painted cream with strips of pale blue; conventionalized fruit-filled baskets and designs of flowery wreaths decorate them at intervals. The great roof has drapings of white muslin, and square, engarlanded shades make the light shine softly on the blue-clad men coming and going, coming and going." Faced with serving one thousand men, she found her work uplifting: "As I look out over the big room I feel that in the whole world it is the only place to be. Around me surged those blue waves; the light caught helmets and drinking-cups; there was the mist of breath and smoke; the familiar

"Outside Canteen."

sound of laughing, disputing, humming. That strange atmosphere of fatality hung over each and every one, yet with a merciless confusing of destinies in the extreme anonymity of it all."[10]

Such idealistic reports on canteen work encouraged American women to support the war effort and to volunteer in hospitality huts. In November 1917, Charles Norton reported on the Red Cross canteen offerings in an interview with the *New York Times*:

> French officers praised without reserve the Red Cross canteen work at a railroad centre near the front, where Miss Margery Nott and her assistants are doing a wonderful work. A freight shed beside the station has been converted by the soldiers themselves, many of them Beaux

Arts men, into an attractive hotel, where a shower bath, a clean bed, and a good supper can be had for 20 cents or less. Formerly those troops on their way home for a six-day leave would arrive at and leave this important junction tired, dirty, and hungary [sic]. If they bought anything it was at highwayman's prices. Now they go home clean, fed, rested. That helps morale.

Norton continued enthusiastically, "Every American who has given a dollar or has done one bit of work for the Red Cross has helped to win this war, for in so desperate a struggle morale is all-important."[11]

The night of September 25, the day Margaret Hall arrived, a major Allied assault began. French general Henri Gouraud warned the *directrices* of the canteen that afternoon, but the French soldiers had already spread word as they passed through. Tremendous crowds of soldiers besieged the women at the counter, "clamoring for saucisson, or fromage or chocolate." Within a few days, Anna Mitchell noted that her "cantiners" had broken all records serving seven hundred meals, in addition to hundreds of cups of coffee or hot chocolate, in two to three hours.[12] The canteen was incessantly busy, except when it was temporarily shut under bombardment, sending the soldiers and workers into their air-raid shelters or basements. Two bombs in early October that struck a nearby French evacuation hospital killed over five dozen men and wounded one of Hall's colleagues. Historian Susan Zeiger attributes some "dissatisfaction" to canteen women who worked with hungry men on leave, impatient to be fed. Canteen workers were left drained by the long hours of heavy work, the discomfort of the rudimentary unheated housing without running water, and the roar of bombing raids that disrupted sleep. Women unaccustomed to lifting twenty-pound coffee pots found themselves exhausted by the domestic work of cooking, cleaning, and serving without interruption.[13] Indeed, the thirty-two-year-old twin Cromwell sisters, with whom Hall worked, were so depressed at the end of their stay in France that they took their lives, leaping from the boat on their way home. Their deaths triggered public discussion of shell shock among female war workers.[14] Because the transport center of Châlons lay close to the battle lines and came under regular attack, the French government awarded ten of the twenty Croix de Guerre given to Red Cross canteen women to colleagues Hall knew at Châlons, Epernay, and Reims, including the Cromwells. The city of Châlons-sur-Marne itself was awarded a Croix de Guerre in 1920.[15]

Cantine des Deux Drapeaux,
Châlons-sur-Marne,
September 25 to October 12, 1918.

I was called at six o'clock on the morning of the 25th. Mrs. Earle came to the train with me, which was a great help. The station was the most confused and the gayest looking place; officers of all kinds and descriptions, in their grand clothes, trying to find their trains. Three important trains left at the same time and were all packed full of officers. The Red Cross had reserved a seat for me, so I was next the window. They also paid my fare, which was almost nothing, as we have military rates. In the compartment were three officers, a priest, and another Red Cross woman going to the Châlons canteen.

It was, of course, a thrilling journey. At Meaux were the first signs of the Germans; as we went farther we realized what an invasion means. Villages half or wholly destroyed, all desolate and awful, but not wholly deserted. Bridges down; old pontoons pulled up on the banks of the Marne, which is only a narrow stream now. I was so surprised when I saw the size of it. There were barbed wire entanglements by the mile, put up with no reason, so far as the untrained eye could see; dugouts and abris along the hillsides, and now and then a soldier's grave with his little cross and his steel helmet upon it. They looked so lonely there on the railroad embankment. Old uniforms were strewn about, trees were in tangled masses, fields pitted with shell holes, and in the midst of it all, little boys and old women were gathering the harvest. We did not see the real battlefield, so the officers told us; but if that wasn't real, Heaven only knows what is.

At Châlons we went to the canteen, which is just behind the railroad station, in a most inviting place for Boches raids, and were then sent in a little Red Cross camion across the river to Miss Nott, the "directrice." We were not expected and no provision had been made for us. They could not take me at the first place to which Miss Nott sent me, so the soldier in her service came with a wheelbarrow and took me to another house, where an untidy French working woman showed me the room she had. I had immediate misgivings, which proved to be well founded, for with the exception of cooties, everything else arrived that night. I slaughtered them by the dozens. When I told the woman the next morning, she only said, "Oh! did they sortis?" So I continued my hunt and now have a room with all the glass in the windows, a thing most unusual for Châlons, and a fireplace also, too small, though, to have much effect in this high studded room. I've bought some wood at a fabulous price, but don't burn it unless I want to get a bath, which so far in my career I feel obliged to do. The downward path is fast, though, they say, and as the weather gets colder, I can't tell just how low I'll sink. I asked one of the girls what she did last winter, and she said, "Oh, I just went into winter quarters, and got a spring clean-up as soon as the weather permitted."

Margaret Nott

Anna Van Schaik Mitchell

Figs. 1-3

This canteen, which was started by Miss Nott and Miss Mitchell, and afterwards taken over by the Red Cross, is a reward for long and good work, and here I am, a greenhorn, settled down in it for the winter! It is for "permissionnaires," soldiers going back and forth on "leave," and is I think the most elaborate of its kind, fascinatingly decorated by French artists. The only trouble is, it is so large that there never is much chance to talk to the poilus. They say Epernay was more "intime."

Besides the big eating room, there is a large reading and lounging room; behind that a moving picture hall, with a stage, most artistic in color and decoration, and behind that a big dormitory where blankets are rented and stretchers given. Shower baths and barber shop are provided, and in the garden there are wine and tobacco kiosks and officers' quarters. Every artist in the world ought to come up here.

It's wonderful, the sight over the counter; the intent expression on the faces of all the soldiers as they wait more or less impatiently to be served. The room is always crowded with poilus, in their heavenly horizon blue, the most truly heavenly color I have ever seen. They form the background, and standing out against them are Algerians, generally in brown with red fezzes, decorated with a gold star and half moon. Senegalese, tall, slim men, black as coal, with shining faces and shining white teeth, in brown uniforms and high red caps, higher than the Algerians. Then there are Anamedes or -mites, whoever they are, I never heard of them before, and Indo-Chinese, one of whom got terribly excited and chattered like a monkey at me the other day, because I told another woman he was an Anamite. He did not calm down until he finally made me understand that he was not an Anamite, but an Indo-Chinese. They all chatter, those Indo-Chinese, in high, shrill voices, so fast and impatiently that you are at your wits' end in no time. I talk English at them as fast as they talk gibberish at me. I have to, out of self protection. We go through all sorts of gyrations and gesticulations and at the end they go off looking entirely unsatisfied. They are little, Chinese-looking men, and everyone dreads a train of them. The French workers call them "insupportable." Besides the French and their colonists, there are groups of Italians in their olive green, often rather sulky, Italian gendarmes, with very forbidding looking Napoleon hats, thoroughly unpopular with the everyday soldier; and then in smaller numbers, but always increasing as time goes on, are our boys, white and colored, in khaki, some wearing service caps, some steel helmets; all nations together, pushing and stretching towards the counter, waiting to be fed. I think I told Mother how the colored boys from around New Orleans, who could speak French, had things their way at Limoges. There were a lot of them there and they went around telling the French that they were the real Americans and to pay no attention to the white boys. Their success was enormous.

On Sunday there was a little fête in the cinema room and as the band stood up on the platform in their long blue overcoats and steel helmets, blue to match their uniforms,

"three long ones"

"brown with our own Khaki"

"trains with equipment"   "baby tanks"

"guns all camouflaged"

"sanitary trains"

"Military procession underneath"

against a pretty stage setting, lighted to perfection, I had to pinch myself very hard, to make sure that it was all real.

We eat in a flat, in a cracked house, where there are no windows left. It is called a Canteen Club; six or seven eat there and divide the expenses at the end of a week. I'm half starved all the time, for I find that working over food, instead of taking away the appetite increases mine, and as the others are very delicate eaters, I don't like to appear like a pig, so curb my desire and have one American-afternoon-tea-slice of bread, instead of a French hunk, which I long for. At any rate, I have no right to eat bread at all, for I haven't my food card yet, as my papers have not come from the French Grand Headquarters and I don't want to stir up trouble by being asked for something that I can't produce. They are frightfully fussy about things like that, and although I was allowed to come paperless, I have nothing to show that I was.

There was no one here to give me instructions of any sort. I was just dumped down and supposed to know it all; probably that was because only trained workers are wanted. However, several of the people have taken pity on me and have given me a helping hand, and when I'm off duty I stay round and try to get some idea of what my next task may be, so I guess I'll get along someway. The "caisse" for "repas complets" from 10.30 A.M. to midnight will be difficult for me, for the dinner costs seventy-five centimes, and they come up and ask for such inconvenient numbers of dinners at a time. One buys for all his comrades often. Some want salad and some don't, and some want meat with no vegetable, and others vegetable and no meat, and some want the "special," all of which cost different amounts, and for one who has shirked mental arithmetic all her life, the prospect is not pleasing. Then the kitchen, too, I don't care to think about, because things are measured out by French weights and divided or cut up into individual weights, which are sold for French money, and that calculation will not be easy to attack. The other things are not bad.

There are such mobs at the canteen all the time that I could give my best friend coffee with my own hands and never know it. My eyes never get above the pitcher I am holding, or the cups I am filling. Hour after hour I do that, coffee in one hand, chocolate in the other, often trying to make change in between. Then if I have soup, it's the same. Bowls are scarce, so they hold up the game sometimes. On top of the soup bowls, we clap a plate of "repas;" meat, vegetable and hunk of bread. Then the men go to the other end of the counter for drinks, and if they want a dessert, they have to buy it and pay for it at the "charcuterie." There you sell sausage; half loaves of bread, eight cents; quarter loaves, four cents; and slices one cent; apple sauce, which costs three cents, but you have to take eight cents for it and give back five when the saucer is returned; grapes, seven cents a bunch, cheese, apples, sometimes so expensive that I blush when I tell the price—perhaps they are a luxury here, though—prunes, etc. That part of the counter one person works. Then there is the "consigne," where forks, cups and spoons are let out for ten cents each article, and money refunded when they bring them back, together with the ticket which is given them when they take them away. Besides the work in the canteen, trains have to be met, troop trains and sanitary trains; both are given coffee, but the sanitary trains have cigarettes too; and the last of the duties, only undertaken if there are enough workers, is to sell stationary and post cards, and rent out magazines and books in the reading room.

The first thing you notice in the town are the ruins left by the air raids. Wherever you look, there they are. It's a favorite place for attacks. They got fifteen hundred bombs in four days in March, more than any other town in France. There is no roof on the station, and near the house where I first went is the biggest bomb hole any of the military men have ever seen. Châlons has been shelled too. I don't see how the canteen workers have stood it. Every night for weeks they were carted out into the country to sleep in the open air, and if it rained, they had to be packed together under some kind of a shelter. Poilus tried their beds during the day, and they took the consequences.

I think I have given you all the calm side of life here. Of course the other side is the one of interest, but that I must be careful in writing about. I really haven't any military information of importance, though. We can tell when an attack is coming by the kind of troops going up. Colonials are good shock troops, but don't hold well, they say. (Two guns have just gone off right here. Wonder what's up!) We know when the attack is to begin, because someone is apt to tell us, and there is no mistaking the moment it does begin, I can assure you. I think so often of Mother when I am coming back from supper and the sky is red with flashes and the guns are roaring like distant thunder. They say that life here is a cure for nervousness about thunder storms. I believe it.

The first night I came the great offensive of this section began about ten o'clock, and the guns went all night long. I was told the barrage was so heavy that even the French couldn't stand the concussion and some of the guns had to be silenced. The next night I was awakened by my old landlady calling, "Get up, Mlle. quickly, the alerte! You will be hurt!" So Mlle. flew up and into her clothes and together with Mme. Hennocque and her young daughter, very charming French people who are staying here to do canteen work because their own house up town is damaged, rushed out into the backyard and over to the canteen by the back way, which the enemy has very kindly opened up by dropping a bomb on the iron fence which shut us off before. The street was full of black shadows of soldiers, rushing in the opposite direction to the town wine cellars or "caves." We went to our little "abri" made for us by the engineers of the French army, after a night Mr. Davidson spent in the canteen under bombardment. There we stayed listening to our own special "75s," the rat-tat-tat's of machine guns, and occasionally heavy dull booms which they said were German bombs. After the thing quieted down, Mme. Hennocque

Marie Hennocque
Madeleine Hennocque

Reed M. Davidson

asked if I would like to see the town "caves." No one at home can ever have any conception of what I saw. It was 3.30. We went in through the court of the "fabrique," one side of which was lined with the kind of open plumbing they are so fond of over here, which at the very entrance made the air unpleasant, to put it mildly. Then we passed through a stone gate built in the hillside and in a few seconds turned and looked down an endless gallery lined on both sides with beds, put as close together as possible, with little night lamps burning at intervals, giving just enough light to keep the place from utter darkness. There were all kinds of beds, elaborate wooden ones, iron ones large and small. Some people had no bedsteads, just mattresses on the damp ground. Others were wrapped in blankets sitting up in folding chairs, and still others, whom I took to be town paupers, were stretched out on top of great wine vats, with no coverings whatever. All the beds were occupied by one or more persons, all in different degrees of soundness of sleep and different degrees of loudness of breathing, and all had placed beside them in a pile their most precious possessions; the children their little toys, the women, great bundles of what I took to be household linen. Some of them even had brought their choicest articles of furniture for safe keeping. Mme. Hennocque took me up and down some of the galleries. We were not allowed to talk and she told me to use my flashlight on the ground only. Off the main galleries (I don't know what they are called—long passageways) are many short blind ones called "chambres séparées" and used perhaps for only one family. Some of the canteen workers go every night to one of these, in a not very popular part of one of the "caves." Last night they had rats pattering around their beds. I put my hand on the walls. They were damp and wet, simply dug out of the clay hills. The cellars are arranged in long connected lines, some are over two miles in length when all measured up. There are five in all, each belonging to a different "fabrique" of wine, and all equally crowded.

They say that now they are nothing compared with what they were during the German offensive of March. Then the whole population was forced to go to them under penalty and there was scarcely room to move.

Now everyone who can has left Châlons and taken their furniture with them. That is why it is so hard to find places to live in, plenty of vacant flats, but no furniture. My old woman proprietor, sixty-eight years old but looks eighty, keeps her "chaise pliante" and pillow constantly beside the front door, ready to snatch up at a moment's notice in her flight to the shelter of the "caves." That night was a strange experience, and when they say, "Mlle. we have suffered, c'est une vie de misére," I can well believe it.

It has been a life of excitement for me. To stand on top of the railroad bridge is the most entrancing thing I have ever done. Everything goes over and under, the military procession on top, the military procession underneath, and the military processions in the air.

They say they have never seen anything like the movement here before, in troops, trucks and trains. The railroad platforms—there are three long ones—change every five minutes. Sometimes they are all blue, poilu blue, then olive green massed with Italian troops, and again brown with our own khaki. Sometimes they are mixed, one platform of each color, when the different troop trains happen in at the same time. Then there are the trains with equipment, guns all camouflaged, big and little; box cars shut up tight; whole lines of flat cars filled with baby tanks. Then, too, the sanitary trains go through every little while, which are always met by one or two workers. I almost pull my arms out "doing" these, carrying the heavy pitchers of coffee, handing them up to the men nurses, and rushing back for more. The "infirmier" will tell you the number of wounded he has, and you leave him coffee enough for all. The German "blessés" get coffee, too, for the kindly old French "infirmiers" say, "Mlle., they are all wounded, French and Boches alike." But when it comes to cigarettes it is a little different. Sometimes we ask the French wounded whether or not to give them to the Boches; sometimes we pass them by, which even now I don't like to do; and sometimes they say, "Allemand," to us, and these are apt to get them as a reward for what may be honesty, or perhaps is only haughtiness.

Over the bridge passes a continuous procession of everything that has to do with war, all camouflaged and all absorbing in their different interests, from a little caravan of carrier pigeons, a sweet little circus parade all of its own, to the biggest of big guns; ambulances rushing to the front and back with the wounded; camions full of different kinds of remarkable and strange things; officers flying back and forth in fine cars covered with mud; a double line going and coming, with no beginning and no end. Sometimes gay French artillery rattle by, horse drawn, and for two or three days the procession coming this way was interrupted by a long, bluish green line made up of young, weary looking German boys in rags, and so unadorned, stripped as they were of all their equipment, that they seemed pathetic; footsore too, as you could tell by one who had discarded his shoes altogether and was carrying them around his neck. They were so young that the French exclaimed, "Why, Mlle., they never have had any hair on their faces." (It's like a thunder storm here now; flashes of lightning and a distant roar; Mother wouldn't like it. Some nights I can't sleep it is so noisy, and everything in the room vibrates. They are going it full tilt, just begun). Their escort, French soldiers who have been wounded and cannot be sent back to the front, marched at regular intervals on each side of the line, some with guns with bayonets fixed pointing straight ahead, some on horses with long medieval-like lances carried straight up and down, and some with swords drawn and held at "attention." All the population came out to watch. There were posters in shop windows to tell when to expect them and the streets were filled with blue poilus and black civilians, who for the most part watched in silence. They were all polite; only one woman whom I saw became excited. She told one of the prisoners what they had made her suffer; a man beside her stopped her, exclaiming, "You must not tell them that," and another man near me grumbled out, "Ten thousand more good loaves of bread a day gone to the devil."

Above the bridge go the aviators. It is thrilling to see them fly by, always in battle formation. Add eleven to grandmother's last birthday (95) and you will know the number I counted in less than ten minutes the other day. They come out of the sky like flocks of wild ducks with their leader ahead and little scouts flying around and above them. I find myself jumping up and down with excitement, as each new escadrille appears, all coming from different directions, all going off in the same, to the German lines. Every fair day they go. I wonder how many come back. There is always a buzz in the air. At about eleven every day lately a German comes over and takes a look at us, and our "75s" send a few shells after him, which make little white puffs in the sky. Mme. Hennocque showed me a piece of shrapnel which just escaped her face yesterday.

It is about 7.30 A.M. and I am sitting up in bed wrapped up in everything I own. Had a compromise night last night; went to bed half dressed because I couldn't decide whether to stay entirely clothed, or pretend that I was leading a calm life and go to bed in regulation fashion. As the night was very bright and favorable to the enemy, I made my plans for a possible midnight visit. Our own sausage balloons were up and our gun mounted on an automobile, ready and waiting. They did not come, but at 5.30 I was waked by the guns, thundering out all along the line, and after I am once waked up by them I can't sleep again. They stopped about 6.30 or 7, and now perfect calm reigns for the time being, except for the rumble of the camions. I am off duty until 1 P.M. this week, so am not going to get up early, as I need the rest; I wish I could make up lost sleep but

I rather think that has gone for good, for I couldn't possibly settle down to sleep in the day time. I tried one day and lost 10,000 Boches prisoners by doing it. However, I'd seen a lot before. Every day, too, little groups go up and down.

Of course I have no perspective on the war at all. What is Russia doing? We don't hear a thing about that. Mrs. Earle has gone to Digne and was a little dejected about it, I think. I did my best to get her out of social into military service, for the social service will go on as long as humanity lasts, and this war will, I hope, not go on quite as indefinitely as that. We went to different Red Cross departments and no place seemed to fit her exactly, so she took what they gave her. Think of it, she speaks all the warring languages, even Flemish, and is put down in the south of France to take charge of refugees, whom I imagine are sent back from the occupied country through Switzerland; people undesirable for the Germans to hold and evidently undesirable for the French to take back, for no township or department wants them. Politics enter in, too, and the mayor who is smart enough to keep them out, or can arrange to have the smallest number quartered in his district, is the popular man. I know that, because I went to a lecture at the Red Cross given by the wife of a Sorbonne professor, who has studied conditions in order to teach them to the refugee workers. It seems like a waste of good material, doesn't it?

I don't remember when I last wrote home and don't know whether or not you see the letters I send. They are always written in such feverish haste that I'm afraid they aren't worth seeing. Don't say the interesting letters must come from me. I'm in one of the places with the strictest censorship. Even Mme. Hennocque's letters from her husband, a famous cavalry general, are censored by military authorities before she gets them.

I'll send this letter down to Paris by Miss H. One by one the women go down to get fixed up by the Paris doctors. Two went yesterday, so we are short handed again during this terrible rush. I told you in a postcard that nothing happened the night after I wrote. It <u>did</u>, only I was too worn out to wake up. The next night I did not take off my clothes at all, nor last night. Night before last (October 1st) we caught it three times, our most war-like horror.

We had an "alerte" while I was at supper across the river, and did not have time to go to a shelter before the barrage began. After that it is not safe to venture out. I watched it a little from the front door, saw the tracers go up and shrapnel explode. It's wonderful to see, but the experienced people have words of contempt for any one who wants to look, so I accepted their better judgment and went down to the cellar. Neither Miss Pond nor Miss Coryn, old hands at it, seemed satisfied with our position, but we couldn't help it. Forty-five had been killed by staying in a cellar like that, and they seem to feel that we should be much criticised if we met a like fate. We stayed there, however, while a terrific firing went on outside; "seventy-fives," machine guns and other guns, and we heard the German machines and the bombs they dropped. Finally it calmed down and we thought

Marie Brockway Pond
Marjorie Stella Coryn

things were over, so I went home and was sitting on my bed later, writing a letter, when I heard the front door rattle violently, a boom, boom, boom, and M.H. found herself on her feet with her hair standing on end. The old woman downstairs, who had come back from the "caves," thinking the excitement of the night over, screeched up to me to come down quickly, got me into her room, shut the door, and wailed and moaned and kept crying out, "Oh, I'm so frightened, why did I ever come home from the 'caves'!" First she dashed to one side of the room and then to the other, and all the time outside there was the terrific explosion of shrapnel and bombs. You feel a little helpless at such a time. I tried to calm her but couldn't. After a while the thing stopped and we heard voices in the street and people walking by, or running, rather. She gasped, "They are going to the 'caves'," and like a flash, grabbed her chair and pillow and was gone. That left me alone in the house, a thing I didn't care any too much about, so I rushed up stairs, opened my windows—I'd risk my life any time to save my window glass—grabbed my papers, my money and steel helmet, put out my fire, and flew for the canteen. They were all down in the "abri." I didn't know my way to the canteen very well in the pitchy blackness and made several dives down blind passageways, ran round and round the fence trying to find the gate, and felt I'd explode of nervousness if I couldn't find some way in soon. It was like a nightmare for a moment.

The minute an "alerte" sounds, the canteen is cleared. The soldiers have to go down to their shelters, the money boxes are snatched up, and the workers go into the "abri" made for them. I hadn't been in ours many minutes when the rumpus began again. We could hear the Germans very plainly and whenever the sergeant and the other men who look out for the canteen came into the "abri" with us and shut the door (a very heavy affair) we knew they were feeling a little nervous. They always gave as an excuse for shutting the door—which made us airless—that the candles smoked in the draft, but we knew better. The two workers I had been with in the cellar after supper were supposed to be on night duty, but they were caught in the street when those first three bombs fell. They saw them come down, threw themselves flat on the side walk against a house, head to head, and stayed there until that attack was over. Then after the next one, which they had spent in a shelter on their side of the river, they came to the canteen and brought the news that we have a war "blessée." One of the women had had her finger cut to the bone by shrapnel, on her way from the house to the little "abri" in the garden, only a few steps away.

There had been no "alerte" that time to give us warning that the Germans were about and it is said that they attached themselves to a French escadrille and came over the lines with them under the protection of the French signals.

About 3 A.M. the Hennocques and I started to go home, when we heard rumors that twelve bombs had fallen just across from our house. We went to see what had happened

Mme E. E. R. De la Croix

and found that a bomb had fallen into the cinema room of the evacuation hospital, into which the wounded men had been crowded that night, waiting to be evacuated. There were ambulances all about and hushed excitement; no one would say a word except that we couldn't help. In the darkness we could see poilus standing round tagged with big white tickets, stretchers lying about, but I couldn't make out whether they were the wounded from the front or the dead and dying from what the French insist on calling the "accident."

The next day Mme. Hennocque and I went over. My Red Cross admitted us, but when we got to the door of the cinema, the doctor in charge said, "Mme. it is no sight for a woman to see, nor for a man, either." This woman didn't want to see it.

Two American officers came out and said they were glad they had been in, for now they were "thoroughly mad." I thought it had taken quite a while to make them so. The doctor said that in all his four years' experience at the front he had never seen anything to equal that. He had asked for permission to evacuate his hospital in the day time, and said he would take no responsibility for the result if it were not done. He had had no answer, only the result. They say he is almost crazy. If the Germans had come twenty minutes later, the room would have been empty. I rather think it was the worst thing of the kind that has happened at all. They say the news flew like wildfire over the front and the men are fighting like mad for revenge.

Since then the members of the canteen have either gone to the country in our little camionette for the night, or to the public "caves," or stayed as I did at the canteen, for I was on duty at 4 A.M. and couldn't leave. Military headquarters has ordered the canteen closed from 8 P.M. to 4 A.M., so I slept either down under ground or in the office of the canteen on a couch, ready to descend at a moment's notice. I am always too tired to have the "alerte" wake me. The guns do, though. It is 9 P.M. now and I am sitting up wrapped in all my clothes,—a sweater, my quilted wrapper and fur coat—and still my hands and feet are cold, but flowers are blooming in the garden, so you see the cold weather hasn't really begun yet. Everyone seems to be sick more or less. There is a horrible kind of grippe about that lasts forty-eight hours and always ends the same way. The guns are going again tonight. The house is rattling, which is always disquieting. I don't wonder that the people here get nervous. One of the women who came up with me said the other day, "You and I don't look the same as when we came." She was looking at me when she spoke. I have had two bad colds since I landed. I am getting over the second one now, but am terribly tormented by fleas. Only Mother knows how I suffer, but I had made up my mind that I was to take my share of vermin.

A day or two ago President Poincaré and General Pétain came here. It was all published in the papers, so I suppose I can mention it. They came to decorate the Mayor and Bishop of long suffering Châlons, and hard suffering too. You would realize that, by

Joseph-Marie Tissier

a walk around the town, where in some parts nothing but ruins are to be seen, and then again by that pathetic procession which begins about dusk every night, of the people going to the wine cellars to sleep. Old bent-over women hobbling along, carrying their possessions done up in sheets slung over their backs, some wheeling their belongings in wheelbarrows, others in push carts or baby carriages; some leading little children by their hands, and others using their hands for the canes which help them make the same trip night after night after night. You feel a great physical weariness yourself as you watch it all, and are glad to stand a few moments on the bridge over the Marne and watch the sunset and beautiful French sky reflected on the quiet water on one side, and on the other the wonderfully picturesque clumps of tall grass and the ever present French fisherman, standing in his boat among them, fishing the river which has become so famous.

I've tried to give you a perfectly true, unexaggerated view of the life here. It is probably paradise compared to the life at the front, but we are certainly living under war conditions, as Mme. Hennocque says. On September 3rd, 1914, as the Germans walked into Châlons, Mme. Hennocque and her daughter walked out, leaving everything behind, and they've never had a moment's rest since. We even find food hard to get; no butter, no eggs, no milk, chicken prohibitive in price, meat terribly tough.

It is after 11, and I must get some sleep somehow. Perhaps the guns will stop soon. They have been going for quite a while. They are really not loud, but wearing, they are so continuous. You could not say they are going every second, because they go much faster than that, dozens a second. The same question again, shall I undress or sha'n't I? I've asked some of the others today what they do, and they say that on clear nights they take off their skirts and boots and leave the rest on, and on stormy nights they turn in. That is about the way I figured it out.

My steel helmet always hangs on my bedpost, and my little knapsack is always packed with my papers, etc., ready to grab to take with me when I make my midnight excursions. Sometimes I go with my steamer rug and sometimes without it. My boots are always put where I can jump into them, and my fur coat arranged so I can find the sleeves with no difficulty. There often is not much time between the "alerte," which is sounded when the Germans fly over the lines, and the time they get here. After that we can't go out. My helmet seems to have taken the place of my life preserver. I'd rather take my chances any day with a submarine, though, than with a bombing machine in the air. They do such devilish things.

The American Expeditionary Force

When Margaret Hall embarked on the SS *Chicago* in August 1918, she estimated that a thousand American soldiers had just gone on board. By mid August of that year, a million American troops had already arrived in France, with 250,000 or more arriving each month.[1] The military balance in western Europe had begun to shift, and one of the key reasons was the entry of the American Expeditionary Force (AEF) into combat, as part of the Allied armies' push north and east towards the French frontier.[2] Military histories of World War I on the Western Front trace a shift in 1914: first, German troops made an initial and rapid advance to a position roughly thirty miles from Paris, crossing the Marne River and seizing Châlons-sur-Marne and Reims on September 4 and 5; next, on September 5, in the First Battle of the Marne, an Allied counterattack halted and pushed them back. Mobile warfare then yielded to over three years of static trench warfare.[3] The new front formed a rough arc, running from the North Sea near Ostende in Belgium to Ypres, Lens, and Arras to near Compiègne, then turning eastward past Soissons, Reims, and Verdun, before turning southward along the boundary of Alsace to the Swiss border. Trench warfare not only led to a tactical war of attrition but generated technical demands for more powerful artillery, tanks, and advanced aircraft, all of which became key factors in the conflict by 1918.

The spring of 1918, however, brought a return to large movements. Gen. Erich Ludendorff profited from the German treaty with Russia, which had been signed at Brest-Litovsk on March 3, to move troops to the west in order to "punch a hole" in the Allied front before the arrival of American forces could tip the scale in France.[4] Only three American infantry divisions were then collaborating with the French in a quiet zone south of Verdun.[5] On March 21, 1918, Ludendorff thus launched a massive, five-stage offensive using storm-troopers to penetrate the British and French fronts. The first of these attacks, Operation Michael, created a huge bulge, or salient, almost forty miles deep, capturing the entire Somme River area and reaching Montdidier. The German advance threatened the main communications between Paris, Amiens, and the north. This shocking rupture of the French and British lines on the Somme was compounded by the psychological impact of aerial bombardment and the new long-range "Paris guns," whose shells started to terrorize Paris on March 23.[6] Hall was told that even Châlons-sur-Marne had received hundreds of bombs during four days in March 1918, at the beginning of the German thrust, although the town was far from the offensive in the Somme.[7] Then, on April 4, Ludendorff redirected his forces to the northern sector between Ypres and Bethune, where a second offensive (Georgette) began on April 9. That attack along the river Lys in Flanders ended April 29, after three weeks. Despite—but also because of—the gains in territory, Ludendorff was repeatedly obliged to order a withdrawal, when his over-extended lines of communication and supply put his shock-troops at risk. German casualties in the Michael offensive ran to almost 240,000, and the losses were heavy among his elite units in each subsequent offensive, to the same extent.[8] After a pause, at the end of May a third German attack (Blücher) struck southward over the Chemin des Dames ridge and crossed the Aisne River. German troops broke through to the Marne at Château-Thierry and Belleau Wood, in what the French called the Aisne-Marne battle. With this, the Germans reached the same position they had attained in the First Battle of the Marne in September 1914, dangerously close to Paris. If the legendary Paris taxis symbolized the successful resistance to the Germans in September 1914, in June 1918 the arrival of American soldiers provided material for a second legendary rescue at Belleau Wood. Although a small battle, it was psychologically important for both the Allies and the Germans.[9]

As Ludendorff's spring offensive engulfed large regions, the Allied command had to address the acute question: how would the AEF contribute to the war effort? During the preceding winter, small numbers of American troops were gradually placed in service with Allied units as part of their training. Although largely unengaged until late May 1918, when almost 650,000 U.S. troops had arrived in Europe, these units picked up experience with seasoned Allied troops and practiced using French and British weaponry.[10] With the exception of African American units, which he agreed to place with French colonial troops, where they were very successful, Gen. John J. Pershing resisted placing his men under Allied command. Ludendorff's dramatic offensives exposed the need for American contributions to compensate for French and British losses. In response to the crisis, the American general reluctantly agreed to the temporary amalgamation of a few American divisions led by American staff officers under British or French command; his goal was an army under an American flag and under his own leadership, a goal he would reach in August 1918.[11]

Selected units of the AEF fought under the direction of Allies in several places along a line that stretched, like an open L, from Belgium in the north to Compiègne not far from Paris, to Lorraine in the east. In March, after a joint operation with French troops, the 42nd Infantry Division (the "Rainbow Division") thus assumed responsibility for a sector southeast of Verdun. At the end of May, in the first planned engagement of the Americans, a regiment of the 1st Division captured the hilltop village of Cantigny in the Somme near Montdidier, supported by the French.[12] But the main American concentrations were farther south between Soissons and Château-Thierry, near Reims in Champagne, and above Verdun along the river Meuse running north in the wooded hills of the Argonne, about forty miles east of Châlons-sur-Marne. Following the German advance at the end of May to a point under forty miles from Paris, a brigade of American marines from the 2nd Infantry Division held the line with the French XXI Corps in the Battle of Belleau Wood, where they arrived June 1 and fought until June 26. Just to the east—next to Château-Thierry—the 2nd and 3rd American divisions helped the French block the German advance along the Marne.[13] On July 4 to 5, Americans gained further experience in the Somme when two regiments joined the Australian 4th Infantry Division, commanded by Gen. John Monash, in a quick victory at the Battle of Hamel that harmonized tank, air, and infantry and suffered few losses.[14]

The Second Battle of the Marne, initiated with Ludendorff's final offensive from July 15 to 17, had two prongs. On July 15, the German army struck briefly to the east of Reims but was halted by Gen. Henri Gouraud's Fourth Army, to which the Rainbow Division was attached. To the west of Reims, in the large bulge between Soissons and Château-Thierry that had been created in the offensive of May to June, the new line of attack also ground to a halt—and was quickly canceled by Ludendorff. On July 18, the tables were turned, leading many to consider this the turning point of the war. Gen. Ferdinand Foch ordered a counteroffensive in the Aisne River sector and in succeeding weeks pressed the Allied commanders to pursue the Germans during their orderly withdrawal; he was honored with the title of maréchal on August 5. By August 4, the French and Americans had retaken Soissons and captured roughly twenty-nine thousand Germans.[15]

Another turning point was marked on August 8, 1918, at the Battle of Amiens in the Somme region. There British technical superiority and the coordination of Allied forces across a long front enabled advances of six miles on average and the capture of about sixteen thousand German prisoners in a single day.[16] The collapse of German morale and of the bulge in the Somme forced General Ludendorff to recognize that his gamble of concentrating his remaining forces had failed; he described August 8, 1918, as the "black day of the German army."[17] Over the course of the summer, he had exhausted his reserve manpower, run short of military supplies, and faced erosion of his troops' strength by the influenza. French advances that wiped out the German salient from the Aisne to the Marne made August 20 "another black day."[18] The last salient Foch hoped to wipe out was a smaller bulge in the German front at Saint-Mihiel, south of Verdun, which the French had failed to recover in 1917. This task was given to Pershing and the newly constituted 1st Army of the AEF—finally a force under his own command.

In Paris in September, Hall witnessed bombing raids that drove home for her the urgent need for American military support. On her arrival, she heard about another "big offensive" being prepared by the Allies. Shortly afterward, the AEF launched its first major engagement as an independent army, from September 11 to 13. Supported by French infantry divisions, Pershing attacked the German salient at Saint-Mihiel. A German decision to retreat a few days earlier made it possible for the Americans and French to take this position swiftly and to capture over thirteen thousand Germans in two days.[19] Parisians were exhilarated by news of the battle of Saint-Mihiel. The rapid success of the attack was a boost to the morale of the Americans as well as of the French.[20]

While Hall was in Paris, she took note of what we might today call the "lived experience" of the war, rather than its military record. Her visits to hospitals, to a hospital train unloading the wounded, and to a military cemetery underscored for her the costs of the summer battles. One of the trains she met with food and blankets was carrying 340 wounded soldiers. She was shocked by the severely wounded in surgical wards, the sick in a hospital for pneumonia, and gassed patients in a tent-hospital. The war at sea also came home to Hall in Paris, when she met a sailor who had survived the September 5 U-boat torpedo attack on the USS *Mount Vernon*.

September 25, the day that Hall reached Châlons-sur-Marne, was also the first night of a fresh joint offensive, which General Gouraud announced earlier in the day to the *directrices* of the Châlons canteen.[21] That night, Hall heard the opening artillery barrages of the French and American forces in Champagne and the Argonne, the beginning of a battle that would last until November 11. Continuous flashes lit the sky, and air raids in the following nights repeatedly interrupted everyone's sleep in Châlons, except perhaps that of the people who took refuge in the famous Champagne wine cellars underground. This broad Allied offensive ran along the entire front from Flanders in the north to the Meuse in the east. On the northwestern wing, two U.S. divisions fought with the British at Cambrai. On the eastern wing, fifteen divisions fought under Pershing in the Meuse-Argonne sector, east of the French in the central Champagne sector, driving northward under Gouraud, who came back to the canteen exultant about his progress, having captured over ten thousand Germans in the first two days. Pershing's goal was to push north to Mézières and Sedan, one of the military headquarters that Kaiser Wilhelm II had used during the Battle of Verdun and a center of rail communications for the Germans. As Pershing intended, the Americans drove north, taking Montfaucon, a hill northwest of Verdun, in a relatively quick advance.[22] But momentum in the Argonne stalled for most of the month of October, as the Americans worked their way north through the forest to reach Romagne, which would become the site of a vast American cemetery. American soldiers described arduous fighting to Hall when they returned from pushing uphill above the valley of the Meuse, north of Verdun. They faced two kinds of problems, with high human costs: a dense German defensive system, which delayed and exposed advancing soldiers to cross-fire, and poor American organization. The men struggled in rough terrain riddled with German dugouts, concrete machine-gun posts, barbed-wire traps, and other fortifications that limited the use of tanks. They pressed forward in hand-to-hand combat, sometimes without artillery support, maps, wirecutters, or basic supplies. Compounding the inexperience of incoming troops, the AEF suffered from material deficiencies, uncoordinated attacks, poor roads and communication, and inadequate air support.[23] At the beginning of November, renewed movement permitted them to reach the outskirts of Sedan, where they stopped to allow the French to retake this city, symbolically reversing a major French defeat in the Franco-Prussian war. By the suspension of hostilities on November 11, over 26,000 American soldiers had been killed and nearly 96,000 wounded in the Argonne.[24]

Although the battles on the ground were fought to the north and east of Châlons, the Allied advance in Champagne and the Argonne invited German attacks on the rail lines serving the Allied troops. German aircraft regularly bombed the zone of Châlons, passing close enough to see that they were targeting nurses wearing white veils or orderlies carrying stretchers, according to reports by Hall's coworkers.[25] Civilians and soldiers in transit all became accustomed to blackouts and sirens. On moonlit nights in the fall of 1918, women knew they must seek shelter in cellars or *abris*, some bringing children and bedding with them. In a night raid on October 2, 1918, over sixty wounded soldiers were killed at Châlons by a bomb that hit an evacuation hospital. Hall notes angry hospital administrators' reaction to the violation of international treaties protecting the wounded.

Situated on the main route between Reims and Verdun, Hall's canteen gave her a front-row view of the military traffic through the railroad station and provided her with rapid reports on "pushes" by French and American troops. Hall observed the forward movement of soldiers on foot, by train, and by truck. And she photographed what she saw on the passing trains, including machine guns, "baby tanks" (small Renault tanks), and carrier pigeons in charming wicker houses. In spite of censorship about where battles were taking place, Hall had ready access to information about the "awful sacrifices we are making" (63). Papers that described both the military actions and political negotiations over a possible armistice were distributed along with coffee and cigarettes to soldiers in the canteen reading room and in nearby hospitals. Hall was therefore able to follow official reports about major military movements, in addition to the unofficial reports by the soldiers who came to the canteen.[26] She marked up her National Geographic map of northern France to show the progress of the Allied front in 1918 in the weeks before the Armistice. Her densely colored and cross-hatched map corresponds to neat black and white military maps of advances. Over the final one hundred days, the Allies would take 363,000 prisoners of war in the measured of the German army.[27]

(Diary) September 29, 1918.

Great bombardment all night. People couldn't sleep. My sleep disturbed, for when that is going on you feel that something is wrong and you can't rest calmly. It is certainly a nervous life. I don't take off my clothes at night now. Am eaten alive with fleas and suffer untold agony. Scarcely have time to wash my hands or do my hair; am a perfect pig to behold, but there is so much doing that I couldn't shut myself up for long enough to do anything. Tried to fix my room. Shifts at the canteen have changed and I am to go on at 4 AM so must sleep there tonight in the office on a cot. After supper stayed a few minutes at the club, and the "alerte" sounded. We did not move immediately as we thought it would be nothing, but the guns began so we went to the cellar. The girls didn't like that as it was dangerous and we are not supposed to. The thing didn't last long, just some Germans passing over, I guess. Saw the sweetest procession go over the bridge today; a little circus parade, each little cart drawn by a big sturdy horse. They were carrier pigeons going up to the front in their little houses, which were very neat and freshly painted. They had windows to look out and it was the only soothing thing I've seen in the long endless moving stream. Later a French artillery detachment went along and seemed very warlike, all camouflaged. Even the sanitary trains are camouflaged. I saw one with all the windows broken yesterday, a perfect wreck. The guard told me the Boches had done it. Saw also about a hundred dogs going up to the front. They were walking round the streets here, two to one master, looking awfully sweet and young, all different kinds, but so affectionate to their masters. They had little tin boxes on their collars. I hated to think that they had to catch it too.

September 30th.

Had a miserable night at the canteen; couldn't sleep much. Thought I'd die between 4 and 7. No time to drink a cup of coffee before I began, so I got almost to a state of fainting from exhaustion. Had to pour coffee and chocolate steadily without a moment to find my handkerchief even, for three hours, lifting those heavy pitchers and rushing madly about to keep all the poilus satisfied and not let any feel neglected. Miss Porter and Miss Bennett had been doing the same thing from 11 P.M. on, without time even to take a drink of coffee themselves—eight hours without one second off!

From 7 to 8 the canteen is closed to be cleaned and the cook gave me a little breakfast. At 8 I had to go into the "caisse" to sell coffee, soup and chocolate checks, until 10.30. Thought I'd die of the responsibility. It was as cold as Greenland and I had a chill. Was a wreck all day and tried to lie down in the afternoon, and lost Boches prisoners who marched through. Great firing on the front. It begins all of a sudden, from perfect calm and quiet, to a glare of light and continuous rumble of thunder. It's wonderful the way it breaks out everywhere at once, even the house shakes. Sometimes it begins

Catherine Rush Porter

Emily Marion Bennett

at 10 P.M. Sometimes at 11, sometimes at 4 A.M., and occasionally through the day. Always aviators overhead. Don't know whether they are enemy or not, and whether or not we'll be bombed into Kingdom-Come any moment. One perpetual rush from one thing to another until you are worn out with the excitement and fatigue of it all, and the reconstructing of life along war lines. If I could only keep clean! But I can't and that's the end of it.

October 1st. (German raids)
October 2nd.

Mme. Hennocque came to the canteen after me to take me to the coal man to order wood. We went to the hospital first to see what had happened. The platform outside the cinema room was filled with the roughest kind of coffins just slung together, which poilus brought up one by one as fast as they could, shovelled clean sand into the bottom, put them just inside the door, collected (on stretchers) what they thought might belong together, and nailed the lid on. Ordered a little wood for $13. Mme. Hennocque showed me rue Carnot and the terrible ruins there. Invited me to go to luncheon with them at the "Angleterre," which has been hit by a bomb and is more or less of a wreck. Interesting eating there and good to get different food. Place full of officers of all sorts, very grand affairs, with huge silver sunbursts on their bosoms, a mark of great honor, I'm told. Had to rush back to service at one o'clock. Before I got home at 4.30 the wood had arrived, so I made a fire and got a hot bath, which made me late for dinner, but felt like a new woman. On the way to dinner, passed the procession going to the "caves." Some have been doing it for years. All workers who could go were taken to the country for the night. I had to stay as I am on duty at 4 A.M. Miss Mitchell and I slept in the office of the canteen. Two others down in the "abri" and Mme. Oblin and Mme. de la Croix, her cousin,—our war "blessée"—went to the "caves."

October 3rd.

Slept in the canteen. Almost died of my cough, which I tried to smother so not to disturb Miss Mitchell. Have not taken off my clothes for a week except twice for the decency of a bath in a hand basin. Was called at 3.30, got dressed, which means putting on my shoes and shaking down like a dog. You're not here more than a day or two before you lose all fastidious habits. Generally get my face washed after a fashion and teeth brushed. Also managed to get a cup of coffee before I began work today. Poured chocolate and coffee with one hand and took in the money as fast as I could with the other. It's about as hard work as I could do and keep it up. At 7 A.M. had to fix up my counter and money boxes. Then ran home, washed my hands, fixed my hair, had coffee and bread, and flew back to the "caisse" until 10.30. Can't do much after that, as it takes forever for me to make up my cash tray and to try to balance an account that won't balance.

At luncheon I heard that there was to be a military funeral, for the sixty-four men killed by the bomb at the evacuation hospital. Went to the military cemetery in the camion with some of the others. All the coffins were done up neatly in white cloth, with flowers on them and arranged in a double row in front of the big monument. We were ushered into the place reserved for the General and officials. They stood on one side of the monument and we on the other. There were French nurses, Y.M.C.A., two or three English women ambulance drivers, besides the Red Cross. When General Gouraud and other important officers came in, the bugle sounded. There were two speeches. Then the ecclesiastical party came in, the Bishop, the choir boys with candles, and they went through their part of the service. I got another coughing fit and almost passed away again. Was mortified to death. At the end the bugle sounded again as the General went out, and after him the Bishop. The interment was later, done without ceremony, I believe.

This morning at 4 A.M. a great offensive began on our front. General Gouraud told us an important hill near Rheims had been taken, and everything was succeeding splendidly. Shook hands with him. He has only one arm. Lost the other in the war.

Rushed back to do sanitary trains, with Miss Coryn. Waited a long time. Finally one came on a track where we didn't expect it, so we grabbed our pitchers—heavy as lead—and hobbled down the tracks between trains, where we weren't supposed to go. The wounded were all on stretchers, just from the front, with first dressings on. Some cars smelled dreadfully. We got coffee to them all. Then we took cigarettes, climbed up into the cars, and handed two to each of the men who wanted them. A few were too sick to take them and I'm afraid others were not able to smoke what they took. One especially looked as though he was suffering awfully. They all seemed to be badly hurt, but all their faces brightened a little when they heard the word "cigarette." They were put in three or four deep, the lowest row almost on the floor. I didn't know what to do about giving the Germans cigarettes, looked rather blank, and the "infirmier" said, "Oh, give me two or three and I will give them to the prisoners." I feel rather sure that they went into Mr. Infirmier's pocket and not into the Germans' mouths. We managed to do the whole train, twenty-one "blessés" in each car. After that had gone out we waited for another, talked to one of our boys whom I had seen in the canteen and thought queer and unattractive, he was so toothless. Found I couldn't judge from appearances. He has been wounded twice, had had his jaw and teeth blown away, and had a silver plate for

Gen. Henri Gouraud

Joseph-Marie Tissier

Marjorie Stella Coryn

a jaw. His skin is drawn so tight underneath that he says it makes him uncomfortable, but the jaw plate does not hurt. Can't eat hard things. He is behind the lines for good now. Talks in a muffled way, has been gassed also. Did next train as well as we could and rushed back to supper. Went to the canteen again, and slept in the "abri" under ground.

October 4th.

Didn't sleep any too well. They say French hospital conditions near here are frightful. Nurses came down to see if they could get eggs, etc. from us, but we never see an egg. Lots of our boys around here have been rounded up by the M.P.s. They are all away on "French leave," over a hundred of them. Have their meals sitting Indian fashion outside the canteen gate, which makes it rather difficult to get in at times. Lots of boys say they have not been paid for months. "No money" and "no mail," is their great cry. Lots haven't enough money to buy a meal, so naturally we give it. Some come out of the hospitals with no money. The deserters simply say they have lost their divisions or companies and stay on here. Guns going now and "avions" flying over. About two hundred at a time go over every day, towards the front at about the same time. Miss Coolidge seems to be ill. Three others have left since I came, all worn out. Miss Coryn gone to a hospital to make a little canteen. Sick of sleeping in a smoky, cindery atmosphere at the canteen, so will chance it on my bed, all dressed except shoes. Got a balance on my account at the canteen, but probably never will do it again.

October 5th.

* * * All the soldiers ordered to sleep in the "caves" tonight. Am on at 4 AM tomorrow, so went to the canteen to sleep. Miss Nott and Miss Mitchell on cots there when I arrived. Went down into the "abri" with the Hennocques. Was waked up by Miss Nott asking the sergeant where the soldiers were. He said, "All in the 'caves,'" so I knew there had been an "alerte." Miss Nott and Miss Mitchell came down into the "abri" and conversed until things were quiet again.

Margaret Nott; Anna Van Schaik Mitchell

October 6th.

Gained an hour's sleep last night, for winter time is on. Up at 3.45 and worked until 7. Was offered the rest of the morning off, but thought I'd get more practice at the "caisse" so stayed. Heard that Poincaré was to be here at 2 o'clock. Saw grand automobiles coming down, so watched at the station. Saw Pétain, Poincaré and Gouraud get into their cars. General Gouraud stopped and spoke to Miss Porter. He is the great man of the moment, because of his Champagne drive, which was tremendously successful. Rheims was out of shelling distance yesterday. Thank goodness, night duty is over for me for a while! This morning the station platform was filled with new stretchers, which shows what is expected. A woman has just come in and told me that I was a great target for

Gen. Henri Philippe Pétain; Pres. Raymond Poincaré

Boches "avions", as my shutters were open. I thought my old woman always shut them, but guess lately she has been in too much of a hurry to get to her "cave" to do anything. They say we have given ten thousand "repas" a day sometimes in the canteen. Town absolutely given over to the "militaire." People who have horses and carts go to the country every night, put straw in the bottom, and pile the whole family in on top of it. See them starting out before dark. Always terrific bombardment going on at front, and always camouflaged lines of camions passing. One lot had camouflage for roads, which looked like rolls of grass, etc., like stage settings. Another was like a street cleaning brigade, huge brushes like those used for that, each drawn by one horse, and behind them carts filled with big, long, very long handled spades, shovels, etc. Often great trucks full of American boys, grinning generally when they pass their country-women.

x x x x x x

Just a line to tell you that everything seems to be going well. I haven't reached the stage yet where I'm used to the work. I don't have any of the hard cleaning or cooking to do, but standing up for six hours steadily, pouring out coffee and chocolate, or dishing out soup, or handing out "repas" or consigning "couverts" or sitting in the "caisse" is wearing in the end, because of the impatience with which you are viewed if you don't serve each individual the moment he appears on the scene; good natured impatience, generally, but still you are aware something is expected of you which you can't for the moment accomplish. Many of the poilus joke; some tap the counter with their cups; some call out, "I've been here since yesterday morning," or some other pleasantry. Some to attain their ends even try flattery, calling you pet names. "En masse" they are certainly entertaining and loveable. One came up today and insisted on shaking hands with a sister "Republican."

All the boys are charmed with the way things are going at the front; frightful losses, but much ground gained. The Germans have been pushed out of their concrete quarters by the terrific bombardments which we've heard lately. We hear that "no prisoners" are being taken now, an order from headquarters. It seems horrible, but everything is horrible. Jeanne, our maid, has been crying all day because she has had a letter from her brother, a prisoner in Germany, signed, "Your little brother who is starving." None of the food they send him gets there.

I may go to a hospital near here next week; one where men are dying from neglect—not our men, I think—because there are not enough nurses to help. I sha'n't nurse, but help Miss Coryn with the little canteen there. Also, I <u>may</u> <u>not</u> go, as Miss Nott said we must be in good health and my cold is not well. However, it's as well as it will be this winter, I guess, as no one here is ever without one entirely, I imagine.

My French papers have come (October 11th) so I can get my bread, fuel, oil and sugar cards now.

Écury, October 13th.
French Ambulance No. 5.
Field Hospital.

On Sunday morning I got up at six, shook out, and went down to the cellar for wood to make a fire. Found my woodpile in such a mess that I fixed it all up, and just as I started away, the whole thing fell down, so I spent another half hour building it up again and incidentally squashing each finger in turn.

At noon Miss Nott came to ask if I'd like to go out to the hospital at Écury to replace Miss Billings. She warned me that it was very primitive and to prepare for real camp life. Why she chose me I don't know, as it is generally the old workers who are given such

Figs. 9–11
Florence Billings

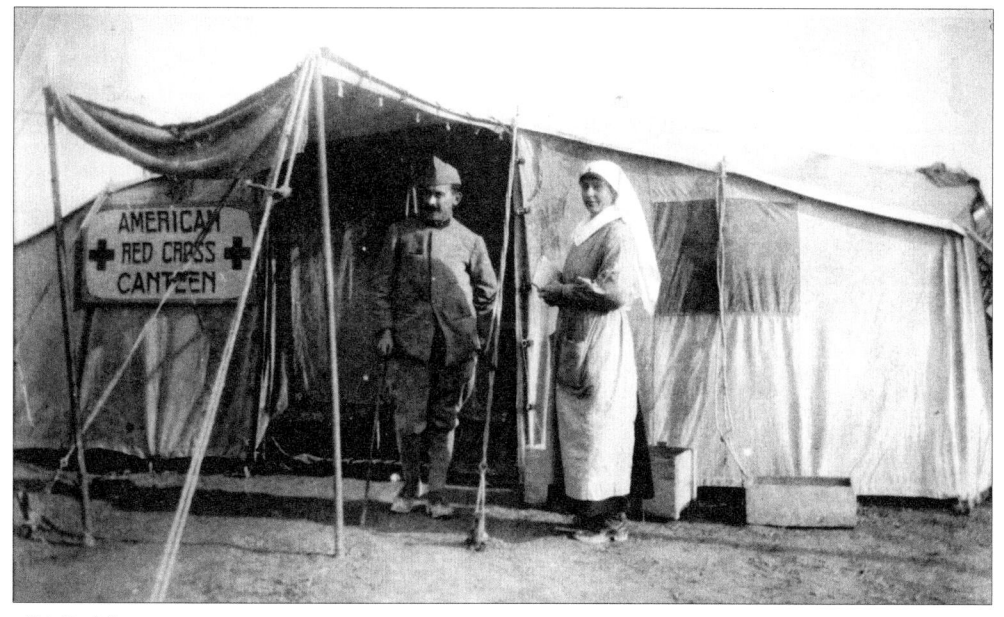

"M. H. at Ecury
Oct. 13. 1918. French Ambulance No. 5."

opportunities. I can't say I was overjoyed at the prospect because of my tendency to pick up grippe whenever it is around, and at present the place is a den of infection, but I wouldn't say "No" for anything, so packed up my camping outfit and started off in the camionette with Miss Mitchell and a lot of supplies.

It is an evacuation ambulance, so technically they are supposed to have no patients stay there longer than a few hours, but in reality many have to stay much longer, because of lack of transportation and often because they are too badly wounded to be moved immediately. As long as no one is supposed to stay, very little food is provided, so the nurses in real distress came down to us to see if we couldn't send up food and workers to make a little emergency canteen.

When we arrived at the hospital we found nothing but the bare ground where the canteen had been. The house was gone, not a trace of anything left. Finally Miss Coryn came wandering up, glanced at me, and remarked, "Oh, you'll be colder than that yet." And then told us that one of the ambulances had moved out a little while ago and as the portable house used for our canteen belonged to them, they had taken it, but another ambulance was going to give us a tent, as the "Medicin-Chef" wanted us to stay—in a French field hospital there are several ambulances, each comprising five doctors, their nurses, "infirmiers" and equipment. I stood shivering, first on one foot, then on the other, while the men put up our tent. We thought we'd have only the muddy ground for a floor, but by and by they took pity on us and brought some wooden slats, making walks for us to move and stand upon—a great comfort. Then they brought back our tables, benches, marmites and boxes, put up our stove, and we were at it again, all in an hour's time.

The most important thing after that, was to arrange our entrance so that no light could escape at night, and to fix the camouflage for our oiled silk windows, so that the German aviators could not spot us too easily. Such details were all so interesting to one new to the ways of war!

After the camionette had gone, we heard a most terrific noise and rushed out. Everyone was looking towards Châlons, where there was a great column of smoke rising like an enormous geyser, an explosion of some sort. Miss Coryn began my instruction immediately, and took me to visit the "grands blessés" wards. We gave the men grapes and cigarettes, and it almost killed me to see the agony on some of their faces. Then she said she would go to see two more patients in the next ward, but that I'd better not come. I did, though, and the horror of that sight! A huge tent, scarcely lighted at all, bare ground, empty except in the middle a little bit of a stove, with a little bit of a fire burning in it, and near it two cots, on one a Frenchman, and on the other an Arab. Their wounds were infected and they would have been too offensive to have had in a ward with others, so they were left alone here to breathe out their lives in as long a time or short a time as nature would allow.

That night, feeling excessively out of place, I dined on awful food with the French nurses—some ladies, some not—in the nurses' barrack, and heard that the explosion we'd seen in the afternoon was a camion filled with hand grenades. After dinner they pulled out their cigarettes, had a sociable smoke, and then went back to their quarters, and Miss Coryn and I spent the night in luxury on stretchers in an officer's room, where there are electric lights, running water, and a stove with enough fire in it to make the room really warm. The only out was, that it is next to the "triage," the great receiving ward for the patients, where they are sorted out, and all night long stretcher bearers were walking back and forth past our door.

In the morning I was waked up by a cheerful voice calling through the wall, "Did les dames Americaines sleep well?" And soon after one of the "infirmiers" announced to the "Medicin-Chef" the number of deaths that night, nine.

While the canteen was in the little house, the girls had had to sleep on stretchers on the floor, a rather uncomfortable thing to do, as all the men who used the place were "petits malades," all with grippe or influenza, and all with habits so untidy that the floor must have been soaked with germs by the millions. I am glad to have escaped that. When the tent was put up, it occurred to the French mind that it would be thoroughly improper for two women to sleep in that, so other quarters were provided in the barracks, with our one or two nights of luxury in between.

After a breakfast with the nurses, who in the lamp light the night before were charmingly pretty, but in their half-dressed early morning untidiness were less attractive, my duties began. I piled a big tray full of delicious grapes, and was told to go to certain "malades" wards while Miss Coryn took the "blessés." When I reached the wards, I found the "Medicin-Chef" making his visits. I had read in Red Cross directions never to go into a ward while the doctors are there, so I stood outside under the canopy which connects the long row of tents, where the very sick patients are. They are great long white tents, with sheets hanging between every two cots, for the "malades" don't like to see each other die; it depresses them. The "blessés" don't mind, so they die before the whole ward.

It seemed as though the doctor spent hours in that ward. I watched the old "infirmiers" clean up the dreadful receptacles which they brought out of the tents, pouring their contents on to the ground. I didn't see how any of us could escape the disease when such methods were used, but I supposed it was the best they could do. Then I watched the stretcher bearers, carrying their great piles of used linen away from the wards, and occasionally some carrying off stretchers filled with old, worn out, dirty uniforms, a very depressing sight. And then I watched a young aviator flying over the hospital, a cousin of one of the doctors, who came to give us a little treat. It was the most wonderful flying I have ever seen,—loop the loops, spirals, nose diving, flying at every angle imaginable, sometimes lower than our highest tents, swooping up just in time to save himself from dashing into eternity. All the French exclaimed, "He is master of his machine," and a little French aviator told me afterwards that he had never seen anyone do such reckless things. Finally the doctor came out and I began my visits, and I can assure you I saw that frightful disease in every one of its frightful stages. The minute I approached a cot, a terrible fit of coughing would take place. It never failed, and I walked into whirlwinds of deadly germs of every variety. A few, a very few, were able to give me a faint smile of thanks. Some nodded their heads only, and as I passed some, the old "infirmier" who was with me would shake his head and say, "None for him," and I knew what that meant.

In the afternoon I went back to the wards with orange juice, filled the drinking cups, which were so dirty and untidy that I could hardly bear to pick them up to hand to the men.

From that time on, my trips grew easier. I lost much of my great horror for hospitals, and now I can smile at times and even make a few remarks.

All that day, while I was making "tartines" for the boys in our little tent, and pouring out their coffee, I heard the coffins being nailed together in the coffin house almost opposite. Luckily none of the very sick wards are near us. We are tucked like a little sideshow of a circus in between two enormously big tents, which hold two hundred beds each and are used by the "petits malades," the walking cases—those without sheets on their beds, the doctor told me. They are our "clients." They can crawl into our tent, read our magazines, play our games, drink our coffee and eat our "tartines," as many as they like, and in that way get a little change from their dismal hospital quarters, which are always damp and cold. There is a little stove at one end of our tent, which makes it warm, and on which is a large "marmite" kept full of coffee, until we close at ten o'clock. We have one electric light, two long tables where the men sit, and a smaller one in the corner, behind which we sit or stand all day,—when we are not in the wards, making "tartines,"—(a slice of bread with apple marmalade or a piece of sausage applied)—and pouring out coffee, which is sweetened, a great boon. Sometimes we leave the pitchers on the table, and say to the boys, "Serve yourself," and they smile and say, "Just like home."

It is about nine P.M., and I wish you could hear the coughing and groaning and moaning going on in the tents beside us. I am sitting in our little tent with a crowd of poilus about, also coughing. Tonight they are laughing and joking and rather gay. It is the first time since we have been here that there has been much more than a whisper uttered in our little "foyer."

The second day the "Medicin-Chef" gave us a room in a barrack, and even had an American Red Cross sign made for us and put on the door, but when we went to it that night we found it occupied by two women already in bed, who said it had been given to them, so we had to go back and get Lambert, our canteen orderly (who helps with the fire and carrying our water) to take out our belongings, and hunt up the "Medicin-Chef," who put us back into our first quarters. I hoped the doctor whose room it is would not come for his bed that night.— He didn't!

The next day the "Medicin-Chef" ushered us again into the same barrack, showed us another little room, with cardboard walls, pinned our American Red Cross sign on the door, and said that would be our quarters. There were two cots in it, nothing else. My wash basin, which luckily I had brought from U.S.A., had to be placed on the floor, and we knelt to wash our faces. There was no camouflage for the window, so Miss Coryn nailed her blanket across that. I should never have thought of it, but she is well trained in war ways.

It has been raining all day and the clay ground is so slippery that we skid at every step and literally need chains on our shoes.

There are a lot of English women ambulance drivers over here, strong and breezy and nice, who do their work well, I'm told. They come to the canteen in Châlons for food sometimes and one has just stopped here to get warm. She said there are crowds of Japanese convoys on the road today.

Our days are more or less the same. There are always crowds of aviators in the sky. Today an escadrille flew by, blowing their sirens, and such a weird noise as it was, like a flock of huge wild geese, quacking the way they do when they fly over us at Cohasset going south in the fall; only this was a wail, bloodthirsty and bloodcurdling.

An American boy, a patient, who drives a French ambulance, comes into the canteen often. He gave me a shoulder strap off one of the first German prisoners taken in the Champagne drive. Two German prisoners come occasionally, also. We give them coffee and a piece of bread, but if they linger too long, we show them the door, because we can't have them taking the seats of the French boys. One is an unattractive sort of a man, the other rather a nice young boy, who speaks French and with whom the poilus seem to enjoy talking. I am sorry I can't hear what he says, for the conversations look interesting. He was in the trenches one day and taken prisoner the next; that was his war experience.

We talk to the poilus and hear interesting tales. A sweet little aviator comes in, one who has just become a pilot and is waiting to be placed in some escadrille. He has been brought up by an English nurse and speaks so well and is such a gentleman that it is a pleasure to have him come. He was a "petit malade" and ready to go soon. He's not strong, though, and I know war will not be good for him.

One of the poilus I talked to has been for years at the source of the Amazon, doing topographical and other work on the boundary between Brazil and Peru. He is very interesting; tells me about the birds, flowers, animals; how they hunt ostriches with dogs, etc.

Two French officers stationed here, a captain and a very charming young doctor, come in often for English lessons. The doctor is so eager to learn that it is quite funny. Indeed, they sometimes come too often; I think they find their young teacher, Miss Coryn, too attractive to leave alone.

Today our supplies ran short, so we did not go through the wards. I always wear my raincoat into the sick wards and take it off for the wounded, not to carry infection. We were promised a hot bath in a bathtub this afternoon, but it never came off; the bath orderly has grippe.

The front has been quiet since the big offensive. Now we are hearing the guns again, but not many. Two poilus have just been talking together and I've been listening to their conversation,—an older poilu and a young chasseur. The older one had been with the division which had liberated the town where the younger one lived, they discovered, and the boy was trying to find out whether his home was still standing. Finally in the course of the discussion the young one complained that it was hard not to know whether he had a home or not. "Hard! You don't know what hard is. I have not seen my wife or daughter for four years. They are with the Boches. My home is gone, my town is gone, and everything else is gone. You have had a place to spend your permissions. I have had none. Four years of this. It's too long; I've had enough." And he looked it; war-worn, worried, with not the faintest look of hope in his face; nothing but impatience and suffering.

Ten or twelve die every night. Each morning at breakfast the nurses announce the number of deaths. Whenever a strong, heavy man is brought in, they always say, "Only a question of hours for him." Sometimes I watch them unload the ambulances. Those able to walk are made to do it; the others, the "couchés," are taken in on their stretchers, covered with their big coats, and all their possessions piled on top of them. You can generally tell from their looks how it will go with them. Sometimes, too, I watch the evacuations for a while. They take hours. Only the most severely wounded are kept here. One day for three hours a steady line of stretcher bearers went back and forth from the wards to the sanitary train at the hospital station. Today, also, everyone was evacuated who could be moved at all. Soon we may be evacuated, too. It is rumored the ambulance which owns our tent is ordered off.

* * * * * * * *

I was interrupted by two men who appeared and told us they had orders to take the tent down. When we expressed surprise, they said, "Why, haven't you been told we are to go and must have our tent immediately?" So off they took it, and left us homeless for a second time. We were put into one of those horrible great newly evacuated pest houses beside us, where night after night we had listened to the coughing and the groans of exhaustion and discouragement of two hundred poilus resting on two hundred cots with only boards for springs, until we thought we'd go mad. It was too awful for words. I couldn't even sit down there, so Miss Coryn and I packed up our most valued possessions, cigarettes, and went out to take a walk.

The sense of freedom I felt when I passed those hospital gates was very strange. Fresh air to breathe, beautiful fields all about us, no coughing, no disinfectant, no hammering in of nails, nothing but beautiful country with a beautiful sunset in the sky, and a heavenly, picturesque little village near by, where troops and their horses were quartered "en repos" in every corner and shelter it possessed, and wherever you looked you found a Belasco stage setting with a fascinating group of poilus cooking their evening meal over their fires, lighted by twilight outside or by candle light inside. It was a wonderful picture and it is hard to realize the fearful tragedy of it even while living in it.

David Belasco

That night we sat over a tiny stove in that huge tent and felt too dismal to speak. Miss Coryn had a slight "cafard," (poilu for an attack of the blues). There was a bright moon and about midnight I was waked up by aeroplanes going over the hospital, flying very low. Everyone was walking round and talking and I couldn't make out whether they were French or German "avions." The hospital had been bombed and swept by machine guns and I must confess to a near attack of knee-shaking for a while. It's a most peculiar feeling to have no shelter to go to. If they were Boches they kept their bombs for another place that night. They stayed round for an hour or so and then went off.

The next morning we carried newspapers, grapes and cigarettes to the "blessés" ward. I talked to a nice, red-haired American boy from Texas for a while, and gave him some of the "Camels" which Phil had stuffed into my pocket on the dock in New York. He looked so delighted, and asked me how I knew they were the only kind of cigarettes he smoked. I think he must feel lonely there, all surrounded by French, but he said they have a sign language which they understand very well. He had had his leg amputated, and looked very frail, and his mind often wandered.

Philip Hall

Many of the "blessés" died while I was there. I used to miss them each day. There was one poor man who never changed; he was suffering frightfully; both his hands and arms bandaged up, one leg off, and it was doubtful whether the other could be saved. He looked like death as he sat propped up in bed, always in the same position, always with the same expression of intense suffering on his face.

In the afternoon the "Medicin-Chef" offered to give us an ambulance to take us back to Châlons, so we packed up and went to say goodbye to our "blessés," but from the sounds which came from the ward we knew that their wounds were being dressed, so we didn't go in. The last thing I heard was the American boy screaming, "Don't pull that so tight!"

Châlons, October 20th to 26th.

The country was attractive as we speeded through it, back to Châlons; just because it was country, and I hadn't been in a car for so long. We saw some of the "75s" which shoot at the Boches aviators when they fly over Châlons.

When I got home I found to my despair my precious window panes gone; the skylight gone, and the house more open than ever to the Châlons winter, and when it rains now, a small Niagara rushes down the stairs. It was done by the explosion which we had heard at Écury of the defective hand grenades, a whole camion load of them. Seven persons were killed; nothing at all found of the driver, and the poor town was more wrecked than ever.

Miss Coryn asked me to dine with her and Col. R. at the Angleterre in the evening. It was interesting to hear him talk. He had just come down from the front and had given the Germans a trouncing that morning with his heavy guns. He was worn out from being up there two weeks, and said, if any man said he was not afraid when he was under fire and under bombing planes, that he lied. They may not show it, but they are, just the same, no matter what they say. He told us that the Argonne forest is going to be terrible to clear, the hardest along the whole line, and that that is the key to the German situation.

On our way to the hotel our car was stopped by a guard, and the chauffeur ordered to put out all the lights. When we came out from dinner, the foyer was pitchy black, not a soul about, and we found there had been an "alerte," which we had not heard. The place was like a dead city as we drove home, through the dark streets in our unlighted car, not a living creature anywhere. The Germans went to Bar-le-Duc, though, instead of Châlons, and gave them a little treat.

I lunched with Miss Nott yesterday. She told me that Gen. Gouraud thought the reason we were so badly bombed the night the evacuation hospital was struck (seventy-eight deaths in all, as a result) was reprisals for the triumphant procession of German prisoners through here. Since then there have been no processions. They have been smuggled through at night, a few at a time.

I've suffered through the kitchen this week, "Chef d'équipe" they call it, and I'm thankful it's over. Such a chaotic week as it has been for me; cutting and weighing "saucisson," weighing "confiture," cutting bread in 8¢, 4¢, 1¢ "repas," and soup sizes; making chocolate, keeping the door of the storeroom closed and locked. The first day I thought I'd go mad between the cat and the brains. Every time I went into the storeroom and butcher shop, the cat would make a dive in after me, and I had to go hunting for her behind carcasses of every description. When I succeeded in capturing her, I went back to weigh my "saucisson"—(I never want to hear that word again)—and always found my scales occupied by the cook and her staff weighing brains. Of course my work didn't progress, and there was a perpetual cry of, "More chocolate, please," "No more confiture," "Coffee all gone," "Please see that the 'repas' come through more quickly," "Will Mlle. please unlock the door." In fact, do a thousand things at once, but "don't stir from serving the vegetable" until Mlle. in despair was ready to stow away on the next boat bound for New York.

The boys often remark, "You ladies work very hard, harder than we," and the American boys sometimes say, "We don't know what we'd do without you," which is very pleasant to hear.

"Oct. 27 1918. 1. Where I spent hours this week cooking chocolate by day and having nightmares about it by night.
2. where the meat is cooked
3. coffee
4. vegetables washed
5. kept full of boiling water
6. soup
7. Mme Bach the cook
8. storeroom door which gives me palpitations every two minutes for fear I've left it unlocked.
9. door out to the canteen where things are served
10. under which I stand by the hour weig[h]ing sausage 11. door out into the office where I sleep when I'm on 3:45 a.m. duty Other women help cook and wash dishes in much confusion all day long. More places to cook which aren't seen in this picture. 8 or 10 separate fires going all the time. MH"

Mrs. Earle wants to come here if she can. She wrote to me that one of the girls who was in her cabin coming over has already died of the grippe and is buried in the little graveyard where we went, outside of Paris. She was a very strong girl and boasted about it. This disease seems to be worse than the black plague, it is so universal and deadly. My cold has gone; being with grippe and influenza seems to have had a curing effect. It is midnight now, the guns are still going, and our sausages are up, with aeroplanes flying around guarding them. It's a fine night, with a bright moon, and the Germans are expected.

October 27th to November 1st.

The guns are banging away at the front. It is much farther away but we can hear them still, and they always disturb one's nervous system. We've got the hardest part of the line near us, where there is terrific fighting and terrific mortality. Everyone from the front says the same thing, that it is awful up there. Think of being so near to it that we can hear it thundering on!

The "avions" have been rushing past all the afternoon (the 28th) and flying so low that they made an awful noise. Just before midnight word came to the canteen that Austria wants a separate peace. There was great rejoicing. Everybody told everybody else the news.

Each day brings some phase of war new to me. The canteen is always packed and we work like mad to feed the boys and to send them up to the lines as comfortable as possible. Every time I hand out a hot dinner, I feel it may be the last the boy will ever have. You will get some idea of the crowds we shelter when I tell you that one morning I asked an American boy if he had found a place to sleep that night. "Oh, yes," he said, "at three o'clock a Frenchman got up off the floor and I took his place." They are on the tables, under the tables, and balanced on the cross bars that support the tables; every chair is full, every bench crowded; those who cannot find enough floor space to lie upon are propped up against the wall, goodness only knows how. The dormitory, large cinema room, "salle de lecture," the restaurant, and a long corridor where they check their belongings, are all the same, and some have to sleep out of doors. It's awfully cold!

There never has been anything real about my life over here. I can't believe that it is I who am seeing it with my eyes, living in something that is a reality and not a dream. It worries me sometimes for I am afraid it will disappear out of my memory like a dream, and I don't know just what to do to hold on to it.

Our nights have not been comfortable. We hear that the "Richthofen circus," the best German flying squadron, has been moved down opposite us, and there are frequent "alertes"—all electric lights in the canteen go out, and we have to clear it by candle light, snatch up our money boxes and fly to the "abri," after making sure not a poilu is left above ground. Telephone messages come, "Germans at Epernay, expect them in twenty minutes," etc., and sometimes they come and sometimes they don't. Then we have the reports from the front, only two hours old often; reports of frightful slaughter going on there, of the awful sacrifices we are making to take the Argonne, and the terrible fighting near Verdun. We can hear the roar of the guns day and night. The military and troop trains go up and the wounded trains come down, and we always have platform work to do outside, besides the canteen work inside, and nurses who are rushing from one sector to another, to feed in the office.

My one spree was a day when I was on night duty. Miss Coryn and I packed up a luncheon, took a chance at getting out past the guards, and went to L'Épine, to see the wonderful church, with fascinating gargoyles, one of the most interesting small ones in France. It was a whole day of freedom, beautiful sunshine, warm green fields, and country that seemed lovely, but isn't really very pretty. We were given a lift by American officers, who dropped us at the church and said they were going back again in the afternoon and would take us home. We ate our luncheon in a field where we could see the church spires through the pines, listening to the guns, watching the aeroplanes overhead, and the blue lines of poilus marching by in the distance, and felt thoroughly at peace with the world. It is strange how quiet and peaceful you can feel with such things going on all about. I suppose it was seeing the country and breathing the country and being away from the constantly changing mob at the canteen that was calming to our nerves.

The church is a beauty. If you are ever in this part of France you must see it. In the thirteenth century the Virgin appeared to the people and bade them build a church over a spring on that spot. There are two or three German graves in the churchyard. We explored the trenches behind the church, where the people go during raids, I suppose. The town has been bombarded and somewhat destroyed, but the church escaped, one of the few which have in this part of the land.

We occasionally see Japanese and Portuguese soldiers. Anamites, with purple coats and mustard brown puttees and hats, which give a good bit of color, are always working at the station.

I've bought a French army blanket from the army stores. I'd like to buy two or three more, one for a curtain at my door to keep the hurricane out, one to put over my broken window for the same purpose, and one to put on the floor for my feet, also one over my bed. That's all a wild dream of luxury, which I sha'n't have, of course. I just happened to be thinking on paper.

November 1st to 6th.

Fig. 4

On All Saints' Day I went to church. I was too late for the service, but in time to hear the organ at the end of Mass. We had just heard of Turkey and hopes of peace, and

France triumphant was in the heart of the organist. He never could have played like that six months ago. I could scarcely keep my self control. It's too much to grasp. Not one soul in the whole world who has not had to suffer! We are used to it now. Peace we are not used to, and the emotion of having the agony over will almost kill some people.

In the late afternoon I went to the military cemetery. The graves—thousands of them—were almost all covered with beautiful growing crysanthemums. Many of the French crosses were decorated with those bead flower wreaths, sometimes with the boy's name on them and "Regrets" written under it in big bead letters.

The Algerian graves are marked by boards with tops carved in a certain shape and painted white with black hieroglyphics. Our graves had no flowers. I thought they would be cared for as they were in Paris, so did not think of carrying any for them, and it was too late to get them then. On each was a little green plant something like parsley.

The next day—the Fête des Morts de la Guerre—we as a canteen were invited by the Bishop to the ceremony at Notre Dame, and were seated with the nurses and women ambulance drivers directly behind the officers. I was fortunate enough to be off duty so that I could go. The altar and choir were hung in black ceremonial hangings. Flags were in all the niches above the altar, and in front of it was a large catafalque draped in a flag and surrounded by many candles. Three beautiful French flags brought in by the procession were held over the catafalque. The service was solemn and impressive. The body of the church was filled with "militaires," officers and soldiers, French and American. On the side aisles were the civilians, women draped in crêpe, men in the blackest of black clothes. "May peace be with the dead, and after the war may peace be also with us," so preached the Bishop. He, as many others, is evidently much worried about the condition of France after the war, and he besought his people to preserve "social and religious peace",—otherwise the sacrifice they had so splendidly made during the four years of war would have been made in vain.

It is fine to hear about nothing but "after the war," and to know that everyone feels the end so imminent. Now we are just waiting to see what Austria will do.

Two little bits of poilus, very gay ones, were in the canteen tonight, and led a lot of singing. After a while they came over to the counter and sang to each other there. Their "camarade" told me they were brothers and suggested that I ask for Tosca, which I did, but they said they weren't in the mood for that, so their "camarade" told me confidentially that they had had a little too much "pinar." He didn't have to be so confidential, though. They sang snatches of operas, with their good trained voices, acted to each other, and were quite amusing.

I was so surprised to see Elizabeth White walk into the canteen office one day. I showed her around the canteen and the town. We bought some "Madeleines" which we ate on the street; they are the only things we can get with sugar in them. She is at the French military hospital here, to take care of the American boys.

Coming over from supper I saw a torch fall through the air, which an aviator in distress had thrown out. He was too far away for us to find and it was so dark we could not see him, only the torch which was like a Roman candle.

I took my fur coat to be fixed today, and the woman who mended it told me how the Germans had been quartered all over Châlons, in 1914, and how none of the French people left their houses for eight days. At the end, the officer who was quartered in her place went away in such a hurry that he forgot his fine embroidered linen, which was being washed.

The canteen certainly is amusing. Today there were crowds of Algerians in their khaki and red fezzes, and a great many Poles who could only communicate with me in German, and some grinning, friendly Chinese whom our boys jollied up to the amusement of all hands. The poilus have a charm that never will exist again. They are quick and intelligent, nothing misses them. They know just how far to go and when to stop. Someone played the violin with guitar accompaniment this morning most charmingly, the Thäis "Meditation," etc. I have been talking with a Senegalese and a Frenchman, who said the Senegalese were fine fighters. I think the African had complained that they were put too much into the front lines. They are used for attacks and the Germans don't like to see them. The French soldier said he adored Americans, thinks them brave, generous and fine to come to a strange country—not their own—to help and that the great victory that is being won is due to them.

Austria capitulated at 3 P.M. today.

Now they are beginning to talk of the war being over in "days;" soon it will be "hours." It was weeks and months a little while ago.

A little baby porcupine was brought into the canteen tonight and passed around. He was all done up in a tight ball, with his little head drawn in and feet so well tucked up that we couldn't see them. A poilu walked off with it, I am afraid to make a late supper for himself. I hope he won't, though, as it was quite sweet.

If I don't write often, don't worry. It's hard to write, as I am never very comfortable in my room.

November 7th.

I went up to Corbineau Hospital with Mme. Oblin to see some of the boys. In one ward which we were going to omit there was a black, black Senegalese with white, white teeth, in bed. He grinned at me so invitingly that I had to go in and talk to him. We had a nice little conversation and I received a fine salute when I left. They all adore to see people, it breaks the monotony for a moment. When I got back I saw Miss Bennett going out to do troop trains and asked if she wanted help. Two or three trains were in, so we had lively business. Some of the men had made little shelters on the flat cars under their guns and camions, with straw to lie upon and canvas for sides. They were very comfortable, but crawled out of their holes for coffee, which is generally much approved of by the poilus, who address us with polite little words of endearment, "petite dame," etc.

All of a sudden another train pulled in. The poilus were all shouting and calling out to us in great excitement, "Est-ce la paix, Mlle. est-ce la paix?" The air was electrified. They shrieked and yelled back and forth from one train to another, cheered, shouted "la guerre est finie," "c'est la paix," waved their hands and their hats, and I thought they had all lost their minds, but when I went back to the canteen it was empty, not one single poilu there. They had all gone home! It was peace; they had gone home, and that was all there was about it; so it seemed to me, and it was the strangest sensation I ever had. Never before had I seen the canteen empty.

I had always thought the war might end suddenly, but not quite as suddenly as this. I knew that the Germans were in flight; that the French had had to follow them in camions and automobiles in this part of the country, but we did not expect the end quite so soon, and it has come too soon. A few days more and the whole German army in this section would have been taken.

I knew, too, that French hearts were lighter, for some Americans had told me a few days before that the poilus had come out of the trenches singing, and I had heard the organist at Notre Dame play his organ that day Turkey capitulated. There was victory in his touch, every note rang out victory.

Soon the poilus began to straggle back to the canteen. There was a general expression of pleasantness on their faces, but no great excitement. No one knew just what to believe, but we all felt that something was about to happen, even if it hadn't; and then we learned that hostilities in one part of the line were to cease while the Germans came through to ask for an armistice.

Of course we all waited with great impatience for eleven o'clock on November 11th. Some of the men said they could not even wait two hours, "two hours more of war was insufferable," they said, with a smile, and yet this ending is not satisfactory to the great majority of people. They wanted Germany to know a few of the things about war that they knew.

Fig 1. In the garden.

Fig. 2. Six Nationalities

Fig. 3.   Outside Canteen.

Fig. 4.   Algerian graves.

Fig. 5.   Châlons ruins.

Fig. 6.   Châlons hard suffering

Fig. 7. Station platform.

Fig. 8. Camouflage. (Road to Douaumont)

Fig. 9. Coffee.

Fig. 10.   [*Écury canteen*]

Fig. 11. Écury—

Fig. 12.   Champagne forest.

Fig. 13.   Train of prisoners—
Germans— Turks— Bulgarians.

Fig. 14. "France triumphant rising out of her ruins"

Fig. 15. Camouflaged trench—Douaumont.

Fig. 16. Road to Rheims.

Fig. 17. American Army.

Fig. 18.   Landscape near Vaux—

Fig. 19.   Death Valley—between the two Forts—

Fig. 20.   Varennes ruins. (Mme Oblin)

Fig. 21.   Our Abri. [*Left: Marjorie Coryn. Right: Frances King.*]

Fig. 22.   Ypres.

Fig. 23. Living over a Railroad Station.

Fig. 24.   German.

Fig. 25.   German tank.

Armistice

On November 11, 1918, in Châlons-sur-Marne, "flags burst out from every house & on all automobiles & camions" and the constant thundering of guns stopped and street lights came on at night, ending the blackouts of many years. Amid the stillness of peace, the poilus were "rather rollicking about," in Anna Mitchell's assessment.[1]

From the first year of the war, proposals for a truce had failed. Pope Benedict XV had urged a general Christmas truce in 1914 to end "the suicide of Europe," but the political leadership ignored this, as well as a seven-point "Peace Note" that the pope sent to the belligerent powers in August 1917.[2] In 1915, two pacifists, the Dutch physician Aletta Jacobs and the American social worker Jane Addams, convened the International Congress of Women at The Hague, where according to the official report 1,136 participants from twelve countries met from April 28 to May 1, to prepare proposals for peace negotiations. Among the principles to end the war that they circulated among heads of state (proposals that may have influenced President Wilson's later peace program) were that territory should not be transferred without the consent of its people, that international disputes should be settled by arbitration, and that women should be granted equal political rights.[3] A year later, on December 12, 1916, when the German military position seemed to be very strong, German chancellor Theobald von Bethmann-Hollweg offered to negotiate through Wilson, then president of a neutral nation. Although the terms were never spelled out, the Allies understood that the Germans anticipated the rights to occupy Belgium and northern France, and to keep Alsace, Lorraine, and the German African colonies.[4] The offer was rejected. One week later, on December 18, Wilson proposed a League of Nations.

Another year passed before British prime minister David Lloyd George restated his country's position, on January 5, 1918, calling for "the right of self-determination or the consent of the governed."[5] Three days later, Wilson laid out his Fourteen Points for peace negotiations, which would include "open covenants of peace," free navigation on the high seas, free trade, reduction of national armaments, consideration of popular interest in deciding the sovereignty of colonies, and the German or Austro-Hungarian evacuation of Russia, Belgium, France, Romania, Serbia, Montenegro, and Poland. Although Wilson did not use Lloyd George's term "self-determination," he did call for the free "autonomous development" of the "peoples" under the control of the German, Austro-Hungarian, and Ottoman empires.[6]

When fighting ceased in 1917 on the Eastern Front, the related agreements came on German terms. In March 1917, the abdication of the tsar shook Russian resolve and weakened army discipline, and after the October Revolution (November 6 to 7, 1917), the Bolshevik seizure of power led to a ceasefire signed by the Central Powers on December 5, 1917. This was quickly followed by an armistice between Romania and the Central Powers on December 9. In the Treaty of Brest-Litovsk, signed March 3, 1918, the Bolsheviks agreed to pay Germany a million gold rubles and to surrender Finland, the Ukraine, Bessarabia, the Baltic States, Galicia, and Crimea. The former Russian empire began to break up.[7]

Germany also seemed poised for victory on the Western Front during the first half of 1918, in spite of food shortages and economic fracture lines. On July 3, 1918, at a meeting in Spa, Belgium, Kaiser Wilhelm II and his high command still believed that appropriate peace terms would include the annexation of Luxembourg and the French iron and coal fields in Lorraine.[8] In July, however, the Allied victory in the Second Battle of the Marne, followed by the successful offensive at Amiens in August and the American victory at Saint-Mihiel in early September, changed the options for peace.[9]

In the weeks before November 1918, fresh reports and rumors came to Châlons-sur-Marne that promised an end to the war. The soldiers themselves eagerly repeated such stories to Margaret Hall, and the canteen buzzed with word of each country dropping out of the war as Central Europe began to break up. The final cascade of truces began with the Bulgarian agreement, which took effect on September 30, followed by the disintegration of the Austrian empire in October. On October 6 a South Slav government was proclaimed, and the next day the contest among different groups for control over a Polish state began. On October 28, Czechoslovakia was declared a republic, and the Allies signed the Ottoman armistice at Mudros on October 30. During the same period, the Austro-Hungarian empire came apart—a Hungarian republic being declared even as Karl I authorized an emissary to settle peace terms in Italy. German mutineers broke down military control in Kiel and Berlin, and Kaiser Wilhelm II, who had continued to rely on the loyalty of the troops, was told by Chancellor Prince Max von Baden and by the Socialist leader Friedrich Ebert, his successor, that he must abdicate.[10] As Hall observed at the canteen, scattered soldiers began acting in anticipation of peace, going AWOL in the days before the general Armistice was signed by German, French, and British representatives on November 11.

What were the terms of the Armistice? Wilson's Fourteen Points in January 1918 had stressed demilitarization, a return to previous frontiers, and a League of Nations. After a mistaken report on November 7 that an Armistice had been signed, the Germans negotiated minor revisions of the terms proposed by the Allies.[11] Unusually detailed in its provisions, the Armistice of November 11 established the grounds on which the Peace of Versailles in June 1919 would be laid out, but it nonetheless left room for German misunderstanding of the terms on which they would be forced to sign the treaty seven months later. It also left room for disagreements among the Allies during negotiations in the spring of 1919, when principles such as the Fourteen Points competed with the Allies' diverse territorial goals. The preliminary agreements set out in the Armistice provided for the termination of military hostilities within six hours after the signing, at 11 A.M. on November 11. All German troops were to evacuate France, Belgium, Luxembourg, and Alsace-Lorraine within fifteen days. The west bank of the Rhine, as well as eastern bridgeheads (with a roughly nineteen-mile radius) at the cities of Mainz, Coblenz, and Cologne, would become a neutral zone, to be occupied by Allied and U.S. troops who would move forward, following the Germans at a distance of six miles. Immediately upon the signing, the treaties of Brest-Litovsk and Bucharest were rescinded, reestablishing Germany's eastern boundaries of August 1, 1914. German East Africa was surrendered unconditionally, to be evacuated by all German forces within a period to be fixed by the Allies; negotiations at the peace conference assigned former African colonies as "mandates" to Britain, France, Belgium, and Portugal, under the supervision of the League of Nations.[12] "Return of prisoners of war without reciprocity" would send thousands of Allied soldiers and civilians home. The German fleet was to be interned, and massive amounts of military materiel were to be surrendered, including howitzers, machine guns, mortars, airplanes, locomotive engines, and railcars.[13]

The accord did not spell out the amount of reparations that would be imposed, or the loss of territories that would strip Germany and Austria-Hungary of much of their territory and part of their German-speaking population. The blockade stayed in place, and German prisoners of war were not released. Those issues would be negotiated among the Allies over the next seven months. Without final treaties in place, the shifting political status of emergent republics in Central and eastern Europe compounded the destabilization of territories by wandering irregular troops and civil war.[14]

French reactions to the cessation of hostilities were ambivalent. On November 11, Clemenceau declared, "We have won the war, and not without pain, but now we must win the peace, and that will be perhaps more difficult."[15] While townspeople in Châlons decorated the streets and crowds enthusiastically celebrated peace in Paris on November 11, women in black carried a message of mourning. Some French and Americans expressed disappointment at not crossing into Germany, to inflict revenge for the sufferings of the preceding four years. General

Pershing, for example, believed the German army should be defeated, rather than accorded a truce.[16] Thus the Armistice was seen as a troubled preliminary peace. In France, the joy of victory was closely knit to crushing grief, while in other nations such as China and Italy, peace seemed mutilated by the failure to achieve territorial war aims.[17]

Starting in November, the consequences of the Armistice were visible in Châlons-sur-Marne. French and American troops regrouped and marched forward, pushing into recovered lands and heading north to establish the occupation of the west bank of the Rhine. Other troops and refugees passed back through the train station as they returned home. Seized German weaponry traveled westward. Auxiliary troops and laborers, who included African Americans, Portuguese, Italian, Chinese, and Annamite colonial units, traveled north and east into the formerly occupied regions to begin to rebuild roads and rail lines, clean up the polluted battle terrain, and clear military debris and waste (such as unexploded shells, grenades, and thickets of staked barbed wire) from agricultural lands wherever possible.[18] Canteen workers were called upon to serve the troops occupying Germany—the Americans at Coblenz and Trier and the French at Strasbourg. On November 12, Hall would be able to hitch a ride to visit Reims, and several months later she would visit Strasbourg and the Rhineland. Thus renewed mobility was the most immediate consequence of the Armistice for a canteen worker in the war zone, like Margaret Hall.

11 o'clock, November 11th.

Armistice signed. Kaiser in Holland, and Crown Prince passed over.

This was the day of all days that I wanted to be in France to see the celebration, and I had to stay in the canteen, so that I never heard a church bell or a single thing except one cannon! When that went off at eleven o'clock, all the soldiers cried out, "C'est la paix! C'est la paix!" "La Guerre est finie!"—and continued to eat their "repas complets!" No throwing up of hats, no singing of the Marseillaise; <u>nothing</u>. France is too sad, and the price it has had to pay is too great to have any real demonstration of joy. There <u>is</u> no joy here. It is simply an awful relief to have the slaughter stopped. That is all. They all felt more like crying than celebrating, and I think that most of them did. One of the French women in the canteen said she could not be gay it was such a sad peace. "Look at the poilus; they are not rejoicing, they have lost too many of their families and friends to be lighthearted." And it is perfectly true. When I went out at one o'clock, there were a few flags about, but when I came home after luncheon, the city was hung with them, and when I started out on my tour of the town, all alone, (with my little silk American flag) so I should not have to control my emotion too much, I hardly knew Châlons. There were flags from every window, the Hotel de Ville was covered with them, and in every group our flag with theirs was in the middle. (Our troops have been in this sector). Boches prisoners had to decorate the cathedral! People were all out on the streets carrying flags, camions flying through the town full of shouting poilus, waving French and American flags; American trucks so covered with flags that you could hardly see any truck at all, filled with grinning American boys.

It was hard not to feel a little emotional at times, but I took to the side streets always until I recovered. In the town square an old man caught hold of my flag and kissed it, saying, with tears in his eyes, "C'est ça que j'aime." They were all wonderful about the Americans. They give us full credit for the victory. Not one man I have ever spoken to has belittled our part in any way. They always say, "Thanks to you Americans." And that night at the canteen they showered so many attentions on one poor American boy that he almost died of embarrassment. Wherever he walked he was surrounded by an admiring mob. They kissed him first on one cheek and then on the other; they formed circles round him; patted him, shook hands and fêted him until he had to seek refuge somewhere out in the dark. His embarrassment was quite attractive to watch, he was so nice and modest.

On my way home I stopped at the Hotel de Ville to watch the camions go by, and to look at the flags and people, especially the American officers who had come in flocks from the camps about to get a supply of champagne for their celebration that night.

That evening I walked back to the canteen in electric light! Two lamps had been strung across the main street, one at one end and one at the other,—the first time in four years that a ray of light had ever penetrated the darkness of this town, and the first time since I left home that I had seen one ray of light anywhere at night. It was a wonderful sight and wonderful to see the people gazing at it as though they had never seen one before. There were posters on the Hotel de Ville, saying that owing to the armistice the order forbidding lights had been repealed, so the few shops which were inhabited, left their windows open, and it was a real celebration externally, but not internally. The people weren't really gay; there was no spontaneity to speak of. A little singing in cafés only. The noise was made by small boys. The star shells and tracers used for fireworks that evening were fired off by small boys. The others had suffered too much and victory had cost them too much, to be lighthearted.

That evening there was a concert at the canteen, a calm one, but after it, a poilu started to play the "Marseillaise" on an accordion; another grabbed a big French flag and waved it, and the crowd joined in and sang. It was the only really spontaneous celebration that I saw, and it was great, as it rang out through that big room and made the cold shivers go up and down your back. The place quieted down almost immediately, and after that they would only come up to you and say, "La guerre est finie, Mlle." "On les a." (We have them). Men were in the canteen from Mézières and said that the guns did not stop until the dot of eleven; that before the end the Germans sent a most terrific barrage of gas shells into the town and killed a great many civilians, men, women and children, as well as soldiers. How dreadful for the ones who had to be killed in those last few hours! That is about all I can tell you of the peace celebration in Châlons. It was not much like America, I imagine. Here there is always the black background of mourning, and if a little feeling of lightness and cheer creeps into your soul, it is quickly driven out by the tragedy all about.

I'll never forget the impression I got on the rue de Marne that day of the armistice. Flags were all out, the sidewalks crowded with the gaily dressed "militaire," camions flying by all flag bedecked and full of cheering soldiers, when suddenly two young women swathed in crêpe from head to foot stepped out of the crowd like black ghosts. They were gone in a minute, but the impression that they left will never go. It was the great dramatic touch, the real France which showed itself for a moment and then disappeared.

The next thrill I had was a trip to Rheims the day after the armistice. About ten of us piled into a big camion and were sent over. Very soon after we left Châlons evidences of war began to appear. Big camps along the side of the road where troops and horses put up for the night; the huge war hospital at La Veuve, the most God-forsaken place I've ever seen, the evacuation hospital for thousands of wounded in this section, and a little farther on, the camouflaged roads began. From there on, all the way to Rheims, we were travelling beside the camouflage. It was not hung over the roads here, but a great screen on the German side, sometimes made of branches, sometimes bunches of straw or raffia tied on wire screens, and sometimes regular made camouflage, a wall ten feet high, I should say, so that the German balloon observers could not see the traffic on the road—unbroken except where the stone walls of farms and little villages took its place. The roads which ran off from ours were camouflaged, too, but they were screened on both sides, and it was a wonderful sight to see lines of blue poilus with their shining steel helmets winding through these screened roads. Soon we began to see shell holes in the fields, and places in the road which had been repaired. Once in a while there was a camion, standing upside down in a terrible state of wreckage in the gutter, and sometimes dead horses. Next the tops of the trees seemed to have disappeared, and then the trenches (the Gouraud line of defense) with barbed wires entanglements in front, began to appear. Trenches seemed to go in every direction through the fields, with long things that looked like clothes horses made of iron and all covered with barbed wire, lying near them, which we were told were to be used by a retreating army. The last men to leave must pull them down to impede the forward rush of the enemy. The woods were full of dugouts and "abris." Little niches were cut out in the banks along the roadside, where men could take shelter if the road were bombed.

We went through little villages all shot to pieces, with not one house standing which was inhabited or inhabitable. Some were all down, some had great shell holes through them, and some of the stone walls had little holes through them, too, made by the French to shoot through if the enemy should pass by that way.

The nearer Rheims we got the more battered up things were. Nothing but stumps were left of the trees. The little village graveyards, or rather what was left of them, were full of soldiers' crosses. I tried to take a picture from the back of the camion of a regiment of poilus we passed on the road. They were led by their band and had their flags and whole fighting equipment with them.

Rheims was a dead city. The silence was appalling, not a civilian in the place. Occasionally—only occasionally, though—a soldier of some nationality would straggle by. They say there are only eighteen houses intact in the place. That must mean absolutely without a crack, for of course there are many streets with the houses standing, but damaged to a greater or lesser degree. The nearer we got to the centre of the city, the more battered it became, and finally when we turned into a side street, the cathedral appeared in front of us. France triumphant rising out of her ruins! The French pennant

Fig. 14

was flying from one of the spires out into the sunshine against the blue sky, and an exquisite little group of French flags was arranged under the rose window, as exquisite and delicate as the rest of the cathedral. That was all. It was almost the only color we saw in Rheims that day. Perhaps there were four other flags hanging from windows in the midst of the ruins, but they only emphasized the loneliness and desolation of the place.

Nothing at all is standing near the cathedral. I wonder if you know Rheims. That beautiful square where the statue of Louis XV stands is one of the strangest sights there. The facades of all the buildings on every side are standing, but when you look through the glassless windows, you see nothing but blue sky; no roofs, no sides, no insides, nothing but the front wall, and every single building on every side of the square is the same.

The general outline of the cathedral is not much hurt, but there is scarcely a square foot on the outside which has not been hit, and most of the detail is destroyed. The inside was more or less cleaned up, at least the débris was collected into big piles. There were enormous holes in the roof, through which flocks of birds were flying in and out. The valuable glass windows were practically saved, and are in Paris now, but the souvenir hunters, always expectant, still spend their precious moments in the cathedral with their eyes glued on the floor hoping that by some glorious chance the visitors before them might have overlooked a splinter of pigeon blood red or sapphire blue glass from the old rose window.

Only the main thoroughfares are open to traffic. The other streets are so full of mountains of débris that even entering them is impossible. It would be easier to begin a new city than to try to reconstruct that, I should think. There are such queer freaks, too. I looked up at what was once an inside wall of a house, and saw three rows of saucepans hanging exactly as they were left on the wall when the people walked out; nothing remained of the house but that wall and the saucepans. All the doors are open and loot is plenty for anyone who feels like taking advantage of an opportunity like that. I did not go into any of the handsome houses but was told there were beautiful vellum bound books, wonderful pieces of embroidery and laces, lying round, things which the soldiers of the Allies did not think it worth while to take, and which I hope the women in our party at least had common decency enough to let alone. I know some of them went back several times, with longing in their hearts, to look at certain things, but the result of their visits I never heard.

One of the French women who works in the canteen here, the wife of the Rabbi of Rheims, an adorable little person, stayed there all through the German occupation. During the day she was made to nurse German wounded and at night she took care of eight French wounded she had hidden in her cellar. "If the Boches had discovered it, I should have been stood up against the wall," she answered when I questioned her about it. "Tant pis." They have lost many things. Among them a wonderful collection of medieval books beautifully bound, priceless I imagine, but she only says, "What difference does it make, we have France." She had nursed and nursed and nursed under shell fire until she couldn't do it any longer, and when ordered away from Rheims finally, she came here for a change of occupation. If any woman ever deserved the Croix de Guerre, it is she, but the ones who really deserve it, by their steady and untiring devotion, are not the ones who always get it.

Mme Hermann

While we were wandering around the streets, a mounted French officer came clattering up behind us. He wanted to know if we had met anyone walking about near by. I think the noise of his horse's hoofs as he galloped off must have resounded through every part of the city. Such silence is uncanny.

After we had seen about all we could in a short time, and I had taken a few pictures, I asked our French soldier if we couldn't go out to see the German lines. "No, quite impossible—défendu"—and we would get smashed up going home in the camion after dark. I didn't like to say much else, but a little later I remarked that we were going to have a bright moonlight night, and when we started for home I noticed that we didn't start back in quite the direction we came in. Finally someone spoke of it and he said no, we were going in quite the opposite direction, out to see Fort Brimont, the one from which the Germans shelled Rheims for so many months.

It seemed as though we had scarcely left Rheims when we stopped to get out to see a big German tank mired on the side of the road, in perfect condition, with a big iron cross painted on each side. Then we went on through the battlefield of years, flat barren country, nothing but desolation, nothing growing, trenches, barbed wire, shell holes, all mixed up together for miles and miles; shell holes so close that you could not distinguish one from another. We passed a big German prison camp (I imagine the prisoners were to clean up the country), and then a procession of baby tanks on its way towards Rheims, the discipline of which we broke up slightly by tossing their drivers cigarettes. It was hard to distinguish between the German and French trenches, for some days they belonged to one side and some days to the other, and they were pretty well shelled up, too, in some places.

Fig. 25

Fort Brimont is a low hill, not far away. Just as we got there some French officers appeared most inopportunely on the road, and our guide, whose respect for a man in officer's cap is unfailing,—like all the French soldiers—seemed to grow visibly pale, remarked that we had no permission to be there at all, and that we absolutely must not get out, so we drove on past the fort. All that we could see was a shelled up mound of earth. When we turned round to come back, we noticed all the road signs around the fort were in German, and as they were the first I had seen they seemed very exciting.

Of course Rheims is a wonderful and horrible sight, but the little villages are to me the really pathetic ones. Rheims is big and rich, and you feel that the people may have a little something besides what you see there, but in the little villages you know you are looking on everything they have left in the world—a pile of débris. If any rooms were left standing, their contents have been removed long since by the French soldiers, who did the plundering so that the Germans might not have that pleasure too!

Coming home we passed artillery regiments drawn by horses. It was interesting to watch them moving along in the gorgeous sunset, with their field kitchens cooking their "soup" and coffee, leaving trails of hot cinders along the road, and to see them turn in and wind their way through the camps, hundreds of them, until it seemed as though the places could take no more. This was war on the country road, which I had not seen before.

We got back about six o'clock. I substituted at the canteen that evening. The Algerians were all together giving a concert and the poilus were standing around listening. My "filleul" brought me a German bayonet and a "Gott mit uns" buckle, and his friend gave me a "bidon."

Refugees and the Repatriated

On landing at Bordeaux in September 1918, Margaret Hall immediately sought out a family of refugees, the Oliviers, who had fled from the Pas de Calais region in the north in 1914. Hall's aunt, Emma Coleman, had sponsored the grateful family during the war as a "godmother." In a system that started in France and then spread to other countries, "godmothers" sent their soldier-protégés letters and packages of necessities such as soap (and tobacco!), and in some cases financial support.[1] At the end of her year in France, Hall sent her remaining French money to the Oliviers. The family were just a few of the many civilians in 1914 who had been terrorized by the initial sweep of German soldiers into Belgium and the departments of the Nord, Pas de Calais, Somme, and Aisne, as invading troops who suspected sniper fire had engaged in punitive executions, arson, and the use of human shields.[2] More commonplace incidents of drunkenness, plunder, and rape threatened civilians in the path of advancing soldiers.[3] Whenever possible, civilians fled ahead of the German advance. Thousands of Belgians took refuge in England, and by the time of the Armistice, 140,000 Belgian refugees were officially registered there.[4] Roughly 200,000 Belgians and 400,000 French fled southward into unoccupied France, where they might seek shelter in a French "foyer," or home.[5] Among other American philanthropists who responded to the overwhelming needs, Edith Wharton in 1914 founded the American Hostels for Refugees and the Children of Flanders Rescue Committee for Belgian orphans.[6] Part of Margaret Hall's work for the American Red Cross in Paris concerned refugees from regions that had become battlefields and who were in need of beds, food, and medical care.

Over four years, each renewed offensive had triggered new waves of refugees. Thus, the Smith College Relief Unit at Grécourt had worked to reconstruct and resettle villages following the First Battle of the Marne, only to flee with local inhabitants at the time of the German Michael offensive in spring 1918, as Hall knew from conversations with Ruth Gaines on her trip to France and in Paris.[7] In September 1918, Hall encountered twenty refugees from Amiens when she visited a Paris canteen, where one woman described her husband as "crazy from shell shock" (17). She also visited a refugee center at the church of Saint Sulpice, which housed fifteen hundred each night; during the German advance in spring 1918, two to three thousand refugees had flooded in, "whole towns at a time" (23).

Just as the war began with hundreds of thousands of refugees on both the Eastern and Western Fronts, it also ended with a flood of refugees in November 1918. An exodus of French inhabitants finally able to leave their shattered homes in the occupied regions of the north flooded into the heart of France seeking family and food. These internal civilian refugees brought a sober reminder of harsh wartime conditions. Hall was quick to note the "mental suffering" of refugees from the occupied zone (significantly, a woman and her daughter were speechless) (82). At the canteen, these refugees arrived in waves of 175 to 200, poorly clad and reduced to "skin and bones" (83). The economic and psychological plight of civilians trapped in the occupied northern zones of France has been compared with that of French prisoners of war suffering from "barbed-wire" neurosis in Germany.[8] By November, the destruction wrought by German troops as they withdrew had caused an additional flood of refugees from the occupied zone in Champagne and the Argonne.[9] Because the military were still cleaning up battlefields that had been fought over for four years, many civilians who had fled could not immediately return when the Germans drew back.[10] By May 1919, some would begin to head "home" to a place lacking any shelter. As one elderly couple explained, "Oh, nothing, Mlle., there is nothing left, no house, no garden, nothing, but it is the only home we have, and we'll put up a little barraque and start again" (149). Reporting on her trip north in May, Hall underscored the difficulty of such returns: "Often the destruction of towns is so complete that it is impossible to tell where their house stood" (149).

An especially important group in the flood of refugees were prisoners of war. By one global estimate, from seven to eight million prisoners of war had been captured between 1914 and 1918, and in November 1918, almost two and a half million Allied soldiers were held by Germany.[11] After the Armistice, a new kind of traffic through Châlons-sur-Marne took place, which Hall was careful to record. The Armistice mandated immediate, non-reciprocal repatriation of all Allied prisoners of war. Moving south and west, skeletal French and British, as well as a few American, prisoners of war arrived from Germany. Emaciated, blank-faced former prisoners of war had simply been released without food, coats, or shoes; they struggled through the November weather to return home on foot. Hall notes that some of the surviving Frenchmen were wearing the 1914 uniform with red trousers, which the French military had quickly abandoned for the less conspicuous uniform of "horizon" blue. Meanwhile, Allied troops continued to move to the north and east in order to reestablish French control up to the frontier, or they entrained directly for Germany, where the Allies would occupy the Rhineland.

Because of the severe depression experienced by those held for several years, the Red Cross and the Vatican had earlier sought the repatriation or internment in Switzerland of all French prisoners of war older than forty-eight who had been held longer than eighteen months. Starting in 1915, exchanges of several thousand medical staff had taken place between Germany and the Allies, along with the repatriation of some severely wounded or sick soldiers and of some interned civilians.[12] Yet large numbers still remained in camps in November 1918. Out of an estimated 600,000 French prisoners of war seized by Germany and held in northern France or occupied territories of the east, at the Armistice over 520,000 still remained in captivity or had died.[13] Others among the released soldiers who returned through Châlons belonged to the 185,000 British and 2,450 Americans who came back from the camps.[14] Hall recognized as shell shock what historians today describe as the trauma of prolonged imprisonment that destabilized some of those who returned. Strikingly, Hall diagnosed a drunken soldier who pestered her while she was writing a letter as a "wreck," like others who had lost their families and comrades, and who were suffering from "too much war, too many shocks" (102).[15] Some French civilians had also been held hostage in German camps such as Holzminden; others had been sent to perform forced labor in Germany or transferred to work camps elsewhere in occupied territory. These civilian hostages all went on the road to return home in November 1918.[16]

A wave of illnesses beset Europe in the fall and winter of 1918-1919 and weakened those passing through Châlons. Because Germans suffered from food shortages due to the blockade, their prisoners lived with hunger, making them vulnerable to diseases; perhaps 17,000 French had died in the camps of malnutrition, typhus, or cholera.[17] The tent hospital at Écury, where Hall had served in October, continued to care for wounded men and repatriated soldiers with virulent diseases in November. The number of deaths due to the flu in the military could only be roughly estimated, in part because of wartime censorship.[18] Typhoid, tuberculosis, pneumonia, and influenza continued to decimate populations who were underfed, without proper housing, and crowded in shelters or public transport as they migrated across frontiers. Some American nurses noted the irony of men continuing to die on November 11 and afterwards, of their wounds or of the influenza pandemic. Shirley Millard, who was caring for flu patients, wrote, "I am glad it is over but my heart is heavy as lead."[19] In Hall's descriptions from mid November 1918, the return of refugees captures this ambivalence: the return that had been longed for was darkened by traumatic memories that would linger for decades. While Hall was quick to note the psychological trauma of prisoners of war, she also described the healing effect of comradeship, particularly in the case of an English and Irish pair. Their friendship may have been particularly striking to her in light of the Easter Rising of Ireland against England just two years before.

What Hall observed was not exceptional during this total war. Mass displacements of populations accompanied military scorched-earth tactics and ethnic purges across Europe during World War I. The largest exodus began in Ottoman Turkey, on April 24, 1915, when the Armenian population was rounded up and either executed or deported on death marches into the desert.[20] Hundreds of thousands of Armenians were disarmed and Armenian women and children driven east on foot. Despite protests by Germans as well as Allied powers, an estimated one to one and a half million Armenians died. In August 1915, Russians burned fields as they retreated, precipitating the flight eastward of tens of thousands of Polish refugees. Russian military commanders deliberately deported Germans, Jews, and Poles from the regions of the empire along the Western Front.[21] By 1917, six million refugees and deportees created an emergency for relief workers.[22] The number of people who died in this forced migration is unknown. Similarly, in the November 1915 retreat of the Serbian Army, tens of thousands of civilian refugees fled into Albania, with casualty rates perhaps as high as two hundred thousand.[23]

Paradoxically, it can be argued that the crises of refugees led to the rise of institutions of humanitarianism.[24] In the postwar period, famine and displacements in the Soviet Union drew relief from Herbert Hoover's American Relief Administration, the International Committee of the Red Cross, and the American Friends' Service Committee. While Hall's memoir never mentions refugees in other countries, she kept in touch with those of her colleagues who, like Anna Mitchell, continued doing relief work in Europe. Hall continued to correspond with Mitchell, the co-director of the canteen at Châlons, who went in 1919 to the Pas de Calais to work with returning families, then from 1921 to 1936 worked in Istanbul with the Nansen International Office for Refugees.[25] When she returned to Boston, Hall herself supported Armenian relief.[26]

Chālons, November 14th to 27th.

After the armistice we wondered if there wouldn't be a let up in our work, but in a day or two prisoners began to straggle in, one or two at a time at first, and then more and more and more, until we had to cry for help. We were swamped literally and absolutely, and the town had to come to the rescue and provide some way to care for them; feed, clothe and give them medical aid.

It was on the 17th that the great influx began. That was a terrific day. At eight, when we opened the canteen, we were flooded with them. It was the big day of celebration in Paris. I had had a sneaking desire to go down to see it. Some went, but thank Heavens, I didn't, for that was a day I know I really did help.

Of all the wrecks I've seen here, these prisoners were the worst—human wrecks. No one who has ever seen their faces could ever forget them, and no one who has not could ever be made to know what they were like that cold morning, as they stood over the counter waiting to be fed. They came by the hundreds, starved men, scarcely human; cold, emaciated, coughing, many with suspiciously bright spots on their cheeks, unshaven, filthy, smelly, with big, dark eyes that seemed to see nothing, faces that expressed nothing, hands cold and clammy. They all felt the same, those hands, as they grabbed the bread I offered them. Each time I had to turn round to fill my pitcher, I was thankful, for it gave me an opportunity to try to control my face. The agony of a "blessé" train is nothing to this, for their agony is quick and sharp, and this has been a slow death of starvation and exhaustion. I'm sure many will not live much longer. There was generally no change of expression when you spoke to them, and often no response. When they did talk, it was so excitedly and so fast that I could scarcely understand what they said.

None of the men had underclothing, overcoats or blankets. The Germans had taken away their boots when they were captured, and many of them had walked miles—some a good deal over a hundred—to get to the border and reach Chālons, the first town which could feed them.

I poured and poured; I wish you could have seen the receptacles they held out to be filled; old cooking utensils, old wash basins, big and little, broken bits of china, old tin cans, anything that would hold water which they had been able to gather up along the way. That collection in itself was enough to make you cry.

There were no places ready for them anywhere. It seems to have come so quickly that the government was not ready and it is a problem that is still to be solved. They all ought to go to hospitals to be examined before they are allowed to go among people, for no one knows what they are bringing with them. They need comfort and rest and food, and I wonder where they will get it. Probably something will be provided somehow.

Six Americans came in, in the same condition,—no hats, no coats, one with a blanket over his shoulders like an Indian, all looking as forlorn and as though they had suffered as much as the French; not quite as much, perhaps, for they looked as though they would soon pick up, and the French looked as though they never would.

They ate and drank and ate and drank, and all day long we were trying to fill them up, cautioning them not to overdo it. How they coughed! It was like Écury. I thought I was back in that nightmare of a place.

When the Armistice was signed, the German guards took the cartridges out of their guns and told the prisoners to go. Nothing was given them; no means of transportation and no directions. Many of them even had not been told they could go. They thought they had escaped, and wandered for days in the woods in the awful cold that we were having at that time, with no shelter and no coverings; travelled at night and hid in the daytime. I think those first ones who got back were in the worst condition. Those who came later had had time to pick up a little, or had had more food, or were more accustomed to the prisoner's life. The first who came were nearer the borders, and many had been prisoners for months, not years.

The English prisoners were really in the worst shape, but I don't think on that day there was much choice. I met an officer from Mailly, a big camp and hospital not far away a day or two afterwards, and he told me they came there by the thousands, in much the same condition in which we got them, only worse, covered with vermin, covered with ulcers from lack of nourishment (they ate mostly beets and "horse vegetables"), full of disease, and feet frozen. I wish that the German prisoners, who look so fat and rosy here, could be made to look at themselves and then look at the returning French. It might suggest a few things to their obstinate minds.

That evening when I started for home I saw some women refugees going back of the canteen and followed them to see where they were going. I found a long barrack, with two long tables down the middle, filled with "rapatriés" (civil refugees just liberated from the invaded country), being fed from our canteen. There must have been about two hundred of them, men, women and children; young men, who at the time of the German occupation were too young for the French army, but since then have grown up, and were on their way to enlist in it now. There were little lights at intervals along the tables, to give the room a suggestion of cheer, but the faces about the tables were worn, haggard and unshaven, and as painful as the faces of the soldier prisoners in the canteen. At one end of the room were a few women, old and young, some with babies, one with a little baby very sick and quite immovable, and another with a little girl of about eight. Mother and daughter looked alike and the expression of suffering and agony on the older face seemed only intensified on the younger. I can't understand how a face so young could express as much as that, for it was mental as well as physical suffering which showed there.

Mme. Oblin, an attractive little French woman who works with us, goes tomorrow to see her brother, who has returned after six months in a German prison. He is a doctor and should not have been held at all. He wrote that many from his camp would never return, and that he could not have held out much longer.

Very many of the prisoners died on the road trying to reach the frontier, and some even died at canteens while they were waiting for food, but none at Châlons.

The refugees from the occupied countries, too, were a great problem. They swarmed through the canteen, old and young, women with children who were cold and hungry. They filled up our kitchen and were under our feet wherever we turned. I know, for I was doing kitchen work that week, "Chef d'Équipe" they call the job, to give it a stylish sound, but it is anything but a stylish position to hold, and to have to stop my work and hunt up bowls and plates and babies' milk, while every single worker at the canteen was shouting at me at the same time, to attend to their needs, was almost more than I could stand, and my heart did not seem to soften much to civil refugees that week.

Finally one night the "Chef de Gare" rushed over to the canteen in great consternation and said, "A very disagreeable thing has just happened to me. One hundred and seventy-five refugees have been landed at the station, cold and hungry, and I don't know what to do with them." So finally, after much talk, we decided that the men who were able to walk were to come to the canteen, and that we would take marmites of soup and coffee and baskets of bread over to the waiting room of the station and feed the old men, women and children there. It was about 12 o'clock and we worked until 1.30, feeding them and making them comfortable, as comfortable as they could be, lying in bunches all over the station floor. Most of the babies and children were too tired to wake up to eat. We never were able to make some of them take a thing. The different families had brought with them all the possessions which they had left, and they were sitting or lying in pathetic groups on them. Old, old women and men, who could scarcely hobble about. Women nothing but skin and bones, hatless and scarfless, most of them, all clad in queer clothes which had no suggestion of warmth. Babies sick and cold, lying on their laps, or in little piles beside them, all crowded into that big, cold, dismal waiting room, lighted only by two dim lanterns. They were all grateful for the hot food we gave them, and when we left, in the early morning, ambulance drivers—splendid English women—had come up in their ambulances to take them off somewhere; I never did know where, but they were all gone the next morning, when I went down to the station to meet Georgia Read, who was to pass through on the Paris train.

The train was late, and I saw two boys in American uniforms waiting round, so I went up to speak to them. They turned out to be two war prisoners, an English and an Irish boy. They had left England together, August 12th, 1914. They had gone through all those awful Belgian battles, and most of the other hard fighting in the war, and were taken prisoners at Verdun six months ago. They had managed to stay together through thick and thin. I talked a long time to the English boy. He said they had been horribly treated; flogged for no reasons whatever; made to work until they could scarcely stand; almost no food; German bread not fit for pigs, even; potatoes mixed with sawdust; and that was all except "horse vegetables." One day when they were working they saw some poilus pass by. The Frenchmen called out, "La guerre est finie," but the boys paid no attention to them. The next day a German officer rode up to their guard, said something, and the interpreter turned to them and told them they could go. The Germans had treated them as they treated all other prisoners; their shoes had been taken away the instant they became prisoners; also all their good clothes, so they were turned loose like the rest, with practically nothing, and had walked many miles through Germany, Luxembourg and Belgium, down to Châlons. The canteen had given them their American clothes before I saw them, and let them spend the night in our "abri" (which, by the way, has never been entered since by any of us!), so they were more decently clad and a little refreshed when I saw them. The English boy was of a stocky build, and although thin had stood the hardships better than the Irish boy, who was tall and of a more delicate makeup. He could not stand up without support, so leaned against the wall of the station. When I remarked to the English boy that his companion looked sicker than he did, he said, "Yes; I was brought up on a farm and he wasn't. I had an advantage to begin with." I watched the Irish boy for a while; he looked so faint and ill, and his color was bad, and the far-away expression in his eyes was very noticeable. The English boy was watching him too, and finally slipped away and spoke a few words to him. "I just told him," he said to me when he came back, "not to lose courage now that we are so near to dear old Blighty; we shall soon be in Paris and get all fixed up in a hospital there." Then he went on to say, "I thought I had lost him yesterday in a hospital, but I managed to keep him with me. When we get to England I am going to take him home to the country with me and feed him up on milk and eggs before I let him go back to Ireland." It was the sweetest little war episode that I'd seen, and I'll never forget the devotion in the English boy's eyes as he watched and guarded over his friend. I gave them a box of American cigarettes and left them smoking peacefully on the platform, waiting for their train to Blighty.

It's worse than war at present. The excitement is over and now we see the results and the ravages on people and property. All through Châlons today I have seen little groups of people with a prisoner in their midst, telling his experiences. I can't understand much except that they all think Germany is on the point of starvation, and not many of them complain of any especial cruelties being shown them by the Germans. They seem to think they didn't have the food to give them, and many of them said that the Germans did not fare better themselves; that the soldiers who went home to their families on "leave," in the north, had had to take enough food with them from the army to last the whole length of their stay. Many would not go home at all because they knew they would have nothing to eat. They say the Germans are as arrogant as ever. Of course, all I see and hear is from certain localities. In some places the war and civil prisoners have not fared badly. I talked one night to a woman and her very pretty young daughter, who had been with the Germans for four years. They were passing through and came to the canteen to rest in the kitchen. They had cultivated the fields all summer and done farm work in the winter, threshing, etc. They said the officers were awful, but the men not so bad.

After the English prisoners, I'm told the Russians caught it worst, then the Italians, French and ours. There was no mercy of any kind shown the English. The Germans called them the "Straf" regiment, and whenever anything in the war went against them, they took it out on those prisoners. They had enormous wooden clubs, which they used for beating them. One of the prisoners brought one with him. Lots of samples of German bread have come down. It looks as though it were mixed with sawdust, and they all swear it is sawdust. It's black and hard and awful.

It was interesting to see Châlons open up and blossom forth after the armistice. Three electric lights now hang over the rue de Marne. We have had a week of beautiful sunshine and moonshine, the first moon for four years which the people of Châlons have found beautiful. The others have all meant nights of suspense and "alertes," and often bombs. The thought of a moonlight night was the most unpleasant thought in the world for them.

The day after the signing, my old landlady's daughter, who owns the house, came back with her two children, and in a few days all her best furniture arrived from the part of the country where there had been no fear of bombardment. The Châlonais not only went away themselves, but they took all their belongings; the householders their furniture, and shopkeepers their merchandise. More and more young women and children appeared on the streets. You can't imagine what a strange feeling I had when I saw the first baby in its carriage; I realized then that it was the first I'd ever seen in Châlons. Soon the shops began to open up, one by one, and it was possible to do a little more shopping in the town.

I have had the "caisse" in the evenings, with the usual terrific mob at the window. It is very exhausting to see it seething, pushing and crowding up in front of me, a regular football crowd, and to hear them say, "pas vite." I am not "vite" on purpose, as they can't serve at the counter as fast as I can sell tickets, so it's better to be a little slow. Can't say I feel altogether at home with centimes and sous, either. "Three repas and four chocolates" still drive me to distraction, for I do "repas" in centimes, and chocolates in sous, and to get them together is almost beyond my mental capacity.

It is interesting to see the old coins which the poilus bring in to spend at the canteen. I'm told they are the savings which have come out of the old stockings of France.

A crowd of American hoodlums came in this evening, made a flying wedge, pushed all the Frenchmen out of their way, and acted like the devil. They had no money. They said they had come from the hospital and wanted free meals. They'd had enough money to get drunk on, however. Even Miss Mitchell remarked that they were a disagreeable lot. I never dare say a word about what I think, opinions are so strong and so varied here that it is best not to express any, I find. However, I'm no fonder of a hoodlum here than I am of a hoodlum at home.

Thanksgiving,
November 28th.

I wonder where you all are now. At this present moment I know you are fast asleep somewhere. In fact, it must only just be Thanksgiving Day with you, as I'm writing very early in the morning, sitting up in bed, as usual somewhat cold, but not quite as cold as usual at this moment, for the warmth accumulated during the night has not all escaped, and then I don't believe it is as cold outside as it has been. I've a north room, over a dampish garden, and that, together with the lack of window glass, keeps the room at an even degree of dampness. My wall paper is almost falling off. Some mornings the trees are bowed down with their ice coverings. Today they aren't, but it is dull and dreary so far; the kind of a day which makes one think of the families at home whose only thankfulness can be that in the future no one else will have to suffer as they have.

Joseph-Marie Tissier

The Bishop invited all the Americans to a service at Notre Dame, given in honor of our holiday. Unfortunately few of us could go, but the church was packed to its capacity with French soldiers and civilians. I was let off duty at the canteen so that I could go. There was a fine triumphant chant and singing, and the preacher who represented the Bishop, who was himself celebrating Mass at the Madeleine in Paris, made us know that the French do appreciate our sacrifices.

I wish that all the American fathers and mothers could have heard what he said; then they would have felt that whatever sacrifice they had had to make to win the war over here, was not made in vain. He expressed the gratitude of France in the most touching way. He told how the French army was disheartened and worn out by the years of fighting they had had; how the enemy was within fifteen miles of Paris, the whole of northern France overrun, and then—hope had come with the American army, and the French and English armies had taken courage, and as our men poured into France, were able to hold the enemy where he was until we could train our army and take our place in the lines. And from that time on, thanks to our courage and our fine men, France began to be liberated. He gave us all the credit for saving his country. Without us, the Germans would have taken it, and France would no longer have existed. "Thank you, Americans. Thank you for your financial assistance, which came at the beginning, all we wanted; thank you for your raw materials, and afterwards for your ammunition, and above all, thank you for your magnificent army which you sent us, with your magnificent men, so big and strong and full of courage. Thank you for everything you have given us, the lives of your sons, the tremendous sacrifices of every kind you have made for us. Thank you—and thank you for the spirit of moral uplift you brought with you."

My Thanksgiving food was brains, badly cooked, for luncheon, and for dinner, liver and sausage, which I don't eat, so Brussels sprouts was all I had!

American boys from the camps near by have been in town all the week, trying to get Thanksgiving provisions, and have come to us for help. Turkey is about $1.50 a pound, chicken $1.20; no eggs, no milk, often no cheese; there is little meat, and no sweets of any kind, so you see it is a hard search for them. One came to me for meat for over a thousand of them, and I turned him over to our buyer, Monsieur Robin. Afterwards he came back and said Robin was going to fix them up, and he was very thankful about it. Yesterday some came in with thirteen thousand francs, which they had collected for a dinner for I can't remember how many, but not many compared with the money.

November 29th to December 11th.

I am sitting in the big recreation room, peddling postcards, etc., and listening to a poilu, who seems to be more or less of a professional musician, play the piano. It is Sunday afternoon, not quite dusk, indeed the setting sun is shining through the open door, but it is still damp. The soldiers are sitting all around me, Italians, French, Americans, playing games, reading and talking; some sleeping in steamer chairs, and others grouped round the piano, listening to the music, their little "musettes"—bags of belongings—stuffed full to overflowing, their "bidons" (canteens) and other equipment, are stacked up all about, and as usual, the scene has a great charm for the eye.

My feet are freezing; otherwise I'm quite comfortable. An American boy has just told me that crowds of our boys have married French girls. He got to Paris the day of the armistice, and in the station, about a dozen "Janes" (I don't know just why they are "Janes") fell on his neck and kissed him. They all say Paris was an open city to Americans that day.

Yesterday a poilu brought me a German gun, and a bayonet with a saw edge, the most cruel instrument of torture I've ever seen.

Your poilu, like most of the others, wanted to get a whack at the Boches in his own country. I think there is much disappointment about it, and if it were not for the loss of life, they would all have wanted to continue the war.

I went up to see Mme. Hennocque a few days ago. Her husband is one of the generals who helped fill the gap when the lines broke between the French and English. She

Marie Hennocque

and her daughter are sleeping on their servants' little iron bedsteads. They can't get a maid; none would come to Châlons, so they are doing all the work themselves, all the work necessary for a camping life like that. They have two or three chairs and a table or two; all the rest of their things have been sent away. Their ceilings are half down, no glass in their windows, and the fireplaces are broken. The house next door was totally destroyed by a bomb.

Mme. Hennocque wants me to go to Belgium with them if they can go. Her husband is there now. It would be great, but of course I couldn't do it. She is a descendant of LaFayette, and has many of his things—authentic. Her face shows the tragedy of life here more than any other I've seen. She has lost her two sons, magnificent looking boys—she showed me their pictures. One, a cavalry officer, was wounded, as was his horse, which fell upon him so that he could not move. When the Germans went by, they shot him in the stomach that he might suffer the more, and when the French drove them back again, he was still alive, suffering indescribable pain from their bullets, from which he died about six hours afterwards. Think of a mother's having to know all that! The other boy was killed outright in action.

I've had another bad cold. They are depressing, for you never can tell what turn they will take, and the idea of going from a "petite malade" into a "grande malade" here is most unpleasant. I even missed half a day's work and went to bed. I was in the "caisse" and knew, with the headache I had, that I never could make change, so accepted the suggestion that I should stay at home that night. I felt so sorry to miss my shift, but knew it was the only thing to do then, as I could scarcely see. There isn't much chance to rest, for our rooms are so cold that unless you go to bed you can't stay in them. Even with a fire in mine, I have to sit in my fur coat, and the drafts on the floor are so bad that I have to keep my feet on my woodpile, and the drafts about my head are so bad that I have to keep my hat on. I never can sew a stitch, as my hands are either too cold or too much swollen, and I wish to goodness I hadn't economized and brought old stockings. They are full of holes already, and never get mended, and when they are entirely gone, I don't know what I shall do. Tell anyone coming over to do reconstruction work, to have their clothes new and strong. I've had more annoyance with mine tumbling to pieces the way they have. That, and the impossibility of keeping decently clean, are the two things that have bothered me most; petty annoyances, I mean. I make myself thoroughly disliked in the house here by demanding a good sized pitcher of hot water once a week. The whole bath process is an affair of hours. I have to make four or five trips down two flights of dark stairs, into the cellar, to bring up my wood. I generally squash my fingers doing that, and almost crack my leg bones trying to break faggots against them. It takes at least two hours for a particle of heat to get out into the room. Then I lug my heavy washstand and water so close to the fire that one side is blistered with the heat while the other is frozen. After the thing is accomplished, I have to do all the mopping up, because the old woman gets so mad if she sees a drop of water on the floor. By that time I'm about worn out, and wonder what's the use of trying. I'm often late for luncheon and sometimes have to cut it out altogether, in order to get to the canteen on time. The other days I cut out cleanliness. It is my bath day about now; that's why I'm writing about it, it is so unpleasantly on my mind. I envy those people who can take a cold bath in a cold room. However, I know it isn't cleansing, so they aren't so much ahead of me after all, although they appear superior.

I am glad to say my meals have come over to this side of the river. The club where I eat has moved, and I am nearer it now. I've taken a room there, but it isn't finished or cleaned yet. Don't know whether or not I'll be more comfortable. I only thought if I were ill, food would be more get-at-able there. Here I did not eat for almost twenty-four hours; had one roll and cup of coffee, my regular breakfast, and a cup of chocolate—extra—given me very reluctantly by my landlady, who said she would do it for <u>once</u>, with emphasis on the <u>once</u>. Here the plumbing is good; there it is unspeakable. I don't know why we don't all die of typhoid; in fact I don't know how we live at all. One of the nurses who was in my stateroom coming over has had a bad attack of pneumonia; another has gone home with incipient tuberculosis. Several have died, and almost all have had either grippe or pneumonia, so you see I'm one of the fittest. Other horrid diseases are about—anthrax, Spanish grippe, trench colds and trench mouth—not here, though, but in some of the canteens. I always carry my own "quart" cup to the canteen.

One evening I went to dinner with Mme. de la T., a French nurse, who lives in a box car which is attached to sanitary trains and goes back and forth from the front to different hospitals in the middle of France. She has been doing it for four years. Her car is a most fascinating place; half of it is a big kitchen with a long stove, etc., where two poilus prepare the food for the "blessés." Her half is all white enamel paint and is attractively furnished. She has a little stateroom and salon, all very comfortably arranged. The next day she was to be attached to a hospital train from La Veuve, to go to Limoges, and wanted me to go with her,—a four days' trip. It would have been an unusual experience, but I felt I could not ask for the time off.

I am a little behind in sleep, as I've had four out of six weeks of evening work. I am always waked up at six A.M. by the racket my old woman makes in the kitchen; at seven the family wrangling begins, and the high-pitched rasping voices always drive me out of bed. The old woman scolds her daughter, and her daughter scolds her, and they both scold the children, and I can't help wondering through how many generations this scolding will be passed down.

A nurse, a friend of Mme. de la T., took me over the evacuation hospital which was bombed. It was full of "rapatriés," four hundred for this one woman to look out for; men, women and children all living in the same barracks, piled in, as many as possibly could sleep in one place,—an awful sight. They told me about their lives with the Boches. Almost everyone says the same thing—that the soldiers weren't as bad as the officers. The women had had hard times, I take it. It was a frightfully depressing sight, to see them all crowded in, regardless of sex, regardless of family; a life capable of absolutely no privacy or decency. Many were sickly and all were underfed and in poor condition. One man was rubbing a woman's leg for her. They needed clothes and shoes and the nurse asked me if the canteen could help her. She told me that fourteen thousand "blessés" went through the evacuation hospital in ten days during the last drive.

I've moved. Jeanne's husband came and helped me. I got a blanket from the Red Cross to put on my bed, to sleep on, and eight towels, one of which I spread out for my head, as there is no pillow, and the towel has a pleasanter feeling than the blanket. There are no sheets here, but I am not used to sheets now; I haven't had any for three months. I roll up in my own blanket, put the French army blanket and my steamer rug over me, and there I am. Bought a slop pail for five dollars or more, a basin for two dollars, and a tin pitcher, which makes my water rusty. Spent days trying to find them, even, as there were none to be had in Châlons.

All this time that the prisoners have been coming down from Germany, the Army of Occupation has been going up. Every morning waked by the bands or fanfare of their trumpets, I rush to the window to watch the regiments go by, pinch myself, and say, "That's the Army going into Germany." Infantry and artillery pass, poilus in blue, and Zouaves and Colonials in khaki and red hats, all in fine form, looking spick and span. Then a little later, a train gets in, which always brings crowds of returning prisoners, most of them in the old red caps and red trousers of 1914, carrying wooden boxes and all kinds of queer bundles. Sometimes Anamites go through, with bundles balanced on the end of long poles, Chinese fashion. Senegalese and Arabs come, too, in their separate detachments, all looking pale,—as pale as pale they can,—thin, sick and thoroughly worn out. Every day for weeks this has gone on, and I fly out of bed to watch. Great cannon rattle up the street, sometimes pontoons carried on camions, and the other day up the canal of the Marne from the English Channel went English submarine chasers to patrol the Rhine. None of our troops come this way; they go up the other side of Verdun.

Paris is said to be wonderful, but there it is celebration, and here it is life, and even with all my love of seeing festivities, I have not wanted to go down. I should like to see the victorious armies march under the Arch. They haven't done it yet,—not until the real peace and the armies return. I should like to see ours land in New York, too, but that would be a sadder sight, for here we do not feel the personal loss as we should at home. Think of it, there are two million dead here!

Battlefield Tourism, Souvenirs, and a Sacred Land

The armistice terms governing the withdrawal of German troops began to open up to civilian travelers those areas that had been the war zone. The same terms also released from de facto imprisonment those who had suffered from the occupation and combat. Travel was still restricted, and in principle certain hazardous areas were strictly off limits to unauthorized personnel. Within fourteen days of the signing on November 11, however, the movement forward of Allied forces heading to Germany converged in the formerly "forbidden" zone with that of a jumble of refugees, returning homeowners, and military labor units heading in to clean up the war zone—and also with the battlefield tourists. Families could be reunited and the home front could spill back into what had been battlegrounds.[1] Margaret Hall was quickly invited to accompany her coworker Mme. Marie Hennocque on a trip to visit her husband, Gen. Edmond Hennocque, who was stationed in Belgium. The press of work was so great, however, that Hall deferred the trip until later in the spring. Starting in November, instead she hitchhiked to visit Reims and nearby battlefields, as well as the area around Verdun; Châlons-sur-Marne was halfway between the two cities. By working at night she could squeeze in short daytrips. In January she also started to take a few short sightseeing leaves. At Verdun she met a military policeman she refers to as "M. P. Baker," from the 77th Division of the American Expeditionary Force, the soldier with whom she would later travel to the sites where he had fought, from Dun-sur-Meuse to Montfaucon, Romagne, Somme Py, and Tahure. Most often she traveled in Champagne, but also in the nearby battlefields of the Argonne and Lorraine. When Hall went later to the northern departments of France and to Belgium, she encountered not only women volunteers she knew who were already in France but the first wave of tourists who had come over from America. Hall's trips overlapped with the beginnings of tourism by nurses, soldiers, congressmen, and curious members of the elite such as the president of Bryn Mawr College, M. Carey Thomas, as well as by bereaved parents and wives who wanted to visit graves or the terrain where their loved ones had disappeared. Indeed, visitors were urged to make—as a 1919 Michelin guide to the First Battle of the Marne puts it—"a pilgrimage, not merely a journey across the ravished land. Seeing is not enough, the visitor must understand."[2] The battlefields were sacred territory, where every step marked a grave.

They were also dangerous. Another Michelin guide, published in 1920, explains, "The ruined villages are as the shells and bombs left them. Everywhere are branchless trees and stumps, shell craters roughly filled in, trenches, barbed wire entanglements, and shelters for men and ammunition. Thousands of shells, shell casings, rifles and machine guns lie scattered about. Corpses are occasionally seen." Despite urgent warnings to visitors and pleas to show respect for the dead, one journalist reported that "never a day goes by without another violent death being recorded."[3] Hall witnessed at least one accident that bloodied a "boy" who had "monkeyed" with ammunition.

Already in 1914, an article in the British magazine *The War Illustrated* comments that "souvenir hunting has become quite an industry."[4] Hall herself was tempted to collect souvenirs on her travels. Souvenirs are trophies of triumph over an enemy, as well as instruments of memory that speak to one's identity, saying "I was there," and in the context of war they connect the civilian spectator to the active, suffering soldier. One study of souvenir culture has described the objects as "both real and symbolic" and also suggested that men collect weapons while women prefer ornaments.[5] Ernest Hemingway, for example, wrote home from the hospital that he had collected "a wonderful lot of souvenirs." He boasted that he had carried back officer's pistols, "Boche" helmets, and "about a dozen Bayonets. . . . The only limit to the amount of souvenirs I could have is what I could carry."[6] As a noncombatant—he drove an ambulance in Italy—possibly he needed to authenticate his participation in the war.[7] Soldiers who passed through the canteen showed Hall some of their own souvenirs, which may have been tokens that stood in for stories they would tell on their return home. Hall passes on the story of an officer who took a spoon and fork from every hotel where he stayed. The ostensibly feminine side of collecting may be represented by Hall's coworker Marion Angellotti, who apparently extracted a brass candlestick from beneath an overturned piano, when passing through the picturesque village of Courteau. Another coworker watched a Red Cross woman remove an enamel sign from a train. In fact, not just men but also women collected military artifacts. Critical of "joyriding" nurses, Hall notes that "two women of the canteen are taking home skulls as 'souvenirs' and some of the nurses pull belts and boots off of dead Germans" (140). She sharply condemns the women's savage fetishism. Some soldiers made gifts to Hall of items that they had picked up—"a German gun, and a bayonet with a saw edge, the most cruel instrument of torture I've ever seen" (87)—but she does not seem to have kept them. In her wanderings, however, she gathered some empty brass 75 mm shells and a helmet with a hole in it, which she crated and shipped home with the help of a prisoner of war. Hall quickly pulled back from looting, recognizing both its risks and its transgression of the owners' property rights, as families increasingly moved back into the ruins that had been their homes. In place of objects, then, Hall collected photographs of the battle zone. She tried to picture how it might have looked to the soldiers who had been there, and she prepared to tell the story of the war as she had seen it.[8]

Visitors to the battlefields sought to gain access to a space where they could imagine and thereby recapture a soldier's actual experiences of history. Travel to those sites became a way to collect indirect memories. In fact, battlefield tourism was—and is—such a powerful postwar activity that cultural critics have begun to study the phenomenon. Historian David Lloyd observes that "One of the recurring themes of travel to the battlefields was that the visit provided an insight into the atmosphere and experience of the soldiers."[9] Susan Pearce suggests

Elsa Bowman, exploring dugouts in Pinon.

that to pick up a trivial object like a piece of shrapnel might serve "to reduce an intrinsically unmanageable and confusing experience to something about which 'sensible' memories and stories" could be constructed.[10] For some mourners, visiting the site where a loved one had fought was a way to imagine his suffering and to unite with him. Even the names of the places resonated with meaning, which visitors sought to pin down by standing on the spot. Anna Mitchell wrote after visiting terrain retaken in October 1918 about how much it meant to see "bits of ground whose names have become familiar to us in the papers all these days past," where one could imagine "plain men, our appealing poilus, pulling themselves out of a muddy ditch . . . on a prosaic bit of bare ground, making their great sacrifice."[11] The battles fought had been chronicled in daily papers and weekly illustrated magazines such as *Le Miroir*, *Leslie's*, or *Collier's*. The sites shown in those photographs could now be visited and brought to life as a shocking physical reality. The chaotic movements of troops, usually censored to reveal advances rather than defeats, could be reinterpreted by visitors who confronted the material hardships men had faced burrowing into the ground.

Travel to the battlefields merged with travel to the cemeteries that were being built, as visitors struggled to understand the war and to construct a memory through their pilgrimages. When General Gouraud accompanied Anna Mitchell on her short trip while the war was still underway, he "stopped to show us a cemetery, just a little collection of graves on the top of the hill." Fresh graves carrying names were dug next to old ones so hastily contrived that they bore no names.[12] Such juxtapositions told a history of the war in their own way. Travel guides gave battlefield explorers advice about telling viewpoints, cemeteries, and accommodations—important details at a time when few hotels had survived among the ruins. For Hall, the urgent task was to collect photographs that could "capture" the past through a visual record of destruction and loss.

Paris, December 12th to 15th.

I came down, not to see Wilson, but to see the tribute France was to pay to America, and everyone says there has never been anything in Paris like it. Miss Angellotti decided rather suddenly to come, too. (I was the only person in the canteen who had not been to Paris, so asked for a three days' permission).

Marion Polk Angellotti

We were both on morning duty, and she had to open the canteen, so got up at five and worked until we left at 11.30. We expected to reach Paris in four hours and to take a chance on getting a room, but we were held up at Chateau Thierry for hours by an accident ahead, had to go back to Epernay, and take a round-about route, arriving at nine o'clock, after which hour no food can be had; so we were not only roomless but foodless, as we had eaten nothing since 8 A.M.!

Everybody had told us we could not get a room and a pleasant French woman in our compartment said if her apartment were in order she would take us to it, but it wasn't. The mobs in the station and subway were colossal; it took a long time even to get a ticket. We had our packs on our backs like all the poilus and "militaires." Miss Angellotti looked very attractive, but I had sunk to almost the lowest stage of my looks, and was so tired I didn't care much.

The clerks at the several hotels near the station smiled at us pityingly when we asked for rooms, so we decided to ask to sit up in the parlor of the Hotel Petrograd, which the Y.W.C.A. had taken. There they offered us two cots in a dormitory of eleven, but when we went up we found only one. The place was distinctly unattractive, and we both decided against it. We asked for food, but they threw up their hands and told us it was forbidden. However, as a great concession they gave us a cup of chocolate and piece of bread, with the first butter we had seen since leaving America. It was nearly midnight, and the room reserved for a woman until then, not having been claimed, was given to us, so after all we were installed in luxury in a single bed. In the bathroom there was only cold water. The maid told me that the American women all washed themselves and their clothes so often that there was never enough hot water even to wash the dishes!

After a fine breakfast we got a cab, gave a big fee, and told the driver to take us over the President's route; Avenue de l'Opéra, rue de Rivoli, to Place de la Concorde, where the mob was so great that we turned off on rue Royale. At the Boulevards we were stopped, but I told the guard we were American "militaires," and wanted to join the American Red Cross, so they let us through, and we drove down the Boulevards in state, the only cab allowed!

It was a fine day. The decorations were much more delicate than ours; there were flags of the Allies out of every window, either alone or in groups, all about the same size, which made Paris very lovely. French infantry lined the Boulevards, cavalry where it was needed, and artillery surrounded the Arc de Triomphe. There we had to get out, but were again allowed to pass, and walked, as only Americans could, in the middle of the Avenue, all the way up to the station. All our organizations were lined up together, and the "blessés," French and American, in wheel-chairs, were on the edges of the sidewalks. Opposite the station were drawn up a detachment of Arabs in gorgeous red robes on white steeds, and drawn up there, too, were Miss Angellotti and M. H., where we could get a view of the whole Avenue du Bois de Boulogne and the Arc in the distance.

The American boys amused the French crowd by climbing like monkeys up into the trees. Each time a boy pulled himself safely up on a branch, they would cry out, "Ça y est," with the utmost delight. The trees all the way down the Avenue looked as if they were covered with huge bunches of mistletoe.

At ten o'clock precisely the guns began to boom. The President and his family stepped out of the station, the Republican guard trotted up, and the party was driven off in carriages drawn by fine prancing horses. There was much cheering and American whistling,—a thing which never fails to shock the French, with whom it is an expression of disapproval.

In a few seconds it was all over, and we could see nothing but a company of French lancers, with their gay little pennants, trotting down the Avenue, through crowds of people, more numerous, it is said, than Paris had ever seen before.

Wilson looked dignified enough, but Mrs. Wilson looked cheap in a cocky hat perched on top of her head, smiling much too broadly, with head and chubby shoulders framed in a big wreath of flowers which had been presented to her and which she held in her hands. (She wore orchids!) "Miss Margaret" was beyond description in cheapness of action. She sat facing Mme. Poincare and Mrs. W., grinning a grin which showed all her white teeth, and shaking "da da's" and "so longs" to the crowd, with her big white-gloved hand. Even one of the American boys looked at me and said, "That doesn't look very dignified for the President's daughter to do," so if he noticed it, I'm convinced that my eyes were not so prejudiced that I've done her an injustice.

We walked down the Avenue and the Champs Elysees. Everything was crowded but there was no uncomfortable pushing. The Place de la Concorde is full of German guns camouflaged, and covered then with little boys watching the show. Strasbourg is gay with flags and flowers; her mourning was taken off almost the very second that the Armistice was signed. Across rue Royale stretched in enormous electric-lighted letters, "Welcome, Wilson the Just," (irritating to me).

In the afternoon we again went forth to view the crowd. It was exactly like Armistice Day, people said. Just a slowly moving mass of people, interrupted every once in a while by the boisterous Parisian students, who swept everything and everyone aside as they dove through the crowds.

About dusk we found ourselves near the Opéra, and heard music, a band at the entrance, so we went up the steps to listen and watch the dense masses in front and all the way up Avenue de l'Opéra. One of the buildings opposite was decorated with electric lights, which spread an attractive glow over the scene. The crowds were so thick that it didn't seem as though another person could get into that square, when suddenly there was a fanfare of trumpets, the crowd parted, and a cavalry regiment wound its way through and out the other side of the "Place." Theatrical—not the wildest imagination of the greatest Belasco could have conceived a scene like that. They went through slowly, led by their trumpeters,—the kind who flourish their instruments in the air between notes,—carrying their pennants, most of them with mimosa stuck in their caps or uniforms, the crowds cheering and waving frantically at them, and the band on the steps playing the "Marseillaise." Finally the field kitchen came along, smoking, preparing their evening meal,—we could almost smell their hot coffee,—and at the end the ambulance. How that man drove his car I don't know. He was sitting on the edge of his seat, leaning out, waving both arms madly at the crowd, first on one side and then on the other, but as I didn't see him stop to pick up a "blessé" I suppose he got through all right.

That evening the Boulevard crowds were out and our boys were the centre of attraction. Most of them had lost their caps, or put them away for safe keeping; lost, I rather think, to the French "Mademoiselles" for "souvenirs."

Châlons, December 18th.

I got back at 1.30 Monday night, very much of a wreck. Found that I was on the evening shift, which gave me free days, so on Wednesday, three of us went to Chateau Thierry for the day, leaving at seven and having a sleepy trip down. It never rained much harder, but we never stay at home for rain, for it never stops. When we got there we escaped the M.P.s, so that we should not be asked for papers and passes. We picked up an American boy in a little open Ford truck, who said he was going out by Belleau Woods and would take us along. In we piled, Mrs. Earle in front, Miss Angellotti and I in back, sitting on we didn't know what, we were in such a hurry not to let the boy escape us. After a while he said he was going to make a round trip through three or four of the destroyed towns, and we could go if we liked. Charmed was not the word for our feelings, although rain was pouring in rivers off our hats, coats, and noses. We passed Belleau Woods and saw great piles of hand grenades and ammunition dumps along the roadsides. The boy told us he was to find an American battlefield burying-ground, and it turned out that he was an undertaker and we were sitting on piles of the little wooden crosses which were to mark the graves of our boys who lost their lives at Chateau Thierry! This boy belonged to a squad who went through the woods and fields, collected the boys from their scattered graves, and placed them together in what is called a "battlefield cemetery." There are many of those little cemeteries all around Chateau Thierry, and many little lonely American graves still unfound. One half of Belleau Woods is full of our dead, the other half full of Germans.

We had a wonderfully interesting drive, found loot in the way of old shell cases, and saw little towns much flatter than any near Rheims. We dined at the Hotel de Cygne with a lot of United States Congressmen who were touring the country. We wanted to go to Soissons, but there was no time, and we heard that the Germans had set time fuses in the ammunition dumps near there, so the road was dangerous for the moment.

In the afternoon we walked to the little town of Courteau, all shelled up and picturesque as the dickens, talked to an old man and woman, whose house, just outside the town, had been destroyed, and who lived all in a mess in an awful old hole in their barn, with a little stove and nothing much else. Some of the family were killed in a bombardment, and the grave took up about the whole space in their little courtyard.

The town was wholly deserted except for one American soldier, a nice boy, who was wandering round alone, dreaming.

Miss Angellotti went through agonies trying to decide whether or not to take a brass candlestick off a piano which was upside down in a destroyed house. They never would have been used again, so it seemed perfectly all right to take it.

From there we climbed by a foot path up to the hill just above Chateau Thierry where our boys had fought so hard, and we tried to picture how it looked down in the valley of the Marne and across on the other hills those summer days when they were rushed there from all quarters, almost pushed off the trains, told to place their cannon and fire, where or in what direction they didn't know, and no one else seemed to know, so I've been told over and over again. It was a real battlefield, not much cleared up; old guns, old clothes, old equipment strewn round everywhere; trees shot down, great shell holes, so deep that if you'd fallen in you'd never have come out; and above all, the constant unpleasant reminder that there had been no time to take proper care of the dead.

We crawled back by train to Châlons, loaded down with loot—German loot—which I've since had a Boche prisoner case up for me, in hopes that I can land it somewhere in the U.S.A. We were almost dead when we got back, at half past ten, but went to the canteen for an hour and a half, that our substitutes might go home.

Vouziers, Somme Py, Sedan.
December 22nd.

    I hadn't in the least recovered from the extreme fatigue of the Paris and Chateau Thierry trips, when a chance to go up to Sedan turned up for Mrs. Earle and me, and naturally we took it. We went up with a nice boy from Chestnut Hill, in a little Ford camionette, all three on the front seat. We drove right through the Champagne battlefields, where the Germans had had their same lines and trenches for four years, from which they couldn't be budged until the last terrific drive; through little towns so flat that at night our boy told us you never knew you were going through a village; but not so flat as one we passed through later, where in broad daylight I had to be told I was going through a town, and even then I couldn't seem to see it. Our companion was nice and patient, and let us get out whenever we wanted to; showed us artillery emplacements, and explained how things were as much as he could. Warfare will never penetrate my brain, though. I simply can't think what it is like. We walked through the trenches, saw little listening posts, and shelves cut out in the sides which were marked "Explosives." Went down into the dugouts, saw human bones all about, and many little crosses with helmets, French helmets, hung on them. The boys were buried, evidently, where they fell. Here the German and French lines were very near together; barbed wire entanglements were in front of all, and spread out round the country besides. The trenches themselves were not as deep as I thought they would be—not the French ones, but the German were different; much deeper, and the dugouts much deeper, with steps and sides made almost of matched boards, they were so well constructed. Between the two lines of trenches—No Man's Land—there was nothing but white ploughed-up clay, which looked like the Bad Lands in our Petrified Forest. Land turned over and over and over; barren, desolate, awful; not a sign of life anywhere, not even one blade of grass which just happened to escape,—nothing!

    On the German side there were crosses, too, in the midst of the desolation, but bigger ones, more ornate, made of iron, with bigger steel helmets on them, often gaudy with their camouflage. I was crazy to go down into their dugouts. In the back line trenches they come with great regularity; I should say about fifty feet apart, and were at least thirty feet deep, with steep wooden steps, almost chute-the-chutes in their steepness, leading down into subterranean rooms. It didn't seem best to take the risk, though. There are all sorts of snares and traps left behind for the unwary; electric connections which can be made by stepping on certain places, and in a second you are nothing but pieces; hand grenades left on top of doors, ready to tumble off at the slightest provocation and maim you for life. People are injured and killed all the time hunting souvenirs. The Germans were aware of this American passion, and did many diabolical things to catch our boys during the war. There is great danger even now. I have seen a girl pick up a German "potato masher" (a hand grenade of the most dangerous variety), and run after me exclaiming "Do look at this funny thing!" "Hands Off" and "Watch Your Step" are the rules for battlefield conduct, and it's annoying to a party when some of its members do not observe them.

We saw all sorts of dugouts; one of the most interesting a German regimental kitchen, all concrete, with big stoves, shelves and tables; quite an elaborate affair. The tops and entrances of all the dugouts were camouflaged. The French had corrugated iron roofing, with camouflage of painted canvas and branches over that. I didn't notice the German.

We went through the little town of Somme Py, where only the ruined church is standing. On its wall is still the figure of the Virgin. We could tell where the Germans had made a stand in their retreat to Sedan by the way the towns and country were shot up. Vouziers is pretty much destroyed, not a whole house there, I imagine. But after that they must have gone pretty fast. All the bridges are down, and flimsy temporary ones are in their places; telegraph poles down, and trees felled flat, for no visible or conceivable reason, for they are lying in the fields and never were meant to obstruct the roads. There were great holes in the roads, especially at the cross roads, all of which were mined. Some mines have not yet gone off; there are red flags to indicate them, and to suggest that the passerby does not linger there. Many have gone off, and to pass them you have to take to the fields and mud, as the road there does not exist. Crowds of ammunition has been left, too. The roadsides are lined with it, and the woven baskets which the Germans used to bring up their shells in, are lying all about. I wanted to bring one home, but they were too bulky. The question of doing your own lugging puts a damper on collecting salvage, no matter how enticing it is. All along, too, beside the roads and in the fields near by, were the little graves, so pathetic in their loneliness.

We got lost and took a longer way round, but it was interesting. We reached Sedan about dark. I had thought the Americans entered Sedan first, but it seems they stood aside and let the French go in, as was right.

Nothing had been destroyed but the railroad station. We went to the Red Cross place and were lucky enough to get one room, and had our food in a room where the Crown Prince had his whenever he went through Sedan. The beer mugs used for our water had crowns in the bottom.

The Red Cross gives away food here. At the table with us were the boys who are working on the railroad, trying to get some connection with the outside world.

Sedan is almost foodless. The question of feeding the people in the districts evacuated by the Germans is a great problem. No railroad tracks go up to them. French camions are in none too good shape after their four years' service, and there is almost no way to get food into these towns. The people really suffered less under the Germans than they do now, although their fare was scant enough before, goodness knows.

As soon as we got to Sedan we hunted up the S.S.U., to try to find transportation back, and discovered a sergeant whom Mrs. Earle knew, who was going back to Epernay the next morning and said he would take us along.

I got up early and had time to walk up to the old Château, all in ruins; not the ruins of war but of age; and to see the Meuse rushing through the town.

Then in the back of an ambulance we drove through Mézières, Charleville, and Rheims, where we again went to the cathedral, and had a tussle with the cranky old guardian, who as usual nagged us to death. We passed the interesting vineyards on the hillsides near Epernay, where we caught a very much belated train, and got to Châlons in time for service.

"German trench and barbed wire. Champagne Front."

When we start off on these trips, we never know when or how or where we are going to land. We generally take bread and food enough to tide us through, and trust to luck that some shelter can be found at night, and some means of transportation back in the morning. It's nervous business, especially as you always have a shift waiting for you at a certain hour, which you must take, and by the time I land in Châlons I am much more of a wreck than when I start out. But why be here in the midst of it and not see it, even if it kills you in the end!

Châlons, December 24th to January 12th.

Period of Demobilization
(and Demoralization)

The night before Christmas we had two large trees. The poilus sang Christmas songs standing around them, and on top of all the tables near by. On Christmas with every meal we gave a cigarette, and in the afternoon some of the workers carried little decorated trees through the hospitals.

New Year's eve was much the same, but there was not much spontaneity about the singing. That day we gave free dinners, little calendars, and bunches of cigarettes (five in a bunch), but the poilus and Italians came in such mobs that we had to stop giving out the cigarettes, for some came a second and third time. Things are always spoiled by some selfish creatures in the crowd. In the afternoon Mrs. Earle, Miss Worthington and I took cigarettes, cakes and mirrors out to La Veuve to give to the "blessés." The boys seemed to like the things. It's an enormous hospital, with railroad tracks running all through it. There are trenches dug between the walls. Mrs. Earle gave a mirror with Pershing's picture on it to one of the Boche prisoners, and had to go back when she found out he was a German, to get it. She was afraid he would stamp on it when he found out what it was. It was most awkward, as he thought she was going to give him something else when she held out her hand to get it back. She told him it wouldn't interest him. The hospital is one of the most depressing places I've seen over here, filled with the wreckage left after the storm!

Conrad Butler

I'm selling postcards this evening, the first time for ages, so between customers I can write a few words. A Russian has just gone out to get his "camarade" who can speak English, to talk to me, so my letter will probably be a little disjointed. Yesterday I got a letter from Conrad from Germany. I had given him a little lecture on not liking the Germans too much, and he said he wouldn't. Their propaganda in our army is dreadful. A drunk has just come up and <u>would</u> sit down in the chair beside me and get very close. I did not know how to get rid of him, so told him I would have to write my letter and he could come back afterwards, and he went smilingly away. We have a great many "zig zags" in the evenings now. Two nights ago an American Indian, a Cherokee, went up to our apartment, took the key out of the door, and told an M.P. later on as a great joke that he had locked up two American women and one Frenchman together. Luckily, though, he did not lock the door, for if he had, I'd have had to sleep on the stairs, as I always keep my key in the kitchen. * * The drunk is back, standing over me grinning, but I'll pay no attention to him and hope he'll depart. He wants me to be good to him, he says. Just this instant a crazy man has come up to shake hands with me, and now has gone away, shaking hands again, to drink chocolate. There have been two around the canteen lately. They have lost all their families in the war and are hanging round because they don't know where or how to find their regiments. There will be lots of wrecks like that in France; too much war, too many shocks, for their brains to stand. That old drunk! I've told him this is to be a long letter and to go away and sit down, but he murmurs that he likes to watch me, and something about Mrs. Wilson.

The work is hard in the canteen now. Mobs most of the time about to be demobilized, and as usual I'm on evening duty. Tonight I stay until midnight and begin again at six in the morning, which means about five hours' sleep for me. It's been awfully cold here, freezing weather. Tonight it is a little warmer and there's a snowstorm on. We are all tired; everyone in canteen work gets tired at intervals. They sink to a point where it doesn't seem as though they could go on, and then start up again.

I hear the French are less cordial about Wilson's visit than they were in the beginning. They think he is rather German in sympathy. He hasn't been yet to see the devastated region; says he doesn't want to be prejudiced by it, the newspaper says. Wish he'd had a little taste of German bombardment, and then see how he'd feel. The old drunk is back again! He told me I was writing too long a letter. * * He has gone away, and will return presently!

I'd like to go up to Verdun, but it seems hard to get away, and harder to get transportation when we do get off for a day. That drunk will drive me to drink! Keeps talking about Mr. Wilson, so I've told him I'll write and tell Mr. Wilson he won't let me finish my letter. * * Can't shake him. All the rest of the poilus are much interested, and if he keeps on much longer I'll shut up shop and go home.

Got a letter from Annie, also one from Miss McDermott, today; they come through better now; aren't sent to a post office which doesn't exist. That old drunk makes me nervous. He's very pleasant, thank goodness, and not of the cross variety. Now he keeps sticking his watch in my face. Guess I'll go. He furnishes too much amusement for the room, and my French is not equal to the occasion. Perhaps it's just as well.

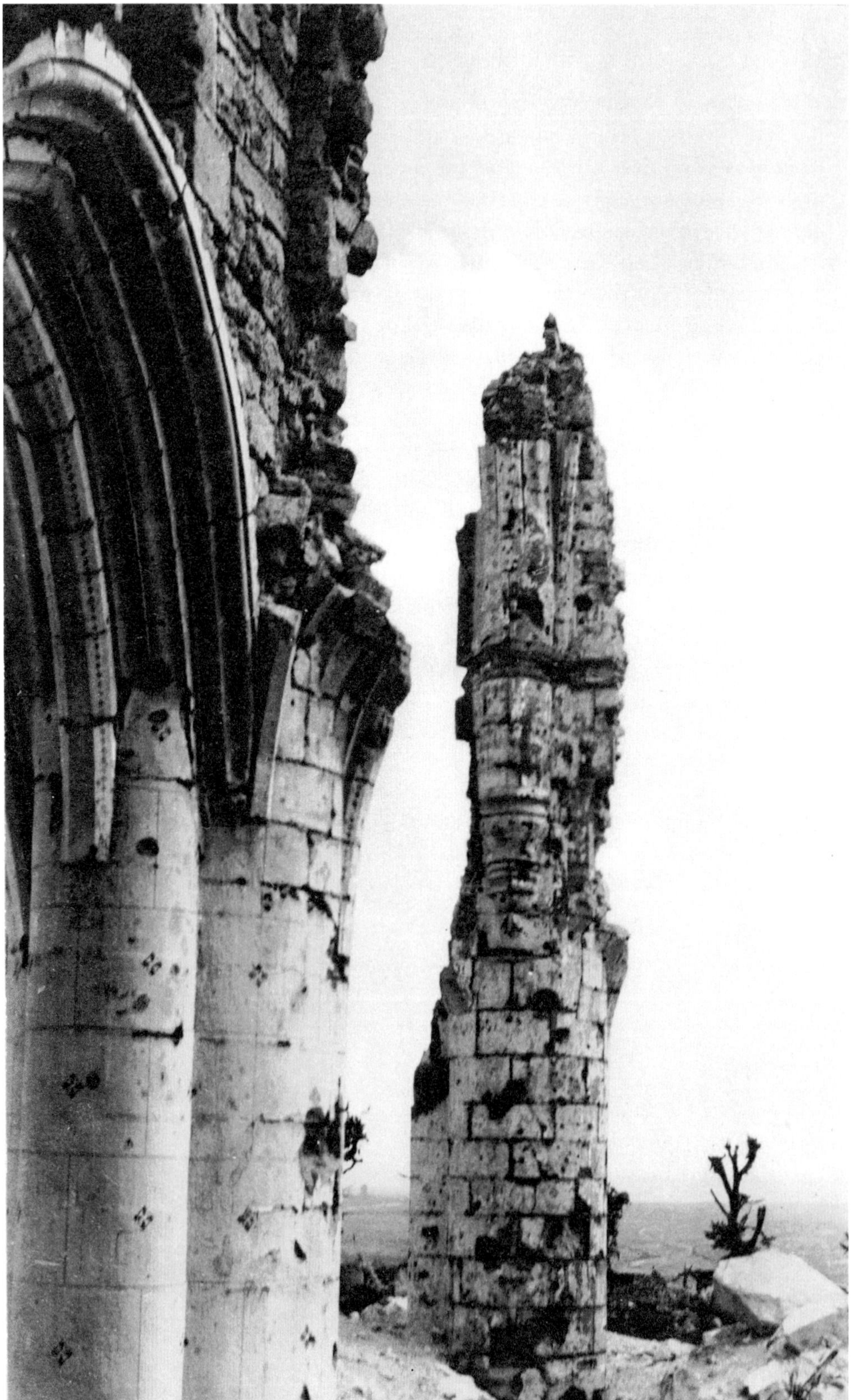

Destruction and Reconstruction

Margaret Hall's photographs extensively document the destruction of northern France and the attendant obliteration of distinctions between town and country, military and civilian, old and young, the living and the dead. "Total War" is one way to describe the collapsed boundaries between military and civilian spaces and the mobilization of entire economies for the purpose of military destruction. War requires reconstruction, however difficult. Despite the apparent stasis imposed by trench warfare, between 1914 and 1918 the systolic and diastolic rhythm of destruction and recovery took place repeatedly in northern France, following the movement of battle lines during major offensives, and especially during the German retreats of 1917 and August to November 1918. The entire northern zone of France—where not only had fields been torn up but villages and cities had been reduced to rubble—came to be called the "devastated regions."[1] Already in 1914 the destruction of the cultural patrimony, central to local identities, led to the publication of illustrated booklets on devastated villages or "cités meurtries" (battered cities).[2] In the violent retreats of 1918, a reversal of the opening invasion, "the end of the war evoked its beginning and this resulted in a hardening mood of retribution."[3] French infantry was outraged by evidence of German scorched-earth policies in "destroyed and pillaged villages" with broken windows, dead animals, and fruit trees that had been sawn down.[4] Four years of industrial war made the landscape unrecognizable in the north.[5]

Several months later, as he walked across the formerly occupied countryside, the deputy commander of the American Red Cross in France, George Ford, who had become an advisor on the reconstruction of the war-devastated cities Reims and Soissons, observed,

There was hardly anyone in Chauny, for the whole city had been systematically and thoroughly blown up by the Germans before they left. Of the great glass-works of St. Gobain nothing whatever was left. All the afternoon, alone, I walked through this beautiful country. Every field was pitted with shell-holes, or criss-crossed with trenches; every home was a moldering heap of stones; there was hardly a tree that was not more or less shattered; everywhere were the litter and waste of battle. Not a living creature of any sort did I meet; there were even no birds. . . . [A]round me was utter desolation.[6]

The physical landscape became a powerful symbol of apocalyptic ruination, as it was photographed and depicted by official journalists, soldiers, and war artists, and civilian observers like Hall. After the cessation of fighting, these regions were reclassified: officials distinguished a "red" zone, which needed to be sifted for abandoned live munitions, and other zones that could be rebuilt after appropriate elimination of hazards. An estimated sixteen million acres were cordoned off because the dangerous remains of weapons polluted the soil, the aquifers, and the crops growing on the soil.[7]

Just as it is hard for us to imagine the numbers of individual soldiers killed, it is hard to imagine the new level of physical destruction entailed by this conflict.[8] Four years of intense industrialized trench warfare with heavy artillery, bombardment, flame-throwers, and other chemical weapons such as gas contaminated the landscape of northern France. Shrapnel shredded trees, leaving symbols of violence in a world whose landmarks changed every week. The mud, every soldier's enemy, became polluted with metal and corpses. The concept of a war of utter destruction, extrapolated from the Prussian military theorist Carl von Clausewitz, was pushed to an extreme in the management of this conflict. At the Battle of Verdun, Gen. Erich von Falkenhayn's goal was to "bleed the French white."[9] The attack on Verdun in February 1916 was launched with a stockpile of 2 million shells and one thousand heavy guns along a front of eight miles. Between the beginning of July and mid September 1916, at the height of the Battle of the Somme, the British fired over 7 million shells. In the last hundred days, at the canal of Saint-Quentin, during an eight-hour attack, 126 shells from field guns fell each minute on every 500 yards of German trench, for a total of 60,000 shells, many of them unexploded because of defective manufacture.[10] Every square meter in the French war zone received an average of one ton of explosives. Over 700 million shells were fired there between 1914 and 1918, littering fields with live as well as exploded shells—which it is estimated would take centuries of work to remove.[11]

In the course of successive offensives on different fronts, soldiers in many armies pillaged homes, destroyed buildings, and contaminated the terrain, even though such acts contravened The Hague conventions concerning civilians. On the Eastern Front, when the Russians pulled back across the Polish and Russian countryside, they followed a scorched-earth strategy that forced peasants to flee with them.[12] On the Western Front, when Gen. Robert Nivelle attacked in spring 1917 on the Chemin des Dames, retreating Germans despoiled the countryside and scattered booby-traps.[13] Allied forces likewise destroyed bridges to prevent German advances and shelled towns they were attempting to retake.

During the last month of the war, hoping to secure an armistice on advantageous grounds and foreseeing that war might recommence after a temporary truce, Chief of the General Staff Paul von Hindenburg and Gen. Erich Ludendorff sought to continue *Endkampf*, that is, a sustained battle that would leave behind a wasteland.[14] In the northern departments, the Germans had removed industrial machinery by the trainload, requisitioned livestock, cut lumber from the forests, and confiscated tools, stripping the land and reducing the capacity for manufacture. The final weeks of the war, however, accelerated the destruction of the occupied zone, leaving a surrealistic lunar landscape of dead houses, dead fields, and dead men. On October 6, German leaders agreed that "the occupied areas will be given over to devastation."[15] Soldiers laid mines at crossroads, poured water into coal mines, and released poison gas that would contaminate the ground for decades.[16] On November 8, the German government's caravan of emissaries with its white truce flag arrived twelve hours late for its meeting with Gen. Ferdinand Foch, because German demolition teams had mined intersections and felled trees to block the roads. As he passed through the lines, Maj. Gen. Detlef von Winterfeldt had to order the roads cleared.[17]

Civilian reconstruction was a compelling vocation for many American women volunteers.[18] Already on her arrival in France, Margaret Hall knew about the social work performed by the Smith College Relief Unit and by Anne Morgan's American Committee for Devastated France. By the end of the war, Morgan's group had distributed roughly five million dollars in war relief. During her postwar travels in July 1919, Hall observed their continuing relief and reconstruction work. Several colleagues from Châlons stayed in France after the war to reconstruct French villages, resettle refugees, restore schools, and provide medical services. Others went east to Constantinople, where they worked with refugees from Russia. Hall's close friend Ethel Earle joined Herbert Hoover's American Relief Administration, which organized shipments of food for millions of starving people in Germany, Central Europe, and famine-stricken areas in Russia.

One large question was whether to replicate the old or to construct a modernized version that might improve the lives of the inhabitants. To leave the ruin could shape a monument that would mark popular memory and attitudes.[19] Debates over sites that had been annihilated generally foresaw a reconstitution, with a few exceptional salvaged ruins. At stake in these debates was the financial responsibility for reconstruction, which many anticipated would be paid for by German reparations. Great architectural monuments, most agreed, demanded to be replicated. Reinforced concrete, however, replaced many original materials, and the rebuilding would take decades.

In her memoir, Hall's photographs document the scarred landscapes and the detritus of war such as unexploded ordnance. Although she brought two brass shells home, she commented often on the dangers to those who would collect such souvenirs. Indeed, much of the hazardous reconstruction of the French landscape was at first a military project. Until December 1919, the removal of unexploded munitions in the "red" zone was performed under military control. From 1920 on, the work was performed under civilian authorities.[20] After the Armistice, colonial and Allied troops helped clear the land of metal, mines, and shells. In Châlons, many of the Italians Hall observed probably belonged to the first of four groups of unarmed engineering auxiliaries ("Truppe Ausiliarie Italiane in Francia") stationed there for construction and maintenance. In August 1918, General Foch called these men "indispensable" to the recovery of the "terrain devastated by the enemy," as the French Army moved forward.[21] When Hall drove through Picardy in July 1919, Chinese labor battalions were firing explosives they had found. She also saw German prisoners of war in labor battalions, men whose task it was after the November ceasefire to clear barbed wire and ordnance from Belgian beaches and French battlefields. Because the French relied heavily on German prisoners of war to reclaim their land, they delayed prisoner repatriation. Cleanup units created dumps of live munitions, empty shells, the abandoned wreckage of vehicles, concrete reinforcements, and barbed wire. Some explosives were recycled for both metal content and explosive powder in factories at Coucy-le-Château and Albert. Despite sustained sifting operations searching for tell-tale metal over nearly a century, nine hundred tons of unexploded arms are still removed annually from French fields by farmers, resulting in still more war-related injuries and dozens of deaths. In 1990, six months of cleanup work for a new French high-speed rail line unearthed twenty-three tons of shells.[22] Near Verdun, the danger of chemical remains has led to the closure of selected regions.[23] The dangers that Hall confronted in her walks over the battlefields continue to surface as the ground shifts over time.

Verdun, January 11th.
Four days' "permission."

My next venture was Verdun. I asked to be allowed to use four days of "permission" to go up there. We went by train to Bar-le-Duc and then took up our stand beside an American M.P. on the Verdun road and waited. M.P.'s can stop all cars on the road, so it's best to shift responsibility to them. Finally, rather late in the afternoon, we found transportation, a Ford truck going up to a camp outside of Verdun. It was thrilling going up the "Voie Sacrée"—the magnificent road over which all the troops marched up to Verdun. It was dark when we got near Verdun, and as we didn't know where to go, we let the boy land us where he thought best—in his barracks. We had thought of staying at the Y.M.C.A. If women visitors get there in time, they put up cots for them in the office, and if there happens to be an extra blanket, they can have it. If not, "tant pis." I knew we were too late for that. The boys thought we could stay in their camp (I didn't), so they kept us, fed us to coffee and squash pie, then took us to their Y.M.C.A. and turned us over to an officer. We had struck the camp—the 13th Engineers—the great night of their sojourn abroad, the night when the moving picture called "Smiles" was to be given. Probably you know about it; the one where all the mothers, fathers, sisters, brothers, sweethearts, wives and babies of the Chicago boys marched in front of the picture machine. The 13th Engineers were for the most part from Chicago, so you may imagine the impatience with which they had awaited that film. The hall was packed early. The newly assembled band, with magnificent shining brass instruments, played American tunes, which I had not heard since I've been here, out of tune, but so grand to hear! Every once in a while some delighted boy would shout out, "Hello, Dad!" or "There they go!" The Lieutenant who had us in charge found his mother and sister, and was going to hunt for his wife the next time the film was given. It was to stay until every boy had seen it enough and felt satisfied.

We found our Lieutenant had helped to build the Châlons canteen, so he was especially nice and gave us a car after the show to take us to Glorieux Hospital, just outside of Verdun, where I knew I could stay, as Miss Frances Mitchell, who had been in our canteen, had asked me to stay with her if I came to Verdun. We were put into a stoveless room with four cots in it, one already occupied, in the nurses' quarters. It was dismal, there's no mistake about it. It seemed queer to be with Americans, and to see all the little towns on the way up filled with Americans, billeted there, all standing up in line as we went through, waiting for their suppers, and to meet American darkies, labor battalions, fixing the roads. It was all American, the whole way from Bar-le-Duc to Verdun. The boys cheered us and waved to us and we were so glad to see each other, as we flew by.

The next morning we had an American breakfast, served by a nice American boy, after which we got a truck into Verdun. There are no civilians there, and it is very much shattered; not as badly as Rheims, I should think. The ruins are older than those at Rheims, softened by time, and some almost moss covered. The streets were full of American soldiers. All nationalities—Russian, Bulgarian, Austrian and German prisoners—in fact were there, but Americans were in charge. We wandered around the town and into the citadel, through which we were taken. Of course, it's an enormous place, with accommodations for twenty thousand or more soldiers, a chapel, Y.M.C.A., Foyer de Soldat, a huge bakery where thousands of loaves are baked, all under ground, but it's just a modern fortress which you can see at any time. The troops went through there, but there were never many who stayed. I had an idea they lived there the whole time, in multitudes. The top of the citadel was ready for the enemy, trenched and barbed wired, but it was very much shot to pieces, the place had been so continuously shelled. The man in charge of the Foyer de Soldat was one of the most pathetic I'd seen in France. He looked so pale and sick, and by his color you could tell that sunshine was what he needed, and not the artificial light and artificial air of subterranean life. His "cafard" was beyond cure. He had lost every friend and companion he had—all killed, he told us, and life for him was too dismal to be endured, and it didn't look as if he'd have to endure it much longer.

"Verdun."

In the afternoon we thought we'd like to see the country outside of Verdun, so placed ourselves again on the road and procured transportation up to Stenay. A nice boy in an ambulance said he was going up to the hospital there, where we could spend the night, and come back in an ambulance the next day. We lost no time in climbing in, and had another wonderful trip along the Meuse, through all those battlefields and ruined towns, towns so flat that we only knew there had been a town by a signpost with its name on it.

There were always the same holes along the road where individual boys had dug themselves in when the road was shelled. The same piles of used and unused ammunition, the same "abris" under the ground, the same little crosses by the roadside, only with American helmets on these, and the same little narrow-gauge railroad which you see all over this part of France, used to take supplies and ammunition to the front. (Germans had the same). Some of the destruction here had been caused by American guns, for this was the edge of our great battlefield, the Argonne, across the Meuse. Dun-sur-Meuse, on a hilltop over the river, was a dream of picturesqueness, if you can call anything so dreadful picturesque. Here, too, the bridges and telegraph poles were down, and the long lines of beautiful old shade trees cut down, to complete the systematic ruin of northern France.

American negroes were salvaging the country all about, and there were hundreds of them along the way. Soon the road signs all became German. It's the queerest thing the way the French have left the German signs up everywhere. Even little pasteboard signs pinned on doors are still there.

At Stenay we stayed in what was originally French barracks, which had been used for a German hospital, and had the big Red Cross painted on the roof. In all the rooms were German slates, which had been used over the beds of patients, with the patient's name and list of his wounds written on them. In several rooms there were pictures of the Kaiser, Crown Prince, Hindenberg, etc. painted on the walls, life size, and in another building, in a room evidently used as a bar, the walls were covered with frescoes and portraits of the Royal family and celebrities. German signs "Silence" and "Shut the door" were still up; a German piano was in the nurses' room. In fact, from all appearances, you might have been in Germany. Outside the hospital near by was a big German rifle range. We were told not to step off the driveways, for the grounds were thought to be mined. Quite regularly we heard great reports, like cannon, and explosions go off; mines or ammunition dumps being exploded. It was almost like being under fire, they were so near. The sky was lighted by them at night, and some sounded and looked as though they were just outside of the hospital yard. The doctors and nurses had been called up there for typhoid pneumonia and accident cases. Some boys were so sick! Two died while we were there.

Gen. Paul von Hindenburg

In the evening some of the nurses, doctors, Mrs. Earle and I went down to Stenay to see a Y.M.C.A. show, the first any of the boys had seen over here,—three girls and one man. One girl whistled and danced and acted, and seemed professional; the others were not, I think. Of course the little professional had "pep" and was most popular, and she was pretty, too, and nice to watch. The remarks of the boys were sweet. "I want to go home!" they wailed out when they first saw the girls. "That's what we have in America." "Why don't you give us shows like this once in a while?" "We wouldn't mind staying if you treat us this way," etc., etc. The hall was packed and icy cold, but the show was an enormous success.

That night we slept on the night nurses' cots, just rolled up in blankets, and the next morning took a chance, let the ambulance go off without us, and went down to Stenay to see the Château where the Crown Prince had lived for thirty months. He had kept the same French caretaker who was in the house when he came, and she showed us about. We saw his seat at the head of the table used for officers; his bedroom and the fine bathroom he had had put in. The other bedrooms belonged to officers; one to the General who took Fort Douaumont. She said the Crown Prince wasn't bad, he stole nothing, but his officers took what they wanted. All the magnificent silver was gone and many other things of value. Whenever the Emperor came, he and the Prince would dine alone in the salon, never with the officers. Father never spent the night. He had a very hard, stern face, so the woman told us. I asked if there had been much revelry, and she discreetly said she had always been downstairs in the evening and did not know what had happened upstairs. The thing that pleased me most was the "abri" which the gentleman (!) had had built for himself under the house,—of steel and concrete, and to which he had had to retire sometimes twice in one night! It was an underground cellar, with a long deep passageway which opened far out into the garden, so he could escape through that if the house were destroyed.

Means of transportation back to Verdun were rather scarce, so we had time to walk along the road for quite a distance and examine the American graves. One especially I remember, covered with all the boy's possessions, even his old woolen gloves. Finally we got a lift as far as Dun. There some American boys took us in, fed us, and let us warm ourselves by their enormous improvised stove, which took up practically one whole room. From there on we had very stylish transportation, in a much camouflaged White automobile, which whirled us into Verdun in no time. That night there was a little entertainment at the hospital by K.C.'s.

Knights of Columbus

The next day we decided to make a try for Fort Douaumont or Fort Vaux. When we asked the Colonel for permission to go into Verdun in an ambulance, he told us he was going in himself and would take us and drop us on the right road, but he never did drop us until we got as near Douaumont as an automobile can go; quite far away, really. We drove on and on through the country so famous for its battles, in and out and up and down, through those barren, desolate, gray hills, all shot to pieces, without a tree or a living thing anywhere for miles and miles; trenches near by and in the distance, going round and over the hills, barbed wire, shell holes, and all along the road everywhere, as close as they could be put, emplacements for guns, all camouflaged over, and "abris" for men to live in. Neither of us dared to speak for fear the charm would be broken, and the Colonel realize that we were to have been set down on the road to find our way up alone. Finally we landed on top of a hill, Fort Sousville, a hole in the hillside. Then I <u>was</u> upset, for I thought the Colonel would give up the search

Fig. 8

for our road, but no, indeed; he persevered and landed us beside a little narrow-gauge track, where there was a sign "Fort Douaumont." It was raining cats and dogs; there was not a sign of human life or any life to be seen; we had come a roundabout way into the hills; there was not a landmark of any sort to guide us on our homeward walk, and when the Colonel murmured, "Can you get back all right?" I said, "Yes, indeed," but I thought, "Oh, heavens!" The loneliness, the desolation, the devastation, the silence, of that spot is greater than any other spot in the whole world, I think. The automobile turned around and disappeared. I watched it go, and then we were left by ourselves, in an unknown country, in the pouring rain, in the Verdun mud, not any too early in the day, alone with the dead. It is hard to describe it. It seemed as though we were up in the mountains too high for vegetation to grow; that there had been a terrific upheaval which had torn the ground into horrible holes, and that the dead brought up with it, either alone or in little groups, had been quickly covered by a sprinkling of earth, and left to the end of time,—each with a little wooden cross decorated with the French cockade, to show that it was "for France" that they were there. We followed the little railroad, stopping every few moments to look out over the hills, to try to grasp the vastness of it all, or to take little side trips to see the graves or to explore the dugouts on the side of the hill. We half walked, half tumbled, into those gruesome caverns, feet down under the ground. Some were very large, with connecting rooms, large enough each for fifteen or twenty men to sleep on cots, which were still there. The old straw and mattresses were there, too, and the tables and shelves, and on one of the shelves a bottle of Parisian perfume. At one place not very far from the top of the hill was a sign, "Poste de Secours," outside of which were piles of all kinds of old uniforms and cooking utensils, broken glass and equipment; inside a long table, we imagined an operating table, and a few steps away from the entrance there was a larger group of graves, one or two decorated with those wonderful French "couronnes," masterpieces of beadwork. Someone who cared had found them!

After a while we discovered the trenches, magnificent ones, with basketwork sides and board walks, full of telephone and electric wires. We walked through them for some distance, taking side trips out to the artillery posts (or observation posts, I don't know which), down into their dugouts, and up over the top of trenches, where the dead had been left unburied; only their belts, boots and bones were left. All the time we had to pick our way along very carefully. The ground was slippery, and the mud deep. The shell holes full of water, deep enough to drown anyone with perfect ease, and the hand grenades and unexploded shells were constantly under our feet. The grenades that were lying in the water on the sides of shell holes looked like schools of fish taking a rest on the sides of their pools. Tracks of the little railroad lower down than ours were torn up, twisted and a complete wreck. The fascination of it all was wonderful.

The entrance to Douaumont seemed more like that of a mine than anything I can think of. I called in at the door and a nice soldier came out and said, certainly we could enter, and he and a "sous-officier" showed us over the fort, took us into the officers' rooms, gave us "pinar" (red wine) and hot coffee, allowed us to eat our luncheon there, and were most cordial. I was surprised at the fewness of the guns in the fort, only one big one and several seventy-fives. It may be that they didn't tell us or show us all their secrets. The Germans had held that fort and Vaux for eight months, and in one place a French shell had entered the fort during the German occupation and twelve Germans are still buried in the débris. The top of the fort is in the same shelled-to-pieces condition that the top of the citadel at Verdun is in. We could look down into the valley and see the trenches where the Germans had been, their nearest approach to Verdun.

Fort Douaumont

Our trip back was, to put it mildly, difficult. I suppose just what the boys have had to endure for years. The rain was beating in our faces, our clothes were heavy with water; I had on my uniform coat, my fur coat and raincoat, the two upper ones soaked through. Then I had borrowed some big rubber boots from the head nurse in the hospital. They wouldn't stay up, so after each step I had to give them a pull. Finally they both sprang leaks and I had to walk in mud oozing up both inside and outside. We didn't know our way, but we took what we thought the right direction, and luckily it was. We trudged on for miles and miles. When anything on the side of the road looked especially inviting, we took a look in. The rats which were exploring the dugouts as we were, made my hair stand on end when they jumped from one rattly thing to another suddenly. Any noise in that stillness so far under ground was a little upsetting to the nerves, and each time I got out safely I felt I had something to be thankful for. There were trenches all along beside us, the little railroad on the down side of the road, and on the upside, artillery emplacements. The back side of the hill was a choice place for all purposes, for the enemy shells go over and seldom land there. Not a human being was in sight to ask if we were right or wrong. Soon, though, as it began to get dark and we began to get tired,—very,—a poilu appeared and told us it was about seven kilometers more to Verdun and advised us to go a little out of our way to get on to the Stenay road, where there was a chance of picking up a truck. The "little" out of our way was miles out of our way, it seemed, and when we did reach the road we were both about "all in," but it was getting dark and I didn't dare to sit down and wait, so we crawled on. In a few minutes I heard a toot behind me, and saw a little train going along through the fields on a narrow gauge. It was impossible to get to, but in a second it turned, crossed the road at our feet, and stopped for us to get on when I screamed "Verdun" to the engineer. If our luck had deserted us then I doubt if you would ever have had this letter. They dropped us not very far from the hospital, and every poilu I met on the way back turned round as I passed and said, "Fatiguée, Mlle.?" and Mlle. gasped back, "Boucoup fatiguée." Mrs. Earle seemed to have more lasting power than I, although I passed my physical test A No. 1.

The next day we beat our way down from Verdun to Bar-le-Duc. It took four different conveyances to get us there, but we finally made it, thanks to a very kind American officer, an hour after our train was supposed to have left, but not feeling at all nervous, for we knew we were in plenty of time, and as it happened the 4.30 train never did come. We left the station at 11 P.M. on another train entirely. That is the way we travel here. If we hadn't told some American soldiers who were standing that they could have our seats at Châlons, we should have gone on to Paris, because we were both alseep. That's what happens to our boys; they ride up and down the tracks until they happen to be awake at the place where they want to get out. We reached Châlons at 2 A.M., went to the canteen for mail, and then to bed.

From my letters I rather think you'll wonder whether I ever do any work. If I tell you a little about the vicissitudes of life in the canteen after the armistice, I hope you will real-

Margaret Nott

ize that our difficulties were not our fault. We had hard and stormy sailing for a while. Immediately the morale in the kitchen collapsed, servants didn't care whether they did their work or not. Miss Nott, the directrice, was invited by General Gouraud to open a little canteen at Strasbourg, so she and three of the oldest and best workers accepted the invitation and left, and took with them on and off our Lieutenant Robin, who is the one and only one who runs the "ravitaillment" of the canteen. Nothing went here. Everything gave out; it just happened so. The coal wouldn't burn, so we had scarcely any fire, and couldn't make soup. The meat gave out. The chocolate gave out. The cheese gave out. Even the horse sausage gave out, and finally the electric lights gave out and we had to pour coffee holding a candle in one hand and the pitcher in the other. Think of me sometimes when you begin your luncheon at one o'clock, at intervals through the afternoon, and again at seven after you have finished your supper, standing always in the same place, always pouring coffee and chocolate, sometimes both hands going at once, and often without time enough even to push back my veil. Finally it got to a point where we wrung our hands in despair, and then Miss Mitchell, the other directrice, went to Strasbourg for a visit, and we were left to our own devices. Then our workers were grabbed away by the Paris office for Germany, in twos, threes and fours, and the rest of us had to do extra work. Even the poilus were different after the armistice. Their morale had disappeared; they were rude, impatient and "zig zag," and it was discouraging to spend your hours waiting on drunks. (They are all right again now). It seemed for a while that they were a different class of men.

Anna Van Schaik Mitchell

Then, too, one by one our canteen force of "militaire" were demobilized. We had had the older men to help us in the canteen, and of course they went first, so we were left with a constantly changing stream of new men in the kitchen, to start the fires, fill our "marmites" and do the heavy work. That was charming for the kitchen women, cooks and dishwashers, for it gave a new and varied crowd to flirt with each week, and life never became dull for them except when we had to call for cups or spoons or ask politely to have a "repas" handed out to us. Then the Misses Lansing came over from Epernay and stole away from our apartment our own angel of a little Breton cook, a most adorable little creature who always wore her Breton cap and what was still better, a cheerful smile. On top of everything else, rumors began to fly around that the canteen was to be closed, and there was the terrible question to decide in one's own mind whether to try to grab another job before all the good ones were gone, or to resign one's self to fate and stay on. Well, here I am, and things seem to be picking up a bit. We have a fresh lot of workers from America, young and untrained, but at least they lighten the work.

Emma S. and Katharine Ten Eyck Lansing

The most worrying thing of all at present is the attitude of our boys coming back from Germany. They adore the Germans and hate the French. (Modify that sentence a bit, please). It is discouraging and alarming, and makes me feel that we have made a great mistake to let our armies go into Germany, especially the men who have not fought and have not seen the war. Nothing is too good for the American boys. Instead of doubling the prices of things, as they say the French have done, the Germans are halving them. The best the house contains is laid at their feet. It is appalling, and makes me think that we have defeated our own ends and the Germans are going to be the victors as far as we are concerned. They are devils, aren't they? If they don't get you one way they will another. German prisoners who work at the canteen are most pleasantly treated by the French, who, as a nation, are easy going and don't carry their grudges very long. Those in the South will forget more quickly than those in the North, who suffered more. The Germans say, "Just wait for six years!" I think they have no intention of remaining a conquered nation longer than that.

Châlons, January

There is a log of wood in my fireplace that is supposed to be burning, but every five minutes I have to stop, go down on my hands and knees and blow it. Then there is a weak blaze for a minute or two, two or three minutes of extreme nervousness on my part for fear I'll lose my last red cinder, and then another frantic blow, so you see I don't have much chance to put my mind on letter writing. It has been cold here, even skating in the "Jard." The ground is covered with snow every morning, but that does not last. There is never sunshine. My feet are so cold now that I'll have to put on arctics soon and my idea of cleanliness has been given up long ago. I've stopped fighting and resigned myself to European ways. I rather think everyone does in the end, only some admit it and some don't. Lately I've had a rest from colds, but one is going through the canteen, and I'm having my turn at it. I've hung on here much longer than some who come. The climate has been so bad for three or four that they couldn't stay. If it were not for the question of losing sleep the way I do, I'd be all right. Food costs so much it doesn't seem right to eat. Meat outrageous, $1.50 a dozen for eggs; we have each had two to eat within two weeks, a great luxury. They are the first I've had. If it weren't for the chocolate at the canteen I think I'd die of starvation. We have food enough, but I don't think it is of a nourishing nature. The chocolate, though, takes the place of anything we lack. And when we couldn't get that, life was a different matter,—almost empty.

Of late I haven't been far away from the canteen. We've seen our enormous naval guns go down, taking up almost two cars for one gun, and some of the five thousand locomotives which the Germans are obliged to give over to the French. The engineers who bring them down come here for food, but we say, "Verboten." They should get it at the railroad station, as it's the business of the government not the Red Cross to feed them. (Later we were told to do it).

Very many are being demobilized. They march up from the station with all their war possessions and accumulations of four years on their backs, looking like old men, sometimes led by a band.

Many of the girls are crazy to go to Germany. I have not put in an application, for I am such a new worker. Those who have been here longer have the first chance to go with our army. So many have already gone from here that I shall soon be the oldest worker. I don't really want to leave France, either.

All our boys who come from Germany think it grand there, and I know they will be made so comfortable that they will wonder why we have been fighting such nice people!!! The Yale Unit went through yesterday on their way home, and such smiling boys as they were.

I talked to a poilu who was to be demobilized today, and remarked that he must be very happy. "Not at all," he answered,—where would he get his food and his good clothes now! I asked if he had any children and he said one, but he'd never have married if he'd known what a trouble it would be.

Sometimes now it is hard to tell when to sell tickets and when not to, as there are frequently civilians who come in to try to buy our food. When I asked one of them if he were "militaire," he said yes; yesterday he was here as a poilu, today he would be discharged. I told him this would be his last canteen dinner, then, and he said yes, but afterwards came back for another ticket, saying that as long as it was his last chance, he'd make the best of it.

Yesterday we had quite an exciting day, watching German officers waiting for their trains on the platform. It was icy cold. They were there walking up and down for hours, looking frozen and mad as fury. They all lined up on the platform to watch a long German train go through. Suppose the prisoners at the canteen vow vengeance every time they see German trains go by, filled with German ex-possessions. One was all flat cars with aeroplanes on them.

Châlons-sur-Marne, February 11th.

I'm in the height of misery at the moment, sitting on the floor in my room, in front of a fire waiting for the water in my basin, in front of the fire also, to get warm enough to put my hands in without weeping. Oh, it's so cold! Yesterday there were icicles two inches long inside the window of our living-dining-room combination. It is <u>supposed</u> to be warm, as it is next to the kitchen, and has a fire, such as it is, in the fireplace all day long. Of course all the water in the pitchers is frozen. Work at the canteen is piling up more and more, and as far as creature comforts go, there are none. I notice the different workers growing darker complexioned daily, and have been fascinated by the dimple in the cheek of one of the girls; each day it grows darker and darker, and her neck matches it, but all around the front of her face, in a little circle going in front of the ears and half way up the forehead and around the front part of the chin, her complexion is fair. The rest is that of a very dark brunette. Her aprons, veils, cuffs and collars are always immaculate, however. She probably has the same decision to make that I do every morning. I use the water in my hot water bottle to wash my face, and more often than not find the remains of the vegetables of the night before floating round in my basin. I always look and hesitate before I make the plunge, but it's that or nothing, so in I go. This life is not for the fastidious. When I get home I'm going to write an essay on French plumbing as I've seen it. I've had one bath in a tub in five months. I know now about that "downward path." You have to go through a certain amount of fight at first, because being creatures of habit, it is hard to let the old ones go, but when once you've been conquered, it's all up and you just sink lower and lower and lower until life in the slums isn't in it compared to yours.

Our one joy used to be the French bread, but we've a new "Prefect of Police" now, and for some reason or other he has spoiled that. I've a great excitement to look forward to tomorrow for breakfast, though—butter. Our little "femme-de-chambre" seems to have a liking for me and has smuggled a pat of butter from somewhere for me to have as a wonderful treat. I am cautioned not to let anyone know or see it.

I've got on my arctics, sweater, fur coat and hat, and can't bear to move, for it starts the cold currents of air going, and that is so agonizing. The snow never melts. Somehow I never thought France was so cold. I'm much relieved to think that the boys are out of the trenches, and like much better (for the time being!) to think of them in German feather beds, with three feather beds on top of them, as one of the boys told me he had had. "Gretchens," feather beds, or any other old Boche thing, is preferable to cold and feeling as miserable as I do. It's not complaining; it's just facts!

I've had an awful afternoon in the "caisse." For over seven hours I've been selling tickets steadily, and the last two I thought they'd break down the walls, they acted so; pushing, flying wedging, elbowing and knocking each other out of the way; all in good nature; screeching at me like crazy men, until I held my head in utter despair. When one got his tickets, he would stoop down and make a dive out through the others' legs somehow. There seems to be more room close to the floor. I had a new system of tickets also, to try to keep straight.

Yesterday Mrs. Earle and I talked to one of the German boys, and the lies they've been told! That the French began the war; that the French began the gas; and thousands of things like that; that the war was inevitable because all nations had been preparing for it and it had to come. He is convinced that he will go home within a month or two at most, or else the war will begin again. Germany <u>will</u> have her prisoners back, he says. He's a nice, industrious boy, but <u>German</u>, and they never can be changed; they will always wish to push their Kultur onto others. He told us their government was the best, and we'd all have to come to it sooner or later. I really felt quite hopeless after I'd talked to him. There is one prisoner in their barracks who speaks French well; he reads the papers to the crowds and they put their German interpretation into the articles and can see nothing as it really is. Otto said it made his "heart bleed" to see the ruin in France.

It's most interesting to see all the different nations. Poles went through again today. A crowd were held here last week because it was thought they might be Bolsheviki propagandists. They could only speak German. Lots of Americans are here now on "permission" passing through. Châlons is so full of "militaire" there are no beds or shelters for them at times, and a dormitory is being made at the Y.M.C.A. for Americans.

Our station guards are Algerian at present, and at night I feel I ought to take a guard home with me to protect me from the guards. They are awful looking men, and when they come to the canteen and try to get tickets, it is beyond description. They helped to wear me out last week. We couldn't strike any words in any language which conveyed anything to our minds; even signs failed to please them, so I used to give up in despair and ask the French what they wanted, who invariably answered, "Oh, they don't know what they want," and passed on. I'll be glad when they go and we get another detachment. The town is full of them, picturesque as the Old Nick in colors and everything else, a perfect feast for the eyes, but not for the nose. I watched for a long time an old man who came down the street with his head all done up in some kind of cloth, his brown steel helmet sitting far up on top, his greenish brown camels' hair cloak, with red stitchings, over his brown clothes, and his whole equipment—brown—packed high on his back. He stopped beside an old brown fence to talk to some friends (dressed the same) standing down below the brown bank, under brownish green trees, the most perfect color scheme, without a single false note anywhere to be seen. If I were only an artist, life at Châlons would not have to go out entirely, the way it will. It's the most awful sin that artists don't come up. You've never seen anything like the types here. No one could ever imagine it, and each day I feel more what a crime it is to let such opportunities slip by. In our country character does not show in the face as it does here; we don't have the distinct types.

A week ago Sunday Mrs. Earle, Mrs. Richard Mansfield and I went to Rheims. There were Algerians quartered in all the towns we passed through. It was one of the coldest days of the winter and the poor things looked perished. In Rheims we went through the usual amount of talk necessary to get the guardian to open the door of the cathedral. I've always had a sneaking desire to climb up into one of the towers. "Défendu," I suppose, but as I passed by, the door was there, and I was there, and no one was looking, so I "entréed" and "montéed." Why not?

Beatrice Cameron Mansfield

Figs. 14, 16

It seemed as though we must have met all the artillery in France that day on the road. The country was covered with snow, and I tried to take some pictures, but my rubber bulb was so frozen that it wouldn't squeeze, and my hands so cold that they wouldn't work, and my feet so cold that they wouldn't take me where I wanted to go, so I'm afraid I didn't get much. We went out to German lines we had not seen before, where there were more concrete dugouts and Red Cross quarters, wonderfully steeled and concreted. The trenches are being filled up as quickly as possible; soon there will be none left. One of the things most wearing to me is the desire to get out to take pictures, and the impossibility of doing it. I know I could get such wonderful things.

The other day the Châlons regiment came home. Everyone was out on the streets to greet them. It was rumored that Pétain was to be here, but I didn't see him. The General of the Sixth Army and his staff rode by us on their way out to welcome the regiment, the 106th Infantry and 25th Artillery. As they marched into Châlons with their band playing, there were met with a deadly silence; not a cheer, no clapping of hands,—nothing. Some had big bunches of flowers and some little bunches, but that was all. Twenty-eight men, all who were left of the original regiment, marched alone behind the music, and the only sounds heard in the streets were sobs. I think it was the saddest thing I've ever seen. The husbands of our two maids were in the regiment, but did not come back. The women were wonderful in their self control. The regiment marched up to the Hotel-de-Ville, where many generals and officials had assembled, and were officially welcomed, after which the band played and they all, infantry and artillery, marched around the square and off to their barracks. The next night there was a torchlight procession, which I missed.

That day I had an awful decision to make, whether to go up the Marne on an English submarine chaser as far as Vitry-le-François or to go to the Argonne. I chose the Argonne. I had been on the English boats several times, to tea, etc., and knew the river more or less from the train, and although it would have been a fine trip, I thought the Argonne more interesting. The English officers on the submarine chasers were very nice and entertaining. They had all chased submarines for years, and some had never seen one at all. I doubt if as many were captured as we were led to believe. They had an awful time coming up the Marne, because they couldn't go slowly enough to make the turns in the river, and were continually getting smashed up.

Mrs. Earle had asked the M.P. to let her know if a car was going up to the Argonne, and that morning the sergeant came flying down to the canteen while I was there, to say that a seven-passenger Fiat would call for us in fifteen minutes. She had already gone on board the boat, so I took Mme. Oblin with me, and we had a wonderful trip as far as Monfaucon, through all the country our boys had fought in so hard. Some of the hillsides were like little checkerboards where the individual men had dug themselves in.

Fig. 30

The towns are utterly destroyed and deserted. Monfaucon is wonderfully situated on a high hill. Nothing remains but ruins, and under them the German shelters where they lived. They say that Verdun quivered all the time the Americans were bombarding it. We did our work well. The officer we were with went up to hunt for his cousin's grave, but we could not reach the town where it was, as the roads were so bad. We were fortunate in having four big strong American men in our car, for otherwise we'd still be up there stuck in the mud. One spring was all but gone when we reached Châlons. The whole country is absolutely deserted and I can't tell you how charmed I was to get a chance to see it. We were gone all day. Luckily I thought of taking a loaf of bread, a box of paté and some chocolate; otherwise we'd have had nothing.

Once in a while I am invited out to dinner at the hotel, which is a pleasant diversion. My French never improves; it gets worse. Sometimes one of the German prisoners comes up to do some work in my room, and I try to talk to him, and after that I'm dumb, for I can't think of any word in any language. Lately I've had a variety of Poles brought to me in the canteen, as I was the only one on the shift who understood German and I had to get them straightened out. Great big Russians come, too, sometimes, and I try to help them, for they often know more German than French.

Our German prisoners say that Germany will always be a republic now, but they say anything they happen to think wise at the moment, I guess.

The Allied Occupation of the Rhineland

One of the most important provisions of the November 11 Armistice, and one of the most contentious, was for the immediate occupation and demilitarization of the Rhineland region in Germany. Previous German treaties on the Eastern Front had imposed similar terms on their opponents. Likewise, the kaiser's peace offer of December 1916 had proposed a permanent occupation of forts in a demilitarized Belgium and the German seizure of railways and ports in a Belgian protectorate.[1] This turning of the tables in November 1918 shocked many Germans, who had perceived the situation more as a temporary truce than as a defeat.[2] Margaret Hall frequently remarked on an air of defiance among captured German officers. A German offer of peace, distributed in a flyer in late October 1918, had proposed an evacuation from Belgium and France, not reparations or the surrender of other territorial gains.[3] From the perspective of the French and Belgians, however, this occupation was needed to create a buffer zone, in order to impede another invasion.[4] From the perspective of Rhinelanders, the occupation imposed by the Allies seemed to symbolize German military impotence. In addition, the Germans had requested in November 1918 and again in April 1919 that the French exclude colored colonial troops from service in the occupation—a request that was refused.[5] Already before the war, German xenophobia demonized the threat of Slavic peoples and of French colonial troops.[6] The defeat of the Germans in 1918 psychologically mirrored the defeat of the Belgians and French in 1914, which had often been called a symbolic rape in a "gendered vision of the national community."[7] In addition, the Allied forces occupying the Rhineland faced tensions because of the widespread political instability of Germany, where conflicts broke out among mutinous armed sailors, Bolsheviks, reactionary militias, and striking workers. While many civilians in the region welcomed the order brought by the Allied troops, others carried nationalist resentments and extremist ideas into the streets. In spring 1919, when it seemed possible that Germany would not sign the Versailles Treaty, tensions rose and Allied soldiers eager to be demobilized were placed on alert, as Hall noticed.

Even before completing the occupation of the Rhineland in 1918, the French reentered the provinces of Alsace and Lorraine that had been lost in 1871. Before the end of November, French troops under Gen. Henri Gouraud had occupied Alsace and Lorraine at the invitation of the Social Democrat Jacques Peirotes, a former deputy to the parliament of Alsace-Lorraine, who was named mayor of Strasbourg on November 10 by an anti-communist faction. Following an uprising and strikes by communist workers and soldiers that started on November 9, Francophile Alsatians called for the French military to restore order.[8] Advancing on foot, French soldiers arrived over roughly a week and Gouraud imposed French military rule. The impact on the Cantine des Deux Drapeaux was immediate. Gouraud (who had commanded the Fourth Army in Champagne with his headquarters in Châlons-sur-Marne) asked Marjorie Nott to establish a canteen at Strasbourg to serve his troops, bringing several of the Châlons canteen workers with her. Anna Mitchell, who stayed on as directrice in Châlons, was increasingly shorthanded, as refugees streamed through the station.[9] Hall was extremely conscious of the resulting demands on the workers who remained in Châlons.

While Gouraud moved in November into Alsace and Lorraine, other Allied troops began to follow the retreating German troops into the Rhineland.[10] The Armistice allowed the German army a breathing space of six days to evacuate France, Belgium, Luxemburg, Alsace, and Lorraine. Meanwhile, Allied armies regrouped for the occupation. German troops were banned from the Rhineland, but German authorities retained administrative control and German police maintained order among their own citizens. These arrangements were confirmed later by the Treaty of Versailles, which barred Germany from fortifying the Rhineland and from having any armed forces there.[11] The primary area to be occupied under the Armistice was the left bank of the Rhine. Along the right bank of the river, a neutral zone six miles wide ran from the Dutch to the Swiss frontier. More important, the occupiers also controlled a set of three strategic crossings of the Rhine at the cities of Cologne, Coblenz, and Mainz with "bridgeheads," that is, three areas each having a radius of almost nineteen miles on the right bank. The purpose of this occupation was twofold: military security and an economic guarantee that Germany would pay reparations for damage done during the war.

In 1920, the civilian Inter-Allied Rhineland High Commission assumed supreme authority over the occupying armies stationed in four unequal sectors of the Rhineland.[12] The Belgian Army of the Rhine was assigned a strip in the north and west, in a sector contiguous to the Netherlands and Belgium itself, opposite the Ruhr valley; Belgian headquarters was established at Aachen. The British Army of the Rhine settled in a small ellipse centered on Cologne, the northern bridgehead. The American Forces in Germany (AFG), with an initial force of 240,000 men, held a large sector spanning from Luxemburg to Coblenz until January 1923. The French Army of the Rhine (a force of 250,000 in 1920) occupied the largest sector, running from Coblenz to Alsace in the south, including the bridgehead at Mainz (across from Wiesbaden), and in 1923 took control of the American sector.[13] The beautiful old Rhineland cities at these bridgeheads became an attraction to the soldiers and to tourists like Hall, who visited each of them on her trip to Germany.

Seven months after the Armistice, the continued occupation of the Rhineland under civilian control was confirmed in the Versailles Treaty, after some fear in June that the Allied forces would face renewed hostilities with Germany (as Hall noted). The dominant powers at the Peace Conference discussed the details of the occupation extensively, torn between the French demands for security and the pragmatic concern of the British and Americans that a protracted occupation might intensify German resentments.[14] The participation of the American forces was expected to extend the wartime collaboration to protect France. In the British view, an American presence would also offer a counterweight to the French expansionist interest in encouraging an independent Rhineland state that might weaken Prussia within Germany and develop stronger economic ties to France. Indeed, Gen. Ferdinand Foch had been explicit about his desire to occupy and integrate the Rhineland.[15] Instead, the French misread political support for separatists in the Rhineland in 1919 and encouraged local leaders who had few followers.[16] By 1924 a political turn favorable to French interests was no longer possible.[17]

In response to the French reintegration of Alsace-Lorraine into France, their support for separatists, and their claims for reparations payments in coal and lumber, Berlin instigated resistance to the French and repeatedly defaulted on those reparations.[18] Both right-wing agitators and communist workers incited violence in the official neutral zone in 1920 and later.[19] Secret arms depots and the rise of paramilitary forces violated the terms of the treaty.[20] In the Belgian zone, one bomb attack on a military train killed ten soldiers and wounded forty.[21] Some Belgian as well as French troops were accused of sexual assault.[22] German veterans' associations became actively engaged in military drill and occasional brawls broke out between Germans and Frenchmen.[23] Among other measures, the French used military incursions into unoccupied Germany to control local uprisings and to enforce reparation payments. Since their own coal mines and forests had been damaged during the war, the French needed the German coal and timber called for as compensation under the Versailles Treaty. French war debts to the United States were due for repayment, and German reparations were expected to help cover these costs.[24] Then, faced with civil unrest in the region in 1920, a section of French colonial infantry from Morocco killed a number of Germans in Frankfurt.[25] Here another factor, race, came to dominate relations between France and Germany and triggered an explosion of racist political propaganda about "black" French troops present in a "white" land. The American commander, Gen. Henry Tureman Allen, was called upon by the U.S. secretary of state to respond to a set of allegations about rape and murder that circulated in newspapers and flyers; after an investigation, he dismissed these as a "violent newspaper campaign" whose indefinite and exaggerated accusations had been refuted in part by responsible German officials.[26] He indicated that the French had dealt appropriately with cases of alleged assaults and pointed out that German and French women had married black French soldiers. The bitter propaganda campaign left a legacy in the 1930s, when under Hitler, policies of racial cleansing would be implemented against the children of those unions.[27]

Few such problems were encountered by the AFG, led first by Maj. Gen. Joseph Dickman, and then by Gen. Hunter Liggett until July 1919, when General Allen assumed command, as the force was rapidly drawn down and troops were sent back to America.[28] Under the Armistice, the "right of requisition" provided that the Allied troops would be maintained at German expense, a measure that corresponded to the German occupation of France, in which troops were billeted on locals and food and other goods simply requisitioned. The upkeep of the troops of occupation in the Rhineland could be charged to the German Command. In fact, both British and American commanders responded to German food shortages with soup kitchens for children. American troops, no longer slogging through mud or suffering from problems of food supply, naturally relished the new conditions. Most found themselves welcome, even though some considered the Germans sulky.[29] Margaret Hall emphasizes that as a militarized member of the Red Cross, she has the right to free transportation on German trains and free hotel rooms; she savors the creature comforts of hot water and featherbeds after her long deprivations at Châlons. Both American and French soldiers appreciated the modernity and cleanliness of German homes and farms.[30]

As a rule, Americans enjoyed friendly relations with the Germans: rather than stay in barracks, they found inexpensive, comfortable rooms in German homes and fraternized with the Fräuleins.[31] In exchange for gifts of soap, chocolates, and cigars from the commissary, American soldiers were treated to roast goose and cake for Christmas, and everyone sang carols together in their own language. Although curfews were imposed, soldiers and their German friends managed to slip around them with good cheer and relative calm. In the words of one nineteen-year-old marine, the family in Neuwied with whom he stayed were "the nicest bunch of enemies a soldier ever had."[32]

American soldiers were eager, however, to return to the States. The AFG responded to increasing restlessness among the troops by offering a range of activities, which included cultural tourism, athletic competitions, and social entertainments, such as dances and jazz concerts. When Hall visited the Rhineland, she performed some light tasks at canteens that she visited, but she was particularly impressed by the number of dances and cultural events that were being organized to maintain morale and order. Some soldiers who were given passes to travel in France came through Châlons, where Hall met and fed them. In February 1919, General Pershing ordered the creation of a postwar system of education to shape a "citizen army" ready "to take an active and intelligent part in the future progress of our country."[33] Libraries and theaters were set up and attached to recreation huts; divisional technical schools offered skills in automobile repair and telephone wiring; and an American Expeditionary Forces University was established at Beaune, France, for those who wished to pursue their education. Progressive ideals of social justice, public service, and self-improvement were the goals of the university commander, Col. Ira J. Reeves, who set up a weekly one-hour lecture, distributed and read aloud at all of the schools, along with a wide range of other courses. During a few months, over 9,500 American students profited from this opportunity.[34] All these structured activities help explain why American soldiers returned from their stay in the Rhineland with memories far more positive than those left by the difficult months of fighting in France, when the casualty rates had been exceptionally high. Both Margaret Hall and Anna Mitchell felt compelled to defend the French, whose homes in the war zone had been devastated and whose experience of food shortages they knew quite well, against negative comparisons to the welcoming Germans.[35]

In retrospect, we may say that the occupation of the Rhineland failed to achieve its goals. The fifteen-year occupation was curtailed to ten years, and all the Allied forces left by 1930.[36] In spite of the Belgian and French occupation of the Ruhr from 1923 to 1925, for the purpose of enforcing the treaty, Germany paid only two-fifths of the reparations originally fixed by the Reparations Commission, and most of the payment had been in goods such as coal and lumber.[37] Although limited officially to an armed force of one hundred thousand, Germany covertly resumed military training in the 1920s, doubled its force by 1926, created stockpiles of arms, and rapidly rebuilt its army under the Hitler regime.[38] Neither economic restitution nor military security had been achieved. Nor had hearts been won. In a plebiscite held in 1935, 90 percent of the Saar electorate chose to rejoin Germany.[39]

March 13th. (Ex-Germany).
Palace Hotel,
Maison Rouge,
Strasbourg.

Here I am in Strasbourg, enjoying a few days of luxury in bed, at the rate of ten dollars a day! It was impossible to rest in Châlons. I had morning work the week the clock changed, so it really got me up every morning about 5.30, and that, together with my cold, made me a perfect wreck, and ready for my permission, which was due.

Paris offered nothing but exertion and annoyance, because of the crowds and discomforts, so I decided to take a chance and turned to ex-Bocheland, feeling sure I could get here the creature comforts I want. I came with Mme. Oblin, who is at this moment entertaining French generals, while I am just as happy staying in bed, gazing into my tiled bathroom.

We spent the first night at Nancy, at the Red Cross Officers' hotel. They have taken the best hotel in the place for officers, and won't allow a Red Cross woman a room by herself; we must sleep in dormitories. It is quite a fascinating place,—"Little Paris," they call it. It has been bombed but none of the valuable old buildings destroyed. The next day we went to Metz. Had to stand up all the way in the train, while all the French officers who could get seats had them. I didn't care, but Mme. Oblin was worn out, after her four years' nursing and canteen work, and looked so tired that two American officers spoke about it. French officers—some of them—certainly aren't what they are cracked up to be as far as manners are concerned. The train crawled along, so we could see the trenches and battle lines very well. I had had Metz put on my travelling order, luckily, for I knew it was forbidden to Americans. I had also bought a military ticket, two dollars from Châlons to Strasbourg, but not by way of Metz. Mme. Oblin's pass didn't take her that way, either, so we had quite a lot of fun travelling ticketless and passless. We wore our veils and went out the military exits, and when a Boche started to object a poilu spoke up with great indignation and said, "Infirmières," so out we went. We found a good room at the hotel, and then went out to see the sights.

When we sat down to dinner that evening, the waiter and proprietor both rushed up and asked me for my ticket. I said I hadn't any. They told me it would be impossible to have dinner without one; that they had not known I was American until they read my registration after I left the hotel that afternoon, and that I must get a ticket from the M.P. in order to eat or sleep in the place. I was almost dead, and told them I wouldn't move until I had eaten, and finally they served my dinner, after which I went out on the street, picked up the first M.P. I came across, and told him I wanted a pass for the place. He took me to the Provost Marshal's office; I showed my papers—nobody understood them—and they asked if I were attached to the French army. I thought it would simplify things to say yes, and after more talk between themselves, they handed out my permission to eat, sleep and walk around the town. It's interesting there, and we had a beautiful day. We went to see the cathedral where Kaiser Wilhelm had had the head of one of the statues removed and his own put in its place. His hands are at present chained together with iron chains.

The next day we went to the Bureau de la Place, and boldly asked the French army to telephone to Strasbourg for a room for me. While we were waiting there a regular Boche, who had been arrested, was brought in and questioned. He was more sullen than I've ever seen anyone before.

We had to beat the railroad again, having no tickets, so we put on our veils and entered the station through the "sortie" as though we did it every day. No one peeped. While we were waiting, Mme. Oblin saw Miss Nott and Miss Mitchell pass by. I felt like a truant anyway, leaving work, and Mme. Oblin also was expected straight through from Châlons, so we were rather taken aback when we were caught in the act of detouring a little.

Margaret Nott; Anna Van Schaik Mitchell

We went through parts of the Vosges Mountains, which were lovely. The French are keeping Alsace and Lorraine for themselves. Americans aren't allowed here, so I may be really safer in my bed than out of it. I wasn't wrong in my idea that I'd find creature comforts here in Strasbourg. I've got the cleanest room and most immaculate linen, and a spotless bathroom with all the most modern appliances, a maid to run in at any moment, and a waiter at table to put everything on my plate, so my exertions are reduced to a minimum.

Last night while I was making arrangements for my room, I heard a band out in the square. It played "Madelon," and the proprietor was left talking to himself until the excitement was over. I didn't even have time to say I was going. Such a mob as there was! Cavalry first, to clear the way, then the band, and more cavalry, and then crowds and crowds and crowds following on. This hotel was the worst old Boche place in Alsace. None of the real Alsatians had ever stepped inside it until after the armistice. During the war it was practically an officers' club.

It makes me mad to hear German all about, and French with that awful staccato Boche accent is even worse than pure German. There are over twenty thousand real Germans here still, although crowds have left. It's easy to tell a German soldier even without his uniform.

I'm going to try to go back via Coblenz and Treves, but I've no papers and don't know whether I can make it. I can get on the train all right here, because Mme. de la Croix (Mme. Oblin's cousin) knows the Commissaire de Gare, but how the Boche and the American M.P.s will be at the other end, I don't know. (The Germans are running the railroads). All the M.P.s I know have told me to try it. Mme. Oblin will, I hope, go with me.

Adélaïde-Gillette Billet Dufrénoy

I spent four dollars on twenty-three books today, and Heaven only knows what I'll do with them. They were on the counter of a shop where I went to get postcards. A collection of little books made by a Mme. Dufrenoy in 1818, to show that women in order to be good wives ought to be able to talk about a little something with their husbands. They are quite interesting and I've looked for them in the New York library when I was doing suffrage work. I travel with that knapsack I brought from home and another I borrow from Miss Coryn, hung over my back like a poilu, but now with my twenty-three books, too, I'll have a harder time, I imagine.

I asked the chambermaid if she saw the Germans go out of Alsace and she said yes, that they looked very sad, and the officers, who were usually so proud, hung their heads. I'm enclosing some Alsace Lorraine money which I think rather interesting. The question is whether if they were to make it themselves now, they would have such pleased expressions on their faces. The inevitable grumbling has begun.

I am waiting for Mme. Oblin to come in, as we are going to the Bureau of Circulation to see if we can get papers to circulate in the zones of the Armies of Occupation. General opinion seems to be that it will be harder for me to get them than for her.

It's snowing now, but the trees are coming out. They don't seem to wait for warm days, as ours do. The town, or rather city, for it's very big, and all except the old part very modern and comfortable, tries to be entirely French. On the great majority of shop windows are signs saying "Maison Française," but on the streets we sometimes have difficulty in finding people who speak French, and I can't always understand their Alsatian German. There are a great many women who still wear the native costume, some of them very elaborate.

The servants here, being of Alsace and Lorraine, were immediately demobilized from the German army after the armistice. It's a good time to be in hotels because the waiters have new, spotless dress suits. One of them told me that they had been sent to Russia, where many thousands were smothered in the snow; they went to sleep, and being too tired to wake up, were never found until spring.

It is strange to be in this city which has been the centre of so long a controversy and to find it calm and untouched. It is now filled with the French army, and it is hard to realize that only a few months ago it was the headquarters of the army of the Kaiser's third son. He lived here all the time, occasionally taking an afternoon trip towards the lines to see if his army were still there. He never spent a night there, and when Miss Nott asked why not, she was told that he thought the trenches a very dangerous place. He spent much time here in revelry, as did all the German officers. The elevator boy can't stop talking when he once begins to describe them and their ways. He says that iron crosses were given for favors done behind the lines, such as stealing for their officers, treasures from French villages, to send back to their friends at home.

Cercle des Officiers de Wiesbaden.

We were ready to leave Strasbourg without passes, for we were asked to go to a canteen at St. Wendell, where help was needed. At the station Mme. Oblin met a friend, Capt. de la Giclais, who is stationed near St. Wendell, who told us to wait and go up with him next morning, which we thought better, as it was to be our real entrance into Bocheland. That evening, however, our passes came,—sent to us by General Gouraud by private messenger from his headquarters at Colmar. Capt. de la Giclais, who is of the family who owned much property in the Place Vendôme, induced us to lunch with him at Homburg. He gave us delicious butter, and said the weekly butter box from home had never failed to reach him during the four years of war. Pretty good record for French mails!

Jean-Marie Joseph Magon de la Giclais

We arrived at St. Wendell at about seven, requisitioned rooms in the hotel, ate at the officers' "popote," and were taken to drive by the French officers through beautiful woods the next afternoon. Our work at the canteen consisted of standing around for ten minutes.

On Sunday Miss Nott and Mrs. Francis came up from Strasbourg to see Capt. de la Giclais. He sent over for us, too, so we went to Homburg, slept in more requisitioned rooms, and dined most formally and stylishly with the Colonel. The next day we all escorted Miss Nott and Mrs. Francis back over the French border, in a powerful automobile, lunched again with Capt. de la Giclais, and went back to St. Wendell late in the afternoon. By that time I was a complete wreck and had to go to bed immediately, dinnerless, exhausted by life in the French army.

Jane Brown Fuller Francis

The next morning we took a train for Mainz and then a tram over here. We arrived too late for any of the festivities in the Kursal, so stayed over today. If I didn't hate to give the Boches my money, and also if I had any to spare, I'd make a few purchases; the mark is worth one half a franc exactly, so you can imagine the bargains there are here.

Talk about the Germans being starved and miserable! I've looked carefully in every village and place I've been, and see no signs of misery. The shops are fine, the people well fed and well dressed and well booted, and twice as well cared for as many of the people in France. And now we talk about feeding the Germans! The idea of saying they are becoming degenerate because of lack of food! Plenty of people are vegetarians and aren't degenerate. Their bread isn't much, I guess; neither has ours been anything very fancy lately. Of course, I'm only judging from appearances.

The German army seems to be demobilizing. At the railroad stations there are crowds of returning soldiers, in uniforms with the military buttons cut off. It's not a very savory looking crowd of men. You've never seen anything like the children here; every place simply crawling with them. Mother and I have never been in the dirty little German villages during our travels. They are awful and I'm so sorry for the men who have to be quartered there.

We never pay any railroad fares in Germany; we're not supposed to. Never pay for any hotel rooms, either; not supposed to. Here we went to the Bureau de la Place, signed up, and were given orders for rooms at the Palace Hotel. We have our bathroom, with mineral water baths, even. It's very chic! And will spoil me for other kinds of travel.

Tonight we've been to "Butterfly" given in German, beautifully staged, beautifully sung, and the house full of German women handsomely dressed, and Allied officers of all nations. Tomorrow we start at eight o'clock, and go either to Cologne or Coblenz; haven't decided which. After this life of luxury, I don't know what Châlons and its squalor will seem like. My cold is not well, but my cough is; can't smell any or taste much.

The Boche nurses aren't a bit attractive. There were two very fashionable French ones at the Kursal, sitting almost next to two awful looking Germans, and it was interesting to see the difference. At St. Wendell we went to the moving pictures one night, and saw a French film, and after that a German one which was very coarse. I'll be glad to get with English speaking people tomorrow, and let Mme. Oblin take her turn at being tired. She can't speak a word of English, and I'm worn out speaking bad French.

Everyone told me it was impossible to cross the Rhine, but here we are, and no questions have been asked. I'll have a harder time with the American M. P. than I've had here, but my French papers ought to take me along. So far I've only had to show them, to get a free room here. Think how the people must hate us. All civilians have to be in the house at 11 P.M.

Don't think of anything else to tell you now. Have no papers for Cologne, but shall try our luck with the English army. This is a fine place for the men quartered here; always something to do,—morning and afternoon concerts, theatre and opera in the evening. It's as cold as winter. Snowed every day at Strasbourg and St. Wendell and is icy here.

The Red Cross is supposed to have grown very strict, so perhaps I'll "catch it" for taking a little trip like this, but I sha'n't care, for I've wanted to see Germany occupied, and now I have.

We took the train on the Wiesbaden side of the river up to the town opposite Coblenz, passing through a neutral zone on the way. I thought I'd get along better with the American M.P.s on that side of the river than on the Coblenz side, and I had no difficulty as they accepted my French pass at our sector, unquestioned. An American officer escorted us across the river and told us where to go to get rooms.

We found our billeting officers not nearly as cordial as the French. They instructed us to leave town as soon as possible, and would only give us a room until Saturday evening—two nights—because all the American officers from the country about come down to Coblenz to spend Sunday and must have rooms. After we were settled at a horrid hotel, where there were no maids, only German men provided to take care of the rooms, we went to hunt up Miss Worthington at the Red Cross canteen in the sta-

Louisa Skinner Worthington

tion. Miss Angellotti and Miss Bates were there too. They had come up to Coblenz for a few days off, to rest away from the social whirl of the Treves canteen, so we all four went across the Rhine in the afternoon to Ehrenbreitstein in a one horse cab. Luckily we found an American truck to take us up the hill. As we were looking at the view of the country, and feasting our eyes on the Stars and Stripes flying over the Rhine, some officers came up, and with no ceremony whatever, invited us to a dance that evening. Evidently there were to be several rival dances, for they appeared much afraid that we might be grabbed up and taken elsewhere. I don't suppose there are girls enough to go around, so there is great anxiety on the part of the promoters of a dance until they land safely in the hall all they have succeeded in collecting.

Bertha Bates

Our new friends took us back to our hotel, where we had an unattractive meal, and came for us promptly at eight. Mme. Oblin found some American women at the dance whom she used to know at Epernay.

The next day I rushed around to the French authorities to get my pass signed up for Cologne. It seemed better to work through the French, as my papers were French, and they are more polite than Americans are. They sent my papers to the American authorities and got them back in time for us to catch the Cologne train. An American M.P. wanted to throw me out bodily, saying my papers were no good. I told him I had spent all the morning having them stamped and made correct and I had no intention of getting out, so sat down in my seat, and finally he went off.

Cologne is full of the English army. We had no trouble and no one asked for papers. We went to the Cathedral and St. Ursula, ate luncheon at the Officers' Club, and stared at the Scotch officers to see how they arranged their skirts when they sit down. After lunch, sight-saw, and went back to the Club for tea. They were all most polite to us. Perhaps they were glad to see a woman or two, as there was not an English woman anywhere about. Somewhat different from our zone! Went back on a late afternoon train. Some American nurses were in our compartment, and one of them soon after we started invited a nice American boy to "pet her." He had no idea of "petting" before, but accepted the invitation, and they went away from the station in Coblenz arm in arm.

We lunched the next day with Miss Angellotti, Miss Bates, and another Red Cross woman, who gave us some insight into the finances of the Red Cross in Germany. Tead with Mme. Oblin's friends, Mrs. Schenk and Miss Watriss at the Aviation Camp, and took a train along the lovely Moselle River, down to Treves, where we found the billeting officer more polite.

Louisa Schenk; Martha Watriss

The Red Cross is <u>the</u> organization in Treves, the Y.M.C.A. in Coblenz. They have very fine quarters, and the food at the canteen is delicious, like our own most elaborate afternoon tea parties. Too much pampering of the boys, I think. In Germany all the Red

Cross food is given away, which seems foolish, as it only gives the boys more money to spend among the Germans.

We found Miss Pond at a dance. She invited us to luncheon the next day at the house where the canteen girls stay, and took us round in a camionette to see the different work the Red Cross does there. That evening we had to escape the M.P.s at the station, so Miss Pond escorted us to the train, and got us on board all right, much to her relief, I imagine.

We stopped over night at Luxemburg, and another night at Nancy, and at Tours had time to see Miss Andrus and the wonderful work she has done in her canteen there.

On April 1st we landed at Châlons, not knowing quite how we should be received. My contract with the Red Cross was up, so I thought they could not be too severe. Nothing was said, however, no matter how much was thought. Found Châlons cold and covered with snow and ice, with no signs of spring, and half an inch of mould on everything in my room. It snowed part of almost every day we were away, but in spite of the bad weather, my cough is gone and I feel much better for the change.

Cemeteries and Commemoration

Almost immediately after the Armistice, Margaret Hall witnessed the labor of laying the dead to rest in permanent cemeteries in northern France and Belgium. Indeed, the work of remembrance actually began with the outset of combat and took many forms, both private and public.[1] Mourners from all the nations engaged in the conflict gave expression to their losses in local memorials (some as far away as Dakar), as well as in traditional rituals such as All Saints' Day services.[2] These "sites of memory," as Pierre Nora calls them, recalled sacrifices in sites around the globe; they indicated ties to the colonies as well as to contested terrain.[3] They could also voice tacit colonial claims for recognition following the defense of the "motherland." Not only did Hall note the presence of soldiers from many French colonies at her canteen and in nearby camps, but she also photographed individual graves where they rested in France. For Australia, New Zealand, and Canada, the vast cemeteries in the Somme and in Gallipoli held special significance, since their contributions to the war shaped their sense of national identity and marked a stage in their movement toward independence.[4]

In France, roughly 300,000 bodies (out of almost 1.4 million dead) were brought back to the villages and towns like Châlons from which the soldiers had come.[5] On Memorial Day in 1919, Hall photographed American graves dug next to those of local and colonial soldiers. Over three quarters of the French dead, however, were not brought back. So many of the dead were scattered or entirely vanished that commemorative practices became highly symbolic, subsuming individual mourning into a larger narrative.[6] The massive loss of life called for communal monuments and for sculptural designs that might confer meaning on loss. Memorials set up by comrades, governments, and social institutions included isolated wooden crosses, plaques on the walls of schools, stacks of arms captured in battle, and the plane of the fallen French ace pilot Georges Guynemer. In October 1919, the French government offered subsidies to every commune for local monuments.[7] While many sculptures were mass produced, some towns strove to express local sentiments. The functions of local village monuments and services were therefore widely varied, and some sculptures were pacifist, while others stressed military courage and sacrifice.[8]

Paradoxically, the hollow, anonymous form of a cenotaph could permit the union of mourners around an empty space that suggested millions of absences.[9] On July 13, 1919, Hall photographed the French catafalque, a huge bier erected temporarily on the Champs Elysees in Paris for the national Bastille Day celebration the next day. On November 11, 1920, the "unknown soldier," chosen from among eight unidentified French soldiers who fell in eight battle sectors, was buried under the Arc de Triomphe to symbolize losses shared by all. The British Cenotaph that architect Sir Edwin Lutyens designed for Whitehall, with its sober, abstract geometric forms that stretch upward to a tomb, was first made of wood and plaster for the July 1919 parade; when the government realized the popularity of this temporary monument, it ordered a copy in Portland stone that was erected and celebrated on November 11, 1920.[10] In a ceremony at Châlons-sur-Marne in October 1921, the American Unknown Soldier was chosen for interment at Arlington National Cemetery in a similar abstract monument.[11]

The struggle to come to terms with the numbers of war dead also took physical shape in graveyards created at the end of the war, primarily in France and Belgium. War graves commissions were set up to create and maintain both small and large formal cemeteries, organized by nationality and religion. Such sites of memory at once level the dead, in their extensive assembly of gravestones, and elevate the stature of those soldiers who disappeared without leaving a physical trace. In retrospect, the vast death toll helps to explain the mutinies and surrenders that marked the last two years of the war, when the number of men in active divisions roughly equaled the total number of deaths over four years. Scattered remains were reburied in large cemeteries, and in later years cemeteries were consolidated further into mass graves, as at the German military burial ground at Vladslo, Belgium (near Langemarck), created in 1952. This collective grave for over 25,000 Germans who died in various battles, including the first Battle of Ypres in autumn 1914, faces Käthe Kollwitz's beautiful statues of kneeling and weeping "Parents."[12] Kollwitz had mourned her son Peter since his death early in the war and explored repeatedly forms that could express her grief. A highly political artist, she also engraved *Krieg* (*War*, 1923), a portfolio of seven powerful images depicting the cost of war—another visual form of war memorial. At Verdun the French created a national "necropolis," the largest French cemetery of the war, with over 16,000 graves (a small part of roughly 230,000 dead at Verdun). In a collective ossuary, skeletal remains of 130,000 unidentified French and Germans are displayed, beneath a 150-foot tower.[13]

Half the dead of the British Empire around the globe were never found or identified.[14] The Imperial War Graves Commission buried 500,000 men and commemorated another half million who simply disappeared. Small British garden cemeteries as well as massive memorials record the extent of British sacrifice along the length of the Somme, as well as the sacrifices of Commonwealth countries.[15] Almost one thousand cemeteries thread through the countryside from the North Sea to the Somme, tracing a map of where men fell.[16] Once recovered from where they had fallen and identified, if possible, bodies were transferred to large cemeteries. The Menin Gate memorial in Flanders, erected in 1927, honors almost 55,000 Commonwealth soldiers whose bodies were unidentified or missing after the repeated battles at Ypres. At Passchendaele, 12,000 soldiers killed in the Third Battle of Ypres were reburied in the Tyne Cot Commonwealth Cemetery, which also commemorates 35,000 whose bodies were not found.[17] Colonial units, Chinese laborers, and German prisoners of war performed this reburial for the Allied dead. The British Memorial to the Missing of the Somme at Thiepval likewise inscribed 72,000 names on the tall, arched walls of a structure designed by Sir Edwin Lutyens. The British architect designed 140 different cemeteries in Flanders and northern France, all drawing on similar classical forms but adapted to their individual sites. Rudyard Kipling, who like Kollwitz had lost a son, chose the inscription used on British cemeteries: "Their Name Liveth For Evermore."[18]

While the British were unable to repatriate bodies of the dead during the war, and so decided to collect them in large cemeteries near where the men had fallen, the Americans, who had far fewer dead, repatriated 70 percent of their fallen. To collect and rebury their remaining dead, the American Expeditionary Force relied on African American labor battalions, men whom Hall frequently encountered on her travels in the Argonne.[19] At Romagne, she heard the "colored band" playing at their tent camp. She hitchhiked in the truck of an African American undertaker, sitting on the wooden crosses he was bringing to a collection site near Château-Thierry. The largest cemeteries, such as the one Hall photographed at Romagne as it was still being constructed, display an immense architecture of death. Smaller cemeteries offered families a harmonious, simply designed garden-memorial that enabled peaceful meditation on the men they had lost.[20] These oases drew an aura of calm order out of the chaos of the battlefield.

On the Eastern Front, few soldiers were interred in formal cemeteries, due to the political instability following the Armistice and the shifting terrain of combat.[21] By contrast, on the Western Front, postwar tours of the cemeteries organized by official as well as commercial touring agencies attracted Gold Star Mothers and widows, families, Legionnaires, and schoolchildren, who visited in groups. Through such collective mourning, officials may have hoped to build a sense of the nation. Physical performance of collective memory—the pilgrimage to the site, retracing a name on a stone, laying a flower or artificial wreath, tucking a note into the gravesite, or writing a few words into a shared booklet—all these actions remind us that "remembrance" is work undertaken to give meaning to the past.[22] Even today, classes of children, descendants of soldiers, and veterans of other wars visit the war museums at sites such as Péronne and Verdun, and leave symbolic poppies on monuments across northern France and Belgium.

Throughout her year-long stay Hall paused to perform rituals of respect for the war dead and to photograph gravesites and memorials. During her first weeks in Paris, she visited a hilltop cemetery, where she found that the American graves had already been decorated by local families. On the train ride to Châlons-sur-Marne she glimpsed "now and then" little crosses topped by a steel helmet by the tracks in the "Zone des Armées." At Châlons she attended funerals, and she went to a memorial service conducted around a catafalque at a mass on November 2, 1918. Hall was impressed by the dignified efforts of the French to honor the American dead as well as their own. On All Saints' Day, she photographed the military cemetery at Châlons where thousands had been buried, including Algerians in their own separate section. Again on Memorial Day, 1919, when the American graves were decorated and honored, she photographed the military procession. Over her many outings to the battlefields outside Verdun and near Reims, from November 12 onward, she photographed unburied bodies and skeletons, "lonely" graves on embankments and hillsides that had been hastily marked with two pieces of wood, as well as larger cemeteries taking shape over the course of the spring. She focused on American graves at Belleau Wood and Stenay and north of Verdun. During her trip along the Somme she photographed crosses on the Butte de Warlencourt (a prehistoric burial mound that had changed hands during the war until it was retaken by the Allies at the end of August, 1918). At the same time, she took a picture of a memorial for the Durham Light Infantry. At Ypres, she recorded the white crosses of a little English cemetery and a little "tank cemetery" on the Menin Road, where remnants of destroyed tanks were clustered; at the Craonne end of the Chemin des Dames, she stopped again to photograph a gravesite. On her trips to Verdun, she repeatedly photographed the mythic "Bayonet trench," where a line of soldiers reportedly had been buried by shellfire. Her photos show first a simple row of projecting rifle muzzles, then a memorial stele flanked by rifles, and third, the site eventually surrounded by a protective fence. That sequence testifies to Hall's interest in the stories that built a myth around the war, her awareness that memory and memorials are malleable constructions, and her choice to substitute photography for the souvenir-hunting that was, in part, responsible for the desecration of the site.

Châlons, April 1st–July 1st.

I thought it would be hard to get back into work again, and it is. Nothing seems very interesting, and the work is more like drudgery than ever before. We go often to the war hospitals near here, to take food and cigarettes to the blessés. On Easter we piled a camionette full, and each patient in Corbineau had quite a variety of little presents. We each had different things to give, and for the men who were out of their wards at the time, we left little piles, which looked very gay arranged prettily on the tables.

I start a great many letters to you, but they never seem to get finished and sent off. Your cable has come. What in the world did I say to make you send it? When I say I'm tired or have a bad cold, it is nothing more than I have at home. It is only annoying to think I can't get over them. It is the same with everyone. I wish you could see the girls in Germany. Some of them are absolute wrecks. Dancing to order does not seem to agree with them. Many of them hate it there, and some who have come back say it was absolute misery. The Châlons workers who stop here on their way home begin to smile again when they land in the station.

All America is joy riding over here, either in automobiles or on trains. Rheims and Verdun are the two ends and aims of American travel, and we are the halfway point between them, the stopping off place. The American army, the American nurses, and all other American organizations pour in. We hear all kinds of talk and opinions, many very annoying, especially when our boys attack the "Frogs." There is an element here who thinks that there were no other battles in the war except the ones we were in. They forget that private property was none too safe in our own camps at home, and seem to think that the French are the only ones who "remove" the belongings of others. They forget that we have profiteers in America, and that the French people are not really responsible for their climate. They forget, also, that they are apt to "requisition" anything they take a fancy to here. An American officer told a friend of mine that he had taken as souvenirs a spoon and fork from every hotel he had stayed in, in France, and one of the Châlons workers on her way to Germany saw another Red Cross woman in her compartment take a little screw driver out of her bag and remove one of those little enamel signs on the doors of German trains used to show which way to close the door.

Discontent is rampant in all branches of the service and among all nations. It's a most deplorable ending to the four years of agony. Not one definite thing accomplished, Allies loving each other less than ever. Perhaps when we know what the peace terms are we'll all feel better.

I want to hire a donkey and go from Switzerland to the sea, via the trenches. (An awful explosion just then! They are blowing up old ammunition all the time, and exploding mines).

Today the sun is out, but there is little feeling of spring softness. I am going to find a Boche prisoner now to fix up my souvenirs. Two women of the canteen are taking home skulls as "souvenirs," and some of the nurses pull belts and boots off of dead Germans. Sometimes the feet come off in the boots, but that seems to be no objection! Talk about the Germans becoming a degenerate nation because of lack of food, what have we become through our passion for "souvenirs!"

Am enclosing myself at the field hospital after an evacuation one day. Have several sweaters underneath, so don't think I've grown as portly as I appear.

You asked about the Cromwells. They were terrified here all through the months of bombardment, but could not be induced to leave. They let nothing interfere with their work, and were wonderful in their generosity. When they left Châlons they were very much depressed, but no one realized to what extent. I think they had no idea of ending their lives until they were on the boat. Then probably in an attack of depression the opportunity presented itself, they worked each other up to the point, and did it. Supersensitive people should not come here. There are too many things which must be overlooked or not seen at all in order to keep oneself from becoming morbid.

Dorothy and Gladys Cromwell

About the only things which break the monotony of life now in the canteen are the entertainments given in the cinema room once or twice a week by the theatrical troupe of the Sixth Army sometimes, and sometimes by the talent of the 106th. There is a fine comedian in the troupe who always makes up the same way and does the same act, but is a constant joy to the crowd. "Tu m'énerves," we call him. Whenever he says that he brings down the house. He has an umbrella with no stick in it, which he hangs on his arm, a most ridiculous looking affair, so wiggly, just like himself. There is one man, very sleek in a dress suit and large boutonière who sings songs, serious and sentimental. He furnishes the classical part of the entertainment. Then there is a "Raconteur," who tells tales always beyond the limit, which never fail to bring a "C'est un peu trop fort" from Mme. Oblin. I am spared the shocks which the French and the accomplished Americans receive during his contribution to the evening entertainment. Most important of all the troupe is the soprano—the prima donna. He is dressed in the conventional opera singer décolleté and sings the soprano arias quite as well as the ordinary operatic soprano. He is easily the favorite and his voice and feminine charm always win for him wild applause. On or off the stage he never loses the mannerisms of the grand prima donna.

Whenever we see a poilu walking down the street with a ladylike switch to the tail of his horizon blue overcoat, we recognize our friend of the opera troupe. There is always a small stringed orchestra which accompanies the performers, and a brass band, which plays one or two rousing good marches during the show, with "Madelon" in between, so the audience may take its turn also.

Other evenings there are moving pictures in the cinema room, but I almost never go to those. We take turns going to the vaudeville when we are on evening duty and business is quiet. Some of us go to the first half of the performance and some to the last half,—except those who "forget" (!) and stay for the whole of it.

Verdun and The Argonne.

I have been off on another little trip up to Verdun and the Argonne with Frances King. I wanted to take some pictures, so I asked Miss Mitchell if I might hire as a substitute a French woman who has worked a long time in the canteen. She agreed to let me, so the end of April we started off for Verdun in the early train, 6.30 A.M. Went directly to the Y.M.C.A. to engage cots, as it is the only place where one can eat or sleep in Verdun. There were about sixty in the dormitory, some already occupied by nurses stretched out on them even then. There were two or three dirty looking wash basins on tables, and the whole thing seemed too messy to endure, so we made for Glorieux Hospital. There we found only twelve or fourteen cots in the visitors' room, taken mostly by French nurses. It was as cold and cheerless as when I was there before.

The next morning we went out to Douaumont, standing up in the Y.M.C.A. truck, bumped about and blown to bits by a frightfully piercing wind, which hurled snow and hail into our faces until we could see nothing. There was such a crowd with us, that F. King and I decided to leave them and walk to Vaux alone, through the shell holes. I found my adjutant friend in Douaumont, who remembered me quite well, gave us more coffee and wine, and showed us the direction to take for Fort Vaux. Luckily the sun came out, and it grew warmer. The walk from one fort to the other was the most thrilling I've had. The battlefield was covered with violets, great, big, wonderful ones, and the larks were singing high up in the sky, but the dead were everywhere in our path. At one place there seemed to be a skeleton in every shell hole. I think we saw dozens of them. We explored all the dugouts we came to, found some very deep ones made entirely of concrete, with double walls of concrete sometimes. In one I found posted the directions for a telephone operator in case of gas alarms. There was furniture and beds—springs on wooden supports—in all of the dugouts, and all kinds of ammunition lying about, which made our walk in the dark a little nerve racking. We crossed Death Valley on some boards, and then started up the hill towards Fort Vaux, getting mixed up in barbed wire more or less all the way.

Frances H. King

Fig. 18

M. P. [Louis?] Baker

Fort Vaux is more interesting than Douaumont. It took the Germans seven days, I think, to take that fort, and we saw quite plainly where they had fought in the narrow underground passageways. There are holes in the sides of the walls made by hand grenades and the bullets from machine guns, which the French had placed behind steel screens in order to guard the ends of the passages. The French only surrendered because of lack of water and because of the stench of the dead, whom they had put in a room far down in the fort, being unable to get them out.

M.P. Baker was to meet us at Vaux at four o'clock, but as we did not get there until six, he had given us up and gone back. We thought we never could make Verdun on foot, but walked almost in before we were picked up by some poilus and driven into the city. When we got back to the hospital we found that M.P. Baker had been telephoning all about the country to see if we had gone to any other camp. He was afraid we might have been blown up on the battlefields, as long as we didn't turn up at Vaux when we said we would.

Mort Homme, the hill which the Crown Prince was supposed to have had tunnelled to take Verdun was the next most interesting trip near by, so we joined the Y.M.C.A. party and went out there the next morning. We each had our own candle, and walked through the whole length of the hill underground. It was a little muddy in spots, but while the Germans were living there it was kept in perfect condition. Besides the rooms, which were large sleeping quarters, there were shelves all along the sides of the main tunnel, where many men could sleep if necessary. In the middle of the tunnel there was a big concrete engine room, with American engines still there, and a large concrete bathroom filled with shower baths, etc. Thousands of men could have lived in that tunnel, ready to march on Verdun when the time came. We ate our luncheon when we came out at the other end. Took a picture, but the weather was no good for pictures. Wandered round the hill, and back to the "town," to catch the train. The town doesn't exist, so you have to guess where the train will stop.

As we wanted to see the American camps back of the lines, M.P. Baker came the next morning and took us to Souilly and the others in the vicinity, and then up to Clermont to see where his division, the 77th, had started into the Argonne. He showed us where he had slept the first night and took us over the line of march they made the next day. The roads were awful and when we reached Varennes, he did not dare to take us farther, so the Y.M.C.A. girls put us up for the night and we ate at an officers' mess. About ten of us

Fig. 20

slept in one room that night and I guess I was the only warm one. Every one else seemed to have suffered agonies, but I can keep warmer asleep than awake, I find.

We had breakfast at the officers' mess, and one of them found us transportation to Romagne in an ambulance. When we got to the outskirts of the American camp there, our driver was held up by M.P.s, so we hopped quickly out and walked right along as though we knew exactly where we were going. Finally a Cadillac stopped near us and a grand officer asked if we'd like a lift. In we piled. He seemed interested to know how we had gotten into the camp, and said we had no right to be there, but as long as we were, that we might as well wait until we were put out. He thought, though, that the commanding officer would not allow us to stay. He seemed very agreeable and left us at the Y.M.C.A. There we told our tale, how we had come up to the camp not suspecting for a moment that it was forbidden ground. A nice lieutenant who happened to be there, and a Y.M.C.A. man, held a conference. One said he would feed us if the other would sleep us, and it was finally arranged that we were to sleep in the Y.M.C.A. quarters in town outside the camp, and were to go to the lieutenant's tent for food. Then the great question of how to stay at all without permission was discussed, and we decided to face the music and go to the Major ourselves to ask for passes. It appears that a good many women had been up there, watched the men bringing in the bodies, and went away with sensational tales about how few were really being identified, etc., which the officers said were quite untrue.

Figs. 31-32

The nice lieutenant took us to the Major. We explained that we had come up to see the Argonne and Madeleine Farm, especially, and not the cemetery. After a few moments of silence and serious thought, probably to impress us with his importance and our sin, he remarked that the country was much too dangerous, too many colored troops in the vicinity for us to wander about in alone. So he asked our lieutenant if he could take the day off. "I don't detail you, only request it," he said, with a smile. We thanked him and went with the lieutenant to his tent, where he and some friends gave us a fine dinner, cooked by a darky cook and served by the darky orderly.

After dinner the officers took us all around the country there, and we got a fine idea of a battlefield quite unsalvaged. There were dead horses about, and still men unburied. I never thought I could look at stray legs without collapsing, but I can. Boots with feet in them are so common that you never think anything about them, and it is not at all unusual to see German boots sticking out of the ground and know that the rest of him is only an inch or two down.

Very hard fighting had taken place around Madeleine Farm. The Germans had apparently used the house as a club. There were evidences of great luxury—panelled walls, comfortable corner seats, a bar, etc. Back in the woods they had the sweetest little bungalos, with pianos, porcelain bathtubs, electric lights, and concrete walks. I can't think of anything nicer than to take a camping trip through there and live in those rustic camps. Outside each house there's a shelter dug deep under ground, and on top of the ground, piles of German ammunition of every variety.

The men threw hand grenades for us, one potato masher caught in a tree, and they screamed to us to drop, which we did in a hurry. Then they tried setting off all sorts of queer smoke things. One they thought was gas, and I must say I was glad when they stopped experimenting. Brought back a little shell with a parachute in it. Hope it is nothing more dangerous than a smoke screen.

All around the outskirts of the woods were shallow trenches where the Germans had hidden to fire on us. They were in the same mess they left them in, everything thrown around, old helmets, uniforms, guns, etc.

We saw the "digging up" squad at work in the distance. Each squad starts out with a truck load of six coffins (made by German prisoners) in the morning, and when they are filled, go back, line up beside a long platform, and unload. There a crowd of undertakers with rubber gloves on are waiting to identify the bodies. They say ninety-nine per cent. are identified correctly. It is most unpleasant to meet the trucks on their return trips. I believe there are sixty of them already in use and sixty more expected soon.

The officers led us back through the cemetery. They said it was not allowed, but they took us right along. We had to walk on narrow ridges between the trenches, some of which were already filled with coffins not yet covered. It was as much as I could do not to slip into the holes myself.

The trucks were all back when we reached the camp and the men on the platform were working intently. Those who had been identified were being carried up to the trenches by four colored men each. All night long and every night that goes on. I don't know how people live breathing that air. The poor darky soldiers must have been ready to give up the ghost when they were landed in that place. Our guides rather wanted us to watch some being identified, but naturally we wouldn't. (I've seen some women who watched four or five coffins opened and the bodies searched).

The officers gave us a good supper and then handed us over to the Y.M.C.A. man, who took us to our quarters. By the time we got there a raging blizzard was in full blast. In a room down stairs there was a small stove surrounded by the usual big strong Y.M.C.A. men. We were taken to a room upstairs. It looked as though it had not been cleaned since the war. There were bloody cloths in the fireplace, an old German canteen in one corner and an American in another. We were thankful to see only two cots in the room. Our host hustled round, brought us blankets, a small wash basin and some water, and told us not to feel nervous, for we should be safe.

After he left we looked about. Water was dripping down from the roof, snow was blowing in drifts through some old burlap which had been nailed up to make a wall on one side of the room. The only thing which suggested comfort was the stovepipe, which came up from the stove below through a hole cut in the floor, so we pulled our cots as near that as possible and sat with our feet over the hole in hopes we cold get a little warm before we turned in for the night. At least we were alone; that was a comfort and a luxury. Whenever I woke that night, which was often, I heard the white guard walking up and down in front of our room.

The next morning we breakfasted in our officer's tent on good coffee and <u>hot</u> <u>cakes</u>. They found us an ambulance going to Dun-sur-Meuse, where we took the daily train to Verdun, and then back to Châlons.

From a photographic point of view, the trip was almost a failure, as it rained or snowed every day. But from the point of view of interest, it was the best yet.

At this moment I ought to be trying to sleep. I have slept two hours in forty-eight. I'm on night duty and can't sleep in the day time, so it makes it hard for me. Begin at 11.45 P.M. and work until 7.30 next A.M. Never off my feet for a moment. I'm the only one on this week, the first who has had night duty alone.

* * * Just fell asleep for about an hour. Since I've been on night duty the weather has become beautiful and spring is really here. It's bad luck to have to be in bed these wonderful days when I want to be out taking pictures. I don't like this mixed up life; there's never any tomorrow or yesterday for me.

A little while ago I heard the clicking of German boots on the pavements, and saw crowds of prisoners with all their baggage on their backs going down to the station. I wish I could have seen the 26th Division come home. I'm awfully sorry about the friction between the French and the Americans since the Armistice, and the tales our boys are taking home. You'll hear a great deal of criticism of the French, some just, but much unjust and undeserved. When you hear it, put America in the same place that France was in when we came over here,—worn out with war, discouraged, many of the soldiers not knowing what had become of their homes or families, with no news of them for three years; thousands with their little fortunes absolutely wiped out; refugees settled down on the people all through the uninvaded country, putting an extra burden on the already over-burdened population there; families having to cope with the hardships, the sorrows and constant suspense of not knowing what was happening, and being at the mercy, more or less, of that class of people who always make their fortunes out of the helplessness of others, the profiteers. You know we have plenty of them in our own country, as it is, and think how the numbers would grow with a chance such as they have had here in France, with so many foreign armies among them, millionaires compared to their own soldiers, who earn now five cents a day. The minute our armies moved into any new places at home, prices began to go up, and the same happened here, often two prices, one for the Americans and one for the French, but in New York if I trade on Second Avenue myself, I am often charged more than if a Second Avenue person buys there, don't you think so? It was the same here. They thought the Americans could pay, therefore why not let them, and the good class of French people fought it. Profiteers have been put in prison for doing it, but a thing like that is almost impossible to prevent, either in America or France, and the French Army and French nation criticize very severely those French civilians who have used the war and the soldiers of all armies for their personal advantage.

Then very few of our boys have had the opportunity of meeting the French people of the better classes. As a nation they are conservative, and the women and girls our boys have been thrown with on the streets are the same class as the girls they meet that way at home. I think I have never heard one of our boys who has been attached to the French army say a disagreeable thing about the poilus or the French officers. They have learned to know their customs, and more or less of their language, are able to understand what they say, and therefore do not misunderstand them or their motives or manners. One day I heard a French soldier make a pleasant little remark to an American when I was selling them meal tickets, and the American shoved him out of the way with his elbow, growling, "Get out of the way, you frog!" The poilu looked at him with utter amazement, and I felt my face flush with mortification and shame. I've wanted and longed so much to have our fine army leave a wonderful impression here in France, but I'm afraid it's the little things like that which have prevented any very close sympathy between the nations. Americans say the French soldiers are robbers, but what about our own boys in our own training camps before they came over? Did they dare to leave anything they valued about? An American officer came down here from Rheims the other day and said that he had left all his valuable clothes, rugs, etc., with some German prisoners up there, and he <u>expected</u> to find them when he got back.

Our boys have had to live in terribly uncomfortable places, in the midst of dirt and filth, in a country famous for its awful winter climate. They have been homesick, disgruntled with their officers sometimes, and generally miserable, and have "taken it out" by blaming the French and running down the "frogs." It does seem strange, doesn't it, that they forget that France has been the battlefield of the war, and that as long as they were living in a country destroyed and devastated by war, it would not be possible to get the comforts and cleanliness that they found waiting for them in Germany. So many compare the two countries, always to the disadvantage of France. Besides, France is an old country, centuries old even before America was known to exist, with old customs, old cities and buildings; houses built hundreds of years ago, when there were none of our modern improvements and comforts, and the people have kept on living in their old homes and are used to it and like it, and we with our new ideas come over and criticise

Fig. 26. Long Wy.

Fig. 27.   Long Wy.

Fig. 28.   Verdun.

Fig. 29. Argonne.

Fig. 30.　Monfaucon—

Fig. 31. German Prisoners—Romagne.

Fig. 32. U.S.A. National Cemetery. Romagne— Argonne.
         June 1919.

Fig. 33.   Plank road near Tahure—

Fig. 34. Lens.

Fig. 35. Armentières [*actually, Arras*]. (narrow gauge r.r. in street)

Fig. 36.   Forest d'Houlhulst. Belgium.

them and wonder why we must be so miserable and uncomfortable, and how they can be so far behind the times.

I've met such sweet American boys when I've been on night duty, and we've had such nice talks, and they have all been so broad minded in the view they have taken about France, that I'd like to have hugged them. It's the boys who think beyond their own personal comfort and have a sympathy and intelligence in their outlook on life who appreciate what these people have gone through.

So many of our boys say, "The French lie down and don't fight; they exposed our flank and made us lose a lot of men by not advancing," but it never seems to occur to them that France had been at it for three years, holding back an enemy who had been forty years preparing for this war, that they had been through the suffering, the despair and agony that only those who have had to retreat and have fought in what seemed at times a losing battle know and feel; that they had held their lines for three years waiting for their enemy to get worn out, because neither their strength nor their numbers allowed them to waste their armies in rash attacks, that in those three years of war they had learned discipline and to obey orders, and that after they had taken their objective, they were to stop and wait even if the next point were almost in their hands, because if they didn't they would spoil the whole game. Our boys with their fresh enthusiasm and courage and American independence, didn't always stop. That was the cause of some mistakes. Then I've been told by American officers we were to be the attack troops for a while, to give the French a rest, and for that reason our boys thought the French were "lying down."

That country around Verdun is, I think, the greatest nightmare of my life, and I am convinced that every American soldier who stands on the top of Fort Douaumont and listens to the little description which the Y.M.C.A. man gives of the four years' fighting about there, and looks at the desolation of that shell-torn country, knows that "The Iron Wall of France," the poilus, deserve, instead of our criticism, our utmost admiration.

Perhaps you wonder why I've written all this. It's because letters begin to come back here from America intimating that our boys have not been well treated by the French, and that they are saying all sorts of disagreeable things about the poilus. I know all the boys are not doing it, but some do. "No real American would," a boy assured me the other night, "only our army is made up of such a variety that they aren't all true Americans." And another boy told me the same night that he had just received a letter from his mother, saying she guessed the Americans were not very well received over here, and he said, "I just sat down and wrote her that if she heard such things, she could feel sure the company those who said them had been keeping was no good." I always implore the boys who make the slurring remarks not to do it at home, if for no other reason than to spare the feelings of the parents of the boys who won't go home. I don't want them to feel that they have made their sacrifice for a worthless country and worthless people. Our boys have been over here too long since the Armistice with nothing to do to interest them. One grumbles and the next catches it and grumbles a little louder.

Wilson has become most unpopular with all the nations, especially France, and the affection and admiration which the French gave the Americans at first cooled down for a while because of him. But now they see that all Americans do not hold his ideas, and I think they are blaming him as a man and not America as a whole for the delay in the peace. Some think his League of Nations is good enough in theory but thoroughly impractical, and that much valuable time has been lost discussing it. He does not live here, he does not know the conditions, he does not know the people or their characteristics, and he's trying to lay down the law for them, a law which they see no way of carrying out.

I can't say, either, that the actions of all American officers and men, and I'm sorry to add, American women also, in Paris, are anything to be proud of. I've never been able to force myself to go back since those two days I spent there when Wilson came. We rose to the war in a magnificent way, we sent our armies and our boys off in a magnificent spirit, and I can't bear to have those who have gone home and do the loud talking and the grumbling and the criticising, and those who stay here and do the drinking and sporting about in Paris, ruin it for us in America by slandering France and the French army, and by disgracing Americans in the eyes of the French here in Paris.

The French—the English also, by the way—naturally resent it when we say or infer that there had been no fighting done in France before America came in, and they resent our assertions that the war was won in sectors of the lines really short compared with the whole length of the battle line. Ours were hard nuts to crack, and we did it and sacrificed our men to do it, and we did very much towards helping to win the war, but if you were French and had lived the life of a French poilu and had earned through part of the war one cent a day, you would not care to hear too much boasting of what others had done who knew nothing of what had happened before they came. Germany and the German army too had been pretty well worn down, so the German prisoners told me, before we began, and when I asked them, men who had fought the Allies on every front, who their worst adversaries were, they said, "The French; they were the good soldiers." The French gave us great credit at the time of the Armistice, they give it to us now, but they <u>do</u> know that they had had three years of it before we came in. I can see quite well what the disgruntled French officer meant when he said to an American officer in the train one day, "You've taken all our hotels, you've taken all our seats in the trains, you've taken all our women, and now it's time for you to go home." It might make us mad if we hadn't enough sense of humor to know that every word he said was true. He had been unable to find a room in Paris the night before because of Americans; he had had to stand up hours in the trains because of Americans, and perhaps the rest of the tale was just as sad, but he didn't tell it.

Night duty is interesting because the boys have time to come up and talk. Some of the other workers could sleep for a while when they were on, but being all alone I found work enough to keep me busy all the time. Jules, the trusted canteen orderly, was a fine companion and great help. There is always an American mob for breakfast at five o'clock, going to Rheims, and another at six o'clock for Verdun. I had to keep my counter stocked, sell chacuterie, and make chocolate all at the same time, which was difficult, so I did all I could before the rush began. The minute an American train comes in, there is such extraordinary order in the canteen. A line is formed as a matter of course. Most of the poilus catch on and fall in, too; but some sneak up to the ticket window, poilu fashion, and try to get their tickets first. We tell them to "make a tail," and they go obediently to the end of the line and wait their turn. Doughnuts have been added to our chacuterie, much to the delight of the American boys. They are always polite about them and say they are very good, even when they are flavored by mistake with strong peppermint, as they were once when I was on night duty. The poilus like doughnuts, too, but when I have them to sell I always tuck as many as I can under the counter and wait for the American boys to come before I put them out.

Many of the boys going through now are on their way up to our front, or the Argonne, to hunt for graves, often their brother's. Sometimes they sit alone by the hour in a corner of the canteen, waiting for their trains. If it seems best, I take them a newspaper to read. It's hard to know whether or not to disturb them.

We have lost a little of our military air and discipline lately, for the refugees are beginning to go back, and we have been ordered to feed them, men and women. They are so happy to be going back to their "pays." When you see the wonderful courage of the little old couples who go through the canteen almost every day on their way "home"— "Home to what?" I ask them, "Oh, nothing, Mlle., there is nothing left, no house, no garden, nothing, but it is the only home we have, and we'll put up a little barraque and start again;" and when a French mother who has lost three sons on the battlefield says to you, "Yes, Mlle., it is hard, but it would have been harder to have had no sons to give to France," then you know what France is really made of. Often the destruction of towns is so complete that it is impossible to tell where their house stood. In one village I saw the other day, the only place to make a garden was on top of four graves, and there it was being made.

Châlons-sur-Marne,
Memorial Day, 1919.

The French General arranged a ceremony for us on Memorial Day at the Military Cemetery. When we arrived in our camion, some of us chattering and laughing as though we were going to a picnic, we found the French soldiers, picked ones, standing round in silence waiting for us, and also many French women dressed in mourning, who had come to pay respect to our dead. As we got out, I suggested as meekly as possible that we be a little less hilarious, but the laughing and talking only seemed to grow louder. Then while we were standing waiting for the General to give the signal to proceed, and the bugles were sounding, there was another lively conversation going on among us. I ventured once more to suggest silence, and a little respect, and the only response I got that time was, "Rats!"

The graves were beautifully decorated, covered with flowers and plants, a beautiful big bouquet at the foot, and a lovely large silk American flag at the head, all done by the French. After the General had finished his little speech, in which he told us that our dead were their dead, that whereas the French soldier had inscribed on his cross, "Died for France," the American would have on his, "Died for Humanity,"—that the French mother, whenever she sent up a prayer for her sons would never forget the American boys here, etc., the French officers, city officials, and veterans of the War of 1870, bareheaded, formed a little procession and visited each grave separately. Then they stood aside and waited, what do you think for—for us, the Americans, to turn our backs and walk away! As far as the French went, the ceremony was a charming recognition of a sacred American day. As far as the Americans went, it was an awkward failure.

Last night an old woman was brought up to my room. She had come from miles away to see her son, who is in the madhouse here. She had not eaten or slept for I don't know how long. Her son had been in Salonica, had caught the Oriental fever, come back to France, been put in the heavy artillery, couldn't stand the winter climate after the heat, and had caught cold; had gone to the hospital again, and come out with "strange ideas," she said. She had come over to see if she could help him. The doctor told her he might get well, and she could "only hope." Before the war she and her husband had three houses near Soissons. The Germans came, everything was destroyed, their little fortune wiped out, and now here they are, destitute. He is seventy-four years old and not able to do much. She looks about the same age. She has a bad heart and had been told by the doctor some time ago she must have "no emotions." "No emotions," she said, "my life has been nothing but emotions these last years, and now my son is 'fou.'"

She and her husband have hired a "little corner" in a barn which was under a hill near her home and so escaped being entirely destroyed. They have started a little garden, but the weather has been so bad that nothing is growing well for them. Her voice was so sweet and calm, and she was so anxious not to inconvenience us, and so grateful for the food and chair for the night which we arranged for her, that it made me wonder whether we in America could have endured it all so patiently.

Every Sunday afternoon we put on fresh aprons, coiffes, collars and cuffs, and go to the Jard to listen to the music. The Jard and canals through it form the chief charm of Châlons. The garden was laid out by the same man who planned Versailles. Here the military band or orchestra of the Sixth Army Corps play for an hour and a half Sunday afternoons. All the military, French, English and Americans, in the vicinity come to listen to the music. It is a fascinating scene to watch them walking slowly round and round the stand, up and down the paths shaded by the beautiful old trees, or sitting in picturesque groups on the grass near by. It's the one time I realize that for a little while I've really been a part of it all.

Sunday evenings M. Pommeret and a friend of his, officers who are stationed at Matougue near Châlons, generally take Mme. Oblin and me to dinner at the Angleterre, and then to the Arena or theatre afterwards, where we see real French performances. They are pleasant little diversions. One day we were invited to Matougue to their "popote." They sent a camion over for us at 10.30. Their mess is in a little room which is decorated with a frieze of silhouettes of all the officers who had eaten there before them. We went in through the kitchen, where a big fat woman was preparing our delicious luncheon. It was very festive, with the finest of wines to cheer us up. After luncheon we were shown about the town and country, and were urged to remain for dinner, which we did. Getting out of the town was very exciting, for no camions were supposed to leave in the evening, so we had to escape the superior officer and steal a camion unknown to him. I'm sure that he was peeking out at us all the time, though, and afterwards M. Pommeret told us that he joked them about it, but was very nice.

American nurses are flocking through here now on sightseeing leaves. Most of them are impatient and expect us to leave our work and wait on them the instant they appear in our canteen office, where they have to eat. We have no provision for serving meals there, and there are never plates or bowls or spoons enough when they come on those trains which bring the mob of soldiers, so it is impossible to feed them as soon as they wish, and often they get up and go out in a huff. One said that she was sure not an American boy at the counter would eat a thing if he knew we were not serving her. We always tell them that if they'll wait a few minutes, we'll do our best, but although some are nice and considerate, most of them are not. They expect to spend the night in the office, and the floor, chairs, tables and couch are so crowded with them that we often can't open the doors of the closets to get out our capes. They make it into a dressing room. Some even put on nightgowns and do up their hair in curl papers. Finally Miss Mitchell had to put up a sign saying that they were allowed to stay there by the courtesy of the canteen workers, and were requested to remember it was a public sitting room and not a bedroom.

Mme. Oblin and I have been down to Epernay once or twice. We went all over the Moët-Chandon champagne works, saw the whole process and had supper with Miss Lansing. It seems like a very happy placid family there. We asked them if the nurses visited them also, and Miss Lansing said that there they had to be put up in her private dining room, and they used the dining room table for a dressing table.

When we are on evening shifts, we sometimes find camions going towards Fort Pompelle, so we beg a ride and spend the day there, wandering around the trenches and taking pictures. German tanks are still there, with three or four dead Germans near them. I don't know why they have been left there, unless the story is true that when the French started to bury them they found bombs planted underneath, and no one would touch them after that. You can see how they were caught coming out from a shell hole, where they evidently had been hiding.

Yesterday I went to Paris camouflaged, to escape the M.P.s. I wore my old civilian suit and a hat I found in the apartment here. I couldn't bear to stop to "sign in and out" of Paris, and to be asked for "visés" I didn't bother to get. Three of us went down together, all separated in the station, and the one who was in regulation uniform was held up and had to go through the whole performance, using the military exit, while Miss Porter and I walked out unmolested. Went to the U.S. Consul to get some deeds signed, and took the afternoon train back. I found that Miss Billings had discovered an American boy, a courier, who goes to Luxemburg every week for a day, and had asked him to take us along. The day we expected to go he had a car full, so Miss Billings and I beat our way up to Vouziers, where we took some pictures of a German field hospital under a hill, and got back in time for service.

Catherine Rush Porter

Florence Billings

There are some nice American postal service boys who live under our windows. They pitch baseball every evening, and the French are such an enthusiastic audience that they block the traffic on the bridge, so the boys have been requested not to play where they can be seen.

One day when I was watching for some celebrity to come up from the station, I saw a Cadillac drawn up under our windows. The sight was too inviting, so I induced Miss Billings to go down and interview the driver. She came back radiant, said that he had a free day, and would take us wherever we wanted to go. I grabbed my camera and we were off in a jiffy up to our front, to explore Somme Py and the country about. Getting "essence" was quite a worry, but we found a man who let us have some, so we were able to go to Rheims along the German lines, a most interesting trip. The first and only inhabitants of Somme Py, the butcher and his wife, gave us wine and were very generous in offering us food, which I hated to take as their "ravitaillment" is most uncertain. Not until fifty come back to a town does the government send food. They were living in a barraque and seemed happy to be there. The country is all very dangerous because of the explosives and grenades lying about which might go off any moment if disturbed. It was the only luxurious drive I've had in France.

The canteen has had a terrible shock. The "prima donna" died quite suddenly one night. He had gone to bed apparently well, only a little tired, and was found dead the next morning. There seemed to be a gloom over the whole canteen. Two or three days after, a few of us went up to his funeral in the diminutive chapel of the Hôpital Militaire. We took up a big wreath from the "Dames de la Croix Rouge Americaine." It was the smallest possible gathering. Three or four women dressed in crepe, and as many men in black, with about six workers from the canteen, and two or three of our kitchen women, a few poilus, not more than five, besides two members of the orchestra, who played Chopin's Funeral March on a violin and bass viol. We all sat so close to the flag covered coffin that we could touch it. After the priest had finished the service, we waited and waited. Finally we heard a rattly cart driven up and back in towards the door. Some men came in for the coffin, put it in the old one-horse cart, we formed in procession, first his few friends of the theatrical troupe, next his family, and then the Red Cross, and walked to the Military Cemetery. There we waited until he was put in his place in the open trench,—(there are always trenches standing open waiting for the next), and left as his mother was sobbing, "Mon pauvre garcon!" It was a great loss to the canteen, and the theatrical troupe did not come back for some time.

The day we really started for Luxemburg was quite cold and there was no windshield in the Ford, so I was about perished by the time we got to Verdun. We went out to Douaumont and again to see the "bayonet trench." Each time I see it is changed. Now there is barbed wire all over it, for the American boys started to dig up the guns to see if the men were really holding them. A French regiment was told to hold its position; they held it, and the trench is marked by their guns, sticking out of the ground. On a monument near by are the words, "ON LES AURA."

Paid my adjutant another call; he gave us some beer and we took a few pictures. Then we drove past Vaux, where I stopped for a few more, and again at Étain. Our driver wanted to show us a German Poste-of-Command in some woods beyond Étain, so we spent a very interesting hour looking at the reinforced concrete walls of the house they had used, and some log cabins made of several thicknesses of huge logs. There were concrete walks all about and a ladder leading up into a high tree to an observation post in the top. We lunched on a German aviation field, and went on to Long Wy, which was a

Figs. 26–27

French stronghold on the Belgian border. We had to cross through a corner of Belgium to get to Luxemburg, but our driver knew the guards, so we got through with no trouble. That evening we walked around Luxemburg and talked to a nice intelligent bunch of M.P.s. One said he never wanted to come back to France, but another disagreed; he wanted to come back to drive by his old campgrounds and say, "I'll never have to sleep in that barn again."

As we were walking home we saw everyone rushing down the street, so I rushed too. Found that the Duchess had just gone into her palace. The crowd waited outside, and in a few minutes the door on to the balcony opened and one by one four daughters and the mother came out and waved to the crowd, which sang the national air.

The next day we drove down to San Mihiel and on to Domrémy, where we saw Jeanne D'Arc's home, etc. Spent the night at Neufchateau. Came back via Colombey-la-Belle, the American aviation field, and Toul.

Work at the canteen is excessively laborous and there is not much of it. The "young ladies" are all the time asking me to change shifts with them so that they can go to dances, and in that way I can arrange to get off without losing my work.

June 23rd.

There is still another hour to wait before we know whether or not we are to be at peace. It will be peace with a little p if we get it at all. Almost everyone is hoping that we sha'n't. Troops and ammunition have been going up to Germany steadily for a few days, and it seems almost like a mobilization again. No French officers are allowed to go to Paris. They are taken off the train here, much to their disgust. Our artillery regiment goes out tomorrow, beginning at six in the morning, and from then on, detachments move every two hours. Our infantry regiment is at Colmar already, all but the Chālons company, which is the last to move. They will be here a few days longer. After that we shall be soldierless. At any rate, the canteen closes on Monday—that is, for the American Red Cross. I don't know what arrangements the French will make about keeping it open.

I've been up to Verdun again for a few days. Got a room at the "Coq Hardi," but they give no food, so I found a little place behind a meat shop where I could eat.

This time the battlefields are garden spots, covered with lovely yellow flowers, and the grass has grown higher, so much of the desolate effect is gone, but the weather is hot, and the battlefield odor is almost unendurable. M.P.B. took me to the Argonne again, up the Dun-s-Meuse road, where much of the German camouflage is still left. At Monfaucon we saw the Crown Prince's periscope, through which he watched Verdun. It's a great concrete chimney affair in the middle of a house. We had to climb up ladders, etc., to get to the top, where there is a wide view of all that part of the country. Had

M.P. [Louis?] Baker

dinner at Romagne. Wherever you go, you meet the huge trucks filled with coffins, and as you pass you always know whether the day's work has been accomplished or not. The French, too, are reburying their dead, and coffins are dropped anywhere along the roadsides. Boches prisoners are doing it for them, our colored troops for us, but the German prisoners are putting the coffins together. We saw where the "Lost Battalion" was lost, and explored some of the German dugouts. They are built in tiers in some places, for officers on the top and men underneath. Some are enormously long tunnels, lined with narrow shelves, where hundreds could sleep. They always have two exits. We found bundles of burlap bags (made of paper), used for pillows, old stretchers lying around, etc.

Mme. Oblin came that night, and the next day we went to Douaumont, and I took her through the shell holes over to Vaux. On our way out she wanted to go to Fort de la Laufée, where her brother had won his Croix-de-Guerre, so we found the little foot path in, and were shown over the fort by some friendly poilus.

M.P.B. took me over the road towards Metz that evening. Each time I go out near the lines, I get more and more horrified, for it only adds new scenes of destruction and distress and desolation to the memories I already have. That night I saw everything by moonlight. The great red moon came up from behind a little white ruined village. The flat country with the barbed wire entanglements still intact, the lingering sunset, the brightest star you ever saw, high up in the sky, and star shells going off every little while up on the wooded hill in the background (set off by burning grass caused by the blowing up of an ammunition dump), was a picture I shall always remember.

A little while ago five mines, set by the Germans during the war, blew up on a road not far away from us, and a party of English graves registration boys almost blew up with them. Sightseers who don't use sense blow up too, sometimes.

* * * This was begun five days ago. I'm now on my way to Paris, 6.30 A.M. It's the day peace is to be signed, so they think. I'm going down hoping to get my pictures, but expect to find the shops closed. If Paris looks interesting, I'll spend the night. If not, I'll go back this evening. Only two more days of the canteen!

The other day we had a Croix-de-Guerre decoration. Three of the canteen workers got them. They were here through all the bombardments. The general opinion, theirs included, is, that their valor did not deserve the Croix-de-Guerre. None the less, they are charmed to have them.

Many celebrities go through Châlons. We have had Lloyd George for five or ten minutes. He bowed, shook hands, and talked very pleasantly to us from his car window. He has a very interesting face and a kindly smile.

David Lloyd George

The day the Germans decided to accept the peace terms, Miss Billings and I went up to the hand grenade station to watch them fire off the guns. They shot paper flags into the sky, which floated down in the most attractive way. We gave the men chocolate and they gave us "souvenirs,"—hand grenades, and explained the workings to us.

There is a nice little carrier pigeon camp out the other side of Châlons which we visit occasionally, also. The men let the birds out for us, and it is quite exciting to watch them fly round and round the camp. Some want to stay out too long and are called "Bolsheviki" by their keepers.

Very little interest is taken in peace, for they all feel it isn't peace. There is general unrest and dissatisfaction with all governments. In the canteen, too, the indecision is trying. No one knows what she is going to do, or what she wants to do. The fascination of this life is hard to give up. Even dirty old Châlons is hard to leave, and I don't know what I'll do when I don't live over a railroad station.

We've been going an hour and a half and have scarcely started. Someone said there had been an accident. I always travel those days, it seems to me. The flowers in the fields are wonderful. The red masses of poppies are so bright that they almost hurt your eyes. Instead of war implements on the trains now, you see farming implements. There are suspension bridges swung across the Marne, where the old ones have been blown up. The shell holes are covered with grass and hay, and the outskirts of the war country seem to be inhabitable and inhabited again. We are getting down towards Chateau Thierry, the Mecca for Americans. It's funny how irritated I get when I hear the remarks of American civilian travellers. It will certainly be bedlam over here when they really begin to come. You ought to have come when I sent for you. I could have arranged to have you and the car come over then if you had only said the word. You'll never have the ghost of an idea now what it has been like.

The greatest luxury in life I have is to sit down all alone and think.

We are at Chateau Thierry now, and the German prisoners on the platform are smoking away and look more insolent than ever.

Versailles Treaty

From January 18 to June 28, 1919, diplomats gathered for the Paris Peace Conference, to design the Versailles Treaty, which would conclude the war with Germany and shape the world to come.[1] The protracted process of peacemaking with all the belligerents in fact stretched on into 1920, in a series of treaties that "took longer than the war itself."[2] While the Armistice of November 11, 1918, had provided an outline of the treaty provisions the Allies were debating, it had not settled frontiers or reparations payments. The diplomats needed to rewrite earlier treaties, such as that between the Central Powers and the Soviets, which had been signed at Brest-Litovsk on March 3, 1918. One of Woodrow Wilson's first priorities was his proposal for a new League of Nations to resolve disputes without war. Such a "society of nations" had been proposed a year before on January 8, 1918, when he presented his Fourteen Points.

The Peace Conference failed to meet the expectations of many participants. Most importantly, the terms the Allies submitted on May 7, 1919, struck the Germans as punitive: they included not only disarmament, the surrender of all territorial gains, and the loss of all colonies, but also an acknowledgment of war guilt and agreement to pay significant reparations to be determined later.[3] When troops had returned home in November 1918, Pres. Friedrich Ebert congratulated them, "No enemy has conquered you."[4] Despite the German army's retreat, the collapse of the German Empire, and the abdication of the kaiser, the German people had not been prepared to recognize military defeat. Instead they were fed by Hindenburg and others a myth of a domestic "stab in the back."[5] Under the treaty provisions, however, Germany would lose one-seventh of its territory and one-tenth of its population.[6] Hall noted in mid June 1919 that it still remained unclear whether Germany would sign: French troops were moving forward to the frontier, in preparation for an invasion of Germany. The German foreign minister Ulrich von Brockdorff-Rantzau pursued a strategy to reject the treaty and resume hostilities but was blocked at the last minute by President Ebert, a socialist, who asked the Supreme Army Command (*Oberste Heeresleitung*) to state whether the military was prepared to return to war.[7] It was not. As it turned out, German representatives grudgingly agreed to the terms on June 28, 1919. Hall took an early train to Paris to witness the celebration.

The Allies have been described as divided in victory.[8] Throughout the spring of 1919, journalists reported on differences in agenda among the Allies that impeded swift agreement during the Peace Conference. The primary French goals were a return of territories lost in 1871, continued occupation of the Rhineland buffer zone, German disarmament, and reparations. The French argued that Germany (with twice the population of France) should demobilize. They also feared political instability spreading from Russia and Germany. The treaty confirmed that, in three phases of withdrawal over fifteen years, the Rhineland was to be occupied by Allied forces (Belgian, British, American, and French), an occupation that had already begun in December 1918. The French would occupy the Saarland for fifteen years, in compensation for the devastation of their coal mines in the industrial northern departments. Initial British aims included reparations; the surrender of the German navy; mandates, or trusteeships, in the Middle East and Africa; and a reduction in German armaments.[9] They would not embrace Wilson's "peace without victory," but they also envisaged a restoration of trade with Germany.[10]

These goals thwarted the desires of the defeated nations and of the peoples whose fate would be decided in the redrawing of frontiers. The talks excluded Germany and Austria, as well as Bolshevik Russia. The "smaller" powers, whose voices were muffled if not entirely silenced, included the Poles, Chinese, Lithuanians, Ukrainians, Bulgarians, Romanians, Turks, Greeks, Armenians, and the peoples of the Ottoman Empire, as well as the colonies in Africa and elsewhere. The five "great powers," Great Britain, France, the United States, Italy, and Japan, debated territorial goals without agreement. From the end of March, President Wilson, Premier Georges Clemenceau, Prime Minister David Lloyd George, and Prime Minister Vittorio Orlando of Italy met in closed sessions; Orlando pulled out of the discussions in April.[11]

Among the muffled voices were those that expected the emancipation and self-determination of subject nationalities. Plans were laid for plebiscites in contested regions such as Schleswig-Holstein, Upper Silesia, East Prussia, Carinthia, Sopron, and eventually the Saar.[12] The vision of self-government, however, included numerous exceptions. The new Czechoslovakia included the Sudetenland, whose German population was not allowed a plebiscite, nor was there a vote in Alsace-Lorraine. In the Middle East, the French won a mandate in Syria, and Great Britain took control over Iraq, Jordan, and Palestine. Queen Marie resisted attempts to carve up Romania by granting autonomy to ethnic minorities; she made pointed remarks to Wilson, a southerner, about the problems of representation for African Americans in the

United States.[13] Wilson rejected Japan's proposal protecting minority rights.[14] Great Britain had its own problems of nationality and empire: the 1916 Irish Easter Rising was followed by strife until Ireland won independence in 1921, and the British Indian Army's massacre of roughly one thousand unarmed Indian demonstrators at Amritsar on May 13, 1919, altered British attitudes toward imperial violence and marked a turn away from British rule.[15] In February 1919, the American sociologist and civil rights leader W. E. B. Du Bois and delegates from fifteen countries organized a parallel First Pan-African Congress in Paris, hoping to achieve a progressive settlement leading to African self-rule in former German colonies. The Versailles Treaty disappointed such hopes, creating mandates under European administration in Africa.[16] The contradictions of the peace negotiations mirrored the divided impact of the war on imperialism itself, breaking up some empires but temporarily strengthening other colonial powers. Inexorably, ideals debated during the conference vanished on paper.[17]

The treaty left undetermined some of its critical provisions. The Germans were held responsible for wartime destruction in occupied lands. Following Article 231 on war guilt, a Reparations Commission was set up to fix appropriate costs after assembling documentation over the next two years. These were anticipated to include pensions for veterans, widows, and orphans. During the German occupation of France and Belgium, machinery and raw materials had been exported to Germany, civilian property and foodstuffs had been requisitioned, and high fines had been exacted for minor or invented offenses.[18] One complication in the calculus of damages was the fact that Allied shelling to recover territory from the German forces had itself wrought terrible damage. The ruins at such famous battle sites as Passchendaele, Soissons, and Dixmude were the result of Allied offensives.[19] In 1921, the sum due was stipulated as fifty billion gold marks, but in fact by 1931 only a little over nineteen billion had been paid, less than one-third of it in cash; payments were suspended by U.S. president Herbert Hoover and ended in 1932.[20]

It was expected that photography would play an important role when the commission determined what indemnification might be claimed. Official photographers flew over the battlefields, and they walked around the craters, along with others like Hall who sought to document the effects of the war. Other evidence came from Germans who had photographed the French countryside, taking pride in the destruction they had wrought, although they also were aware of its shocking nature.[21]

Under Articles 227-230 of the treaty, the Allies also attempted to establish a multinational tribunal to prosecute selected German officials as war criminals under the rule of international customary and moral law. The Dutch refused extradition of Kaiser Wilhelm II. The Germans likewise refused extradition of any wartime officials. Instead, they held a trial at the Leipzig Reichsgericht from May to July 1921 for those accused of violations of international law (which under The Hague treaties protected prisoners of war and medical workers). A small number of men were charged, but they were either acquitted or sentenced to short terms in prison that were not served, in what has been considered a mockery of justice.[22] In effect, key provisions of the Versailles Treaty were modified or not enforced. Moreover, the U.S. Senate voted on March 19, 1920, not to ratify the treaty. Despite Wilson's extensive campaigning, the United States did not join the League of Nations.

As a result of these many thwarted expectations, the treaty left no one happy. It was said to be "too gentle for all that is in it which is harsh."[23] The provisions for reparations have continued to be considered highly controversial, judged as "unclear, contradictory, and undoubtedly shortsighted." Ferdinand Foch, who felt the restrictions on Germany were too lenient, declared, "This is not Peace. It is an Armistice for twenty years," echoing the distrust many had expressed in November 1918.[24] The Germans objected to the "dictated peace," which did not conform to the Fourteen Points of Wilson himself. The American secretary of state Robert Lansing denounced the peace agreement as "hopelessly bad."[25] Treaties signed in the fall of 1919 and in later years with Austria, Bulgaria, Hungary, and Turkey provided for the breakup of the Austro-Hungarian and Ottoman Empires. By reducing the strength of rivals to the east, these treaties actually strengthened Germany's position. Redrawn frontiers and new nation-states fed decades of conflict.[26]

One sign of the continuing demoralization, skepticism, and anger of French citizens in 1919 was Clemenceau's invitation to *gueules cassées*, or facially mutilated soldiers, to participate in the ceremonies for the signing of the Treaty of Versailles on June 28, 1919. Living evidence of the trauma of war experienced by occupied France, these men physically documented the right to reparations; their faces, reflected in the Hall of Mirrors, presented a visible condemnation of Germany.[27] Two weeks later, on July 14, when Margaret Hall was in Paris to watch the Bastille Day parade, disabled French soldiers marched proudly down the Champs Elysées.[28]

Hall calls it a peace treaty "with a little 'p.'" Hall's reactions to the negotiations and the treaty aligned her with the French point of view. Several comments suggest that she considered Wilson "rather German in sympathy," since according to the newspapers, he did not want to see the devastated regions, for fear that the facts might "prejudice" him. He is quoted as having said, "I'm afraid if I visited the devastated areas I would get mad."[29] "Wilson hasn't yet been to see" the devastated regions, she notes. Hall sympathized with the demoralization of those French men and women who perceived the Armistice as a failure to pursue a clear-cut German defeat and who hoped the projected reparations would enable the reconstruction of their country. For many reasons, the Versailles Treaty could not heal the ruptures wrought by the war. In France, one-third of men aged nineteen to twenty-two had died, a literal "lost generation."[30] The number of civilian deaths overall in the war has been estimated at six million.[31] In addition, the influenza deaths left a diffuse feeling of senseless loss that reinforced the "deficit of meaning."[32] Women, for whom the death of husbands and sons meant that the impact of the war would last for a lifetime, also faced in many places the termination of their wartime jobs, as soldiers returned to reclaim their former positions and salaries. In the postwar period some observers noted the difficult readjustment of soldiers to civilian life, not only because of their injuries, trauma, and grief for dead comrades, but also because of what the historian George Mosse calls the "brutalisation" wrought by military service. Harsh militarization led some soldiers to channel their emotions into paramilitary conflicts, in a cycle of political and physical violence that fed subsequent wars.[33] For many different reasons, then, the people Hall encountered felt "it isn't peace" (156).

"Belgium."

Paris, July [*June*] 28th, 1919.
Treaty of Versailles.

Paris seemed inviting, so after I got my pictures, I went up to the Red Cross to meet Mme. Oblin's brother. We batted together all day. When the guns went off at the Invalides, to announce that peace had been signed, we were sitting at a little café on the Champs Elysées drinking beer. There seemed to be no excitement whatever.

In the evening we went out to see the boulevard crowds. It was amusing to watch the poilus form circles and dance around couples, of any age or description, calling out "Embrassez,—embrassez-vous, embrassez-vous," and the victims were not allowed to escape until they had "embrasséd."

The nicest thing I saw was a group of American officers who had dined just well enough to forget their official dignity. One had climbed up an electric light pole in the middle of the boulevard, and was about to direct the singing of the crowd. He asked them to have a little patience, and said that first his friends would give them a short concert of American songs, after which he would ask them to all join in singing the Marseillaise. They sang two or three popular American songs, to a charmed audience, and then the leader took an English flag from some one in the crowd and with it led the Marseillaise. Everyone sang, and my escort in a most pleased voice remarked, "Pas mal, pas mal." It was really very well done, and all nations were very well satisfied.

Am spending the night at the Chatham, and go back to Châlons on the early train, as M.P.B. is to meet me and take me to Somme Py and Tahure, so that I can take pictures.

M.P. [Louis?] Baker

Photo, p. xxvi

Fig. 33

M.P.B. was at the station waiting for me when I reached Châlons, so I rushed home, changed from Paris clothes into trench clothes and went off for a most interesting day, through Souain, Somme Py, Tahure, up as far as Grand Pré. Had supper at Romagne at the Y.M.C.A., and listened to the colored band concert. It was too late to go home, so I stayed at Verdun. Could not get a room in the hotel, so M.P.B. put me up in his house and made me very comfortable.

In the morning he took me back to Châlons for the celebration of the last day of the A.R.C. in the canteen. We had a little reception for the French Red Cross, and a show in the garden. It was a bad day, but I tried for a picture or two.

On July 1st the French took possession of our beloved canteen, and on the 3rd I went down to Paris, buying a return ticket for Châlons, for I couldn't bear to feel that I had cut all connection with it. Came to Hotel Celtic to be with the Kings; got a good room and board for twenty-two francs a day.

The next day, the 4th of July, we had no trouble in getting down to the Place de la Concorde, to see the review in honor of our holiday. We had a splendid view of the whole affair. The French brought out their old battle flags. All the buildings, the Place and the statues, were beautifully decorated for us, done in such exquisite taste, and it was a holiday for all. The Americans march in the solid wall formation, which looks as though nothing could break it. They were all about the same size men, and with their steel helmets they presented a very formidable front. The French march in looser formation, and are more relaxed, which is not as striking in parades. An American boy standing beside me seemed quite outraged that the French had brought out such careless looking soldiers, so I tried to explain that it was their way of marching, and that the French Army had found they could march longer distances a day by doing it that way.

In the afternoon we went to the Embassy for tea. Mr. Wallace is Mrs. Francis' brother-in-law, so Châlons was well represented. The "young ladies" came in flowing blue canteen veils, which were a little conspicuous, to say the least.

Hugh C. Wallace

Notes from Diary.
Somme.

Started from Amiens on a three-days trip in automobile driven by an English officer. Took our luncheon along. Had some difficulty in deciding where to go, as only the main highways were open. The other roads had not been repaired and the officer did not care to risk taking his new car on bad roads. Went through Albert, stopped and took pictures of the church. The Germans had taken away the Virgin which had hung out at right angles from the tower all through the war. Albert much destroyed. Went through Bapaume to Arras, where we were in luck, as the Cathedral door was open, so we could go in and I got a few pictures. Then drove through the city to Hotel de Ville, which was a wreck. Next stopped at Vimy Ridge. F. King and I explored the tunnels the Canadians made to go under the Ridge and place their mines. They were pitchy black and wet, and seemed to go on for miles. Then we climbed to the top of the Ridge and saw the line of huge craters, seven or eight, made when the Canadians blew up the German trenches, and incidentally blew off the top of the Ridge. I asked two poilus to go down into one of the craters, so to get some of the idea of its size in a picture. They were setting off unexploded ammunition near by, and as we went away, there was a frightful explosion, and some pieces of shell whizzed over our heads, disconcertingly near. An officer who had fought at Vimy was on top of the Ridge when we were, so we listened to his description

Fig. 35

Frances H. King

Fig. 34

of the mining and blowing up of the Germans. Ate luncheon in the car. Went through Souchez to Lens, the worst mess I've seen anywhere. Nothing but a mass of débris of bricks and twisted iron. Not one thing standing. Got to Lille the middle of the P.M., engaged rooms and looked about the town. Could press a button while in bed and unlock the door of our rooms. The Germans must have enjoyed that luxury very much. Dined with our captain chauffeur and went to bed early. The Germans have taken away all the brass.

The next morning started at ten, went straight up to La Bassée, across the canal on an English military bridge, through Menin, to Pilcom Ridge, where we got out and explored the trenches. It is right over Ypres, and the Germans were entrenched there all the time. Took pictures of English tanks which had succeeded in getting up as far as this on the Ridge, and of the "Cemetery of Tanks" below the Ridge. There must have been over a dozen stuck down there in the Flanders mud, total wrecks.

Fig. 22

At Ypres we had luncheon in a little barraque. I flew round and took pictures. On the ruins of the Cloth Hall, which are to be left as they are, is a sign, "This is Holy Ground. No Stone of this Fabric may be taken away. It is a Heritage of all Civilized People. (By order of the Town Mayor, Ypres)."

"Cloth Hall–1919– Tommies"
British soldiers marching through Ypres.

The captain showed us "Death Corner" where a German shell had fallen every two or three minutes for four years, and then took us off the road and showed us where he had worked for some time putting in an engine to keep the trenches pumped out. He told us how the men had been stuck in the mud and drowned there. Saw Mt. Kemmel, crossed Messines Ridge, through Poperinghe, through Armentiéres, back to Lille. A good many of the trenches have already been filled in and much of the barbed wire cleared away. Much more cleared up than the French fronts. Felt in more or less of a hurry, as Mrs.

Frances Purviance and Katharine King

King and K. wanted to catch the train for Paris at five o'clock. Frances and I dined again with our English captain, and the next day, in a drizzling rain, started off towards St. Quentin via Douai, Cambrai and Bourlon Wood. We got out there, but the place was so wet that we didn't explore it much. There had been very heavy fighting in those woods. Old guns and cannon about just as they were left. German camouflaged helmets lying around in the ruins. It was very interesting in spite of the day. Went on to Le Catelet and Bellicourt, where the canal goes underground for such a long distance. Thousands of Germans lived in that tunnel. Americans didn't know it was there, so went beyond it on top of the ground, and were trapped. Too late to go to St. Quentin, so we went back to Amiens via Peronne, where we spent the night at the hotel. Were much amused watching a party of American naval officers and women. In the evening we watched the dancing, and the gray haired dignified English officers entertaining French mademoiselles. They say that during the war Amiens was a "den of iniquity."

Took an early train back to Paris. People were all flocking down there for the 14th, so we were pushed about frightfully trying to get on the train, but finally made it. A train of Americans went through the station while we were waiting, and I tossed them all the Camel cigarettes I had, much to their joy.

Train very late. Found the Kings had no tickets for the 14th, so we all decided to go over to the Elysée Palace Hotel (A.E.F. headquarters), and see what we could do there. Miss King only asked for one, for her mother, but after refusing definitely, the officer gave us four passes, so we were well fixed.

On the 13th took some pictures of the Champs Elysées' crowds. M.P.B. came for dinner and took me out. We tried to see the procession round the Cenotaph, but I got tired of balancing myself between a German cannon and a tree, so we didn't stay long enough. Walked from the Place Bastille up town, to see the decorations. Hotel de Ville was lovely. Paris a dream.

When we walked home that evening the Champs Elysées was already crowded behind the ropes. People on camp stools, folding chairs, etc. Babies in hammocks swung from one chair to another, ready for the night. All the trees were full of people. Men with ladders went from one tree to another. When one was full, all connection with the ground was broken, and they were there for the night and until after the parade the next day. Saw "musettes" being swung up, full of bottles and boxes, probably their midnight feasts and their breakfasts. Rue Balzac being on a hill, was already packed full of standing people. Could scarcely get through. The side streets were crowded with all kinds of carts, from Paris and country about, filled with ladders, clothes horses and boards, ready to be put up after midnight against anything that could be found to support them. Such a noise as went on all night under my window, music, automobile horns, people laughing and talking. Got up at five A.M. and at six we started out. It was almost impossible to get through rue Balzac. We pushed and elbowed and finally accomplished it. One cross street several blocks down was supposed to be kept open, so we went there and found it absolutely blocked. However, we got into the crowd, and pushed along towards the Champs Elysées. It was a near panic getting across, and I thought we'd be caught there and not be able to see a thing. The mounted police were ordered to charge on us, and if it hadn't been for a high-up Paris official who was trying to cross in the same place, we never should have made it. I thought Mrs. King would be crushed to death. It was almost as bad getting to the sidewalk after we had crossed the avenue. When we reached the Elysée Palace, the doors were not open, and we had to wait outside there half an hour. Finally got settled in a window on the ground floor, but after the parade started, I went up on the roof, to be able to see the armies pass under the Arch. Had a magnificent view, although to get it I had to make a perilous trip up the roof on an outside ladder. Felt thoroughly satisfied with my position, heard the music play as they came under the Arch, and saw them march through.

In the evening M.P.B. and I went out to see the sights. Missed the torchlight procession. Saw the dancing on the streets, and the fireworks over the river. The sight from the Tuileries garden was one that never will be seen again, I imagine. Wonderful clouds in the sky, lighted up by searchlights from all directions. The Eiffel Tower lighted, the Arc-de-Triomphe lighted with flaming lamps burning all the way across the top. The gardens were illuminated and decorated with lanterns, as were the Place de la Concorde and Champs Elysées. Magnificent fireworks bursting all over the sky, just like fairyland. It was impossible to believe it was real.

A day or so after, Miss Billings and I went up to Soissons. Found an automobile with a woman chauffeur to take us to the Chemin des Dames. Walked towards Pinon through unsalvaged German trenches, went into concrete dugouts, some great round galleries filled with tons of absorbent cotton and bandages. Others were piled so full of ammunition that we couldn't get in. Trench mortars, machine guns, etc., lying about outside. As the Chemin des Dames is impassable for automobiles, we had to walk over to Fort de la Malmaison. It was a long hot walk and we found a very much destroyed fort at the end of it.

Back to Soissons for the night. Hotel more or less shot to pieces. Guests requested not to use any more water than actually necessary, because it all has to be carried into the house.

Next day took our woman chauffeur and her husband and went to see the quarries at Juvigny, where thousands of German soldiers lived during the war, and which we found used now for a German prison camp.

The prisoners had collected every kind of a thing to make partitions for themselves, and many of them had made private cells, which were exceedingly neat. It was damp and dark inside, with only a few little stoves, an awful place to live. The prisoners help with the administration of the camp. We talked to some of the clerks in the office, who seemed cheerful enough. Our French guard let us go wherever we wished, so we watched the metal workers in their little workshop, and inspected the kitchen. On our way out we passed a German officer walking along swinging his cane, looking very haughty and defiant, as they always do.

Coucy-le-Château was our next stopping place. Near the station found a big German naval gun emplacement, one of the biggest they had. The one which fired on Paris was in the Bois-de-Coucy, they told us, the other side of the town. We didn't have time to go there.

Emplacement for a "Wilhelmgeschütze" gun in the Coucy area.

On our way to St. Quentin we passed the Hindenburg line. Went to see Amy Steinner in her little foyer de Soldat there. She appeared very anxious to get rid of me, although we stayed only about fifteen minutes.

Miss B. went off early the next morning, but I stayed on and went with the Y.M.C.A. excursion to Anizy and Mont-des-Singes, attached myself to some American boys who seemed to know what they were about, and they engineered me around through the German trenches on one side of the hill, and the French on the other. All the time we were going up the hill we heard firing of guns and bullets going over our heads, which we found was a Chinese labor battalion off on Sunday leave amusing themselves.

The top of the hill reminded me of Verdun. Nothing but a mass of deep shell holes in the white clay, skeletons in some, feet sticking out of others; all covered with poppies so red that they almost blinded you. On our way down, found a dugout in which were ten or twelve Germans who had been gassed. It was awfully deep and hard to get in. I wasn't sure that I could stand it. It was a puzzle to grope your way along without stepping on those lying in the passage. In the room at the end, some were sitting in chairs, others leaning over the table, still others on the wire beds, or stretched out on the floor,—just as they were when the gas caught them. It seemed only musty down there, not really disagreeable at all. They had been playing cards, and the game was spread

Florence Billings

out on the table, together with their letters and books. Their hands were mummified, but you could almost see the muscles in their broad shoulders. Probably the gas, and being so far down away from the air, had preserved them. Don't know how I ever could have gone into such a place. The only reason must be because they were our enemies, and you don't feel the same about them as you do about anything else in the world.

Found a letter from Elsa Bowman when I got back to Paris that evening, saying that she had gone to Laon and wanted me to go up for Sunday, so the next Saturday went up there. Saw the work of the Committee for Devastated France. Had dinner with Elsa and the next day we went over to Rheims. Stopped at Berry-au-Bac on the way, where we saw Miss Thomas (Bryn Mawr) and Helen Taft. The girls from Laon had taken us as far as that, so when we were ready to go on, we sat by the roadside and waited for transportation of some kind. Spent night at Rheims, went to Y.M.C.A. and watched a dance, and to call on Mme. Hermann.

Sunday took an automobile back to Laon via Craonne, and saw that end of the Chemin des Dames. Nothing whatever left of Craonne. In the afternoon went down to Pinon, where we explored the great underground galleries there. Saw an American boy who had monkeyed with ammunition rushed by in an automobile with face streaming with blood. He had thrown a fuse down, which went off, injuring him and the girls and men near him. Talked to the cousin of the woman who had cooked for the Kaiser when he had lived at Pinon in a château there owned by a French countess. She was evidently a friend of his, because the woman said that the chateau had never been hit while the Germans were attacking Pinon or taking Soissons, and when they left, all the furniture was taken away and returned later unhurt. The owner had come back to her ruins after the French had retaken the place, but was none too popular in the neighborhood. Whenever the Emperor went out to drive while there, the inhabitants left the streets, as they did not care to salute him. Some families had come back, and were living in dugouts. A few had new barraques. They were all very cordial and glad to see us.

Next trip was to the Belgian front with Frances King. Had no papers, but chanced it, and relied on our Red Cross uniforms to take us along and give us military rates. Went to Bruges for the first night. Next morning looked around, saw the Memlings, took boat around the canals, and in the afternoon went down to Blankenburg for that night. Next day went to Seebrugge, saw the Bruges Canal stopped up. Belgian soldiers were taking down the concrete fortifications at the mouth of the canal. The Germans had burned the piers before they left. Then walked over to the Môle, passed Boches prisoners who were gathering up the barbed wire on the beach. Whole coast covered with it. Walked out on the Môle. Took the wrong way and had to climb up on the railing, but with the help of some sailors, made a safe crossing. Saw hole English boat hook had made in the fence when they tried to climb up on the Môle. Also the great hole made in the Môle itself by the English submarine when they exploded it and ten thousand pounds of dynamite. Captain Fryatt's boat "The Brussels" was still there, but the next day they were expecting to salvage it. *Capt. Charles Fryatt*

Had luncheon at the hotel in Seebrugge. I walked back to Blankenburg and took pictures on the way. Got some of the camouflaged guns used for coast defence. Then went to Ostend in the afternoon and found rooms at a hotel on the beach; rather reasonable. In the evening walked along the breakwater, which is still covered with barbed wire, and made arrangements to take a trip the next day over the Belgian front.

Started early in the morning in an automobile with a Belgian man and his wife. (Two hogs). Went to Nieuport, where the Belgians blew up the dykes to flood the Germans out. Crossed the Yser, and took pictures of the German trenches on the one side and the Belgian on the other. Then to Dixmude, Ypres, out towards Mt. Kemmel, Poelcappelle, Forêt d'Houthulst, and Moëre, where the big gun is which was used to fire on Dunkirk when the Germans thought the English needed discipline.

Back to Paris in the train, via Brussels, through Mons and the English front. Before I left Paris, sent all the money I had left to E.L.C.'s filleul. *Emma Lewis Coleman*

Left Paris August 10th for Havre. Sailed on "La France." In station in Paris heard someone call, "Margaret!" and found it was Aimée Leffingwell and her husband. Sat at table with them and Mr. Vinton, a friend of theirs. Arrived in New York August 18th. Demobilized August 19th. *Amy Leffingwell, Kenneth McKenzie* *Warren Jay Vinton*

Appendix 1: Biographical Key

Allen, Miss: An organizer of Red Cross volunteers in Paris, Allen may have been a woman who served in the Paris office of the CARD in 1918–1919.

Andrus, Ida Bourne (1887-1962): A native of Yonkers, New York, and a member of the Smith College class of 1910, from August 1918 to February 1919 Andrus performed canteen work for the Red Cross in Paris and Tours, and did relief work with the Smith College Relief Unit at Grécourt in the Somme region, staying in Europe until spring 1920. With her husband, Wadsworth A. Williams, she settled in Minneapolis. Daughter of U.S. congressman (1905–1913) and philanthropist John Emory Andrus, she became director of the Surdna Foundation he had set up.

Angellotti, Marion Polk (1887-1979): The daughter of Frank M. Angellotti, chief justice of the California Supreme Court, Angellotti joined the canteen at Châlons-sur-Marne in May 1918. In September she worked at Evacuation Hospital No. 13 in Commercy, south of Saint-Mihiel, where she was injured in an accident. Already familiar with southern Europe from travel in 1915 to 1916, Angellotti was one of Hall's traveling companions when on leave from the canteen in December. In 1919, she transferred to a canteen in Trier, Germany. She wrote popular historical fiction and published a wartime spy novel, *The Firefly of France* (1918).

Baker, M. P. [Louis?]: A military policeman in the 77th Division, which went to France in March 1918, Baker lived in Verdun in the winter of 1919. His division fought at Belleau Wood and in the Meuse-Argonne. Hall met Baker first in her trips to Vaux and Verdun. He later drove Hall through the Argonne to Metz, Somme Py, and Tahure, to view sites where he had seen action; he met her in Paris for the celebration of Bastille Day, July 14, 1919. His service information matches that of Louis Baker (1887–1950), a New Yorker, who was thirty when drafted and was promoted to corporal.

Bates, Bertha (1887-1967): From St. Louis, Bates attended Washington University and graduated from Vassar College in 1899, then became a high school teacher. She performed searcher work for the Red Cross in France from August 1918 to June 1919. Hall met her in Germany. She married Carlo Zuccaro and died in Taormina, Italy.

Belasco, David (1853-1931): An American playwright and the producer of over one hundred plays, Belasco was noted for his naturalistic yet dramatic effects.

Bennett, Emily Marion (1884-1977): Of Tyngsboro, Massachusetts, Bennett graduated from Smith College in 1906 and worked as a teacher in New York City. Bennett served as secretary and canteen worker in Châlons and Reims; in 1919, she was decorated at a ceremony in Reims with the Croix de Guerre.

Billings, Florence (1879-1959): A native of Hatfield, Massachusetts, Billings grew up in Redlands, California. After graduating from Stanford (class of 1903), she taught in California and in Germany and traveled in Europe. In August 1914, Billings volunteered with the American Ambulance Hospital in Neuilly, France. From November 1917, Billings performed canteen service with the American Red Cross at Châlons-sur-Marne and Écury, which earned her the Croix de Guerre. She traveled with Hall to Paris, Vouziers, Somme Py, and Soissons. After the war, Billings continued to do relief work in Paris before she left in November 1919 for Turkey, where she taught at the American School for Girls in Bursa, then worked with the Near East Relief organization for refugees until 1923. She wrote a master's thesis on the 1909 Armenian massacre in Cilicia (Columbia University, 1927).

Bowman, Elsa (1874-1960): Hall's college friend from Bryn Mawr (class of 1896), Bowman taught at the Brearley School in New York and was an active suffragist. Hall frequently lunched with her at the Bryn Mawr Club in New York and joined her in suffrage parades in Washington, D.C., and New York City in 1913. Bowman was secretary of the National War Work Council of the YMCA serving the AEF in France and worked at Laon from July 1919 until 1920. Hall traveled with Bowman to Reims, Pinon, and Laon, and the two met to observe the work done by CARD. They toured the American southwest (1914) and the Colorado Rockies (1928). In 1923, they traveled in Africa with Hall's chauffeur, Pierce Butler.

Bradley, Dr. Frances Sage (1866-1949): A pediatrician from the U.S. Bureau in Washington, D.C., Bradley carried instructional films about children's health with her on the SS *Chicago*. She served the Red Cross in France from July 1918 to April 1919. Bradley published several books on child welfare.

Burnett, Miss: A secretary-stenographer in Anne Vanderbilt's Red Cross office in Paris, Burnett worked in France from November 1918 to July 1919.

Butler, Conrad (1895-1947): Pierce Butler's brother, who was in Germany in 1919.

Butler, Pierce (1892-1973): The family chauffeur, Butler was Hall's assistant until her death.

Coleman, Emma Lewis ("E.L.C.") (1853-1942): Hall's maternal aunt, Emma Coleman was an active writer, historian, and photographer. A professional portrait photographer, she taught her skills to her niece as a child and used photography to document New England history and the lives of sharecroppers in South Carolina and Virginia. Her most successful book, *New England Captives Carried to Canada between 1677 and 1760, during the French and Indian Wars* (1925), continues to be cited as a source of genealogical information and has been reprinted twice. She also published histories of Deerfield, Massachusetts, including *A Historic and Present Day Guide to Old Deerfield* (1907), *Epitaphs in the Old Burying-Ground at Deerfield, Mass* (1924), and *Frary House—1685, Old Deerfield, Massachusetts* (1940). Coleman traveled in Europe in her youth and visited France with Hall in 1927. She donated her typescript of Hall's memoir to the Massachusetts Historical Society.

Colgate, Ethel M. (1881-1940): Colgate traveled on the SS *Chicago* to join Anne Morgan's CARD Unit in Laon in 1918–1919 as a mechanic, bringing a car that her family had donated. A concert pianist, Colgate had studied under the Polish pianist Theodor Leschetizky (1830–1915) in Boston.

Coolidge, Miss: A Red Cross worker at Châlons-sur-Marne.

Coryn, Marjorie Stella (1895-1968): Born in London, Coryn became a U.S. citizen when she moved to San Francisco in 1901, where her father became a newspaper editor. Coryn served the Red Cross at Châlons-sur-Marne and briefly at nearby Écury, for which she won the Croix de Guerre. After the war she lived in France, returning to the United States around 1937. Between 1932 and 1954, she published several historical biographies on French subjects.

Cromwell, Dorothea and Gladys (1885-1919): Twins from New York who worked at the Châlons-sur-Marne canteen from February 1918 to January 1919, the Cromwells both won the Croix de Guerre. Exhausted and under stress from bombing raids, they became depressed and broke down while traveling home in January 1919. Despite receiving care from a doctor on the SS *Lorraine*, they committed suicide by leaping together from the deck, after writing several suicide notes. Gladys was a successful poet whose collection *The Gates of Utterance* (1915) was followed in 1919 by a posthumous volume.

Cross, Emily R. (1879-1955): A Bryn Mawr graduate (class of 1901) from New York, Cross served on the executive committee of the Franco-American Committee for the Care of the Children of the Frontier from May 1918 to March 1919. In 1917, she led a colony of ninety-nine girls at Grandbourg and another of thirty boys at Issy-les-Moulineux.

Davidson, Reed M. (1877-1940): After serving in the Spanish-American War, Davidson worked as an editor for the *Ashland Daily Independent* in Kentucky. In 1918, he went to France to perform "home service work" for the Red Cross at Châlons-sur-Marne, where he ordered construction of the air raid shelter. Davidson managed a refugee camp for Russians in Gallipoli in 1920, then served as chief of the Near East Relief headquarters in Egypt.

De la Croix, Mme E. E. R.: An Irish cousin of Mme Oblin, De la Croix was wounded during her work in Châlons-sur-Marne and received the Croix de Guerre.

De la Giclais, Capt. Jean-Marie Joseph Magon (1873-?): Stationed near St. Wendel in Germany, De la Giclais escorted Mme Oblin and Hall to a canteen in Wiesbaden. He had been settled in Canada for nearly twenty years, where he was married to a Massachusetts woman (Roberta Talbot), owned a farm, and was president of the Western Canada Bank Company. When the war began he volunteered to serve in the French Army. He achieved the rank of *général de brigade* and received a distinguished service cross from the U.S. for service with the 42nd Division of the AEF.

De la T.: A French nurse who performed canteen work in a hospital train car between La Veuve, near Châlons, and Limoges.

Dufrénoy, Adélaïde-Gillette Billet (1765-1825): A French author of elegies, natural history books for children, and a history of famous women, *Biographie des jeunes demoiselles, ou vies des femmes célèbres depuis les hébreux jusqu'à nos jours* (1816), Dufrénoy was also the editor of a thirty-six-volume *Bibliothèque choisie pour les dames* (1818-1821).

Duncan, Isadora (1877-1927): A famous American modern dancer, Duncan raised funds for the French war effort and rented her chateau in Bellevue to the American Red Cross for use as a hospital.

Earle, Ethel Deodata (1874-1940): The widow of Prof. Mortimer Earle (Bryn Mawr), Ethel Earle was Hall's neighbor in New York, and the two sailed together from New York City to France. Earle performed Red Cross hospital hut work in Paris and Digne, then joined Hall in Châlons-sur-Marne. From 1918, she performed relief work under the ARC commissioner general for Europe in Czechoslovakia, Serbia, Montenegro, and Poland, while she was also affiliated with Herbert Hoover's American Relief Administration, formed in response to widespread starvation following the war. In June 1920, she went to Belgrade as a field worker for the American Commission to Serbia. In August 1921, she worked with the World Student Christian Federation in Warsaw. She renewed her passport in 1922 in order to do relief work in Poland and the Balkans.

Jane Brown Fuller Francis (1875-1939): Born in Chicago, Francis was a daughter of Melville W. Fuller, the U.S. Supreme Court Justice; one of her sisters was Mildred Fuller Wallace, the wife of Hugh Campbell Wallace (below). In 1899, she married Nathaniel Leavitt Francis, with whom she lived in Washington, D.C. In 1915, Nathaniel Francis enlisted in the Canadian Expeditionary

Force, quickly rising to the commission of first lieutenant and eventually fighting in Lens and Ypres. In 1916, Jane Francis embarked on the *Kroonland* from New York to perform relief work in England and France. She appears to have worked at the Cantine des Deux Drapeaux and then followed Marjorie Nott to open and staff a canteen at Strasbourg in 1919 (116, 131).

Fryatt, Capt. Charles (1872-1916): Captain of the British merchant ship SS *Brussels*, Fryatt escaped two submarine attacks, the second by trying to ram the U-boat. Seized later by the Germans, he was executed as an unlawful civilian combatant in July 1916. In the press, Fryatt's death was represented as an atrocity.

Gaines, Ruth L. (1877-1952): A Smith College graduate (class of 1901) trained in social work, Gaines worked as a librarian in New York City before the war. An original member of the Smith College Relief Unit, Gaines sought to raise funds by publishing *A Village in Picardy* (1918) about their reconstruction work at Canizy, in the Somme region. The German spring offensive of 1918 wiped the village out again and forced the Smith unit to join the exodus of refugees from the region. She returned to France on the same boat as Hall. Following a second tour of relief work in France from August 1918 to March 1919, Gaines published *Helping France: The Red Cross in a Devastated Area* (1919) and *Ladies of Grécourt: The Smith College Relief Unit in the Somme* (1920).

Gibson, Harvey D. (1882-1950): The president of the Liberty National Bank in New York City, Gibson became the general manager of the American Red Cross in 1917, the American Red Cross commissioner for France in 1918, and commissioner for Europe in 1919. As field head of the ARC in Paris from June 1918 to March 1919, he lectured on the organization's work.

Gouraud, Gen. Henri (1867-1946): Gouraud made his career in Africa, then commanded the French Expeditionary Corps in 1915 at Gallipoli, where he lost his right arm. During the Second Battle of the Marne, as commander of the Fourth Army (which coordinated its efforts with the AEF), Gouraud was responsible for fifty miles of the Marne front and came several times to Châlons-sur-Marne. As the commander of French troops in Alsace after the Armistice, he invited Marjorie Nott to open a canteen in Strasbourg.

Guynemer, Capt. Georges (1894-1917): Guynemer was a legendary French ace who shot down fifty-three German planes. A Spad VII in which he downed nineteen enemy planes was exhibited at the Paris Invalides.

Hall, Philip (1881-1969): Brother of Margaret Hall.

H[ennocque], Mlle Madeleine (1901-1978): Madeleine later took the name Hennocque du Mottier de Lafayette, reaffirming her mother's family connection to the Marquis de Lafayette. She married Michel de Larminat in 1927.

Hennocque, Gen. Edmond (1860-1933): Born in Ohio of a French father, General Hennocque led his cavalry division beside the American 26th Division in the assault on the Saint-Mihiel salient in September 1918. He later commanded occupation forces in the Ruhr. Hall notes that the Hennocque family owned pistols that Lafayette had given to George Washington.

Hennocque, Mme Marie (1864-1949): Marie Bonnin de la Bonninière de Beaumont Hennocque was a Frenchwoman who lost two sons in the war, one in 1914 and the other in 1916. Mme Hennocque worked with Hall in Châlons-sur-Marne. At the end of November 1918, she invited Hall to join her in Belgium, where her husband, Gen. Edmond Hennocque, was stationed.

Hermann, Mme.: The wife of Joseph Hermann (d. 1929), the rabbi of Reims and Epernay. Mme. Hermann (first name undetermined) worked as a nurse with the French Red Cross from the beginning of the war. They spent time in Reims, Paris, and Châlons-sur-Marne during the war.

Hindenburg, Gen. Paul von (1847-1934): After his success in commanding the German offensive against Russia in 1914, Hindenburg became chief of the general staff in 1916. Together with Gen. Erich Ludendorff, he assumed control of the military and militarized the economy. He was elected president of the Weimar Republic in 1925, and in 1933 appointed Adolph Hitler as chancellor.

Hoyt, Mary Fellows (1877-1957): A linguist in Hall's class at Bryn Mawr from 1895 to 1898, Hoyt was a cousin of Woodrow Wilson. From 1915 to 1917, she studied nursing and wireless signaling. As an auxiliary nurse in the American Red Cross from July 1917 to February 1919, she worked at the Neuilly hospital in Paris, where her languages proved useful. She spent six weeks as an interpreter for American soldiers at a French Hospital in Beauvais.

King, Frances H. (1876-1970): Daughter of Adam King, consul-general in Paris from 1890 to 1896, Frances and her family spent many years traveling in Europe. In August 1914, she returned from England to New York. She, her sister Katherine, and their mother, Frances P., volunteered with the Red Cross in New York, then joined the Distributing Bureau of the Surgical Dressings Unit in Paris in July 1916. King accompanied Hall on trips to Verdun, the Somme, Paris, and Belgium.

King, Frances Purviance (1847-?) and Katharine King (1875-1959): The widowed mother of Frances H. and Katharine King, Frances P. King enrolled with her daughters in the Red Cross in July 1916. Like her mother, Katharine worked for the Red Cross from July 1916 until June 1919. Although the three originally came from Baltimore, the King family lived near Hall in New York City.

Lafayette, Marquis Gilbert du Motier de (1757-1834): Lafayette was a hero of the American Revolution and a major figure in the French Revolution, for whom a French air squadron of American volunteers, the Lafayette Escadrille, was named.

Lansing, Emma S. (1873-1952) and Katharine Ten Eyck (1875-1933): Sisters of the secretary of state, Emma and Katharine served in a Red Cross canteen at Epernay, west of Châlons-sur-Marne, from September 1917, where Emma was appointed director. They were awarded the Croix de Guerre in August 1918 for their work at the Epernay canteen while it was under bombardment.

Leffingwell, Aimée: See McKenzie.

Lloyd George, David (1863-1945): The British prime minister of the Liberal Party from 1916 to 1922, Lloyd George worked to limit the power of British generals and to secure at the Paris Peace Conference of 1919 reparations less punitive than those sought by the French premier Georges Clemenceau.

Mansfield, Beatrice Cameron (1860-1940): A former actress and a friend of Ethel Earle, Mansfield traveled to Reims with Hall. Her only child, Richard (1898–1918), was an ambulance driver in France who then joined an American aviation unit, but contracted meningitis and died.

McDermott, Miss: Hall's secretary in Boston.

McKenzie, Aimée Leffingwell (1873-1961): As a member of Hall's Bryn Mawr cohort, Aimée or Amy Leffingwell (class of 1897) recognized Hall when about to embark on the SS *France* in

August 1919. She later published a French grammar and translations of French literary works, including the correspondence between George Sand and Gustave Flaubert.

McKenzie, Kenneth (1870-1949): With his wife, Amy, McKenzie met Hall in August 1919. Born in Cambridge, Massachusetts, he was a professor of Italian at the University of Illinois at Urbana-Champaign and Princeton University. From September 1918 to August 1919, he served as director of the Italian branch of the American University Union in Europe, the same organization with which his travel companion Warren Jay Vinton was affiliated.

Mitchell, Anna Van Schaik (1878-1965): Anna ("Nan") Mitchell did relief work in Serbia from July 1915 to March 1916, when her efforts were interrupted by the renewed invasion of Serbia. From July 1916 to June 1917, she worked in Paris with the French Institution for the Blind at Reuilly, the American Hostels Committee, and Edith Wharton's refugee committee, as well as at canteens in Calais and Bar-le-Duc. She co-founded with Marjorie Nott the Cantine des Deux Drapeaux at Châlons-sur-Marne, which she co-directed from 1917 to 1919, often in the absence of Nott. She was awarded the Croix de Guerre for her service. From 1919 to 1920, Mitchell worked with refugees in the Pas de Calais; in 1920, she served with the Red Cross in America; and from 1921 to 1936, she assisted Russian refugees in Istanbul.

Mitchell, Frances (1876-?): Born in Rhode Island, Frances Mitchell attended Bryn Mawr in 1905–1906. She served at canteens in Epernay, Châlons-sur-Marne, and Toul; she then worked at a hospital near Verdun, where she welcomed visits from her former coworkers.

Mitchell, Mildred (1897-1992): The niece of Anna Mitchell, Mildred secured a YMCA nursing certificate, then worked for the Red Cross at the Châlons-sur-Marne and Epernay canteens from December 1917 to January 1919. During the Second Battle of the Marne, she nursed the wounded in an evacuation hospital at Epernay and at Hôpital Temporaire 3 in Châlons. From October to December 1918, she also ran French Ambulance No. 5, a temporary tent hospital at Écury that cared for the wounded and for victims of influenza. In 1920, her family published anonymously her *Letters from an American Girl in the War Zone, 1917–1919.* She married John W. Brock, Jr., who had served in the war.

Moore, Mrs.: A worker in the Red Cross "search" office in Paris whose job it was to locate missing soldiers for their families.

Morgan, Anne Tracy (1873-1952): The daughter of the financier J. Pierpont Morgan, Anne Morgan set up organizations for working women in New York and in France. She lived in Versailles with her friends Elsie de Wolfe and Elisabeth Marbury in a villa that they would offer to the Red Cross for a convalescent hospital when the war broke out. A visit to the region of the Marne in September 1914 inspired her to establish the American Fund for French Wounded (AFFW) and the Comité Américain pour les Régions Dévastées (CARD), which raised five million dollars for war relief and was officially recognized by the French government. With Dr. Ann Murray Dike, Morgan ran her relief network from a rundown château in Blérancourt, which she rebuilt, and which in 1931 became the Franco-American Museum of the Château of Blérancourt. As chairman of the organization, Morgan in 1918 was awarded the Croix de Guerre. In 1932, she was made a commander of the French Legion of Honor.

Nott, Margaret (1878-1957): The daughter of Charles Nott, chief justice of the Court of Claims in Washington, D.C., and granddaughter of two college presidents (Union College and Williams

College), "Marjorie" Nott was a member of the New York Woman Suffrage Party, living in New York City with Frances Mitchell, who also came to France as a canteen worker. Before the war, Nott worked on behalf of settlement houses. A friend of the American writer Max Eastman, she moved in radical intellectual circles. With Anna Mitchell, in June 1917 Nott founded and then directed the canteen for French troops at Châlons-sur-Marne. Their work was honored with the Croix de Guerre. When the United States entered the war, the canteen was absorbed into the American Red Cross network. After the Armistice, Gen. Henri Gouraud invited Nott to open a canteen in Strasbourg, where she served until September 1919. In 1924, she married Victor Morawetz, a wealthy corporate lawyer, and settled in Charleston, South Carolina.

Oblin, Mme: "An attractive little French woman," in Hall's words, who worked at the canteen at Châlons-sur-Marne and at Epernay over the course of the war. Hall traveled with Oblin to Montfaucon, Strasbourg, Matougues, Epernay, Fort de la Pompelle, and Fort Douaumont. Hall visited Paris with Oblin's brother, who won the Croix de Guerre for his service in the medical corps.

Olivier, Mme: Refugees from the German-occupied Pas de Calais region, the Olivier family was sponsored by Emma Coleman. On Hall's arrival in France, she visited the family at Cenon, near Bordeaux.

Pershing, Gen. John J. (1860-1948): As commander of the AEF, arriving in France in June 1917, Pershing allowed some troops to serve under Allied commanders ("amalgamation"), but he strongly supported separate deployment of American troops. Earlier in his military career, Pershing had served in the Philippines, led black troops in Cuba during the Spanish-American War, and headed a search for Pancho Villa in and around Mexico. After World War I, Pershing was appointed to the highest army rank, General of the Armies of the United States.

Pétain, Gen. Henri Philippe (1856-1951): The commander-in-chief of the French Army after the mutinies of 1917, Pétain led the defense of Verdun in 1916, improved trench conditions, and cautiously restricted offensives against the Germans until American troops arrived. As head of state during World War II, he collaborated with the Germans, for which he was later convicted of treason. His sentence was commuted to life imprisonment.

Poincaré, Pres. Raymond (1860-1934): The president of France from 1913 to 1920.

Pommeret, M[onsieur]: A French officer stationed at Matougues, west of Châlons-sur-Marne.

Pond, Marie Brockway (1862-1957): A Red Cross canteen worker from Rochester, New York, Pond served from December 1917 to June 1919 in Châlons-sur-Marne. She then directed a canteen at Treves (Trier). She was the daughter of Col. Nathan Patchin Pond, a Civil War veteran and owner of Rochester Printing Company.

Porter, Catherine Rush (1885-1979): Daughter of the prominent Biddle-Porter family of Philadelphia, and descended from American generals and governors, Porter was a canteen worker from September 1917 to June 1919 at Châlons-sur-Marne and at Reims until July 1920. She traveled with Hall to Paris and was decorated in a ceremony at Reims with the Croix de Guerre. In 1922, she married a French lieutenant, Paul Marthel, in Paris.

Read, Georgia Willis (1881-1965): A friend of Ruth Gaines, Read had dropped out of her class at Smith College in 1901. She served the Smith College Relief Unit as treasurer and as a driver. After the war, she wrote historical studies and coauthored two books with Gaines.

[Reynolds], Annie: A servant in the Hall household, Reynolds had been a governess for Margaret.

Schenk, Louisa: A friend of Mme Oblin, Louisa Schenck worked at the Coblenz aviation camp.

Steiner, Amy L. (1877-1966): A Bryn Mawr graduate (class of 1899), Steiner worked six months at a YMCA canteen in France in the spring of 1919, where she drew on emergency funds raised by Bryn Mawr alumnae in Baltimore. Her father was Baltimore physician and scientist Lewis Henry Steiner.

Taft, Helen (1891-1987): The daughter of Pres. William Howard Taft (who founded the League to Enforce Peace in 1915), Helen Taft was a Bryn Mawr student (class of 1915) and a suffragist, who became dean of the college in 1917 at the age of twenty-six. She briefly replaced M. Carey Thomas as acting president of the college in 1919–1920. After earning a doctorate in history at Yale University, she returned to Bryn Mawr as dean and professor of history. Taft's husband, Frederick Manning, taught history at Yale and Swarthmore College.

Thomas, M. Carey (1857-1935): The president of Bryn Mawr College (1894–1922), Thomas took a year's sabbatical in 1919–1920 to travel with friends through Europe and Asia. Although head of a Quaker college, she gave enthusiastic support to the war and supported the participation of college women in the war effort. In 1908, she had become president of the National College Women's Equal Suffrage League, a cause Hall embraced.

Tissier, Joseph-Marie (1857-1948): As the bishop of Châlons-sur-Marne from 1912 to 1948, Tissier invited the workers at the canteen to special religious services, such as one on Thanksgiving Day. He officiated at the funeral of the wounded soldiers who were killed when a bomb struck their hospital on October 2, 1918. In the same week, he was decorated by Pres. Raymond Poincaré and by General Pétain, who made a special visit to Châlons to honor the "long suffering" city.

Vanderbilt, Anne Harriman Sands (1861-1940): The forceful administrator of the American Red Cross office in Paris, Anne Vanderbilt organized assignments to canteen work and documentation of the missing. The wife of William K. Vanderbilt, she was a leading member of the American colony in France, with two Paris homes, which were used as hospitals during the war, and a château. She initiated a canteen at La Chapelle station in Paris. With the president of the American Hospital in Neuilly, she helped A. Piatt Andrew establish the American Field Service, which created five ambulance sections during the battle of Verdun in 1916. The Vanderbilts paid for ten vehicles in that ambulance service and provided the first airplanes of the Lafayette Escadrille. Anne Vanderbilt also raised funds in the United States for relief work in France. She received the Médaille d'Or des Étrangers in August 1915 from the French Ministry of Foreign Affairs for her service to France, and in 1919 she received the Legion of Honor.

Vinton, Warren Jay (1889-1969): Vinton suspended his graduate study at University of Michigan in November 1917 to serve as secretary of the Michigan Bureau of the American University Union in Europe. He also worked with the Red Cross in the Balkans from January to August 1919. Vinton later wrote a book on the New Deal and was the chief economist and planning officer of the United States Housing Authority.

Wallace, Hugh C. (1863-1931): The American ambassador to France from 1919 to 1921, Wallace received the Grand Cross of the Légion d'Honneur.

Watriss, Martha (1899-?): A New Yorker, Watriss interrupted her junior year at Bryn Mawr to go to France, sailing on November 30, 1917, and served at Red Cross canteens in Epernay and in

Germany until June 1919. She met Hall at the Coblenz aviation camp. After the war, she completed her degree in history at Bryn Mawr (class of 1919). In 1926, she married Sir Henry Thornton, president of the Canadian National Railways, whom she had met in France.

White, Amelia Elizabeth (1878-1972): The daughter of Horace White, the editor in chief of the *New York Evening Post*, Elizabeth White studied Greek and philosophy at Bryn Mawr (class of 1901). She directed the Preparatory Trade School in New York City (1908–1909) and taught English at Bryn Mawr (1912) before the war. She served with the Red Cross as a nursing assistant at a French military hospital in Châlons-sur-Marne.

Wilhelm, Crown Prince of Germany (1882-1951): The son of Kaiser Wilhelm II, Prince Friedrich Wilhelm led the German Fifth Army assaults at Verdun and elsewhere. When his father abdicated at the time of the Armistice, the Crown Prince was barred from the throne and from his military command.

Wilhelm II, Emperor of Germany (1859-1941): The last German kaiser and king of Prussia, Wilhelm II ruled from 1888 until he was forced to abdicate November 9, 1918. He went into exile in Holland, where he spent the rest of his life. His vacillating but aggressive foreign policies and rivalry with his royal British cousins contributed to the outbreak of the Great War.

Wilson, Woodrow (1856-1924): President of the United States (1912–1920), Wilson ran in 1916 on a platform of neutrality. Following the renewal of unrestricted submarine warfare, he asked Congress in April 1917 to declare war on Germany. He visited Paris in December 1918 and returned for the Peace Conference that prepared the Treaty of Versailles, in part based on Wilson's "Fourteen Points" speech in January 1918, in which he proposed a League of Nations and political self-determination.

Worthington, Louisa Skinner (1879-1960): A canteen worker in Châlons-sur-Marne and Coblenz, Worthington was decorated with the Croix de Guerre for her service from February 1918 to May 1919. She published a novel, *Leonore Lends a Hand* (1922), after the war. The daughter of a Cincinnati lawyer, she married Beverly Bond, a professor of history at the University of Cincinnati, in 1933.

Appendix 2: Selected Chronology of World War I

This timeline presents some of the major events of World War I but is not comprehensive. The selection has favored events that took place along the Western Front and that are especially relevant to the Champagne region. Actions taking place at locations that Margaret Hall photographed are underlined.

1914

June 28	In Sarajevo, Archduke Franz Ferdinand of Austria-Hungary is assassinated.
July 28	Austria-Hungary declares war on Serbia and attacks Belgrade the next day.
August 1	Germany, bound by treaty to Austria-Hungary, declares war on Russia, in response to Russia's mobilization in previous days.
August 1/2	German troops cross the border into Luxembourg.
August 2-3	Germany requests to pass through Belgium to France; Belgium refuses.
August 3	Germany declares war on France.
	Germany masses troops along borders to prepare for invasion of Belgium and France.
August 4	Germany declares war on neutral Belgium and invades.
	Britain declares war on Germany.
📷 August 6	German forces move into France to enter <u>Longwy</u> on the Luxembourg border.
	Austria-Hungary declares war on Russia.
	Serbia declares war on Germany.

Siege of Liège

August 4-5	German advance toward city meets resistance from Belgian defenders.
August 6	German military initiates the Siege of Liège with barrage on the city.
August 7	Germany takes the city but troops remain embattled with fortresses surrounding the area.
August 16	Final fortresses defending Liège are overcome.

August 7-14	Battle of Mulhouse France's first incursion into Alsace and Lorraine territory, provinces lost to Germany in the Franco-Prussian War (1871). On August 8, French military capture the city of Mulhouse but withdraw again after a German counterattack the next day. Conflict in the area continues, August 14–24: see Battle of Frontiers, below.
August 9-22	British Expeditionary Force (BEF) disembarks in France.
August 12	France declares war on Austria-Hungary.
August 19	Pres. Woodrow Wilson declares neutrality of United States.
August 20	German forces occupy Brussels, Belgium.

Battle of the Frontiers

August 21-23 — Battle of the Ardennes
On August 21, French armies advance in the Ardennes but encounter unexpected German forces. French are soon routed and retreat, August 23–24. Locales involved include Neufchateau, Briey, Sedan, Stenay, and Verdun.

August 23 — The Battle of Mons opens; it constitutes the first major action of the BEF.

August 23 — German troops execute over six hundred Belgian civilians in Dinant.

August 24-25 — French army continues to hold on in Lorraine and pushes German troops back past Nancy. The French army in Alsace is ordered to retreat and withdraws from Mulhouse, which passes into German hands for the remainder of the war.

August 26-28 — French forces retreating through Sedan and Stenay halt there briefly and engage with pursuing German forces and briefly stall latter's progress. Sedan will remain in German hands for four years.

August 28-29 — Conflict continues around Amiens, Compiègne, Guise, Saint-Quentin, Soissons; during these conflicts many French towns and villages are falling into German hands.

In late August, German forces continue to push westward across Belgium, taking territory from French and BEF troops as they go, including Mons, Charleroi, and Namur; German occupation of Namur sets the stage for invasion of northern France.

August 25-28 — German occupiers sack Louvain, Belgium, including the destruction of its medieval library.

August 26-30 — German forces defeat Russians in Battle of Tannenberg.

August 30 — German plane bombs Paris. Bombing raids of the city will continue through September 1918.

September 1 — German advance southwest across France has brought forces to within thirty miles of Paris. The next day, French government leaves Paris, relocating to Bordeaux until November.

September 2 — Germans take Laon, France.

September 4 — Germans occupy Châlons-sur-Marne and Reims in Champagne. They shell Reims briefly that morning.

First Battle of the Marne

September 6-12 — French halt the German advance toward Paris.

September 12 — Gen. Ferdinand Foch retakes Châlons-sur-Marne, and Germans also withdraw from Reims.

September 7-14 — Germans defeat Russians at Masurian Lakes.

First Battle of the Aisne

German forces in Champagne retreat to Aisne River, where they literally entrench, initiating large-scale trench warfare on the Western Front.

September 13 — France again in control of Soissons and Amiens.

September 16 — Germans take Craonne and are entrenched along the Chemin des Dames; BEF troops at Aisne River also entrench.

182   Letters and Photographs from the Battle Country

1914

September 19	German artillery in the hills near <u>Reims</u> bombard the city, and the iconic <u>medieval cathedral</u> burns.
September 24	Saint-Mihiel taken by German forces, which will hold this position over the Meuse River as a strategic salient (bulge into the enemy's line) until 1918.

Battle of Yser

Along the Yser River in Belgium, north of <u>Ypres</u> and connected with the North Sea (and thereby the English Channel), Allied and German forces struggle to gain the advantage in the "Race to the Sea" and then the Battle of Yser.

October 16	German attack at Dixmude opens the fight for the Yser, although the town continues to hold out until November.
October 26–27	Belgians begin deliberate flooding of the area between Neiuport on the coast and Dixmude, ten miles inland, which holds the German forces to the east bank. Other locales involved include Ostend and <u>Zeebrugge</u>.

First Battle of Ypres

In Belgium, conflicts continue as German forces advance across Belgium, into Flanders, and toward northern France. On October 4, <u>Lens</u> falls to attackers and on October 9–10, Antwerp is captured. The city of Ypres is a critical point en route to the French border and the English Channel. Fighting in October and November takes place across the north-south front in Belgium and down to Armentières just across the border in France.

October 13	British forces are established in Ypres, prepared to defend the city.
November 1–2	Germans take Messines Ridge.
November 11	Germans advance line between Messines Ridge and Menin Road Ridge, engaging BEF, and also begin bombing Ypres.

Although the Germans make important gains throughout the months, including territory directly to the north and south of Ypres, the city itself remains in Allied control, creating a salient that the attackers are not able to reduce.

October 29	Turkey enters the war on the side of the Central Powers.
December 25	"Christmas Truce" is observed by some soldiers on Western Front.
December 20 –March 1915	First Battle of Champagne and First Battle of Artois

A primary French effort of winter and spring 1915, the offensive in Champagne comprises several coordinated supporting plans, including that in Artois. The French attack in both areas opens December 17–20 and continues, with marginal gains, into January, when the German counterattack begins. Engagements in the Champagne region continue into the spring, with no meaningful progress on either side but enormous casualties on both sides.

1915

January 31	Germans use poison gas at Bolimar, Poland.
February 4	Germany announces a "war zone" from the Channel to north of the British Isles for unrestricted U-boat attacks on all Allied and neutral shipping.
February 19 –December 20	Dardanelles Campaign (Gallipoli)
	Allies attempt, but fail, to gain control of the Dardannelles Straits in Turkey.
March 21	First German zeppelin bombing of Paris.

Second Battle of Ypres

On April 22, the German assault opens with chlorine gas attack from Langemarck, north of Ypres. British forces counterattack the next day but meet strong German resistance, including more gas attacks. In the following week, both sides mount drives that gradually make modest gains around Ypres but end in late May with little change in the line of battle. Allies still hold Ypres but Germans have substantially reduced the salient around the city, including taking Pilckem [Pilcom] Ridge.

April 24	The roundup and subsequent genocide of Armenians begins in Turkey.
April 28-May 1	The International Congress of Women at The Hague organized by Aletta Jacobs and Jane Addams drafts resolutions to foster peace, including approval of women's suffrage.
May 7	German U-boat torpedoes British liner *Lusitania*, killing over a thousand people, more than one hundred of whom are American.
May 9-June 18	Second Battle of Artois

Preceded by five days of shelling, a new French offensive in the Artois begins May 8. Vimy Ridge is a prime objective of the French but remains in German control.

May 23	Italy declares war on Austria-Hungary.
June 23-July 7	First of twelve battles of Isonzo, Italy.
September 25 -mid October	Second Battle of Champagne and Third Battle of Artois

Two French offensives launch September 25, both aimed particularly at weakening the German front by disrupting rail lines, with taking Mézières and Vimy Ridge as specific goals. There are substantial casualties but no real territorial gains. France makes renewed attempts in October but with no better results.

October 7	Germany and Austria-Hungary attack Serbia.

1916

Battle of Verdun

When the German assault begins on February 21, French forces hold the city of Verdun, which is protected by a ring of forts, including Douaumont and Vaux. The road into Verdun from Bar-le-Duc, later called la Voie sacrée, is key to French defense as the only supply route to Verdun and this corner of the front. Other critical positions fought over in surrounding months include le Mort Homme, which Germans gain control of on May 29 and hold until August 1917; Thiaumont Farm; and Forts Souville, Tavannes, and Laufée. In ensuing months, a German advance draws close to the city, but the French retain control.

February 25	Germans seize Fort Douaumont.

*Look for **Verdun** to identify other key developments in this battle.*

April 20	France deploys a squadron of American volunteer pilots, known as the Lafayette Escadrille.
April 23-May 1	German occupying forces deport roughly 25,000 civilians from Lille, Roubaix, and Tourcoing in occupied northern France.
April 24-May 1	The Easter Rising in Ireland is repressed by the British.
May 8	Accidental explosion at Fort Douaumont near Verdun kills hundreds of the German garrison.

1916

	May 31-June 1	Naval battle of Jutland in the North Sea confirms British naval supremacy.
📷	June 1-8	German forces take Fort Vaux northwest of **Verdun**.
	June 3	National Defense Act passes in U.S. Congress, expanding U.S. military forces.
	June 4-September	Russian Brusilov Offensive against Austro-Hungarians takes place in what is today Ukraine.
	June 22-23	Germans release a newly developed diphosgene gas on the French lines during the fighting in **Verdun** conflict.

Battle of the Somme

	June 24	BEF and French forces launch preliminary bombardment of Somme offensive earlier than planned to aid French defense of **Verdun**.
	July 1	Allied infantry attack along the front initiates the battle. The date will become notorious for the immense casualties suffered by British troops, especially in their advance along the northern end of the line. After July 1, Somme and Verdun battles will proceed together into the fall.

*Look for **Somme** to identify other key developments in this battle.*

	August 27	Romania declares war on Austria-Hungary.
	August 29	Field Marshal Paul von Hindenburg becomes chief of staff of the German Army, with Erich Ludendorff as his quartermaster-general. Ludendorff's strategy will largely direct the German war effort from this point.
	September 5	German commanders review the situation around Verdun and relinquish the "hold at all costs" strategy that has been pursued.
	September 15	Renewed British attack in the **Somme** conflict, including use of tanks.
📷	October 24	Following a French offensive initiated on October 19, the Allies retake Fort Douaumont and a week later Fort Vaux near Verdun. Fighting continues in the area into December.
	December 7	David Lloyd George becomes British prime minister.
	December 8	Gen. Robert Nivelle replaces Joseph Joffre as French commander.
	December 18	Wilson proposes a "league of nations."

1917

	January 22	Wilson advocates "peace without victory" in an address to the Senate.
	February 1	Germany resumes unrestricted submarine warfare on neutral shipping vessels, which had been suspended for over a year; United States officially severs diplomatic relations with Germany on February 3.
	February 24	With a preliminary manoeuvre on the **Somme**, Germany initiates a major withdrawal of its forces to the heavily fortified Hindenburg Line in order to consolidate its positions on the Western Front.
	March 1	American newspapers publish the telegram of January 16 in which Germany approached Mexico for a military alliance.
	March 5	Wilson inaugurated for his second term in office.

March 8	"February" Russian Revolution begins. Tsar Nicholas II abdicates March 15.
March 14–April 5	Germany implements the major stage of the military withdrawal to the Hindenburg Line, this stage concentrated on the northern part of the front. Troops destroy the territory as they pass through in order to leave as little as possible that the Allies can use.
April 6	Wilson signs Congress's declaration of war on Germany.

Battle of Arras

April 9	BEF infantry attack along the front from Vimy Ridge to south of Arras after extensive preparatory artillery and aerial bombardments of the German line. Over most of a week, fighting pushes the Germans back as far as Lens.
April 9–12	Canadians capture Vimy Ridge, a key point of German defense in the area.
April 16	In coordination with Battle of Arras to the north, French Nivelle offensive along the Chemin des Dames northwest and east of Reims opens in mid April, pushing towards Laon, but gains little territory. By early May, it has petered out.
April–June	French war effort is strained by protests and mutinies within the armed forces on the Western Front as well as civil protests and strikes.
May 15	Gen. Philippe Pétain replaces Nivelle as commander of the French Army.
May 18	Gen. John J. Pershing named commander of American Expeditionary Force (AEF). He lands in France June 13.
July 1–16	Battle of Messines, Flanders: opens on June 7 with the explosion of nineteen mines previously set in tunnels under the ridge, then held by German troops. British forces secure the ridge.

Third Battle of Ypres

mid July	Allied aerial and artillery attacks are underway to prepare for planned infantry assault.
July 31	Advance begins in morning, including an opening assault on German-held Pilckem Ridge, and gains territory by evening. Over ensuing months, poor weather contributes to slow progress.
September 20–25	BEF takes Menin Road Ridge.
November 6	Canadians take Passchendaele village and Passchendaele Ridge soon after (November 10).
August 20	French attack in Verdun recaptures le Mort Homme, which German forces have held since spring 1916.
October 24 –November 10	In the Battle of Caporetto, Italian forces are defeated by a combined Austro-Hungarian and German initiative.
November 7	In the "October" Revolution in Russia, Bolshevik Vladimir Lenin seizes power.
November 16	Georges Clemenceau becomes French premier.
November 20 –December 7	Battle of Cambrai *In a new offensive and incorporating tank warfare into the attack, Allies make initial gains but end the battle having lost most of these to German counteroffensive.*
December 9	Defeated, Romania signs the Armistice of Focșani with the Central Powers.

December 10	Nobel Peace Prize is awarded to the International Committee of the Red Cross.
December 15	Bolshevik armistice with the Central Powers concluded.

1918

January 8	Wilson proposes Fourteen Points for peace negotiation at joint session of Congress.
January 30	German planes bomb Paris. By September 15 over 660 bombs fall in the Paris region.
March	Influenza outbreaks occur at U.S. military bases.
March 3	Russia signs the Treaty of Brest-Litovsk.

Ludendorff Offensives: part 1/ Michael

March 21-April 5	Ludendorff initiates a series of spring offensives with Operation Michael, south of Arras, which is very effective its first day, soon flags, and drags on to April 5.
March 23	Germans begin long-range shelling of Paris using one or more giant Krupp guns known as the "Paris Guns." On March 29, the Church of Saint-Gervais is hit.
March 26-April 3	British and French authorities agree to place armies under unified command for better coordination—French general Ferdinand Foch is designated. Details of command structure are still being worked out through April 14. May 1, Pershing declares that AEF will not be folded into the mix.

Ludendorff Offensives: part 2/ Georgette

April 9	Germans launch an attack along the Lys River in Flanders and break the Allied line, held by the BEF.
April 10	BEF routed from Armentières and Messines Ridge.
April 17-18	Renewed German offensive pushes BEF from Mount Kemmel.
April 22-23	Royal Navy executes raids on ports at Ostend and Zeebrugge on the coast of German-occupied Belgium in an attempt to block the waterways and primarily to disrupt U-boat activity. The effort fails.
April 23	British and French commanders create a military relief plan that will allow troops to rotate sectors.

Ludendorff Offensives: part 3/ Blücher

May 27	German forces attack across the Aisne River, gaining the primary objective, Chemin des Dames, the same day. The advance proceeds well for several days, almost reaching Soissons (May 28) and Reims, but the advance is too quick and compromises the troops' ability to hold their gains.
June 5	Allied resistance has stopped the German advance at the Marne, its southernmost tip at Belleau Wood and Château-Thierry.
May 28	An American division, with French support, routs German forces holding the town of Cantigny in the **Somme**.

Ludendorff Offensives: part 4/ Gneisenau

June 9-14	German attack in the areas of Compiègne and Soissons makes little progress against French forces, which had advance warning of the offensive.

June 5-26 — In the battles of Belleau Wood and Château-Thierry on the Marne, two divisions of the AEF under French command push back the German advance.

Ludendorff Offensives: part 5/ Marneschutz-Reims

July 15-17 — Germans forces advance on both sides of Reims in an effort to close the salient around the city and take Châlons-sur-Marne; the drive fails.

Second Battle of the Marne

July 15-17 — Marneschutz-Reims (see above) fails.

July 18 — Rapid Allied counteroffensive along the Marne turns failed German assault into the beginnings of an extensive rout. Along the Aisne River, American divisions fighting at Soissons in conjunction with French infantry are attacked with gas.

August 6 — Allies have pushed German line back to the Aisne River, between Soissons and Reims, eradicating the salient to the west of Reims.

Battle of Amiens

August 8-21 — Allied forces reduce German salients along the line between Arras and Montdidier. Ludendorff will later call August 8 the "black day of the German army," when over 15,000 exhausted soldiers surrender to the Allies.

August 26 — Substantial swath of the German front between Ypres and Péronne pushed eastward.

September 4 — Allies have gained considerable territory in Flanders, once again reaching Ypres.

September 2 — Ludendorff orders withdrawal of troops to the Hindenburg Line, which will proceed in ensuing weeks.

September 4 — Margaret Hall lands in France.

September 5 — Hall arrives in Paris.

Saint-Mihiel Offensive

September 12-16 — Americans, with French support, capture Saint-Mihiel, the anchor point of a salient that the Germans have held since 1914.

September 15 — Air raid on Paris by waves of planes. Hall watches.

September 25 — Hall arrives at Châlons-sur-Marne.

The Hundred Days: Allied Final Offensive

The culminating Allied offensive of the war encompasses coordinated drives along the front from the north in Belgium south through France toward Nancy. American divisions serve in several areas, but the AEF has responsibility primarily for the line from the Argonne Forest eastward to the Meuse River, a key portion of attack in the **Battle of Meuse-Argonne.** *The assignment anticipates drives north through the Argonne toward Grandpré and also through Varennes and Montfaucon to Romagne, and AEF troops will also advance along the Meuse to Dun-sur-Meuse and then Stenay. Even as ceasefire discussions proceed in October and November, fighting along the Western Front continues, and retreating German forces take a terrible toll on lives and infrastructure.*

September 25-26 — Aerial and artillery bombardments on the German front in the Meuse-Argonne and Champagne prepare the areas for the advance of AEF and French infantry.

1918

September 26	French and AEF divisions advance toward enemy positions, Americans moving north into the Argonne Forest and along a line eastward to the Meuse River.
September 27	American troops take Montfaucon.
September 29	American divisions fighting alongside BEF in the area of Cambrai and Saint-Quentin attack Bellicourt Tunnel, where rousted German troops cause heavy American losses.
September 30	Bulgaria concludes armistice.
October	Influenza pandemic spreads through the military.
October 2-6	The "Lost Battalion" of the 77th Division is pinned down in the Argonne Forest by surrounding German forces.
October 3-4	Germany and Austria-Hungary approach the United States with a request for ceasefire negotiations.
October 8	Allied offensive near Cambrai begins with artillery barrage.
October 10	The AEF has gained control of the **Argonne Forest**.
October 13-20	Hall assists at emergency hospital for the wounded and sick in Écury, south of Châlons.
October 16	American forces have advanced through the **Argonne Forest** and move on their objective, Grandpré, which they will take on October 27.
October 24	Italians are victorious in the Battle of Vittorio Veneto.
October 30	Armistice of Mudros ends conflict between the Allies and the Ottoman Empire.
November 1-7	In a new drive assigned as part of the **Meuse-Argonne** offensive, AEF forces move on to Sedan; French troops enter Sedan on November 7.
November 4	Austria-Hungary ceases hostilities, and armistice with Italy takes effect.
November 9	Kaiser Wilhelm II of Germany abdicates and flees to the Netherlands, with the Crown Prince.
November 11	Germany signs an Armistice with the Allies. Hostilities end at 11:00 A.M.
December 13	Woodrow Wilson arrives to prepare for the peace conference.

1919

January 18	The peace conference at Paris begins.
June 28	The Treaty of Versailles is signed between the Allies and Germany.
July 14	Bastille Day victory parade in Paris.
August 11	Hall boards the SS *France* for her return to New York.

1920

March 19	U.S. Senate fails to ratify the Versailles Treaty. The United States will not become a member of the League of Nations.
August 26	U.S. Senate ratifies the Nineteenth Amendment, granting American women suffrage.

Appendix 3: Places and Monuments: The Geography of War

Albert: A market town in the Somme region, after August 1914 Albert was in Allied hands but very close to the Amiens to Arras line held by the BEF. In the fall of 1916, during the Battle of the Somme, BEF forces assaulted the German line around Albert, pushing the front away from the town. German troops took the town again in the May–June 1918 offensive, and Allies recaptured it at the end of August.

Amiens: The capital of the Department of the Somme, seventy-five miles from Paris, this vital railway junction was contested over four years by the Allied and German forces. Briefly occupied by German forces in August and September 1914, it was in Allied hands for much of the war but always close to the front and suffered considerable damage. On August 8, 1918 (called "the black day of the German Army" by Gen. Erich Ludendorff), British, Australian, and Canadian troops, using hundreds of tanks, made a surprise attack on German positions east of Amiens. Supported by French and American forces to the south and east, the operation weakened German morale and brought an end to trench warfare in the area.

Anizy[-le-Chateau]: A village in the Aisne region, Anizy-le-Chateau is north of Soissons and close to the western end of the Chemin des Dames. Primarily in German hands throughout the war, it was contested in the French attack on the area in April 1917. See also Mont des Singes.

Armentières: An industrial center on the French border with Belgium and ten miles directly south of Ypres, Armentières was in the midst of the battle in Flanders in October 1914. Although not taken by German forces at that time, it was within a few miles of the frontlines for most of the war. In the second Ludendorff offensive in April 1918, BEF troops abandoned the city, and it remained in German hands until October. Almost completely destroyed, it was rebuilt after the war.

Argonne: This forested and mountainous region, between the Aisne and Meuse Rivers and east of Reims and northwest of Verdun, was the area designated for the major American offensive that began on September 26, 1918. The difficult terrain impeded the progress of American troops for several weeks, including the fight to take the strategic hill of the village of Montfaucon.

Arras: About thirty miles directly south of the Belgian border, the city of Arras had served northern France as its primary grain market. Allied forces held staunchly to the city at the beginning of the war and retained it throughout, but it remained close to the front and sustained substantial damage from shelling. As a primary location on the BEF's section of the front, Arras also served as an anchor for the major BEF offensive in the spring of 1917, which included the capture of Vimy Ridge.

Belleau Wood: This forest west of Château-Thierry was taken in the German advance of May 1918, which threatened to reach Paris. In June, the Germans were halted here by American marines with the 2nd Division in an action coordinated with the French Army.

Bellicourt Tunnel: See Saint-Quentin.

Bordeaux: Shipping was directed to this major port city in southwest France in order to evade German U-boats operating in the English Channel.

Bourlon and Bourlon Wood: The village of Bourlon, about twenty miles southeast of Arras and six miles west of Cambrai, was behind German lines for much of the war. Allied attempts to break through the German line took place with the Battle of Cambrai in 1917, in which BEF forces fought German troops in the village and the wood over several days in November and December 1917, although both remained in German hands. The outcome was different in the fall of 1918, when the village and Cambrai were liberated, including a rapid advance through the village and the wood by Canadian troops.

Cambrai: Twenty-five miles southeast of Arras, the town of Cambrai had in its vicinity rail lines, a canal, and nearby heights that made it a valuable and defensible position. Taken in the German advance in October 1914, it remained behind German lines until the end of the war. During the Battle of Cambrai in November 1917, BEF troops came within a few miles of the city but were pushed back by the Germans. See also Bourlon.

Cenon [Senon]: Northeast of downtown Bordeaux, Cenon today is a suburb of the city. The trek across the Garonne River to the old Cenon town hall is about three miles.

Châlons-sur-Marne: Today renamed Châlons-en-Champagne, the capital of Champagne and of the Department of the Marne, this main railroad intersection between Reims and Verdun was bombed heavily in 1918. It was the site of the busy Red Cross Cantine des Deux Drapeaux where Hall worked. During the First Battle of the Marne, the Germans occupied the city from September 4 until September 11, 1914.

Château de Pinon: This château, northeast of Soissons and west of the Chemin des Dames, was headquarters for the German First Army. Kaiser Wilhelm II and the crown prince visited there. The residence was destroyed by fighting in 1917 and 1918.

Château-Thierry: A city on the Marne fifty miles northeast of Paris, and partway between Paris and Châlons-sur-Marne, Château-Thierry was overrun in the German sweep through the region in September 1914. Back in French hands until Gen. Erich Ludendorff's offensive of May 27, 1918, it then became the southern-most point of the German salient between Reims and Paris. There in early June 1918, American forces under French command prevented the Germans from advancing across the Marne and proceeded in later July to push the Germans back to their 1914 line, but the city had sustained considerable damage during the attack and counterattack.

Chemin des Dames: This roughly ten-mile ridge, with a view over the Aisne River and surrounding country, runs from its western point near the village of Pinon to an eastern end at what was the village of Craonne. During the war, the Fort de la Malmaison anchored its western end. Because of its vantage and its proximity to Soissons (to the southwest), Laon (north), and Reims (less than twenty miles to the southeast), it offered great strategic value to whichever army could control it. Aside from various skirmishes, three protracted battles were fought in 1914, 1917, and 1918 over this ridge. Following the First Battle of the Marne, the Germans retreated to this plateau between September and November 1914 and created deep shelters in its underground stone quarries. In an attempt to recapture it in April 1917, French and Senegalese troops suffered 130,000 casualties in a charge on the ridge; large-scale mutinies followed in May. The minimal gains made by the French in April were improved in October, when German troops withdrew a few miles farther north in the face of a renewed French drive. One of the drives in Gen. Erich Ludendorff's spring 1918 offensive captured the ridge again, and in August to October, fighting was renewed here during the final Allied offensive. Some areas along the Chemin were demolished during the course of the war; the village of Craonne (below) was rebuilt in a new location.

Coblenz, Germany: The American 1st Division entered this city at the confluence of the Rhine and the Moselle Rivers in December 1918, in the first phase of the postwar occupation of the Rhineland. Maj. Gen. Joseph T. Dickman made his headquarters as commander-in-chief of the Army of Occupation in the Fortress Ehrenbreitstein on the eastern side of the Rhine. Some American troops began to return home from the American sector of the Rhineland by April 1919, but the occupying American Forces in Germany did not completely withdraw until January 1923.

Cologne, Germany: After the Armistice, the British occupied the bridgehead city of Cologne on the Rhine, which had been a cultural center from Roman times. They retained military control over the zone of the Rhineland north of the American sector under the terms of the Treaty of Versailles and remained there until 1929.

Coucy-le-Chateau: The town of Coucy-le-Chateau, ten miles north of Soissons, was occupied by the German army in September 1914 and remained behind German lines until the spring of 1917. Then, as the Germans effected their withdrawal to the Hindenburg Line, portions of the medieval castle, with its dominating view of the surrounding area, were strategically demolished and the town and nearby villages were also largely destroyed. The occupiers did leave behind, however, a concrete emplacement that had supplied the foundation for one of the German long-range guns.

Courteau: Most likely Courteau was a village on a hill just one mile west of downtown Château-Thierry. Today there is a neighborhood in that location called Courteau Hameau. One photograph, a stereograph, shows the ruins of the village after the war; the *Catalogue of Copyright Entries* from the Library of Congress for 1919 (vol. 14, pt. 4, p. 226) has an entry for the photograph (but an apparent typographical error has misidentified it as "Courteass").

Craonne: A village at the eastern end of the Chemin des Dames, Craonne was on the German frontline from September 1914. It stood directly in the path of Gen. Robert Nivelle's spring 1917 offensives, and although the outcome of the April 16 attack put the area back in French control, nothing remained of the village per se. An arboretum is in the location of Vieux Craonne, and the Craonne that exists today was rebuilt in the 1920s less than a mile southwest of the original.

Dun-sur-Meuse: Northeast of Romagne, the town of Dun-sur-Meuse is partway between Verdun to the south and Stenay to the north; on the Meuse River, it also encompasses the heights of Dun Haut, which afford a vantage over the territory below and a strongly defensible position. It was well behind German lines for most of the war; Allies finally reached the town at the beginning of November 1918, when AEF troops succeeded in crossing the river despite German artillery fire.

Écury: A village five miles south of Châlons, Écury-sur-Coole served as a hospital base for the front in Champagne. In the summer of 1918, Evacuation Hospital No. 5 was set up there.

Epernay: A fortified medieval city famous for its champagne wine production, Epernay is about twenty miles northeast of Châlons and, like the other towns in the area, was briefly occupied in September 1914 and suffered bombardments at that time and again in 1918.

Étain: This town in the Meuse Department, less than fifteen miles east of Verdun, was bombarded on August 24, 1914, by the Germans, who entered two days later and occupied it until the Armistice. During their advance into Étain and the surrounding area, the Germans arbitrarily executed civilians and used them as human shields.

Fort de Brimont: North of Reims, this fort guarded the Aisne canal and the railway line to Laon. The Germans captured the fort, enabling them to shell the city. They held this position, where they kept French prisoners of war, from September 1914 to October 1918, just a month before Hall visited it.

Fort de Douaumont: To the east of Verdun, this fort, protected by heavy gun turrets and a thick, steel-reinforced concrete roof, fell to the German attack on the city in February 1916 without resistance. After eight months, during which the Germans used this vantage point to shell the defenders of Verdun, it was recaptured on October 24, 1916, by the elite Colonial Infantry Regiment of Morocco, with Senegalese sharpshooters and several Somali companies, under the command of Gen. Charles Mangin.

Fort de la Laufée: One of the smaller fortifications in the ring of Verdun defenses, Laufée is south and slightly east of Fort du Vaux. Intense fighting occurred around it during Battle of Verdun, especially in June and July 1916, as German forces repeatedly assaulted Forts Souville and Tavannes.

Fort de la Malmaison: Lying at the western end of the Chemin des Dames, northeast of Soissons, this position was repeatedly contested, despite the fact that the French had deemed the fort unable to withstand modern barrages and chose not to arm it for defense before the war. German troops occupied Malmaison in the sweep to the Marne in 1914 and held it until it was retaken by French Zouaves on October 23, 1917. The Germans recaptured the fort again on May 27, 1918, and held it until September 28, when it fell to the French.

Fort de la Pompelle: Just east of Reims, this unarmed fort was part of a nineteenth-century defensive ring; it was taken by German troops on September 4, 1914, without a contest, and recaptured twenty days later. In March, June, and July 1918, the fort resisted repeated German attacks.

Fort de Vaux: Southeast of Fort Douaumont, Vaux was the second French fort near Verdun to be lost. On June 7, 1916, Vaux fell to gas and flame attacks directed by Crown Prince Wilhelm. Like Douaumont, Vaux had been stripped of much of its defensive artillery. Maj. Sylvain Eugène Raynal led the heroic resistance of a small group in room-to-room combat within the fort, and he surrendered only after exhausting his water supplies. Gen. Charles Mangin recaptured Vaux in November 1916, after retaking Douaumont.

Glorieux: In this suburb of Verdun, American Field Hospital No. 114 conducted divisional triage in a former French military hospital. In October 1918, American Evacuation Hospital No. 15 moved to Glorieux, to receive wounded from the fighting in the Ardennes.

Homburg (Saarland), Germany: Homburg, a town twenty miles from the French border and previously a part of the German state of Bavaria, became a part of the Saarland with the Treaty of Versailles, which redefined that area in order to meet France's postwar need for coal. In the nineteenth century, Homburg was known for its textiles and hospital.

Jard: A municipal garden with a promenade and canals at Châlons-sur-Marne, designed by the landscape architect André Le Nôtre.

Juvigny: The village of Juvigny had military significance because of its position on the road between Soissons, five miles to the south, and Saint-Quentin. Taken during the initial German sweep in 1914, Juvigny remained in German hands, but very close to the frontlines, when positions stabilized in the fall. The Allies reclaimed the village in the spring of 1917 only to lose it again a year later. At the end of August 1918, AEF and French forces launched an attack that led to several days of intense combat before their troops reentered the village and discovered that Germans had secreted themselves in underground caverns. The village the AEF then liberated had been demolished.

Laon: Occupied by the Germans for almost the entirety of the war, Laon was a commercial and agricultural city north of the Chemin des Dames. After the Armistice, Laon became a distribution center for relief, including medical support, and reconstruction activities in the Aisne Department.

La Veuve: A village nearly seven miles north of Châlons-sur-Marne, where an American hospital was located.

Lens: Between Arras to the south and Armentières to the north, Lens is an industrial city specializing in coal and iron. By the beginning of October 1914, as the Western Front settled into the stalemate of the coming years, Lens was at the German frontline, where it would remain until the fall of 1918. When the German occupiers withdrew, they left the city in ruins, flooding coal mines and destroying machinery.

Lille: Ten miles from Armentières, Lille is a center of manufacturing and trade at the border of France and Belgium. Despite fortifications meant to make it a principal position in France's defensive line before the war, Lille fell to German bombardment early in October 1914 and was occupied by German forces until October 1918. During the occupation, thousands of French civilians were deported from the city to provide labor in the occupied territory and Germany.

Long Wy: An industrial city at the French border where Belgium and Luxembourg meet, Long Wy (or Longwy) was taken by Germany at the outset of the war and remained in German occupied territory until the Armistice.

Madeleine Farm: On the road north of Montfaucon and southeast of Romagne, this farm figured prominently in the AEF drive through the Argonne in October 1918. German troops had used the farm to create a strong pocket of resistance, blocking the American advance in the immediate area from October 5 to 8 and taking a heavy toll. On October 9, three divisions managed to break through and take the farm.

Matougue[s]: A village, roughly six west of Châlons-sur-Marne, where French aviation groups, or "Groupes de Bombardement," were stationed.

Metz: An industrial city on the Moselle River, Metz is particularly rich in coal and metals. Metz is situated some thirty miles north of Nancy and thirty west of the border with Germany, in the part of Lorraine held by Germany from the end of the Franco-Prussian war in 1870 until 1918.

Mézières: Situated on an oxbow in the Meuse River, Mézières (today Charleville-Mézières and the capital of the Ardennes Department) is fifty miles northeast of Reims and less than ten miles from the closest Belgian border. German forces occupied the city in September 1914 and set up general headquarters there; the headquarters were bombed in 1915, but the attack missed Kaiser Wilhelm II. The city was also in the path of an Allied attack during the Battle of Amiens in 1918.

Mont des Singes: In German hands from September 1914, this heavily damaged hill in the Aisne region roughly nine miles from Soissons was repeatedly contested and became especially memorable in the April 1917 French attempt to regain the Chemin des Dames: colonial troops that captured the position overnight fell back in a storm; the next weeks witnessed mutinies. The hill changed hands between the French and Germans in October 1917, May 1918, and September 1918, when the Allies finally liberated it.

Montfaucon: This village ten miles northwest of Verdun in the Argonne fell to the German advance to the Marne in 1914 and remained in German hands until the fall of 1918. Situated on a strategic hill, it became an obstacle in the American drive northward through the Argonne, toward Romagne, and was only finally in Allied control at the beginning of October.

Mort Homme: This dramatically named hill nine hundred feet above the Meuse northwest of Verdun was the focus of intense fighting in the spring of 1916, with German and French forces struggling to dislodge one another from separate slopes of the hill in April. Having secured their position by June, the Germans created tunnels to quarter thousands of soldiers. It was retaken by the French in August 1917. The hill is situated west of the now-vanished village of Cumières.

Nancy: One hundred miles east of Châlons, the city of Nancy was occupied by German forces during and immediately after the Franco-Prussian War; returned to France in 1873, it became the capital of French Lorraine and was fortified before 1914 in anticipation of future conflict with Germany. In late August and early September 1914, advancing German forces attempted to take Nancy but ultimately failed, although the city was bombarded heavily. Nancy served the Allies as an important rail center during the war, and the 1st Division of the AEF took over a sector of the frontline at Nancy in October 1917.

Notre Dame-en-Vaux: The collegiate church in Châlons-sur-Marne, built in the twelfth century.

Ostend, Belgium: A seacoast city twenty miles west of Zeebrugge and twenty east of the border with France, Ostend fell to German control in October 1914. Allied efforts to undermine German naval operations would target Ostend as well as Zeebrugge in the spring of 1918.

Paris locations: Avenue des **Champs-Elysées** is a famous street in central Paris. On the western end lies the **Arc de Triomphe**, a nineteenth-century monument honoring Napoleonic generals and their victories; on the eastern end is the **Place de la Concorde**, where in 1920 the French Unknown Soldier was buried. Just north of the Champs-Elysées is **Elysée Palace**, the official residence of the French president, which served as AEF headquarters in 1919. A complex of military museums and monuments as well as a center of veterans' services, l'Hôtel National des Invalides was founded by Louis XIV to house disabled war veterans. It is the site of Napoleon I's tomb. **Bellevue Hospital** was the facility housed in Isadora Duncan's château near Bellevue Station in the Meudon suburb of Paris. Red Cross volunteers cared for patients arriving on hospital trains at **Gare de Vaugirard**, a station near Montparnasse. The **Hôtel de l'Arcade** is one block northwest of L'église de la **Madeleine**, a neoclassical nineteenth-century church. **Joinville-le-**

Pont is a Paris suburb where a pneumonia hospital was set up during the war. An ancient church, **Saint-Gervais** had been badly damaged by the German "Paris gun" on Good Friday 1918 in an attack that killed dozens of civilians. The Church of **St. Sulpice** served as a refugee center during the war. **The Bois** de Boulogne, a wooded park west of central Paris, has been a popular place for pleasure rides since the nineteenth century. To the north of the Bois is the suburb **Neuilly-sur-Seine**, where the **American Hospital** was founded in 1906 to serve the American expatriate community. During the war, a Red Cross mobile hospital was established there to care for Allied soldiers. South of the Bois is **Auteuil**, the site of Grand Prix races before the war; a hospital for gas injuries there (American Red Cross Military Hospital No. 5) was one of the first American tent hospitals in France. To the west, overlooking the Bois, is Fort **Mont-Valérien** in the suburb **Sûresnes**, also the site of an American military cemetery. Located at 33–35 Rue Caumartin, **Hôtel Petrograd** was used by the YWCA for housing during the war.

Pas de Calais: A department in the north of France, many of whose inhabitants became refugees, fleeing the ruins left by constant combat.

Pilckem [Pilcom] Ridge: German troops took this ridge north of Ypres in April 1915. The opening assault in the Third Battle of Ypres, the Battle of Pilckem Ridge, July 31 to August 2, 1917, comprised British and French forces advancing out from Ypres to the north, east, and south. While the Allied troops gained some ground, it was hard won.

Pinon: Between Laon to the north and Soissons to the south, this village near the western end of the Chemin des Dames was in German hands from September 1914 and suffered in several battles for that terrain. Retaken by the French in October 1917, the village of roughly five hundred inhabitants was reconstructed by Anne Morgan's relief group. In February 1918, the 26th Division of American infantry, under French command, held the western side of the Oise-Aisne canal between Pinon and Braye-en-Laonnois; in May 1918, German forces took the area again.

Reims: In 1914, the splendid Gothic cathedral in the city of Reims, where French kings were crowned, was damaged by German bombardment and a fire that destroyed the roof, some stained glass windows, and sculptures. The roof of the nearby Abbey Saint Rémi was also destroyed, and much of the town was leveled. The first shells fell on September 4, 1914, before German troops entered the city. After the French retook the city on September 13, shelling continued and killed German prisoners being nursed in the cathedral. Allied nations condemned the destruction, and the cathedral became a propaganda symbol of German aggression.

Romagne[-sous-Montfaucon]: A village in the Argonne five miles north of Montfaucon, Romagne had been captured by Germany at the beginning of the war and was occupied until AEF troops recaptured the village on October 14, 1918. Today it is the site of the Meuse-Argonne American Cemetery, with graves for more than fourteen thousand American soldiers. See also Madeleine Farm and Montfaucon.

Saint-Mihiel: South of Verdun and sixty miles east of Châlons-sur-Marne, the town of Saint-Mihiel is also a gateway to Metz, today the capital of the Lorraine region. Captured by German forces in September 1914, Saint-Mihiel was the anchor point of a major salient, or incursion, into French territory that the Allies were unable to reduce for four years. In September 1918, the Saint-Mihiel offensive provided the first major American victory, when AEF troops took the town as well as the rest of the area that had constituted the salient.

Saint-Quentin: In late August 1914, as German forces advanced into northern France, Gen. Joseph Joffre ordered a counterattack at the town of Saint-Quentin, but it fell into German control by August 29. Occupation of the area also allowed the German military to incorporate the Saint-Quentin Canal into its development of the Hindenburg Line, the heavily fortified complex of defensive positions built along a ninety-mile front. In 1918, an important struggle took place over this partly subterranean canal structure, where German soldiers were sheltered in the Bellicout Tunnel, thirty feet deep and four miles long: in late September and early October, British, Australian, and American troops broke through the main German defensive line. A famous photograph shows the British brigadier general John Vaughan Campbell addressing troops assembled on the steep slopes of the canal to congratulate them on their victory.

Sedan: Set in a bend of the Meuse in the Department of the Ardennes and less than ten miles from the Belgian border, Sedan was the site of the decisive French defeat by German forces on September 2, 1870, in the Franco-Prussian War. That defeat marked the fall of Napoleon III, the loss of the territories of Alsace and part of Lorraine, and the creation of the French Third Republic. After German forces occupied Sedan on August 25, 1914, it remained under German occupation for four years, and Kaiser Wilhelm II and Crown Prince Wilhelm had headquarters there. French troops reentered the city on November 7, 1918.

Soissons: Sixty-five miles northeast of Paris, on the Aisne River, the town of Soissons stands about ten miles southwest of the western end of the Chemin des Dames. German forces briefly occupied Soissons in September 1914, although bombardment from the frontlines would continue. German forces took the town again in May 1918, when it marked the western end of a salient established during the third Ludendorff offensive. Allies regained the town in August, but it had been looted and mined in the meantime; reconstruction took place in the 1930s.

Somme Py: A village on the road north from Châlons-sur-Marne to Charleville-Mézières, what was known as Somme Py in 1914 is today Sommepy-Tahure, created when Tahure was deemed too expensive and hazardous to rebuild. Intense fighting in this area occurred in the fall of 1915, when the French launched an offensive on the front in Champagne east of Reims. Although the offensive failed in any substantial way, the Allies retook the village of Tahure, but their advance stopped just short of Somme Py. In July 1918, the American 42nd Division joined the battle on the frontline at Somme Py, and the village was recaptured by Gen. Henri Gouraud at the end of September.

Souain: A village east of Reims and northeast of Châlons-sur-Marne, Souain and the other villages in this part of the Champagne-Ardenne region were taken during the German drive to the Marne in September 1914. The wooded area from Souain to Perthes-lès-Hurlus, another village to the east, became riddled with trenches in the following year, and during the French offensive of 1915, French and German troops fought fiercely for every foot of terrain. AEF troops were positioned near Souain in July 1918. Today Souain is known as Souain-Perthes-lès-Hurlus since the latter village was not rebuilt after the war.

Souilly: Village on *la Voie sacrée* (the Sacred Way), the only road kept open for trucks to bring men and supplies to Verdun. In the 1916 Battle of Verdun, Gen. Philippe Pétain made Souilly the headquarters of his Second Army, and from September 21, 1918, it served as headquarters for Gen. John Pershing and the American First Army.

Stenay: A town on the Meuse River between Verdun and Sedan, Stenay was occupied by the Germans from August 28, 1914, to the end of the war. The Château des Tilleuls here was used as headquarters by Crown Prince Wilhelm until February 1918. Stenay was taken by American forces on November 11, 1918.

Strasbourg: A major commercial and industrial center in the Alsace region, Strasbourg had been a point of contest in Europe for centuries before Germany claimed it in the Franco-Prussian War. The Treaty of Versailles officially returned the city to France.

St. Wendel, Germany: Sixty miles northeast of Metz, the city of St. Wendel was a rail center in the Saarland. See also Homburg.

Tahure: A village east of Reims and northeast of Châlons-sur-Marne, Tahure and the hill just north of it, the Butte de Tahure, were the scene of intense fighting in the fall of 1915, when German forces occupied the area, and again in the Allied advance north in the fall of 1918. There was nothing left of Tahure when it was recaptured in September, and the village was ultimately deemed so hazardous that a hundred years later it remains off-limits to casual visitors.

Treves, Germany: The city of Treves, called Trier in Germany, is situated on the Moselle River near the Luxembourg border. After the Armistice, an advance general headquarters of the AEF was established there, and American Red Cross workers arrived on December 8, 1918, to care for released prisoners of war. They remained to serve the Allied occupying forces in 1919.

Varennes[-en-Argonne]: A village in the Argonne forty miles northeast of Châlons-sur-Marne, Varennes was taken in the German advance in the fall of 1914 and remained close behind the German frontline for four years. It was liberated on September 26, 1918, as AEF troops drove north through the Argonne Forest.

Verdun: Situated on the Meuse River, east of Châlons, Verdun had been heavily fortified in the nineteenth century, protected by a ring of forts, Douaumont and Vaux among them. Its defensive features also included an interior fortress known as the citadel, which had been outfitted with subterranean chambers. The German army's initial sweep to the Marne in 1914 approached Verdun but did not take it; instead, German forces dug in north and east of the city, establishing a front that remained relatively unchanged from 1914 to 1916. A German bombardment on February 21, 1916, opened the Battle of Verdun, which would last until December, including a French counteroffensive that began in October. Although Germans forces seized surrounding forts, the French maintained a narrow passage—la Voie sacrée—to defend the city for the rest of the war, and Verdun became a powerful symbol of French endurance. The ten-month battle cost 163,000 French and 143,000 German lives. The area around Verdun was reclaimed by the Allies in September 1918, when the AEF drove northward through the Argonne Forest. Verdun and its forts (especially Douaumont and Vaux) were a symbol of French national pride; Hall visited these sites repeatedly. Today the massive war memorial at Verdun remains a site of pilgrimage.

Vimy Ridge: The high ground just west of the town of Vimy—partway between Arras, on the French side of the front, and Lens, on the German side—was a critical position in the German defense in this area as it looked over vital rail lines. French forces had taken but quickly lost the ridge in May 1915. During the BEF offensive east of Arras in 1917, Canadian troops took the ridge in a celebrated assault in mid April.

Voie sacrée: The "Sacred Way" was the name given to the narrow access route from Bar-le-Duc through which French troops and supplies could be transported north to Verdun.

Vouziers: On the Aisne River in the Ardennes and thirty miles northeast of Reims, the town of Vouziers was taken in the German advance south to Champagne in 1914 and remained north of the German line until the fall of 1918. A rail line passed though Vouziers, and in September 1918, the crown prince's army held this portion of the front during the Saint-Mihiel offensive. When French forces recaptured the town in October 1918, it had been demolished during the German retreat.

Wiesbaden, Germany: Roughly 130 miles northeast from Metz and 100 from the French border, the city of Wiesbaden was occupied by French forces in December 1918. It later became the home of the Inter-Allied Rhineland Commission.

Ypres, Belgium: A city in the province of West Flanders, Ypres had been a prosperous medieval commercial center known especially for its textile production. During the war it was the scene of three major battles, taking place in October and November 1914, April and May 1915, and from July to November 1917. Although German forces held territory in an arc around the city through most of the war, Germany never succeeded in capturing it. Ypres was, however, largely destroyed by 1918 but rebuilt in the years following.

Zeebrugge [Seebruge], Belgium: A seaport on the coast of Belgium, Zeebrugge constituted a strategic position for activities in the English Channel and the North Sea. The German advance across Belgium gained control of Zeebrugge and its port in 1914, after which it was used as a launch point for U-boat attacks on Allied shipping and naval operations. The Allies developed several plans over the years to block or disable access from the port, including possible attacks on the "Mole," a protective structure extending more than a mile into the channel. A major British effort in April 1918 failed in its objective. See also Ostend.

Appendix 4: Period Terms

Annamites: Indochinese from central Vietnam. Forces from the French colony served in France at the front, in medical units, and in factories.

Blighty: Military slang for England and for "home" more generally. It also meant a wound debilitating enough to send the injured home for recovery.

colonist: A soldier recruited from the French and English colonies, serving with the Allied forces.

cootie (slang): Lice.

Dakin: The Carrel-Dakin method of irrigating infected wounds with a diluted antiseptic solution of sodium hypochlorite and boric acid, which was developed during the war by chemists Henry Drysdale Dakin and Alexis Carrel at a hospital at Compiègne.

dirigible: Motorized airships, or German zeppelins, which were used to bomb England and France. They proved inaccurate and vulnerable to anti-aircraft and plane defenses.

Fokker: A German dogfighter, the twin-engine plane flown by the ace Manfred von Richthofen.

"French leave": A leave taken without permission.

Gothas: Large German twin-engine biplanes with a three-man crew that were first used in 1915, primarily in nighttime bombing raids on Paris and London, or on similar major targets.

"Janes": American slang for "girls."

M.P.: Military policeman.

puttee: Leg wrappings between the ankle and knee, used with various military uniforms.

"Republican": A reference to the "sister Republics" of France and America, whose political alliance goes back to the eighteenth century.

Salonica fever: Trench fever, or quintan fever, caused by bacteria transmitted by body lice.

sanitary trains: Hospital trains.

sausage balloon: A tethered observation balloon of the sort seen by Hall as she sailed from New York, and used as well as in the war zones.

75s: 75 millimeter French field guns, which were supplied to the American Expeditionary Force.

shell shock: What today would be called post-traumatic stress disorder. Manifestations ranged from muteness and seizures to verbal tics, fragmented speech, memory loss, and uncontrollable terrorizing flashbacks.

Taube: The *Taube* ("dove") was a German monoplane with bird-like wings with rounded tips. It served in the first months of World War I as a fighter, bomber, and reconnaissance craft. Its lack of maneuverability made it vulnerable to attack, and it was replaced by "Gotha" models starting in 1915.

zigzag: A staggered or back-and-forth movement. Also slang for drunk.

Appendix 5: Foreign Terms

abri: shelter
alerte: alarm, warning siren
allemand: German
ambulance: unit of mobile field hospital
avion: airplane
beaucoup fatiguée: much tired (non-standard French)
bidon: water bottle
blessé: casualty, the wounded
boche: German (derogatory)
bois: woods, park; the Bois de Boulogne in Paris
b[re]loque: "all-clear" signal, siren (or bugle) following an air raid
cafard: depression, "blues"
caisse: cash box, cash register
camarade: comrade, buddy
camion: truck, wagon
camionette: small truck or van
cantine: canteen
cave: wine cellar, basement
Ça y est!: That's it, got it!
centime: cent (1/100 of a franc) in the French monetary system. In 1914 a soldier's pay per day, later raised to five *centimes* (a *sou*) and finally 20 *centimes* in 1917.
C'est ça que j'aime: That is what I love.
C'est la paix: Peace has come, this is peace.
C'est un peu trop fort.: That goes a little too far.
C'est une vie de misère.: It's a miserable life.
chaise pliante: folding chair
chambres séparées: separate or enclosed rooms
cha[r]cuterie: pork sausages, ham, or chopped meats; delicatessen
chasseur: infantry, light cavalry; fighter plane
chef d'équipe: squad leader
chef de gare: station manager
clients: customers
confiture: jam preserves
consigne: deposit

couchés: wounded lying on litters
couronne: funeral wreath
couverts: place settings for the table
dames américaines: the American ladies
décolleté: low neckline
défendu: prohibited
directrice: director of canteen
en masse: in a group, massed
en repos: at rest, on relief
entréed: entered; humorously anglicized past tense of *entrer*
escadrille: squadron
essence: gasoline
Est-ce la paix?: Is it peace?
fabrique: factory, winery
Fatiguée Mlle?: Are you tired, Miss?
femme de chambre: chambermaid
Fête des Morts de la Guerre: November 2, day of the dead, especially war dead in 1914–1918
fêted: celebrated; humorously anglicized past tense of *fêter*
filleul: a wartime "godson," to whom one sent letters and packages
fou: mad
foyer du soldat: soldier's hostel, rest home
gare: train station
Gott mit uns. (G): God be with us.
grands blessés: the severely wounded
grippe: influenza
guerre: war
infirmier: male nurse, orderly
insupportable: intolerable
intime: intimate, cozy
jardin: garden
Kultur (G): culture (opposed to French civilization in propaganda)
La guerre est finie: The war is over.
lumière: light
marmite: pot
méd[e]cin chef: head doctor

militaire: soldier, the military
Mlle: mademoiselle, Miss
montéed: climbed; humorously anglicized past tense of *monter*
musette: satchel, backpack
On les aura!: We will get them!
pas vite: not fast (enough)
pays: country, region, hometown
permissionnaire: soldier on leave
petits malades: patients with minor illnesses
pinar[d]: cheap red wine (slang)
poilu (slang): French foot soldier, bearded and unkempt
popote: mess, kitchen (slang)
Poste de Secours: first aid station for wounded
Quel joli pain!: What lovely bread!
raconteur: storyteller, narrator; public entertainer
rapatriés: those repatriated, returned from imprisonment or exile
ravitaill[e]ment: provisioning, replenishment
repas: meal
repas complet: full meal
Salle de Conversation: recreation hall
Salle de lecture: reading hall
saucisson: cured dry sausage
soldat: soldier(s)
sortir: to exit, come out
sou: 5 centime coin
sous officier: noncommissioned officer
Straf (G): punishment
tant pis: too bad
tartine: open-faced sandwich
triage: sorting patients according to type and seriousness of injury
Tu m'énerves: You're getting on my nerves.
Verboten (G): forbidden
Zouaves: French light infantry, originally Algerian colonists

Notes

Introduction [pages xv-xxx]

1. The correspondence and instructions from the American Red Cross are pasted into Hall's own copy of the memoir. Margaret Hall, "Letters and Photographs from the Battle Country, 1918–1919," Cohasset Historical Society (65.07.01). Hall made the statement about marriage to her great-niece.
2. This portrait may have been taken by Hall's aunt, Emma Coleman, a professional portrait photographer and historian of Deerfield. Coleman gave her copy of Margaret Hall's illustrated memoir to the Massachusetts Historical Society. It is Coleman's copy which has been transcribed for publication here. Some of Coleman's glass plates are in the Emma Lewis Coleman Photographic Collection at Historic New England, Boston, Massachusetts.
3. Hall sent "From Behind the Front," a short narrative about her first four months in France, which is close in tone and wording to the memoir, to the *Bryn Mawr Alumnae Quarterly,* January 1919, pp. 119–124. In the 1920s she created four copies of the full memoir, amply illustrated with her photographs. In addition to the copies for Coleman and for herself, she put together two other versions of these precious volumes for the nephew and niece who lived with her after their mother died. Surprisingly, this lively account of her year, woven out of her letters and diary entries, was never published.
4. The war, Fussell suggests, was intrinsically ironic, because of the disparities between human costs and political benefits, between the idealistic language of propaganda or chivalric heroism and the actual devastation to be observed. See Paul Fussell, *The Great War and Modern Memory* (Oxford: Oxford University Press, 1975). He questions whether women were capable of the "subtler" kinds of irony he found in the great British soldier-poets, in *Thank God for the Atom Bomb* (New York: Ballantine, 1988), 111.
5. Dorothy and Carl Schneider suggest that the American women who volunteered to work in Europe belonged to the type of the "New Woman" that emerged at the end of the nineteenth century: middle-class, urban, well educated, and often single. Dorothy and Carl J. Schneider, *Into the Breach: American Women Overseas in World War I* (New York: Viking, 1991), 4–6.
6. An estimated twenty-five thousand American women served abroad between 1914 and 1918. See Schneider, *Into the Breach,* 287–289.
7. Further information can be found in his obituary, "Gen George F. Hall Dead, Did Much for the Massachusetts Militia and Had Served in the Civil War," *Boston Globe,* March 2, 1915, p. 8.
8. See Michael Neiberg, "One Hundred Days to Victory: Amiens to the Meuse-Argonne," in his *Fighting the Great War: A Global History* (Cambridge: Harvard University Press, 2005), 331–356; John Keegan, *The First World War* (New York: Vintage Books, 2000), 408.
9. For a summary of the battles in summer 1918 and the "black day" of August 8, see Keegan, *The First World War,* 406–411. Hall quotes a comment on German prisoners of war that they were too young to shave (37).
10. Hall listed her address as 120 East 31st Street, New York, in the *Bryn Mawr College Calendar* (1909), 50. In 1908 the college *Quarterly* reported she was a frequent visitor for lunch at the Bryn Mawr Club in New York. *Bryn Mawr Alumnae Quarterly,* April 1908, p. 37.
11. A letter of July 5 from R. H. Stetson of the American Red Cross accepted Hall for Foreign Service and directed her to obtain the necessary vaccines and uniform. The Red Cross correspondence is inserted into the first volume of Margaret Hall, "Letters and Photographs from the Battle Country, 1918–1919," the copy held by the Cohasset Historical Society (65.07.01). On September 24, she was authorized by Francis S. Blake to report to Châlons-sur-Marne. Hall, "Letters and Photographs," Cohasset Historical Society (65.07.01).
12. Philip Hall, Jr., kindly reported and reviewed this information.
13. Hall inserted a copy of this bank draft in her copy of the memoir. Hall, "Letters and Photographs," Cohasset Historical Society (65.07.01).
14. Together with her portrait, Hall kept little snapshots of the elegant family car in which she and her mother had been driven down from their home in Massachusetts to New York City by their chauffeur, Pierce Butler. It appears to be a 1915 Cadillac. Private collection.
15. Hall heard that the Salvation Army sent two teams to the war zone and at one point wished she had volunteered with that group instead of the Red Cross. On women in the Salvation Army, see Lettie Gavin, *American Women in World War I: They Also Served* (Boulder: University Press, Colorado, 1997), 209–240.
16. A great many women suffered from "frontline fever." See Schneider, *Into the Breach,* 31–32, 83; Susan Zeiger, *In Uncle Sam's Service: Women Workers with the American Expeditionary Force, 1917–1919* (Ithaca: Cornell University Press, 1999), 74–75. Nora Saltonstall, whose papers are held by the Massachusetts Historical Society, eagerly sought for positions close to the front. *"Out here at the Front": The World War I Letters of Nora*

Saltonstall, ed. Judith S. Graham (Boston: Northeastern University Press, 2004), 55, 56, 70.

17 Châlons-sur-Marne is about twenty-seven miles from Reims and fifty-four miles from Verdun, two symbolically important cities that were bitterly contested during the war. Hall estimated that she was just half an hour's drive from the front.

18 The crisis arose from the "big American offensive" at Saint-Mihiel on September 12 (18). Directors Anna Mitchell and Marjorie Nott requested help, but when they did not receive it, Nott went to Paris to press further. Meanwhile, Hall's Red Cross card arrived and she could apply for French papers. Anna V. S. Mitchell, diary, September 22, 1918, Anna V. S. Mitchell papers, subseries of Olivia Stokes Hatch Papers, 1859–1993, Special Collections Department, Bryn Mawr College Library.

19 Anna V. S. Mitchell, diary, September 23, 1918, Anna V. S. Mitchell papers, Bryn Mawr College Library. After waiting about ten days, Hall was rushed off with provisional papers from September 6 ("Récépissé de Demande de Carte d'Identité").

20 "Thrills of American Women in the War Zone: Their Trips to the Front from the Red Cross Cantine at Chalons—Lighter and Darker Sides of the Soldier Life," *New York Times Magazine*, February 17, 1918, p. 70; "Fighting Blood Up in Pershing's Men," *New York Times*, November 23, 1917, p. 4.

21 Anna V. S. Mitchell to C., September 22, 1918, Anna V. S. Mitchell papers, Bryn Mawr College Library.

22 Robert H. Ferrell, *America's Deadliest Battle: Meuse-Argonne, 1918* (Lawrence: University Press of Kansas, 2007), 41.

23 An official United States medical report of 1925 explained that mobile hospitals had been sent to other locations because of the risk of bombing: "American surgical teams were sent to a French hospital at Chalons-sur-Marne, where non-transportable American wounded were received; but persistent bombing of this town rendered it a very unsuitable location for the accumulation of patients." M. W. Ireland et al., *Medical Department of the United States Army in the World War*, vol. 8: *Field Operations* (Washington, D.C.: Government Printing Office, 1925), 353.

24 "Red Cross Serves Hot Food to Yanks," *New York Sun*, October 10, 1918, p. 6.

25 Margaret Hall to Philip Hall, October 1918, private collection.

26 *Bryn Mawr Alumnae Quarterly*, April 1908, 37.

27 One wonders whether she told her parents that she had been a picket in the Ladies' Garment Strike in New York, as she reported to the *Bryn Mawr Alumnae Quarterly*. See "News from the Classes," April 1913, p.15. Other wealthy sympathizers of the International Ladies' Garment Workers' Union included Anne Morgan.

28 See the *Bryn Mawr Alumnae Quarterly*, June 1912, p. 152; April 1913, p. 14; June 1913, p. 79. Hall's obituary claims that she staged "country wide parades in 1915." "Miss Margaret Hall, Traveler, Suffragette," *Boston Herald*, January 1, 1964, p. 72. On the suffrage movement, see Jean H. Baker, ed., *Votes for Women: The Struggle for Suffrage Revisited* (New York: Oxford University Press, 2002).

29 Feminist leaders such as Millicent Fawcett urged women to volunteer, in order to earn the vote. In 1917, a parade down Fifth Avenue of nurses who were on their way to France was interpreted by a reporter as a sign of "world-wide forces making for suffrage." "In the face of so much clear-eyed valor and calm, wise sacrifice, the voice of the anti-suffragists sounds forced and strange." "The Red-Cross Nurses," *Literary Digest*, October 20, 1917, p. 28.

30 Wilson urged the Senate, arguing, "I tell you plainly that this measure which I urge upon you is vital to the winning of the war and to the energies alike of preparation and of battle." Woodrow Wilson, *Address of the President of the United States, September 30, 1918* (Washington, D.C.: Government Printing Office, 1918), Cary T. Grayson Papers, Woodrow Wilson Presidential Library (also available online: "Address Supporting Women's Suffrage Amendment, 30 Sept. 1918," http://wwl2.dataformat.com/HTML/30740.htm).

31 The photographs of "mother" and the American Red Cross memorabilia are all inserted in the three-volume copy of her memoir that Hall kept for herself, then left to her chauffeur and life-long companion, Pierce Butler. Butler donated it, together with posters and a few souvenirs, to the Cohasset Historical Society. Hall, "Letters and Photographs," Cohasset Historical Society (65.07.01).

32 Hall's photographs of devastation, which she exhibited after her return to the United States in 1919, could be compared in their purpose to those commissioned by Anne Morgan and CARD (the Comité Américain pour les Régions Dévastées). The CARD images served as propaganda printed in newspapers, in a wide appeal for humanitarian relief. See Anne Dopffer, ed., *Des Américaines en Picardie: Au service de la France dévastée, 1917–1924 / American Women in Picardy: Rebuilding Devastated France, 1917–1924* (Paris: Réunion des musées nationaux, 2002). The Morgan Library and Museum exhibited a selection in 2010, "Anne Morgan's War: Rebuilding Devastated France, 1917–1924," http://www.themorgan.org/exhibitions/online/AnneMorgan/default. Hall, however, arranged her photographs as a narrative sequence in each of the scrapbooks she assembled.

33 This AEF paper signed by Adj. Gen. J. H. Perkins is inserted in Hall, "Letters and Photographs," Cohasset Historical Society, facing page 68. It lists travel to Paris on December 13–20, to Sedan on December 22–24, to Verdun on January 4–25, and to Strasbourg from March 7 to April 1919. It does not indicate permission for her actual travels in occupied Germany.
34 Anne Vanderbilt, "Orders for Canteen Workers," August 9, [1918], inserted in Hall, "Letters and Photographs," 36v., Cohasset Historical Society.
35 Hall tucked into her copy of the memoir a notice from the American Red Cross that states, "All women must make a statement on their passport application that they have no male relatives (husbands, sons, fathers or brothers) in the armed service of the Unites States, either here or abroad, or overseas in the service of any organizations such as the Red Cross, Young Men's Christian association, [or] Knights of Columbus." The *New York Times* reported that the Women's Bureau of the American Red Cross was selecting canteen workers from among applicants "willing to serve without pay and bear their own expenses abroad." It chose "only those of robust health who can speak French and who are willing to undergo hardships and discomforts. In addition applicants had to be between the ages of 30 and 50." "Ask Co-operation in War Relief Work," *New York Times*, September 16, 1917.
36 Verbal communication by Suzanne Hall Diefenbach about a conversation between Margaret Hall and her great-niece in 1952.
37 In later years Hall went camping with Elsa Bowman in the Rockies for six weeks (1923), and they traveled to Japan (1928). She traveled to Europe and North Africa with her aunt, Emma Coleman, and her chauffeur, Pierce Butler, in 1929. Butler accompanied her to France in 1927; to Panama in 1928; to Honolulu and Yokohama, Japan, in 1928; and to San Juan, Puerto Rico, in 1950. See "News from the Classes," *Bryn Mawr Alumnae Quarterly*, June 1916, p. 49.
38 Margaret Hall to Philip Hall, October 11, 1918, private collection.
39 "JMO des Hopitaux d'evacuation (HOE) 1914–1918 au Val-de-Grâce," December 27, 2012, in the blog *Histoire des hôpitaux militaires et du service de santé durant la Grande Guerre* (http://hopitauxmilitairesguerre1418 .overblog.com/archive/2012-12/). See item Hôpital d'évacuation no 2 [de Châlons].
40 Wilson, *Address of the President . . . , September 30, 1918.*
41 The family kept no record of what cameras she used. The size and quality of her prints suggest that she carried one vest-pocket Kodak with 120 roll film and a second bellows camera with quarter glass plates. She may have used a tripod. Out of over 270 images, at least 20 were commercial. These included panoramic views of the canteen, assorted postcards, and photographs of Paris celebrations cut from a newspaper supplement commemorating July 14, 1919. She enlarged well over 100 images to 12" x 20", 14" x 20", and 16" x 20" formats. The enlargements are in the Hall collection, Cohasset Historical Society (65.07.01).
42 Each copy of the memoir presents variants in its scrapbook layout and selection.
43 Anna V. S. Mitchell to C., September 22, 1918, Anna V. S. Mitchell papers, Bryn Mawr College.
44 Program cards for the vaudeville and a Punch and Judy show performed in the canteen theater are pasted into the copy held by the Cohasset Historical Society, facing pages 179–180.
45 Margaret Hall, "From Behind the Front," *Bryn Mawr Alumnae Quarterly*, January 1919, p. 121.
46 Anna V. S. Mitchell to C., May 2, 1919, Anna V. S. Mitchell papers, Bryn Mawr College Library.
47 Ferrell, *America's Deadliest Battle*, 2; Margaret Macmillan, *Paris 1919: Six Months That Changed the World* (New York: Random House, 2001), 198.
48 Pershing told Haig, "it was difficult to exaggerate the feeling of dislike for the French which existed in the American army." Byron Farwell, *Over There: The United States in the Great War, 1917–1918* (New York: Norton, 1999), 272.
49 Two canteen workers came back from Germany complaining about Americans' preference for the Germans: "Everyone agrees that they are getting more and more to hate the French, and to think the German is a good fellow." Those at the canteen felt "the French for the last five years have represented certain fundamental virtues and fine qualities that the world ought to have, while the Germans have stood for equally fundamental defects in national character." Anna V. S. Mitchell to C., April 10, 1919, Anna V. S. Mitchell papers, Bryn Mawr College Library.
50 Ferrell, *America's Deadliest Battle*, 6–10, 16–17, 76, 94.
51 Martin Gilbert, *The First World War: A Complete History* (New York: Holt, 1994), 459–460, 467.
52 Native Americans won ten Croix de Guerre; Choctaw served as telephone operators in the Argonne, foreshadowing contributions by code-talkers in several Native American languages during World War II. Farwell, *Over There*, 160.
53 Tyler Stovall affirms that "the world war did . . . produce the New Negro," whose "increased racial pride and resistance to discrimination" were nourished by the "spectacle of whites willing to treat them with dignity

and respect." Tyler Stovall, *Paris Noir: African Americans in the City of Light* (Boston: Houghton Mifflin, 1996), 28, 26.
54 Farwell, *Over There*, 150–157.
55 Anna V. S. Mitchell to C., November 3, 1918, Anna V. S. Mitchell papers, Bryn Mawr College Library.
56 The story was told us by her nephew, Philip Hall, Jr., who showed us an album with pictures Margaret had taken as a child.
57 The other two recipients of these volumes were not her brothers but the nephew and niece whom she had taken in after their mother died.
58 Arthur N. Fuller's obituary essay about Emma L. Coleman and her work as a historian, photographer, and promoter of basketry in Deerfield is held by the Pocumtuck Valley Memorial Association, Deerfield, Massachusetts. Coleman and Baker were also close to Sarah Orne Jewett.
59 Hew Strachan, *The First World War* (New York: Penguin, 2003), 312. Three thousand light tanks entered French service in 1918, some of which were provided to the AEF.
60 Wilfred Owen, "Anthem for Doomed Youth," in *The Poems of Wilfred Owen,* ed. Jon Stallworth (New York: Norton, 1983), 76.

Chapter 1: American Relief Organizations in France   [pages 1-4]
1 Several orders of nuns wear white, especially when serving as nurses.
2 Susan Zeiger, *In Uncle Sam's Service: Women Workers with the American Expeditionary Force, 1917–1919* (Ithaca: Cornell University Press, 1999), 29. Racism and "nativism" impeded applications by African American women (before 1919 only three worked for the YMCA serving segregated units) and by Jewish volunteers (Zeiger, 28–30). The obstacles that faced African American women are recounted by Addie W. Hunton and Kathryn M. Johnson in *Two Colored Women with the American Expeditionary Forces* (Brooklyn: Brooklyn-Eagle Press, 1920).
3 See Zeiger, *In Uncle Sam's Service*, 63, and Knights of Columbus Committee on War Activities, *Knights of Columbus War Work Service* (New Haven, Conn.: John J. Corbett Press, 1918) (this source can be found online at the Knights of Columbus Museum, accessed April 7, 2014, http://www.kofcmuseum.org/km/en/resources/www1.pdf). This pamphlet explains that "Knights of Columbus buildings, huts and tents everywhere are wide open to men of all races, creeds and color. The society's war workers accept no money for the supplies they distribute in hospitals, in the field, or anywhere else" (3). For information on the YMCA, see William Howard Taft et al., *Service with Fighting Men: An Account of the Work of the American Young Men's Christian Associations in the World War* (New York: Association Press, 1922).
4 For an overview of associations providing "aid and comfort" in Europe, see chapter 5 of Dorothy Schneider and Carl J. Schneider, *Into the Breach: American Women Overseas in World War I* (New York: Viking, 1991), 118–167; they trace disputes as well, 53–56.
5 Zeiger, *In Uncle Sam's Service*, 2, 175-176n4.
6 Julia F. Irwin, *Making the World Safe: The American Red Cross and a Nation's Humanitarian Awakening* (Oxford: Oxford University Press, 2013), 72–73, 69. In the process of consolidation, some organizers such as Edith Wharton complained, although she could no longer finance her relief work. Nora Saltonstall comments on Wharton's complaints in a letter, which can be found in *"Out here at the Front": The World War I Letters of Nora Saltonstall,* ed. Judith S. Graham (Boston: Northeastern University Press, 2004), 60. Overall, women served happily in various organizations, according to Schneider, *Into the Breach*, 54–59. Lettie Gavin agrees that "there was no open competition and there was much collaboration" among social service agencies. Lettie Gavin, *American Women in World War I: They Also Served* (Boulder: University Press of Colorado, 1997), 221.
7 On American nurses in Europe, see Zeiger, *In Uncle Sam's Service*, 104–136, especially 105, 107, 113; and Schneider, *Into the Breach*, 79–117. The Schneiders explain their estimate of twenty-five thousand American women abroad in appendix A, *Into the Breach*, 287–289.
8 Zeiger, *In Uncle Sam's Service*, 52–53. Zeiger states that 2,503 women did auxiliary work for the Red Cross, and 3,198 did auxiliary work for the YMCA (52). The Schneiders estimate a similar total for women serving abroad in a wide array of occupations. *Into the Breach*, 287–288.
9 On "frontline fever," see Schneider, *Into the Breach*, 31–32. Nurse Julia C. Stimson exulted at her "good fortune" "to be in the front ranks" (Schneider, 17). See also Margaret R. Higonnet, "At the Front," in *The Cambridge History of the First World War,* ed. Jay Winter (Cambridge: Cambridge University Press, 2014), 3:121–123.
10 Margaret Darrow, *French Women and the First World War: War Stories of the Home Front* (Oxford: Berg, 2000), 139–141.
11 See Henry P. Davison, *The American Red Cross in the Great War* (New York: Macmillan, 1919).
12 See Davison, *American Red Cross*. On ARC canteens, see Lettie Gavin, *American Women in World War I*, 187–

192. Gavin also discusses women's work in the United States, as do Maurine Weiner Greenwald, *Women, War, and Work: The Impact of World War I on Women Workers in the United States* (Westport, Conn.: Greenwood, 1980); and Kimberly Jensen, *Mobilizing Minerva: American Women in the First World War* (Urbana: Illinois University Press, 2008).

13 Charles D. Norton, quoted in "Fighting Blood Up in Pershing's Men," *New York Times*, November 23, 1917.

14 A long list of prominent American women performing war work in France can be found in Ida Clyde Clarke, *American Women and the World War* (New York: Appleton, 1918), 454–460.

15 The form is included in Margaret Hall's own copy of her memoir, "Letters and Photographs from the Battle Country, 1918–1919," Cohasset Historical Society (65.07.01).

16 Schneider, *Into the Breach*, 14–15, 21. Hall pasted instructions concerning the purchase of her uniform from Abercrombie and Fitch into her copy of "Letters and Photographs."

17 Schneider, *Into the Breach*, 4–5. The generations of women in the late nineteenth and early twentieth century who pursued college education are generally understood today as belonging to a group that social historians call "New Women." See Schneider, 4.

18 Florence Converse, *Wellesley College: A Chronicle of the Years 1875–1938* (Wellesley, Mass.: Hathaway House Bookshop, 1939), 191.

19 On volunteers from women's colleges, see Schneider, *Into the Breach*, 71–78. For the Radcliffe unit, see Giuliana Vetrano, "An Ambivalent Achievement: The Radcliffe Unit in France, 1917–1920" (B.A. thesis, Harvard University, 2009).

20 Ruth Gaines, *Helping France: The Red Cross in the Devastated Area* (New York: E. P. Dutton, 1919); Ruth Gaines, *A Village in Picardy* (New York: E. P. Dutton, 1918). The Smith College Relief Unit was founded by Harriet Hawes, who drew on her prior experience serving as a relief nurse in both the Greco-Turkish war of 1897 and the Spanish-American War; she was inspired by Anne Morgan's American Fund for French Wounded. The Smith Unit was recognized by the Red Cross in 1918.

21 See Florence Billings Papers, Sophia Smith Collection, Smith College, Northampton, Mass. In another typical sequence, Frances Webster served first as a nurse's aide in children's units for the ARC, then as a secretary to the chief nurse of the Children's Bureau in Paris, and finally as a nurse in evacuation hospitals at the front. See the Frances Webster letters, 1917–1918, Ms. N-2267, Massachusetts Historical Society. See also Schneider, *Into the Breach*, 74, 107. Men also shifted from one organization to another. In 1915 the Rockefeller Foundation sent Reginald C. Foster to care for orphans in Germany and Poland; after the United States declared war, he joined the American Red Cross and urged his sister, Hilda Chase Foster, to volunteer with the ARC, which she did in late 1918. See the Hilda Chase Foster papers, 1873–1974, Massachusetts Historical Society.

22 Anne Dopffer, ed., *Des Américaines en Picardie: Au service de la France dévastée, 1917–1924 / American Women in Picardy: Rebuilding Devastated France, 1917–1924* (Paris: Réunion des musées nationaux, 2002), 48.

23 Laura Lee Downs, "War Work," in *The Cambridge History of the First World War*, 3:72–95.

24 Fisher Ames, Jr., *American Red Cross Work among the French People* (New York: Macmillan, 1921), 3.

25 For samples of women's testimony about war work, see Margaret R. Higonnet, *Lines of Fire: Women Writers of World War I* (New York: Penguin Plume, 1999).

Chapter 2: Wartime Paris [pages 11-13]

1 Martin Gilbert, *The First World War: A Complete History* (New York: Holt, 1994), 66–72.

2 The conditions of daily life in Paris from 1914 to 1918, including the topics of rationing, the influenza, and the feminization of labor, are traced by Pierre Darmon, *Vivre à Paris pendant la Grande Guerre* (Paris: Fayard, 2002). For the Taube and Gotha air raids, see Darmon, *Vivre à Paris*, 339–350, 351–366.

3 Three "Paris" guns, designed by Dr. Walter von Eberhardt, were first fired Saturday, March 23, 1918. Twenty-five shells hit Paris on the first day. One gun was knocked out of commission immediately. On Friday, March 29, a shell that struck Saint-Gervais church killed ninety-one. See the detailed study by Christophe Dutrone, *Feu sur Paris: L'Histoire vraie de la grosse Bertha* (Paris: Taillac, 2012), especially 194. The so-called "Big Bertha" guns were smaller, with a shorter range. For the psychological impact, see Darmon, *Vivre à Paris*, 373 and 367–380 passim.

4 Darmon, *Vivre à Paris*, 370–371, 378; Priscilla Mary Roberts and Spencer C. Tucker, eds., *The Encyclopedia of World War I: A Political, Social, and Military History* (Santa Barbara: ABC-CLIO, 2005), 899–900. For the number of guns, see Dutrone, *Feu sur Paris*, 194; Darmon, *Vivre à Paris*, 374; Gilbert, *The First World War*, 407. The barrels were replaced after firing sixty rounds. One super cannon reportedly exploded. Roberts and Tucker, *The Encyclopedia of World War I*, 900.

5 Darmon, *Vivre à Paris*, 386.

6 [Mildred Mitchell], *Letters from an American Girl in the War Zone, 1917–1919* (Princeton: privately printed,

1920), 11.
7   Adrian Gregory, "Lost Generations: The Impact of Military Casualties on Paris, London and Berlin," in *Capital Cities at War: Paris, London, Berlin, 1914–1919*, ed. J. M. Winter and Jean-Louis Robert (Cambridge: Cambridge University Press, 1997–2007), 1:59, 69, 67. Certain groups were exempted from the draft: railroad, police, and postal workers, as well as some skilled workers in essential industries.
8   Françoise Thébaud, *La Femme au temps de la guerre de 14* (Paris: Stock, 1986), 163–165, 182–185; Mathilde Dubesset, Françoise Thébaud, and Catherine Vincent, "The Female Munition Workers of the Seine," in *The French Home Front, 1914–1918*, ed. Patrick Fridenson (Oxford: Berg, 1922), 183–218.
9   Laura Lee Downs, "War Work," in *The Cambridge History of World War I*, ed. Jay Winter (Cambridge: Cambridge University Press, 2014), 3:74–75.
10 Leonard V. Smith, Stéphane Audoin-Rouzeau, and Annette Becker, *France and the Great War, 1914–1918* (Cambridge: Cambridge University Press, 2003), 136.
11 Margaret H. Darrow, *French Women and the First World War: War Stories of the Home Front* (Oxford: Berg, 2000), 294–303.
12 See Jay Winter, "Paris, London, Berlin, 1914–1919: Capital Cities at War," in *Capital Cities at War*, 1:3–24, especially 10–11. For inflation rates, see in the same volume Jon Lawrence, "Material Pressures on the Middle Classes," 229–254, especially 233–235 and table 8.2.
13 Mme Journiac, "Letter to the Minister of Public Works," in *Lines of Fire: Women Writers of World War I*, ed. Margaret R. Higonnet (New York: Penguin Plume, 1999), 92.
14 Winter, "Paris, London, Berlin," especially 11.
15 See Manon Pignot and Roland Beller, *La Guerre des crayons: Quand les petits Parisiens dessinaient la grande guerre* (Paris: Parigramme, 2004); Margaret Higonnet, "Picturing War Trauma," in *Under Fire: Childhood in the Shadow of War*, ed. Andrea Immel and Elizabeth Goodenough (Detroit: Wayne State University Press, 2008), 115–128.
16 Edith Wharton, *Fighting France: From Dunkerque to Belfort* (New York: Scribner's, 1915), 29, 33, 41.
17 Hew Strachan, *The First World War* (New York: Viking Penguin, 2004), 435.

Chapter 3: The Canteen at Châlons-sur-Marne [pages 27-30]

1   Edith O'Shaughnessy, *My Lorraine Journal* (New York: Harper, 1918), 60, 69, 77, 81, 98, 100; Fisher Ames, Jr., *American Red Cross Work among the French People* (New York: Macmillan, 1921), 37–38; Capt. A. M. McKnight, "American Red Cross, List of Directrices of L.O.C. and Aviation Canteens with their Addresses in the United States" and "Summary: American Red Cross Canteen Service, Bureau of L.O.C. Canteens, Army and Navy Department," August 25, 1919, 942.616, Central File of the American Red Cross, 1917–1934, Donated Records Collection, Record Group 200, National Archives at College Park, College Park, MD.
2   "Ask Co-operation in War Relief Work," *New York Times*, September 16, 1917. See also "Thrills of American Women in the War Zone," *New York Times*, February 17, 1918. Mildred Mitchell, the twenty-year-old niece of Anna Mitchell, joined her aunt and then headed the tent hospital at Écury where Hall briefly worked. Mildred Mitchell, passport, November 1917, Ancestry.com.
3   Margaret Hall to Philip Hall, Sr., October 11, 1918, private collection.
4   Maurice Pierrat, *Châlons-sur-Marne pendant l'Occupation allemande, Septembre 1914* (Châlons-sur-Marne: l'Union républicaine de la Marne, 1915), especially 29, 37.
5   A contemporary account of relief work in France can be found in Laurence Binyon, *For Dauntless France: An Account of Britain's Aid to the French Wounded and Victims of the War* (London: Hodder and Stoughton, 1918). The First Aid Nursing Yeomanry Corps (FANY) was a volunteer British group founded in 1909 that received training for stretcher-bearers and orderlies. In the fall of 1917, FANY units went to Epernay and Châlons. The British Hackett-Lowther Unit, founded in August 1917, drew soldiers' rations and transported the wounded to and from evacuation hospitals and stations on the railways. Led by the aristocrat May "Toupie" Lowther and her friend Desmond Hackett, that all-female unit was honored in 1916 with the Croix de Guerre, and six drivers won the Croix de Guerre as individuals in 1918. See Laurence Binyon, *For Dauntless France*, 110.
6   Edith Wharton, *Fighting France: From Dunkerque to Belfort* (New York: Scribner's, 1915), 50–51.
7   Anne Vanderbilt, "My Trip to the Front," *Harper's Magazine,* January 1917, pp. 175–186.
8   "On Canteens," *Living Age*, April 27, 1918, pp. 245–247.
9   "Thrills of American Women in the War Zone," *New York Times*, February 17, 1918, p. 70.
10 O'Shaughnessy, *My Lorraine Journal*, 188, 183.
11 Charles D. Norton, quoted in "Fighting Blood Up in Pershing's Men," *New York Times*, November 23, 1917, p. 4.
12 Anna V. S. Mitchell, diary, September 25, 1918; letters, October 1, 1918, p. 349, both Anna V. S. Mitchell papers,

subseries of Olivia Stokes Hatch Papers, 1859–1993, Special Collections Department, Bryn Mawr College Library.

13 Susan Zeiger summarizes the exhaustion some women, including Margaret Hall, expressed regarding the food service they provided at canteens in her *In Uncle Sam's Service: Women Workers with the American Expeditionary Force, 1917–1919* (Ithaca: Cornell University Press, 1999), 60–61. She also discusses the "dancing problem" endemic to social canteens, like the "dancing to order" that Hall witnessed in Germany (139). *In Uncle Sam's Service*, 72–74.

14 "Cromwell Twins End Their Lives By Leap from Ship," *New York Times*, January 25, 1919, p. 1. Miss Barnett of the canteen attributed their act to "the long strain and high nervous tension under bombardments." See also "Brings Story of Cromwell Tragedy," *New York Times*, January 29, 1919, p. 1; and "Praise the Dead Cromwell Twins," *Boston Evening Globe*, January 30, 1919, p. 3.

15 Capt. A. M. McKnight, "Summary: American Red Cross Canteen Service, Bureau of L.O.C. Canteens, Army and Navy Department," August 25, 1919, 942.616, Central File of the American Red Cross, 1917–1934, Donated Records Collection, Record Group 200, National Archives at College Park, College Park, MD. For the Croix de Guerre awarded to Châlons-sur-Marnes, see l'association du Mémorial des batailles de la Marne, Dormans (51700), Communes décorées de la Croix de guerre, 1914–1918, p. 28, http://memorialdormans.free.fr/CommunesCroixDeGuerre14-18.pdf, accessed May 8, 2014.

Chapter 4: The American Expeditionary Force [pages 43-47]

1 John W. Whitman, "United States, Army," in *The Encyclopedia of World War I: A Political, Social, and Military History*, ed. Priscilla Mary Roberts and Spencer C. Tucker (Santa Barbara: ABC-CLIO, 2005), 1198–1203. When Woodrow Wilson declared war in April 1917, the United States Army had roughly 127,000 troops and just over 80,000 in the National Guard. By March 1918 the AEF in France numbered 318,000 men; that number had increased to 430,000 by the end of April and to 650,000 a month later. David F. Burg and L. Edward Purcell, *Almanac of World War I* (Lexington: The University Press of Kentucky, 1998), 161, 162; Whitman, "United States, Army," 1198; John Keegan, *The First World War* (New York: Vintage Books, 2000), 372; Meirion and Susie Harries, *The Last Days of Innocence: America at War, 1917–1918* (New York: Random House, 1997), 234.

2 Robert H. Ferrell, *America's Deadliest Battle: Meuse-Argonne, 1918* (Lawrence: University Press of Kansas, 2007), 27. See also Keegan, *The First World War*, 392–412.

3 For an overview of World War I historiography and the standard shape of the military narrative, see Jay Winter's "Introduction to the Volume" and "Introduction to Part I," in his *Cambridge History of the First World War* (Cambridge: Cambridge University Press, 2014), 1:11–12, 15, as well as Stéphane Audoin-Rouzeau, "1915: Stalemate," and Robin Prior, "1916: Impasse," in the same volume, 1:65–88 and 89–109, respectively. See also Gerd Krumeich and Stéphane Audoin-Rouzeau, "Les batailles de la Grande Guerre," in *Encyclopédie de la Grande Guerre, 1914–1918: Histoire et culture*, ed. Stéphane Audoin-Rouzeau and Jean-Jacques Becker (Paris: Bayard, 2004), 300–302.

For the rapid German advance in September and the fighting in the area of Châlons-sur-Marne, see Martin Gilbert, *The First World War: A Complete History* (New York: Holt, 1994), 68–69; and Burg and Purcell, *Almanac of World War I*, 24–26. The hasty Allied retreat in August 1914 was chaotic and costly. On the single day of August 22, 1914, the French army lost 27,000 dead, and in one month, 200,000. Stephane Audoin-Rouzeau, "Combat," in *A Companion to World War I*, ed. John Horne (Chichester: Wiley-Blackwell, 2010), 184; Michael Neiberg, *Fighting the Great War: A Global History* (Cambridge: Harvard University Press, 2005), 23–25. As Hall would have known, the Germans reached the Marne on September 4, 1914, and after the French military and many of the townsmen had left Châlons-sur-Marne, Maj. Gen. Hugo von Seydewitz moved into the city. He demanded a security of 506,000 French francs and took leaders of the city and neighboring towns hostage, including an elderly curé who died of mistreatment. The French re-entered the city September 12. Maurice Pierrat, *Châlons-sur-Marne pendant l'Occupation allemande, Septembre 1914* (Châlons-sur-Marne: L'Union républicaine de la Marne, 1915), 29–48 passim.

4 Keegan, *The First World War*, 392–394; Neiberg, *Fighting the Great War*, 317. Like a boxer striking at different parts of the body, Ludendorff struck at a succession of fronts. He gave these attacks the code names "Michael" (March 21- April 5, in the Somme), "Georgette" (April 9-29, between Ypres and Bethune), "Blücher-Yorck" (May 27-June 5, between Laon and Château-Thierry), "Gneisenau" (June 9–14, on the Matz River between Noyon and Montdidier), and Marneschutz-Reims (July 15–17, two separate thrusts to cross the Marne and Vesle), which replaced "Hagen," a planned attack on Flanders. Burg and Purcell, *Almanac of World War I*, 200–212; Keegan, *The First World War*, 394–409; David T. Zabecki, "Marne, Second Battle of the," in *The Encyclopedia of World War I*, 750–752; Cristoph Mick, "1918: Endgame," in *The Cambridge History of the First World War*, 1:144, 147–152. See also the helpful maps in Vincent J. Esposito, ed., *The West Point Atlas of American*

Wars, vol. 2: *1900–1953* (New York: Praeger, 1959), maps 62–66; and Robin Prior and Trevor Wilson, *The First World War* (Washington, D.C.: Smithsonian, 2004), 177, 179, 182–183, 187–188, 193. One interpretation of these offensives is that his primary goal was the English Channel, while other drives were feints; another interpretation is that he struck where he found Allied forces weak, or where he could drive an opening between armies. His push southward to the Marne in May and June, at first a feint, became an opportunistic thrust toward Paris. Burg and Purcell, *Almanac of World War I*, 206, 209.

5 Neiberg, *Fighting the Great War*, 311.
6 For the Paris guns, see Christophe Dutrone, *Feu sur Paris: L'Histoire vraie de la grosse Bertha* (Paris: Taillac, 2012); and Burg and Purcell, *Almanac of World War I*, 201 passim. For the spring offensives synopsis, see sources cited in note 4 above.
7 Mildred Mitchell, working in the canteen in March 1918, recorded that four hundred bombs fell on Châlons in the first week of the Ludendorff offensive. [Mildred Mitchell], *Letters from an American Girl in the War Zone, 1917–1919* (Princeton: privately printed, 1920), 30. The report of 1,500 bombs that Hall heard was undoubtedly exaggerated.
8 Neiberg, *Fighting the Great War*, 317, 330; Robin Prior and Trevor Wilson, "War in the West, 1917–18," in *A Companion to World War I*, 133.
9 For a synopsis of the Blücher offensive, see Mick, "1918: Endgame," 1:150–151.
10 Gilbert, *The First World War*, 420–421. On the AEF training with the Allies, see Harries, *The Last Days of Innocence*, 233. Because American infantry filled the space on transport ships, Pershing depended on British and French manufacture for many kinds of equipment, from helmets to 75 mm field guns, trucks, tanks, and airplanes.
11 Robert A. Doughty, *Pyrrhic Victory: French Strategy and Operations in the Great War* (Cambridge: Belknap Press of Harvard University Press, 2005), 421–423, 465; Byron Farwell, *Over There: The United States in the Great War, 1917–1918* (New York: Norton, 1999), 148–158. The negative side of the black soldiers' story in the AEF is emphasized by Keegan, *The First World War*, 374. On the "overwhelmingly positive" experience of African American infantry under French command, which awarded the entire 369th Infantry the Croix de Guerre, see Richard Slotkin, *Lost Battalions: The Great War and the Crisis of American Nationality* (New York: Holt, 2005), 134, 153–212, 396. Gouraud resisted the imposition of segregation by Pershing's staff and praised his black units. Slotkin, *Lost Battalions*, 253–254. See also Barry M. Stentiford, "Historical Controversy: Performance of U.S. African-American Troops," in *The Encyclopedia of World War I*, 1200. For Pershing and the amalgamation of AEF troops with Allied forces, see Whitman, "United States, Army," in *The Encyclopedia of World War I*, 1199–1201.
12 Burg and Purcell, *Almanac of World War I*, 199; Ferrell, *America's Deadliest Battle*, 28–29; Neiberg, *Fighting the Great War*, 326–327. This small but effective action to capture a hilltop village and observation point instilled confidence about American fighting abilities. Nonetheless, it was described by George Marshall as "of no strategic importance." Harries, *The Last Days of Innocence*, 244.
13 Keegan, *The First World War*, 407; Neiberg, *Fighting the Great War*, 328–329; Burg and Purcell, *Almanac of World War I*, 210–215. Led into battle with no artillery support, the marine advance through wheatfields has been compared to the "unavailing heroism" of the British at the Somme. The brigade lost almost half its men in this battle. Nearby at Vaux, the brigade of the 2nd Division suffered only 128 casualties. See Ferrell, *America's Deadliest Battle*, 29.
14 Neiberg, *Fighting the Great War*, 339–340. Monash found that Germans surrendered willingly and had lost strength, evidence of the high cost of the preceding months' offensives. The Ludendorff offensives had cost the Germans nearly one million men, and around nine hundred thousand Allied soldiers as well. Burg and Purcell, *Almanac of World War I*, 217; Neiberg, *Fighting the Great War*, 355, 317. In Neiberg's view, the great offensive plan had started to fail by April 3. See also Mick, "1918: Endgame," in *The Cambridge History of the First World War*, 1:152–153; and Doughty, *Pyrrhic Victory*, 474.
15 Although they invoke different date ranges (typically July 15 to 17/18 or July 15 to August 4/6), summaries of the Second Battle of the Marne are plentiful. See, for example, Doughty, *Pyrrhic Victory*, 468–772; Mick, "1918: Endgame," 151–152, 153; Keegan, *The First World War*, 409; Burg and Purcell, *Almanac of World War I*, 217; Zabecki, "Marne, Second Battle of the"; and Vatow, "Aisne-Marne Offensive," in *The Encyclopedia of World War I*, 75–76; as well as Michael Neiberg's book-length treatment, *Second Battle of the Marne* (Bloomington: Indiana University Press, 2008). For more specifics regarding Soissons and for Foch as a maréchal, see Doughty, *Pyrrhic Victory*, 470–473, and also Mick, "1918: Endgame," 153; Gilbert, *The First World War*, 447; and Neiberg, *Fighting the Great War*, 337.
16 Caryn Neumann and Spencer C. Tucker, "Amiens Offensive (8–15 August 1918)," in *The Encyclopedia of World War I*, 96–98; Gilbert, *The First World War*, 450–451; Burg and Purcell, *Almanac of World War I*, 219–220.

17 Neiberg, *Fighting the Great War*, 342–344; Ferrell, *America's Deadliest Battle,* 31; Burg and Purcell, *Almanac of World War I*, 219. For more detailed accounts, see Erich Ludendorff, *Ludendorff's Own Story, August 1914– November 1918* (New York: Harper, 1919), 2:326–332; and Alistair McCluskey, *Amiens 1918: The Black Day of the German Army* (Oxford and New York: Osprey, 2008). Ludendorff's volume is the source of the now oft-replicated "black day" quotation (326).

18 Neiberg, *Fighting the Great War*, 330; Doughty, *Pyrrhic Victory*, 480; Ludendorff, *Ludendorff's Own Story,* 2:344. Ludendorff repeatedly overcame his own doubts, however. As late as October 24, he declared that Wilson's demand for unconditional surrender was "unacceptable" to soldiers. Two days later he was forced to resign. Doughty, *Pyrrhic Victory*, 500.

19 Keegan, *The First World War*, 411; Burg and Purcell, *Almanac of World War I*, 223–224; Neiberg, *Fighting the Great War*, 346–347. In their joint attacks, American forces were supplied with weapons by the French, including 227 out of 289 tanks, 4,874 out of 6,364 aircraft, and 3,532 of their 4,194 artillery pieces. Doughty, *Pyrrhic Victory*, 505, 511; Farwell, *Over There*, 208–209. As Farwell also notes, they did not always know how to operate their equipment.

20 For Parisians, see Hall (20); for American confidence, see Neiberg, *Fighting the Great War*, 347, and Farwell, *Over There*, 217.

21 Letter, October 1, Anna V. S. Mitchell papers, subseries of Olivia Stokes Hatch Papers, 1859–1993, Special Collections Department, Bryn Mawr College Library.

22 For an in-depth study of the actions in this period, see Ferrell, *America's Deadliest Battle*, especially 41–49, 54–55, 95–98, 102–104, 125–129. For the American divisions in Cambrai and the prisoners of war, see Burg and Purcell, *Almanac of World War I*, 227; Neiberg, *Fighting the Great War*, 350–351; and "French Have Over 10,000 Captives," *New York Times,* September 28, 1918, p.1.

23 Ferrell provides details regarding poor supplies and poor training: *America's Deadliest Battle*, 6–10, 14–17, 30, 116–125. He also lays out repeated examples of inept command: 28, 106, 109–110, 112. Robin Prior and Trevor Wilson attribute casualties in part to "inexperienced command," in "War in the West, 1917–18," in *A Companion to World War I*, 135. See also Doughty, *Pyrrhic Victory*, 492–493; and Farwell, *Over There*, 221. Stalled by September 29, Pershing himself said his advancing units were "hopelessly swamped." Doughty, *Pyrrhic Victory*, 493.

24 Ferrell, *America's Deadliest Battle*, 131–140; Farwell, *Over There*, 241.

25 Of a German pilot flying low over her tent hospital, Mildred Mitchell writes, "When he saw our white veils, he turned his machine gun on us by way of a salute." Mitchell, *Letters from an American Girl*, 47.

26 See also the September 29, 1918, entry of diary in Anna V. S. Mitchell papers, subseries of Olivia Stokes Hatch Papers, 1859–1993, Special Collections Department, Bryn Mawr College Library.

27 Gilbert, *The First World War,* 499.

Chapter 5: Armistice [pages 67-70]

1 Anna V. S. Mitchell, diary, November 12, 1918; letter, November 11, 1918, Mitchell papers, subseries of Olivia Stokes Hatch Papers, 1859–1993, Special Collections Department, Bryn Mawr College Library.

2 Pope Benedict's first encyclical on the war, delivered on November, 1914, "Ad Beatissimi Apostolorum," deplored the destruction made possible by modern warfare and proposed a Christmas truce. The text of the encyclical is available at the Vatican website, Supreme Pontiffs, Benedict XV: http://www.vatican.va/holy_father/benedict_xv/encyclicals/documents/hf_ben-xv_enc_01111914_ad-beatissimi-apostolorum_en.html, accessed June 6, 2014. His second response to the war, "To The Heads of the Belligerent Peoples," an address delivered on August 1, 1917, was a seven-point peace plan that included disarmament, negotiation, withdrawal from occupied territories, and freedom of the seas, foreshadowing some of Woodrow Wilson's fourteen points. See John F. Pollard, *The Unknown Pope: Benedict XV (1914–1922) and the Pursuit of Peace* (London: Geoffrey Chapman, 1999), 112–139.

3 International Congress of Women, The Hague—April 28th to May 1st, 1915, *Resolutions Adopted* (Amsterdam: Concordia, 1915), 4, 6.

4 Hew Strachan, *The First World War* (New York: Viking Penguin, 2004), 226–227. Expectations remained surprisingly similar in autumn 1918; see John Keegan, *The First World War* (New York: Vintage Books, 2000), 413.

5 David Lloyd George, *British War Aims: Statement by the Right Honourable David Lloyd George, January Fifth, Nineteen Hundred and Eighteen* (London: Hazell, Watson & Viney, 1918). On the sequence of proposals, see Strachan, *The First World War*, 303–304.

6 Woodrow Wilson, "President Wilson's Fourteen Points," Avalon Project, Lillian Goldman Law Library, Yale Law School, http://avalon.law.yale.edu/20th_century/wilson14.asp (accessed June 7, 2014).

7 Helmut Konrad, "Drafting the Peace," in *The Cambridge History of the First World War*, ed. Jay Winter (Cam-

bridge: Cambridge University Press, 2014), 2:608; Vejas Gabriel Liulevicius, "German-Occupied Eastern Europe," in *A Companion to World War I*, ed. John Horne (Chichester: Wiley-Blackwell, 2010), 455–456. On the Treaty of Brest-Litovsk and the breakup of the Russian Empires, see Robert M. Slusser and Jan F. Triska, *A Calendar of Soviet Treaties: 1917–1957* (Stanford: Stanford University Press, 1959), 1; Keegan, *The First World War*, 341–342, 381–383.
8   Keegan, *The First World War*, 408.
9   Keegan, *The First World War*, 411–412.
10 Martin Gilbert, *The First World War: A Complete History* (New York: Holt, 1994), 474; Strachan, *The First World War*, 322. On the cascade of requests for an armistice see Zara Steiner, *The Lights That Failed: European International History, 1919–1933* (Oxford: Oxford University Press, 2005), 4; and Keegan, *The First World War*, 416–417. On the demand for abdication, see Keegan, *The First World War*, 417–419. Other helpful sources on Central Europe at this point in the war include Priscilla Mary Roberts and Spencer C. Tucker, eds., *The Encyclopedia of World War I: A Political, Social, and Military History* (Santa Barbara: ABC-CLIO, 2005); David F. Burg and L. Edward Purcell, *Almanac of World War I* (Lexington: The University Press of Kentucky, 1998); and various essays in Winter's *The Cambridge History of the First World War*.
11 Bullitt Lowry, *Armistice 1918* (Kent, Ohio: Kent State University Press, 1996), 156–162. Hall reports the soldiers' excitement, triggered by the Allied meeting with German emissaries to transmit terms on November 7 (66). See "United Press Men Sent False Cable," *New York Times*, November 8, 1918, pp. 1, 3.
12 Margaret Macmillan, *Paris 1919: Six Months That Changed the World* (New York: Random, 2001), 98–106.
13 On the German surrender of military materiel, see Leonard V. Smith, Stéphane Audoin-Rouzeau, and Annette Becker, *France and the Great War, 1914–1918* (Cambridge: Cambridge University Press, 2003), 157–158; Strachan, *The First World War*, 326–327; Michael S. Neiberg, *Fighting the Great War: A Global History* (Cambridge: Harvard University Press, 2005), 355–360. For overviews of the Armistice terms, see Neiberg, *Fighting the Great War*, 357–360; Macmillan, *Paris 1919*, 158; Conditions of an Armistice with Germany, Official release by the German Government, published in the *Kreuz-Zeitung*, November 11, 1918, in *The World War I Document Archive*, comp. World War I Military History List (WWI-L), Brigham Young University Library, http://wwi.lib.byu.edu/index.php/Conditions_of_an_Armistice_with_Germany, accessed May 29, 2014. For the full terms of the Armistice, see *Terms of Armistice Signed by Germany: Address of the President of the United States to the Joint session of the Congress Monday, November 11, 1918*, Doc. No. 1339 (Washington, D.C.: Government Printing Office, 1918).
14 Keegan, *The First World War*, 419–420; Bruno Cabanes, "1919: Aftermath," in *The Cambridge History of World War I*, 1:193–196; Robert Gerwarth, "The Continuum of Violence," in *The Cambridge History of World War I*, 3:638–662.
15 Lowry, *Armistice 1918*, 162.
16 Smith, Audoin-Rouzeau, and Becker, *France and the Great War*, 156–157; Macmillan, *Paris 1919*, 158.
17 Macmillan, *Paris 1919*, 322–344, 476.
18 Hugh D. Clout, *After the Ruins: Restoring the Countryside of Northern France after the Great War* (Exeter: University of Exeter Press, 1996), 46.

Chapter 6: Refugees and the Repatriated [pages 77–80]

1   See Susan Grayzel, "Mothers, Marraines, and Prostitutes: Morale and Morality in First World War France," *International History Review* 19 (1997): 66–82. Women formed a Soldiers' Godmothers League in the United States. Starting in 1915, two Frenchwomen's associations, La Famille du soldat and Mon soldat, with the help of newspapers paired soldiers with correspondents; even schoolchildren were organized to contribute to the effort—a theme very common in children's books of the period. Hall notes the gratitude of the Oliviers. At the end of the memoir, Hall reports that she sent the rest of her French money to Emma Coleman's "filleul" (godson) before leaving Paris (169).
2   John Horne and Alan Kramer, *German Atrocities, 1914: A History of Denial* (New Haven: Yale University Press, 2001), 179–184, 230; Annette Becker, *Les cicatrices rouges, 14–19, France et Belgique occupées* (Paris: Fayard, 2010), 53–82.
3   Joanna Bourke, "Gender Roles in Killing Zones," in *The Cambridge History of the First World War*, ed. Jay Winter (Cambridge: Cambridge University Press, 2014), 3:159.
4   Peter Gatrell, "Refugees," in *Europe since 1914: Encyclopedia of the Age of War and Reconstruction*, ed. John Merriman and Jay Winter (Detroit: Scribner's, 2006), 4:2187.
5   Horne and Kramer, *German Atrocities*, 184.
6   For lists of American women engaged in philanthropy, see Ida Clyde Clarke, *American Women and the World War* (New York: Appleton, 1918).

7. Ruth Gaines wrote three books reporting on the work of the Smith Unit, in the face of military destruction along an unstable front. See Ruth Gaines, *A Village in Picardy* (New York: E. P. Dutton, 1918), 176 passim; *Helping France: The Red Cross in the Devastated Area* (New York : E. P. Dutton, 1919); and *Ladies of Grécourt: The Smith College Relief Unit in the Somme* (New York: E. P. Dutton, 1920), 129–131.

8. See John Yarnall, *Barbed Wire Disease: British and German Prisoners of War, 1914–19* (Stroud: Spellmount, 2011). For an extended analogy between civilians caught in occupied territories and prisoners of war, see Annette Becker, *Oubliés de la Grande guerre: humanitaire et culture de guerre, 1914–1918; populations occupées, déportés civils, prisonniers de guerre* (Paris: Noêsis, 1998).

9. The plan to retreat behind a "broad swath of destruction" was discussed by the German military from July 1918. See Isabel V. Hull, *Absolute Destruction: Military Culture and the Practices of War in Imperial Germany* (Ithaca: Cornell, 2005), 309.

10. Hall reports meeting an old couple living in the ruin of their farmhouse who were the sole occupants of their village. Anne Morgan's CARD used photographs of stoic villagers, some living in underground storage as the face of fundraising. See examples of such photographs in Anne Dopffer, ed., *Des Américaines en Picardie: Au service de la France dévastée, 1917–1924 / American Women in Picardy: Rebuilding Devastated France, 1917–1924* (Paris: Réunion des musées nationaux, 2002), 12, 14, 20, 92, 135. Gaines's books testify to the slow process of reconstruction that would enable a few dozen returnees to resettle at any one time, over the next five years. Hugh Clout provides an overview of the reconstruction efforts by CARD, the Smith Unit, and English Quakers in the region north of the Marne, where relief workers found villagers living in the misery of ruins that were inadequate as shelters. Hugh D. Clout, *After the Ruins: Restoring the Countryside of Northern France after the Great War* (Exeter: University of Exeter Press, 1996), 71–73, 84. Clout observes that few could return immediately to the British zone, where ongoing military operations inhibited resettlement. Clout, *After the Ruins*, 76.

11. Heather Jones, "Prisoners of War," in *The Cambridge History of the First World War*, 2:269; Uta Hinz, *Gefangen im Großen Krieg: Kriegsgefangenschaft in Deutschland 1914–1921* (Essen: Klartext, 2006), 93.

12. Becker, *Oubliés*, 244.

13. Becker, *Oubliés*, 15.

14. Jean-Claude Auriol, *Les barbelés des bannis: La tragédie des prisonniers de guerre français en Allemagne durant la Grande Guerre* (Paris: Tirésias, 2003), 265.

15. See Becker, *Oubliés*, and Heather Jones, "Prisoners of War," 2:269.

16. Annette Becker, "Captive Civilians," in *The Cambridge History of the First World War*, 3:272–277.

17. Jones estimates that between 17,000 and 38,000 French prisoners died in German captivity. Heather Jones, "Prisoners of War," 2:284.

18. Some estimates run from fifty to one hundred million influenza deaths worldwide, including half of deaths in the American military. John Barry writes, "It is also impossible to state with any accuracy the death toll. The statistics are estimates only." John Barry, *The Great Influenza: The Story of the Deadliest Pandemic in History* (Harmondsworth, Eng.: Penguin, 2004), 396–397.

19. Shirley Millard, *I Saw Them Die: Diary and Recollections of Shirley Millard* (London: Harrap, 1936), 100.

20. Hans-Lukas Kieser and Donald Bloxham, "Genocide," in *The Cambridge History of the First World War*, 1:603–611.

21. Peter Gatrell, "Refugees," in *Europe since 1914*, 4:2188.

22. See Peter Gatrell, *A Whole Empire Walking: Refugees in Russia during World War I* (Bloomington: Indiana University Press, 1999).

23. Gatrell, "Refugees," 4:2188.

24. Bruno Cabanes "1919: Aftermath," in *The Cambridge History of the First World War*, 1:188–189. See also Bruno Cabanes, *The Great War and the Origins of Humanitarianism, 1918–1924* (Cambridge: Cambridge University Press, 2014).

25. See Anna V. S. Mitchell papers, subseries of Olivia Stokes Hatch Papers, 1859–1993, Special Collections Department, Bryn Mawr College. Hall's correspondence with Mitchell's sister is preserved at the Hoover Institution Archives. Under the aegis of the League of Nations, Fridtjof Nansen directed a High Commission for Refugees that provided identity papers for stateless persons. See Gatrell, "Refugees," 4:2190, and Cabanes "1919: Aftermath," 1:187.

26. "Miss Margaret Hall, Traveler, Suffragette." *Boston Herald*, January 1, 1964, p. 72.

Chapter 7: Battlefield Tourism, Souvenirs, and a Sacred Land [pages 91–94]

1. For the flow homeward and outward, and the difficulties of reconstruction, see chapters seven to ten in Hugh D. Clout, *After the Ruins: Restoring the Countryside of Northern France after the Great War* (Exeter: University

of Exeter, 1996). See also Ruth Gaines, *Helping France: The Red Cross in the Devastated Area* (New York: E. P. Dutton, 1919).
2. *Michelin Guide to the Battlefields of the World War* (Milltown, N.J.: Michelin & Cie, 1919), 1:7, cited in Hugh D. Clout, *After the Ruins*, 274.
3. Quotations from *The Americans in the Great War* (Clermont-Ferrand: Michelin & Cie, 1920), 1:40, and "Vers la renaissance des régions dévastées," *L'Architecture* (1919): 501, both cited in Clout, *After the Ruins*, 273–274.
4. Nicholas Saunders, *Trench Art: Materialities and Memories of War* (Oxford: Blackwell, 2003), 130.
5. Susan M. Pearce, *On Collecting: An Investigation into Collecting in the European Tradition* (London: Routledge, 1995), 236, 218.
6. Ernest Hemingway, *Ernest Hemingway: Selected Letters, 1917–1961*, ed. Carlos Baker (New York: Scribner's, 1981), 12.
7. Pearce, *On Collecting*, 220; Margaret Higonnet, "Souvenirs of Death," *Journal of War and Culture Studies* 1.1 (2008): 68.
8. Higonnet, "Souvenirs of Death," 75–76.
9. David W. Lloyd, *Battlefield Tourism: Pilgrimage and the Commemoration of the Great War in Britain, Australia and Canada, 1919–1939* (Oxford: Berg, 1998), 113, 117.
10. Pearce, *On Collecting*, 244.
11. Anna V. S. Mitchell, letter of November 3, 1918, Anna V. S. Mitchell Papers, subseries of Olivia Stokes Hatch Papers, 1859–1993, Special Collections Department, Bryn Mawr College Library.
12. Mitchell, letter of November 3, 1918, Anna V. S. Mitchell Papers, Bryn Mawr College Library.

Chapter 8: Destruction and Reconstruction [pages 105–108]

1. Martin Gilbert, *The First World War: A Complete History* (New York: Holt, 1994), 309; Corinna Haven Smith and Caroline R. Hill, *Rising Above the Ruins in France: An Account of the Progress Made Since the Armistice in the Devastated Regions in Re-establishing Industrial Activities and the Normal Life of the People* (New York: G. P. Putnam's Sons, 1920); George B. Ford, *Out of the Ruins* (New York: The Century Company, 1919).
2. John Horne and Alan Kramer, *German Atrocities, 1914: A History of Denial* (New Haven: Yale University Press, 2001), 307–308.
3. Horne and Kramer, *German Atrocities*, 321.
4. Michael Neiberg, *Fighting the Great War: A Global History* (Cambridge: Harvard University Press, 2005), 331–332.
5. Annie Deperchin, "Des destructions aux reconstructions," in *Encyclopédie de la Grande Guerre, 1914–1918*, ed. Stéphane Audoin-Rouzeau and Jean-Jacques Becker (Paris: Bayard, 2004), 1125–1138.
6. Ford, *Out of the Ruins*, 20–21.
7. Smith and Hill, *Rising Above the Ruins*; Georges H. Parent, *Trois études sur la Zone Rouge de Verdun, une zone totalement sinistrée: I. L'herpétofaune - II. La diversité floristique - III. Les sites d'intérêt botanique et zoologique à protéger prioritairement* (Luxembourg: Musée National d'Histoire Naturelle, 2004).
8. Alan Kramer, *Dynamic of Destruction: Culture and Mass Killing in the First World War* (Oxford: Oxford University Press, 2007), 13.
9. Kramer, *Dynamic of Destruction*, 31.
10. Robin Prior and Trevor Wilson, *The First World War* (Washington, D.C.: Smithsonian, 1999), 118, 135, 199.
11. Deperchin, "Des destructions aux reconstructions," 1125.
12. Peter Gatrell, "Refugees," in *Europe since 1914: Encyclopedia of the Age of War and Reconstruction*, ed. John Merriman and Jay Winter (Detroit: Scribner's, 2006), 4:2188; Kramer, *Dynamic of Destruction*, 47.
13. Kramer, *Dynamic of Destruction*, 49; Prior and Wilson, *The First World War*, 206.
14. Isabel V. Hull, *Absolute Destruction: Military Culture and the Practices of War in Imperial Germany* (Ithaca: Cornell University Press, 2005), 309, 312. Hull cites plans for a "broad swath of destruction across the rest of occupied France and Belgium," 315.
15. Hull, *Absolute Destruction*, 315.
16. Hull, *Absolute Destruction*; Hugh D. Clout, *After the Ruins: Restoring the Countryside of Northern France after the Great War* (Exeter: University of Exeter Press, 1996), 20.
17. Neiberg, *Fighting the Great War*, 357.
18. Peter Grant, *Philanthropy and Voluntary Action in the First World War: Mobilizing Charity* (London: Routledge, 2014). Grant argues that far more working-class activists, especially women, became involved in philanthropic work.
19. Deperchin, "Des destructions aux reconstructions," 1127.
20. Clout, *After the Ruins*, 64.

21 Julien Sapori, "Les T.A.I.F 'Truppe Ausiliarie Italiane in Francia': guerriers ou terrassiers?" *14–18, le magazine de la Grande Guerre* 46 (2009): 72.
22 Clout, *After the Ruins,* 276.
23 Benoît Hopquin, "Le Poison de la guerre coule toujours à Verdun," *Le Monde,* January 20, 2014.

Chapter 9: The Allied Occupation of the Rhineland [pages 123-127]

1 Martin Gilbert, *The First World War: A Complete History* (New York: Holt, 1994), 306. The German proposal, of course, was rejected.
2 Georges-Henri Soutou, "Diplomacy," in *The Cambridge History of the First World War,* ed. Jay Winter (Cambridge: Cambridge University Press, 2014), 2:532; Zara Steiner, *The Lights That Failed: European International History, 1919–1933* (Oxford: Oxford University Press, 2005), 63. The truth was that the army could no longer fight. Gen. Paul von Hindenburg instructed the chief negotiator, Matthias Erzberger, to conclude "at any price," and on learning the details of the armistice, he sent a coded telegram saying, "you must sign all the same." See Michael Neiberg, *Fighting the Great War: A Global History* (Cambridge: Harvard University Press, 2005), 358, 361.
3 See copy printed in Vernon E. Kniptash, *On the Western Front with the Rainbow Division: A World War I Diary,* ed. E. Bruce Geelhoed (Norman: University of Oklahoma Press, 2009), 127.
4 Alan Kramer, *Dynamic of Destruction: Culture and Mass Killing in the First World War* (Oxford: Oxford University Press, 2007), 313.
5 Tina M. Campt, *Other Germans: Black Germans and the Politics of Race, Gender, and Memory in the Third Reich* (Ann Arbor: University of Michigan Press, 2004), 35. German propaganda used a language of "savages" and "pollution" (in contrast to German "Kultur"). See Campt, *Other Germans,* 37, 44, 52, 55 passim. Sander Gilman links the "mirage" of blackness to otherness in *On Blackness without Blacks: Essays on the Image of the Black in Germany* (Boston: G. K. Hall, 1982), xiii.
6 Campt, *Other Germans,* 34.
7 John Horne and Alan Kramer, *German Atrocities, 1914: A History of Denial* (New Haven: Yale University Press, 2001), 306 (see also 199, 302, 321); Joanna Bourke, "Gender Roles in Killing Zones," in *The Cambridge History of the First World War,* 159.
8 On the political upheavals in Alsace, which echoed socialist uprisings elsewhere in Germany, see Jean-Claude Richez, Léon Strauss, François Igersheim, and Stéphane Jonas, *1869–1935, Jacques Peirotes et le socialisme en Alsace* (Strasbourg: BF Éditions, 1989).
9 Anna V. S. Mitchell to C., October 20, November 3, 1918, Anna V. S. Mitchell papers, subseries of Olivia Stokes Hatch Papers, 1859–1993, Special Collections Department, Bryn Mawr College Library.
10 Hew Strachan, *The First World War* (London: Penguin, 2003), 327; Gilbert, *The First World War,* 500; Margaret Pawley, *The Watch on the Rhine: The Military Occupation of the Rhineland, 1918–1930* (London: I.B.Tauris, 2008), 1–2.
11 Gilbert, *The First World War,* 518. For the text of the treaty, see The Versailles Treaty June 28, 1919, The Avalon Project: Documents in Law, History and Diplomacy, Lillian Goldman Law Library, Yale Law School, http://avalon.law.yale.edu/subject_menus/versailles_menu.asp, accessed June 6, 2014.
12 For a general history of the IARHC occupation, see Pawley, *The Watch on the Rhine,* 127–154.
13 Dick van Galen Last, "Rhineland Occupation," in *Europe since 1914: Encyclopedia of the Age of War and Reconstruction,* ed. John Merriman and Jay Winter (Detroit: Scribner's, 2006), 4:2218; Pawley, *The Watch on the Rhine,* 47.
14 Margaret Macmillan, *Paris 1919: Six Months That Changed the World* (New York: Random House, 2002), 158–168, 170–175, 194–198, 465–480.
15 Macmillan, *Paris 1919,* 197; van Galen Last, "Rhineland Occupation," 4:2218; Pawley, *The Watch on the Rhine,* 17; Soutou, "Diplomacy," 2:509–511. Pawley traces the French promotion and funding of separatist movements in *The Watch on the Rhine,* 51–72.
16 The Catholic mayor of Cologne, Konrad Adenauer, weighed pursuit of an autonomous state within the German Republic in February 1919. Steiner, *The Lights That Failed,* 23. Hans Dorten, a former prosecutor from Coblenz, similarly agitated for independence from Protestant Prussia in June 1919. He was briefly named president of a Rhineland Republic, but his support quickly fizzled out. See Stephen A. Schuker, "The Rhineland Question: West European Security at the Paris Peace Conference of 1919," in *Treaty of Versailles: A Reassessment after 75 Years,* ed. Manfred F. Boemeke, Gerald D. Feldman, and Elisabeth Glaser (Cambridge: Cambridge University Press, 1998), 288–289.
17 Van Galen Last, "Rhineland Occupation," 4:2218–2219; Steiner, *The Lights That Failed,* 22–23.
18 Van Galen Last, "Rhineland Occupation," 4:2220. Van Galen Last suggests that the German government coop-

erated with the British and American forces in order to divide the Allies.
19 Pawley, *The Watch on the Rhine*, 42.
20 Van Galen Last, "Rhineland Occupation," 4:2220.
21 Pawley, *The Watch on the Rhine*, 44.
22 It has been suggested that as younger Belgians who had experienced the German occupation were drafted, rape may have served them as a form of revenge or as a masculine rite of initiation. Anne Godfroid, "After 'Teutonic Fury,' 'Belgian Fury'? Fact and Fiction in the Revenge of Belgian Soldiers in the Rhineland in 1923," in *Rape in Wartime,* ed. Raphaëlle Branche and Fabrice Virgili (Basingstoke, Eng.: Palgrave Macmillan, 2012), 96–97, 99. Most black French African troops had left Germany by the time of events alleged in German papers.
23   Pawley, *The Watch on the Rhine*, 130–140; Bruno Cabanes, "1919: Aftermath," in *The Cambridge History of the First World War*, 1:192–193.
24 Jon Jacobson, "Reparations," in *Europe since 1914*, 4:2208. Immediately after the departure of the American forces, in 1923 to 1925, when the Inter-Allied Reparation Commission formally recognized the German default on payments, the French and Belgians occupied the Ruhr area. That strategy of extraction by force failed. See Van Galen Last, "Rhineland Occupation," 4:2220; Schuker,"The Rhineland Question," 305, 311; Steiner, *The Lights That Failed*, 230. Germany may have spent more money rearming than the amount stipulated in reparations that they refused to pay. See Antoine Capet and Spencer C. Tucker, "Legacy of the war," in *The Encyclopedia of World War I: A Political, Social and Military History*, ed. Priscilla Mary Roberts and Spencer C. Tucker (Santa Barbara: ABC-CLIO, 2005), 24–25.
25 Pawley, *The Watch on the Rhine*, 42; Campt, *Other Germans*, 36.
26 General Allen's report on this "political propaganda" was published in United States Army, American Forces in Germany, *American Representation in Occupied Germany, 1920–1921* (1922; London: Forgotten Books, 2013), 1:94–97; "Finds Negro Troops Orderly on Rhine; General Allen Reports Charges Are German Propaganda, Especially for America," *New York Times*, 1921, p. 9. Allen's report finds "French colonial troops . . . quiet, orderly and well behaved," and the High Commission likewise condemned the charges as for the most part "completely unfounded." United States Army, *American Representation*, 1:97, 100.
27 The long-term consequences under the Nazi government included forcible sterilization of mixed-race Germans. See Campt, *Other Germans*, 63–80.
28 Pawley, *The Watch on the Rhine*, 32–33; van Galen Last, "Rhineland Occupation," 4:2221.
29 Byron Farwell, *Over There: The United States in the Great War, 1917–1918* (New York: Norton, 1999), 267–268.
30 Bruno Cabanes, "Démobilisations et retour des hommes," in *Encyclopédie de la Grande Guerre, 1914–1918*, ed. Stéphane Audoin-Rouzeau and Jean-Jacques Becker (Paris: Bayard, 2004), 1053; Farwell, *Over There*, 269.
31 Farwell, *Over There*, 269.
32 From a memoir by Reynold Thomas, "Seeing Tina Home or Beating the Curfew with Military Honors." By permission of Margaret Thomas Buchholz.
33 Mark Meigs, "Crash-Course Americanism: The A.E.F. University, 1919," *History Today* 44.8 (1994): 37.
34 Meigs, "Crash-Course Americanism," 37–39.
35 Anna V. S. Mitchell to C., April 10, 1918, Anna V. S. Mitchell papers, subseries of Olivia Stokes Hatch Papers, 1859–1993, Special Collections Department, Bryn Mawr College Library. On Pershing's view, see Farwell, *Over There*, 272.
36 Pawley, *The Watch on the Rhine*, 179–183. She argues that the mood of isolationism led the Allies to set aside intelligence reports on the rise of Nazism and nationalist rearmament.
37 On the German refusal to pay reparations, and the extensive attempts by the Allies to create arrangements that would facilitate payments, including American loans to Germany, see Jacobson, "Reparations," 4:2205–2209.
38 Pawley, *The Watch on the Rhine*, 179, 183–184; Steiner, *The Lights That Failed*, 247.
39 Frank Marion Russell, *The Saar: Battleground and Pawn* (Stanford: Standford University Press, 1951), 104.

Chapter 10: Cemeteries and Commemoration [pages 135-138]

1   Jay Winter, *Sites of Memory, Sites of Mourning: The Great War in European Cultural History* (Cambridge: Cambridge University Press, 1995), 78; Carina Trevisan and Elise Julien, "Cemeteries," in *Capital Cities at War: Paris, London, Berlin, 1914–1919*, ed. J. M. Winter and Jean-Louis Robert (Cambridge: Cambridge University Press, 2007), 2:446.
2   The memorial at Reims to troops from the colonies (destroyed in World War II by German occupiers) was paired with a memorial at Bamako and another at Dakar. But see also the erasure of memory, as discussed by Bruce Scates and Rebecca Wheatley, "War Memorials," in *The Cambridge History of the First World War*, ed. Jay Winter (Cambridge: Cambridge University Press, 2014) 3:453–454.

3   The landmark study *Lieux de Mémoire*, which gives extensive space to cemeteries, has been translated twice in different configurations. See Pierre Nora, ed., *Realms of Memory: Rethinking the French Past* (New York: Columbia University Press, 1999–2010).
4   Bruno Cabanes writes of the "nationalisation of the memory of war" that "became a true founding myth" for Australia and New Zealand; the Versailles Treaty, he says, "fuelled nationalism" in colonies disappointed by the outcome. Bruno Cabanes, "1919: Aftermath," in *The Cambridge History of the First World War*, 1:184, 181. Guoqi Xu similarly argues that "Indian involvement in the war sparked . . . the rise of Indian nationalism." Guoqi Xu, "Asia," in *The Cambridge History of the First World War*, 1:487. See also Chris Maclean and Jock Philips, *The Sorrow and the Pride: New Zealand War Memorials* (Wellington: GP Books, 1990); J. R. Gillis, *Commemorations: The Politics of National Identity* (Princeton: Princeton University Press, 1994); Ken Inglis, *Sacred Places: War Memorials in the Australian Landscape* (Carleton: Melbourne University Press, 2004); and David McKenzie, ed., *Canada and the First World War* (Toronto: University of Toronto, 2005).
5   Annette Becker, *Les Monuments aux morts: patrimoine et mémoire de la Grande Guerre* (Paris: Errance, 1988), 360. Carina Trevisan and Elise Julien discuss the French eagerness to repatriate the bodies of their dead. See their essay "Cemeteries," 2:436–437.
6   Daniel J. Sherman, *The Construction of Memory in Interwar France* (Chicago: Chicago University Press, 1999), 6.
7   Winter, *Sites of Memory*, 78–116.
8   Antoine Prost, "Les monuments aux morts," in *Les Lieux de mémoire*, ed. Pierre Nora (Paris: Gallimard, 1984), 1:195–225.
9   Winter, *Sites of Memory*, 104; Leonard V. Smith, Stéphane Audoin-Rouzeau, and Annette Becker, *France and the Great War, 1914–1918* (Cambridge: Cambridge University Press, 2003), 171–175. On the symbolism of the cenotaph and the unknown soldier, see Trevisan and Julien, "Cemeteries," 2:455–465; Bruce Scates and Rebecca Wheatley, "War Memorials," in *The Cambridge History of the First World War*, 3:537–538. The powerful charge carried by such a monument is conveyed by Charlotte Mew's poem "The Cenotaph," in her *Collected Poems and Selected Prose* (New York: Routledge, 2003), 40–41.
10 Winter, *Sites of Memory*, 102–105. See also Martin Gilbert, *The First World War: A Complete History* (New York: Holt, 1994), on the unknown soldier as a focus of yearning for the bereaved, 529.
11 In her own copy of the memoir, Hall inserted a postcard of the Châlons-sur-Marne Hôtel de Ville, with a caption explaining that the bodies of four unidentified American soldiers were brought there, and one was designated as the American "unknown soldier" to be buried at Arlington on November 11, 1921. Margaret Hall, "Letters and Photographs from the Battle Country, 1918–1919," Cohasset Historical Society (65.07.01), facing page 81.
12 Jay Winter, *Remembering War: The Great War between Memory and History in the Twentieth Century* (New Haven: Yale University Press, 2006), 148–149. See also Winter, *Sites of Memory*, 108–113. The cemetery built at Roggeveld by German soldiers, where Peter Kollwitz first lay, was consolidated in the 1950s with many smaller grave sites in a new resting place, "Der deutsche Soldatenfriedhof Vladslo."
13 Sherman, *Construction of Memory*, 71. For German cemeteries, see Rudy Koshar, *From Monuments to Traces: Artifacts of German Memory, 1870–1990* (Berkeley: University of California Press, 2000). For English cemeteries in France, see Philip Longworth, *The Unending Vigil: The History of the Commonwealth War Graves Commission, 1917–1967* (London: Constable, 1967). For Australian cemeteries, see Bart Ziino, *A Distant Grief: Australians, War Graves and the Great War* (Crawley: University of Western Australia Press, 2007).
14 John Keegan, *The First World War* (London: Hutchinson, 1998), 451.
15 Trevisan and Julien,"Cemeteries," 2:438.
16 Keegan, *The First World War,* 452.
17 Keegan, *The First World War*, 372.
18 Eccles. 44:14.
19 On American reburial, repatriation, and graves registration, see Lisa Budreau, *Bodies of War: World War I and the Politics of Commemoration in America, 1919–1933* (New York: New York University Press, 2009).
20 Sherman, *Construction of Memory*, 83.
21 Keegan, *The First World War*, 451.
22 Jay Winter and Emmanuel Sivan, *War and Remembrance in the Twentieth Century* (Cambridge: Cambridge University Press, 1999), 10–11.

Chapter 11: Versailles Treaty [pages 157–161]

1   Margaret Macmillan, *Paris 1919: Six Months That Changed the World* (New York: Random House, 2002).
2   Martin Gilbert, *The First World War: A Complete History (*New York: Holt, 1994), 530.
3   John M. Keynes in particular argued that the terms were too harsh, overlooking the precedents set by the

German reparations demands made of the Russians and those imposed in 1870–1871 on the French. See Gilbert, *The First World War*, 518. For the terms of the treaty, see The Versailles Treaty June 28, 1919, The Avalon Project: Documents in Law, History and Diplomacy, Lillian Goldman Law Library, Yale Law School, http://avalon.law.yale.edu/subject_menus/versailles_menu.asp, accessed June 6, 2014.
4 Macmillan, *Paris 1919*, 159; Christine Beil und Gabriele Trost, "Trauma Versailles," in *Der erste Weltkrieg* (Berlin: Rowohlt, 2006), 235–236.
5 Gilbert, *The First World War*, 515.
6 Helmut Konrad, "Drafting the Peace," in *The Cambridge History of World War I*, ed. Jay Winter (Cambridge: Cambridge University Press, 2014), 2:617.
7 John Horne and Alan Kramer, *German Atrocities, 1914: A History of Denial* (New Haven: Yale University Press, 2001), 335–337; Gilbert, *The First World War*, 518; Macmillan, *Paris 1919*, 473–474.
8 Keith L. Nelson, *Victors Divided: America and the Allies in Germany, 1918–1923* (Berkeley: Unversity of California Press, 1975).
9 Macmillan, *Paris 1919*, 98–107.
10 Robert W. Tucker, *Woodrow Wilson and the Great War: Reconsidering America's Neutrality, 1914–1917* (Charlottesville: University of Virginia Press, 2007), 213.
11 Macmillan, *Paris 1919*, 273–278.
12 Yves Beigbeder, *International Monitoring of Plebiscites, Referenda and National Elections: Self-determination and Transition to Democracy* (Dordrecht: Nijhoff, 1994), 81.
13 Macmillan, *Paris 1919*, 487.
14 A formal account of such dissent can be found in the Carnegie Endowment for International Peace, *Violation of the Laws and Customs of War: Reports of Majority and Dissenting Reports of American and Japanese Members of the Commission of Responsibilities, Conference of Paris 1919* (Oxford: Clarendon Press, 1919).
15 Alan Kramer, *Dynamic of Destruction: Culture and Mass Killing in the First World War* (Oxford: Oxford University Press, 2007), 283.
16 Macmillan, *Paris 1919*, 98–106.
17 Macmillan, *Paris 1919*, 158–159; Tucker., *Woodrow Wilson and the Great War: Reconsidering America's Neutrality, 1914–1917* (Charlottesville: University Press of Virginia, 2007), 213.
18 Kramer, *Dynamic of Destruction*, 314.
19 Kramer, *Dynamic of Destruction*, 227.
20 Jon Jacobson, "Reparations," in *Europe since 1914: Encyclopedia of the Age of War and Reconstruction*, ed. John Merriman and Jay Winter (Detroit: Scribner's, 2006), 4:2206, 2208–2209.
21 Kramer, *Dynamic of Destruction*, 234.
22 Bruno Cabanes, *The Great War and the Origins of Humanitarianism, 1918–1924* (Cambridge: Cambridge University Press, 2014), 1; Annette Becker, "Leipzig Trials," in *Europe since 1914*, 4:1636–1637.
23 Jacques Bainville, cited by Stephen A Schuker, "The Rhineland Question: West European Security at the Paris Peace Conference of 1919," in *The Treaty of Versailles: A Reassessment after 75 Years*, ed. Manfred F. Boemeke, Gerald D. Feldman, and Elisabeth Glaser (Cambridge: Cambridge University Press, 1998), 275.
24 Corona Brezina, ed., *The Treaty of Versailles, 1919: A Primary Source Examination of the Treaty That Ended World War I* (New York: Rosen, 2006), 46.
25 J. W. Schulte Nordholt, *Woodrow Wilson: A Life for World Peace* (Berkeley: University of California Press, 1990), 358.
26 See Peter Gatrell, "War after the War: Conflicts, 1919–23," in *A Companion to World War I*, ed. John Horne (Chichester: Wiley-Blackwell, 2010), 558–575; Hew Strachan, *The First World War* (London and New York: Penguin, 2003), 333; John Keegan, *The First World War* (New York: Vintage Books, 2000), 419–420.
27 Macmillan, *Paris 1919*, 476; Sophie Delaporte, *Les gueules cassées: les blessés de la face de la Grande Guerre* (Paris: Noêsis, 1996).
28 Gilbert, *The First World War*, 519.
29 Andrew Scott Berg, *Wilson* (New York: Putnam Penguin, 2013), 531.
30 Keegan, *The First World War*, 423.
31 Kramer, *Dynamic of Destruction*, 251.
32 Leonard Smith, Stéphane Audoin-Rouzeau, and Annette Becker, *France and the Great War, 1914–1918* (Cambridge: Cambridge University Press, 2003), 165.
33 George Mosse, *Fallen Soldier: Reshaping the Memory of the World Wars* (Oxford: Oxford University Press, 1990); John Horne and Robert Gerwarth, eds., *War in Peace: Paramilitary Violence in Europe after the Great War* (Oxford: Oxford University Press, 2012); Stéphane Audoin-Rouzeau and Annette Becker, *1914–18: Understanding the Great War*, trans. Catherine Temerson (London: Profile, 2002), 236.

Appendix 1: Biographical Key

The following resources were consulted in the compilation of these personal name entries: U.S. Social Security Death Index (1935-present); Federal and State Census Reports (1860–1930); New York Passenger and Crew Lists (1820–1954); Boston, Passenger Lists (1820–1954); U.S. Passport Applications (1795–1925). These and all online databases below were accessed by searching by personal name across Ancestry.com.

Also consulted were the following publications and documents: *List of Personnel in the Overseas Service of the American Red Cross: April, 1917 to November, 1919*, vol. 1: *Women* (Hartford: The Connecticut State Library, 1921); Capt. A. M. McKnight, "American Red Cross, List of Directrices of L.O.C. and Aviation Canteens with their Addresses in the United States" and "Summary: American Red Cross Canteen Service, Bureau of L.O.C. Canteens, Army and Navy Department," August 25, 1919, 942.616, Central File of the American Red Cross, 1917–1934, Donated Records Collection, Record Group 200, National Archives at College Park, College Park, MD; *Britannica Student Encyclopedia* from Encyclopædia Britannica Online; *The Bryn Mawr Alumnae Bulletin* (1920–1938); *The Bryn Mawr Alumnae Quarterly* (1908–1919); *The Bryn Mawr College Calendar* (1915–1918).

Additional details of the following individual figures' lives were drawn from the following resources:

Ida Bourne Andrus: "Andrus Daughter Dies at 74 in Minneapolis," *Herald Statesman*, May 11, 1962.

Marion Polk Angellotti: Henry Fitz-Gilbert Water, "Descendents of John Devereux," *New England Historical and Genealogical Register* 74 (1920): 309; "Miss Angellotti Hurt by Mishap in France," *San Francisco Chronicle*, October 10, 1918.

Baker, M. P. [Louis?]: U.S., World War I Draft Registration Cards, 1917–1918 (online database); U.S. Veterans Gravesites, ca. 1775–2006 (online database); "Deaths," *New York Times*, August 10, 1950.

Bertha Bates: *A Catalogue of the Officers and Students in Washington University with the Courses of Study for the Academic Year, 1895–96* (St. Louis: Nixon Jones Printing Co., 1895), 26; *The Third General Catalogue of the Officers and Graduates of Vassar College, 1861–1900* (Poughkeepsie, N.Y.: A. V. Haight, 1900), 134; Reports of Deaths of American Citizens Abroad, 1835–1974 (online database).

Emily Marion Bennett: *The Work of the American Red Cross: Report by the War Council of Appropriations and Activities from Outbreak of War to November 1, 1917* (Washington: American Red Cross, 1917), 90; *Smith Alumnae Quarterly*, vol. 10, November 1918, p. 51.

Florence Billings: "Florence Billings, Pioneer Resident, Passes Away," *Redlands Daily Facts*, September 10, 1959, p. 5; finding aid, Florence Billings papers, 1915–1959, Sophia Smith Collection, Smith College, Northampton, Mass.

Elsa Bowman: *Woman's Who's Who of America, 1914–1915*, ed. John William Leonard (New York: American Commonwealth Co., 1914), 119; "Flint-Bowman," *New York Sun*, October 16, 1895; "Letter to the Editor," *New York Times*, April 22, 1913; Connecticut Death Index, 1949–2001 (online database).

Frances Sage Bradley: Finding aid, Frances Sage Bradley papers, 1893–1965, Manuscript, Archives, and Rare Book Library, Emory University.

Conrad and Pierce Butler: U.S., World War I Draft Registration Cards, 1917–1918 (online database); U.S., World War II Draft Registration Cards, 1942 (online database).

Ethel M. Colgate: "Four Weddings on the Calendar," *New York Times*, December 23, 1923; "Note and Comment," *Boston Evening Transcript*, January 30, 1902, p. 4.

Dorothea and Gladys Cromwell: Susan Solomon, "Gladys Cromwell," in *The Modernist Journals Project*, Brown University and the University of Tulsa, http://library.brown.edu/cds/mjp/render.php?view=mjp_object&id=mjp.2005.01.071; "Praises Cromwell Twins," *New York Times*, January 30, 1919, p. 22; "Cromwell Deaths Now Confirmed," *New York Times*, January 26, 1919, p. 1.

Reed M. Davidson: "Reported Captured and Dead," *Red Cross Bulletin*, November 15, 1920; *Ashland City Directory*, 1917; *Ashland Daily Independent*, Obituary Index: February 26, 1940.

Mme E. E. R. De la Croix: "Red Cross Serves Hot Food to Yanks," *New York Sun*, October 10, 1918, p. 6.

Ethel D. Earle: New York City Death Index (1862–1948) (online database).

Jane Brown Fuller Francis: U.S. Passport Applications, 1795–1925; Boston Evening Transcript, April 12, 1899, p. 3; Frederick S. Mead, A.B., ed., *Harvard's Military Record in the World War* (Boston: The Harvard Alumni Association, 1921), 346.

Ruth L. Gaines: "Smith College Unit to Serve in France," *New York Times*, July 22, 1917. Her letters, diary, and other materials from the war are kept in the Sophia Smith Collection at Smith College.

Harvey D. Gibson: Frequent citations in volume 2 (1918) of the *Red Cross Bulletin*.

Mme Marie Hennocque: Death dates for her sons, Auguste and Gustave, come from a monument at Beaumont-sur-Dême transcribed at MémorialGenWeb, http://www.memorial-genweb.org.

Mme Hermann: "French Rabbi Sends Plea to Chicago," *Sentinel*, March 8, 1918.

Mary Fellows Hoyt: Alice Bache Gould papers, Massachusetts Historical Society.
Anna Van Schaik Mitchell: Finding aid, Register of the Anna V. S. Mitchell Papers, 1920–1944, Hoover Institution, Stanford University.
Mildred Mitchell: "Miss Mitchell Engaged," *New York Times*, August 2, 1923; Social Security Death Index (online database).
Anne Tracy Morgan: Ruth Franklin, "A Life in Good Taste," *New Yorker*, September 27, 2004.
Marjorie Nott: Barbara Bellows, *A Talent for Living: Josephine Pinckney* (Louisiana State University Press, 2006), 126–128.
Marie Brockway Pond: Finding aid, Marie Brockway Pond Papers, 1917–1919, Sophia Smith Collection, Smith College.
Amy Louise Steiner: "Dr. Steiner Dead; Physician, Writer," *New York Times*, November 6, 1942.
Joseph-Marie Tissier: *Catholic Herald*, January 16, 1948.
Anne Harriman Sands Vanderbilt: "Lafayette Escadrille," in *The United States in the First World War: An Encyclopedia*, ed. Anne Cipriano Venzon (New York: Routledge, 2013), 325. "The French-American Hall of Fame: Mrs. William K. Vanderbilt," *La France: An American Magazine*, February 1920.
Warren Jay Vinton: "Alumni Notes," *Signet*, June 1918, p. 96; "Warren Jay Vinton, '11, Appointed for Relief Commission," *Michigan Alumnus* 25 (1919): 282; Congressional Directory; finding aid, Warren Jay Vinton papers, 1932–1969, Division of Rare and Manuscript Collections, Carl A. Kroch Library, Cornell University.
Elizabeth White: Gregor Stark and E. Catherine Rayne, *El Delirio: The Santa Fe World of Elizabeth White* (Santa Fe: School for Advanced Research Press, 1998).
Louisa Skinner Worthington: Ohio, Deaths, 1908–1932, 1938–2007 (online database).

Appendix 2: Selected Chronology of World War I

The dates and descriptions used in the chronology were informed by these sources: David F. Burg and L. Edward Purcell, *Almanac of World War I* (Lexington: University Press of Kentucky, 1998); Pierre Darmon, *Vivre à Paris pendant la Grande Guerre* (Paris: Fayard, 2002); Vincent J. Esposito, ed., *The West Point Atlas of American Wars*, vol. 2: *1900–1953* (New York: Praeger, 1959); Martin Gilbert, *The First World War: A Complete History* (New York: Holt, 1994); John Horne, ed., *A Companion to World War I* (Chichester: Wiley-Blackwell, 2010); John Keegan, *The First World War* (New York: Vintage Books, 2000); "The Nobel Peace Prize 1917," Nobel Prizes and Laureats, Nobelprize.org, www.nobelprize.org/nobel_prizes/peace/laureates/1917/, accessed May 14, 2014; Maurice Pierrat, *Châlons-sur-Marne pendant l'Occupation allemande, Septembre 1914* (Châlons-sur-Marne: l'Union republicane de la Marne, 1915); Stéphane Audoin-Rouzeau and Jean-Jacques Becker, *Encyclopédie de la Grande Guerre, 1914–1918* (Paris : Bayard, 2004); Spencer C. Tucker and Priscilla Roberts, eds., *The Encyclopedia of World War I: A Political, Social, and Military History* (Santa Barbara: ABC-CLIO, 2005); Jay Winter, ed., *The Cambridge History of the First World War* (Cambridge: Cambridge University Press, 2014).

Appendix 3: Places and Monuments: The Geography of War

The information in this appendix is based on the following sources: David F. Burg and L. Edward Purcell, *Almanac of World War I* (Lexington: University Press of Kentucky, 1998); Byron Farwell, *Over There: The United States in the Great War, 1917–1918* (New York: Norton, 1999); Robert H. Ferrell, *America's Deadliest Battle: Meuse-Argonne, 1918* (Lawrence: University Press of Kansas, 2007); Martin Gilbert, *The First World War: A Complete History* (New York: Holt, 1994); Paul and Remi Hess, "La vie a Reims pendant la guerre, 1914–1918," http://1914ancien.free.fr/reimshss.htm; John and Alan Kramer Horne, *German Atrocities, 1914: A History of Denial* (New Haven: Yale University Press, 2001); M. W. Ireland, Charles Lynch, Joseph H. Ford, and Frank W. Weed, *Medical Department of the United States Army in the World War*, vol. 8: *Field Operations* (Washington, D.C.: Government Printing Office, 1925); John Keegan, *The First World War* (New York: Vintage Books, 2000); Michael S. Neiberg, *Fighting the Great War: A Global History* (Cambridge: Harvard University Press, 2009); Hew Strachan, *The First World War* (New York: Penguin, 2003); Spencer C. Tucker and Mary Roberts, eds., *The Encyclopedia of World War I: A Political, Social and Military History* (Santa Barbara: ABC-CLIO, 2005); Jay Winter, ed., *The Cambridge History of the First World War* (Cambridge: Cambridge University Press, 2014); Our History, American Hospital at Paris, http://www.american-hospital.org/en/american-hospital-of-paris/about-us/our-history.html, accessed May 31, 2014; Thomas G. Frothingham, *A Guide to the Military History of the World War, 1914–1918* (Boston: Little, Brown, and Company, 1920); Francis J. Reynolds et al., *The Story of the Great War* (New York: Collier and Son, 1920); *Soissons Before and During the War* (Clermont-Ferrand: Michelin & Co., 1919); *The Battle of Verdun (1914–1918)* (Clermont-Ferrand: Michelin & Co., 1920); *The Americans in the Great War* (Clermont-Ferrand: Michelin & Co., 1920); "Distributes Relief among War Victims," *New York Times*, June 1, 1919 (for CARD in Laon); *Petit Larousse illustré* (Paris: Larousse, 1981); *Encyclopædia Britannica: The New*

Volumes, Constituting . . . the Twelfth Edition (London and New York: Encyclopædia Britannica, 1922), various entries; *Encyclopædia Britannica Online* (London: Encyclopædia Britannica, 2014), various entries; *Gazetteer of the World* (London: A. Fullerton & Co., 1859), various entries; *Red Cross Bulletin*, April 21, 1919, pp. 6–7; "Destruction of the French Coal Mines," *Engineering and Mining Journal*, December 21, 1918, p. 1077; Records of the American Expeditionary Force, Record Group 120, finding aid, National Archives, www.archives.gov/research/guide-fed-records/groups/120.html; Shipley Thomas, *The History of the A.E.F.* (New York: George H. Doran Company, 1920); Alexander Woollcott, "How's It Look over There?" *North American Review*, December 1920, pp. 765–776.

Appendices 4 and 5: Period and Foreign Terms

The list of period and foreign terms has been informed by these standard reference sources: the *Petit Larousse*, *Harrap's New Standard French and English Dictionary*, and the *Oxford English Dictionary* (1933).

Index

106th Infantry (French), xxiii, 121; photograph of, xxiv; theatrical troupe of, 140–141, 153
25th Artillery (French), 121
77th Division (Lost Battalion), 142, 155, 188
accommodations: in Châlons, 31, 34, 36–37, 48, 86, 88–89, 117, 118–119; in Paris, 15–16, 95, 163; in Nancy, 128; in Metz, 128–129; in Strasbourg, 128, 129; in Germany, 131–134; in Verdun, 141, 154, 162; in Varennes, 142–143; in Romagne, 144–145; in Lille, 164; in Soissons, 166
Adalbert of Prussia (prince): Hall mentions, 130
air raids: in Paris, 11–12, 12–13, 16, 21–23; in Châlons, 30, 35, 35–36, 39–41, 47, 51, 62–63; and bombing of evacuation hospital, 41, 47, 60
Albert, 108, 189; Hall visits, 163
Allen, Miss, 15, 171
Alsace-Lorraine, 124, 125. *See also specific cities and towns*
American Committee for Devastated France (CARD), 4, 6, 28, 107, 168
American Expeditionary Force (AEF), xxi, xxiv-xxvi, 43, 44–45, 46–47, 186, 187–188; French express appreciation for, 13, 21, 65, 71, 72, 86–87, 97, 148, 150, 163; African American soldiers of, 32, 109, 111, 137, 143, 144, 155, 162; Hall comments on friction with French, 86, 116–117, 118, 139, 145–149. *See also specific battle sites*; illnesses; injuries; soldiers
American Forces in Germany (AFG), 125, 126–127
American Fund for French Wounded, 4. *See also* American Committee for Devastated France
American Red Cross (ARC), xix, xx, xxi-xxv, 2, 3, 4; Hall notes presence of, 5, 6, 7, 15; in Paris, 15–16, 17, 18–20, 24, 24–25; canteen operations, 27, 28, 30. *See also specific locations*; Red Cross
Amiens, 181, 189; Hall visits, 163, 165
Amiens, Battle of, 45, 187
Andrus, Ida Bourne: Hall mentions, 134; identified, 171
Angellotti, Marion Polk, 92; Hall travels with, 92, 95–98, 133; identified, 171
Anizy-le-Chateau, 189; Hall visits, 167

Arc de Triomphe, 95–96, 166, 194
Argonne battlefields, 187–188, 189; Hall visits, 111, 121–122, 142–144, 154–155. *See also* battle sites, devastation of
Armentières, 182, 186, 189; Hall visits, 164; photograph of, fig. 35
Armistice, 66, 69–70, 71; terms of, 68, 69–70, 91, 123; Hall describes reactions to, 71–72
Arras, 185, 186, 187, 189; Hall visits, 163; photograph of, fig. 35
Austria-Hungary, 65; Hall hears rumors of peace request, 62, 64
Auteuil, 195; Hall visits hospital at, 19–20

Baker, [Louis?] "M.P.", xxv; photograph of, xxvi; Hall mentions, 91, 142, 154, 155, 162, 165, 166; identified, 171
Bates, Bertha: Hall mentions, 133; identified, 171
battlefield tourism, xix, 93–94, 137, 139, 155, 156. *See also* Hall, Margaret
battle sites, devastation of, 31, 78, 92, 99, 105–108, 146, 155, 159. *See also names of specific sites*; battlefield tourism; reconstruction and salvage
Belasco, David, 59, 97: identified, 171
Belgium, 182, 186, 187; Hall visits, 154, 168–169; photographs of, 161, fig. 36. *See also specific cities*
Belleau Wood, 45, 186, 187, 189: Hall visits, 97–98
Bellicourt Tunnel, 188; Hall visits, 165
Bennett, Emily Marion: Hall mentions, 48, 65–66; identified, 171
Billings, Florence, 4; Hall mentions, 53, 152, 156, 166, 167; Hall travels with, 166–167; identified, 171
Bois de Boulogne, 195; Hall visits, 19, 96
boots, with feet in them: commonness of, 143
Bordeaux, 189; Hall arrives in, 10, 14, 15
Bourlon Wood, 190; Hall visits, 164–165
Bouvier, Jeanne, 12
Bowman, Elsa, xviii, 4; Hall travels with, 168; photograph of, 93; identified, 172
Bradley, Dr. Frances Sage: Hall describes, 6; identified, 172
Brion, Hélène, 12
Bryn Mawr: Hall mentions, 16. *See*

also individual students of
Burnett, Miss, 172; Hall mentions, 16
Butler, Conrad: Hall mentions, 102; identified, 172
Butler, Pierce: Hall mentions, 5; identified, 172

Cambrai, 185, 188, 190; Hall visits, 164–165
canteen (general services of) and hospitality huts, 2, 20, 25, 28, 30; in occupied Germany, 126–127, 133–134. *See also* Cantine des Deux Drapeaux; Écury, canteen at; St. Wendel (Saarland); Tours, canteen at; Treves, canteen at
Cantine des Deux Drapeaux (Red Cross canteen at Châlons-sur-Marne), xviii, xix, 27, 28–30, 124; photographs of, xvii, 27, 38, 61, 140, 162, figs. 1–3, fig. 21; Hall mentions, 16–17, 18, 25, 154; Hall describes, 32, 62, 140; Hall describes work at, 34–35, 48, 50, 51, 52, 60–61, 63, 66, 85–86, 102–103, 115–116, 118–119, 139, 145, 149, 151–152, 154; reactions to Armistice at, 71, 72, 116; Croix de Guerre awarded at, 155; final day of ARC participation in, 162
CARD. *See* American Committee for Devastated France
cemeteries, gravesites, and funerals, 94, 135–138, 149; Hall mentions or attends, 19, 21, 25, 50, 64, 97–98, 112, 113, 150, 153; burials at Romagne, 143, 144, 155
Cenon, Bordeaux, 190: Hall in, 14–15
Châlons-sur-Marne (city), 151, 156, 163, 181, 187, 190; photographs of, xxiv, xxvi, 26, 29, 36, 49, figs. 5–7, fig. 13, fig. 23; conditions during war, 27–28, 30, 35–38, 41–42, 47, 48–49, 51–52, 65; grenade explosion at, 54, 60; responses to Armistice in, 67, 69, 71–72, 85; American Unknown Soldier chosen at, 136; Military Cemetery in, 150, 153; Jard, 151
Châlons-sur-Marne, Red Cross canteen at. *See* Cantine des Deux Drapeaux
Château-Thierry, 45, 156, 186, 187, 190; Hall visits, 95, 97–98
Chemin des Dames, 181, 186; Hall visits, 166, 168
Coblenz (Germany), 191; Hall visits, 132–134
Coleman, Emma Lewis, xxvi; letter to,

14; sponsors Olivier family, 14, 77, 169; identified, 172
Colgate, Ethel, 4; Hall describes, 6; identified, 172
Cologne (Germany), 191; Hall visits, 133
Comité Americain pour les Régions Dévastées (CARD). *See* American Committee for Devastated France
Coolidge, Miss, 172; Hall mentions, 51
Coryn, Marjorie: Hall mentions, 39, 50, 51, 52, 60, 63, 130; at Écury canteen, 54, 55, 57, 59; identified, 172 ; photograph of, fig. 21
Coucy-le-Chateau, 191; Hall visits gun emplacement at, 167; photograph of, 167
Courteau, 191; Hall visits, 98
Craonne, 181, 191; Hall visits, 168
Croix de Guerre, 75, 155; awarded for canteen work, 30, 155; awarded to Châlons-sur-Marne, 30; photograph of ceremony for, 155. *See also individual recipients*
Cromwell, Dorothea, xxiii, 30, 140; photograph of, 140; identified, 172–173
Cromwell, Gladys, xxiii, 30, 140; photograph of, 140; identified, 172–173
Cross, Emily: Hall mentions, 16; identified, 173

Davidson, Reed M.: Hall mentions, 35; identified, 173
dances, as recreation for soldiers, 8, 126, 133–134, 139, 154, 168
De la Croix, Mme E. E. R.: Hall mentions, 40, 49, 129; identified, 173
De la Giclais, Capt. Jean-Marie: Hall mentions, 131; identified, 173
De la T., 173: Hall mentions, 89
Dufrénoy, Adélaïde: Hall buys books by, 130; identified, 173
Dun: Hall visits, 112
Duncan, Isadora: Hall describes hospital run by, 24; identified, 173
Dun-sur-Meuse, 187, 191; Hall sees, 111; Dun-sur-Meuse road, 154

Earle, Ethel D., 3, 4, 107; Hall mentions, 5, 6, 8, 9, 15, 31, 39, 62, 102, 119, 121; in Paris with Hall, 17, 21–22, 24–25; travels with Hall, 97–98, 99–101, 109–115, 120; identified, 173
economy: wartime, 12, 13, 17, 31, 49, 52; postwar, 131, 143, 145–146, 152. *See also* food and water
Écury, 191; field hospital at, 53; Hall staffs canteen at, 53–59, 188; photographs of, 1, 53, 58, figs. 9–11
Ehrenbreitstein, Germany: Hall visits, 133
Epernay, 191; Hall mentions, 32, 63, 95, 101, 116; Hall visits, 152
L'Épine: Hall describes, 63
Étain, 192; Hall visits, 153

First Pan-African Congress, 159
Foch, Ferdinand, 45; on Versailles Treaty, 160
food and water, 9, 10, 12, 13, 14, 15, 16, 17, 20, 34, 42, 49, 50, 64–65, 87, 100, 102, 109, 114, 117, 119, 126, 131, 133, 145, 149, 151, 153. *See also* Cantine des Deux Drapeaux, Hall describes work at
Ford, George, 105–106
Fort de Brimont, 192; Hall mentions, 75
Fort de Douaumont, 147, 183, 184, 192; Hall visits, 112–115, 141, 153, 155; photographs of, xxviii, 114, fig. 8, fig. 15
Fort de la Laufée, 183; Hall visits, 155
Fort de la Malmaison, 192; Hall visits, 166
Fort de la Pompelle, 192; Hall visits, 152
Fort de Vaux, 183, 184, 192; Hall visits, 112, 114, 141–142, 153, 155; photograph of, fig. 18
Foyer du Soldats, 2, 28; Hall notes, 110, 167
Francis, Jane Brown Fuller: Hall mentions, 131, 163; identified, 173–174
French Red Cross, and Cantine des Deux Drapeaux, 162, 163
Fryatt, Charles: Hall mentions, 169; identified, 174
Fussell, Paul, xv

Gaines, Ruth, 3–4, 6, 78; Hall mentions, 25; identified, 174. *See also* Smith College Relief Unit
Gare de Vaugirard, 194; ARC services at, 24
gas (chemical weapon), xxii, 182, 183, 187; victims of, 15, 18, 19, 24, 167–168
Germany: occupation of, 70, 123–127, 158; Army of Occupation, 90; American relief workers in, 118, 126; Hall's descriptions of, 131–134
Gibson, Harvey D.: Hall mentions, 16; identified, 174
Gouraud, Henri, 124; Hall mentions, 50, 51, 60, 116, 131; identified, 174

Guynemer, Georges: plane of, 24; identified, 174

H., Miss, 39
Hall, George F., xvi
Hall, Margaret: photographs of, xiv, xv, xxx; about typescript of memoir by, xv, xxi–xxv, xxviii, xxix, 172; biographical summary of, xvi–xxi, xxv; about photographic work by, xxvi–xxviii, 135, 136, 137, 138, 172; in Paris, 4, 12, 15–25, 31, 46, 95–97, 152, 162–163, 165–166; transatlantic passage, 5–10; in Bordeaux, 10, 14; comments on own photographic work, 10, 75, 121, 142, 145, 152, 153, 163, 164, 169; in Châlons-sur-Marne, 31–42, 47, 48–52, 60–66, 71–76, 81–90, 97–98, 101–103, 115–120, 121, 134, 139–141, 145–153, 154, 155–156, 162; in Écury (field hospital), 53–59 ; on reaction to Armistice in Châlons, 71–72; trips to Reims, 72–76, 120–121, 168; support for Armenian refugees, 80; on Wilson, 95, 96, 103, 148; trips to Verdun and surrounding area, 109–115, 141–142, 153, 154, 155; on American attitudes toward France, 116–117, 118, 127, 139, 145–149, 163; on American attitudes toward Germany, 116–117, 118; on her feelings toward Germany, 119–120, 129, 131, 168; trips to Argonne battlefields, 121–122, 154, 155; travels in occupied Germany, 126, 131–134; visits Nancy, 128; visits Metz, 128–129, 155; visits Strasbourg, 128–130; on women's rights, xviii, 130; visits Romagne, 143–145, 154–155; trip to Luxembourg, 153–154; visits Paris for celebrations, 155–156, 162–163, 165–166; trips to Ardennes, Somme, Picardy, and Pas de Calais sites, 162, 163–165, 167–168; trip to Belgium, 164, 168–169; trip to Soissons, 166; trip to Laon, 168; departs Paris for ship to New York, 169
Hall, Mary Elizabeth Coleman, xvi, xx, xxii, 12; Hall mentions, 9, 16, 32, 35, 37, 41, 131
Hall, Philip, Sr., xx, 27; Hall mentions, 9, 59; identified, 174
Hennocque, Edmond, 91; Hall mentions, 39, 87; identified, 174
Hennocque, Madeleine (daughter): Hall mentions, 35, 40, 42, 51, 88; identified, 174

Hennocque, Marie (mother), 91; Hall mentions, 35–36, 38, 39, 40, 41, 42, 49, 51, 87–88; identified, 174
Herrman (Herrmann), Mme. Joseph, 75, 168; identified, 175
Hindenburg, Paul von, 184; Hall mentions, 111; identified, 175
Hindenburg Line, 185, 187
Homburg (Saarland), 192; Hall visits, 131
hospital ("sanitary") trains, 24, 24–25, 37, 50, 89
hospitals, 2, 28; Hall visits Paris hospitals, 4, 18–20, 24, 25, 46; Hall rides in ambulances, 25, 101, 110, 143, 145; evacuation hospital near Châlons bombed, 41, 49, 50, 60; Hall describes field hospital in Écury, 54–59; Hall visits Corbineau Hospital, 65–66, 139; Hall visits hospital at La Veuve, 72, 102; Hall visits Glorieux Hospital, 109, 141, 192. *See also* hospital trains
Hotel de l'Arcade (Paris), 15–16, 194
Hotel Petrograd (Paris), 95, 195
Hoyt, Mary: Hall mentions, 19, 23; identified, 175
The Hundred Days (final Allied offensives on Western Front), xvi, xvii, xxv, 45–47, 187–188. *See also specific battle sites*; Meuse-Argonne Offensive

illnesses, xxii-xxiii, 9, 14–15, 25, 41, 62, 88, 89, 150, 160, 186, 188; at Écury field hospital, 54, 55–56, 58–59; among prisoners of war, 79, 81. *See also* injuries
injuries, xxii; shell-shock, 17, 30, 79, 102, 140; various, of wounded soldiers, 18–20, 24, 24–25, 50–51, 54, 59; sustained by canteen worker, 40, 49; and Versailles Treaty signing ceremony, 160

Jules (canteen orderly): Hall mentions, 149
Juvigny, 193; Hall visits, 166

King, Frances: Hall travels with, 141–145, 163–165, 168–169; Hall mentions, 166; identified, 175; photograph of, fig. 21
King, Frances Purvience (mother of Frances): Hall mentions, 163, 164, 165, 166; identified, 175
King, Katharine: Hall mentions, 164, 165; identified, 175

La Chapelle, ARC services at, 24–25
Lafayette, marquis de: Hall mentions, 88; identified, 175
Lansing, Emma S.: Hall mentions, 116, 152; identified, 175
Lansing, Katharine Ten Eyck: Hall mentions, 116, 152; identified, 175
Lansing, Robert: on Versailles Treaty, 160
Laon, 181, 192; Hall visits, 168
La Veuve, 72, 89, 102, 193
League of Nations, 157, 160; Hall on, 148
Leffingwell, Aimée: Hall mentions, 169; identified, 175–176
Leipzig War Crimes Trials, 159–160
Lens, 182, 185, 193; Hall visits, 164; photograph of, fig. 34
Leschetizky, Theodor, 172: Hall mentions, 6
Lille, 183, 193; Hall visits, 164
Lloyd George, David: Hall mentions, 156; identified, 175
Long Wy, 180, 193; Hall visits, 153–154; photographs of, fig. 26, fig. 27
Lost Battalion. *See* 77th Division
Ludendorff, Gen. Erich, 184. *See also* Ludendorff offensives
Ludendorff offensives (spring-summer 1918), xvi, 11, 43–44, 45, 186–187; Hall mentions, 35, 36
Luxembourg: Hall visits, 154

Madam Butterfly (opera by Puccini): Hall sees, 132
Madeleine Farm, 193; Hall visits, 143–144
Mansfield, Beatrice: Hall mentions, 120; identified, 175
Marne, Second Battle of the, 19, 24–25, 45, 187; First Battle of, 181
Matougues, 193; Hall visits, 151
McDermott, Miss: Hall mentions, 103; identified, 175
McKenzie, Kenneth: Hall mentions, 169; identified, 176
Metz, 193; Hall visits, 128, 155
Meuse-Argonne Offensive, 30, 46–47, 187–188; Hall records evidence of, 35, 37–38, 39–41, 48–52, 58, 59, 60, 62–63. *See also specific battle sites*
Mézières, 183, 193–194; attack on, day of Armistice, 72; Hall sees, 101
military police, 109, 128, 132, 133, 143, 154
military transport, 37, 47, 48, 52, 63, 66, 75, 90, 117, 118; on SS *Chicago*, 5–10; photograph of, 33

Millard, Shirley, 79
Mitchell, Anna V. S., xviii, xxiii, xxvi, 27, 30, 67, 80, 93, 94, 127; Hall mentions, 32, 116, 129, 141, 152; identified, 176
Mitchell, Frances: Hall mentions, 109; identified, 176
Mitchell, Mildred: identified, 176
Mitchell, Miss (unspecified), 49, 51, 53, 86
Moët-Chandon champagne works (Epernay): Hall visits, 152
the Môle (jetty in Zeebrugge): Hall visits, 168–169
Mont des Singes, 194; Hall visits, 167–168
Montfaucon, 187, 188, 194; photographs of, 104, fig. 30; Hall visits, 122, 154
Moore, Mrs.: Hall mentions, 16; identified, 176
Morgan, Anne, 4; identified, 176. *See also* American Committee for Devastated France (CARD)
Mort Homme, 183, 185, 194; Hall visits, 142; photograph of, 142

Nancy, 181, 187, 194; Hall visits, 128, 134
Neuilly-sur-Seine, 195; Hall visits hospital at, 18–19
Norton, Charles D., 3; description of Cantine des Deux Drapeaux, 29–30
Notre Dame-en-Vaux (Châlons-sur-Marne), 194; Hall attends services at, 64, 66, 86–87
Nott, Marjorie, xvii, xxiii, 27, 29, 124; Hall mentions, 31, 32, 51, 52, 53, 60, 116, 129, 130, 131; identified, 176–177
nuns: Hall mentions, 5, 8, 9
nurses: Hall mentions, 5, 6, 19, 24–25, 50, 51, 54, 55, 63, 89, 132, 133, 141, 151–152

Oblin, Mme: Hall mentions, 49, 65, 83, 121, 140, 151, 152, 162; travels with Hall, 121–122, 128–134, 155; identified, 177; photograph of, fig. 20
Olivier family, 77; Hall visits, 14–15; Hall sends money to, 169; identified, 177
O'Shaughnessy, Edith: description of Cantine des Deux Drapeaux, 29
Ostend (Belgium), 182, 186, 194; Hall visits, 169

Paris, 194–195; conditions during war, 11–13, 16, 17–18, 20, 24, 181,

186, 187; Hall in, 15–25, 95–97, 152, 162–163, 165–166; Versailles signing celebrations in, 162; Fourth of July celebration in, 163; Bastille Day celebration, 165–166. *See also individual sites*

"Paris Guns" (long-range cannon), xxii, 11, 16, 44, 167, 186

Paris Peace Conference, 157–159

peace: rumors of impending, 62, 63–64, 65, 68; Hall describes initial reactions to, 66; attempts at, before 1918, 67, 123; on Eastern Front before Armistice, 68; ambivalence about, 154, 156, 160, 161. *See also* Versailles Treaty

Pershing, John J., 44, 46, 185; Hall mentions, 102; identified, 177

Pétain, Philippe, 185; Hall mentions, 41, 51, 121; photograph of, 157; identified, 177

photography, 106, 159; Hall's, xxi, xxvi–xxviii, 10, 47, 73, 75, 121, 135–138, 141, 142, 145, 152, 153, 155, 162, 163, 164, 165, 169

Pilckem [Pilcom] Ridge, 183, 185, 195; Hall visits, 164

Pinon, 195; Hall visits,166, 168; Château de Pinon, 168, 190; photograph of, 93

Poincaré, Mme., 96

Poincaré, Raymond: Hall mentions, 41, 51; identified, 177

Pommeret, M., 151; identified, 177

Pond, Marie Brockway: Hall mentions, 39, 134; identified, 177

Porter, Catherine Rush: Hall mentions, 48, 51, 152; identified, 177

prima donna (of the 106th Infantry), xxiii, 140–141, 153

prisoners of war—Allied and American: military, 52, 78–79, 81–82, 83–84; civilian, 79, 85, 89–90

prisoners of war—German, 15, 20, 37–38, 39, 47, 48, 60, 71, 75, 82, 110, 145, 146, 155, 156; in prison camps and labor battalions, 108, 137, 144, 166–167, 168; Hall encounters, 15, 50–51, 57, 98, 102, 118, 119–120, 122, 140, 148; photographs of, fig. 13, fig. 31

R., Col., in Châlons: Hall mentions, 60

Read, Georgia: Hall mentions, 83; identified, 177

reconstruction and salvage: 4, 70, 78, 107–108, 111, 156, 164, 167, 168; ammunition retrieval and demolition, 111, 139, 144, 155, 163; body retrieval and burial, 137, 144, 155. *See also individual relief organizations*

Red Cross, 80, 132; International Committee of the Red Cross, 80; in occupied Germany, 133–134, 139. *See also* American Red Cross; hospitals; *specific facility locations*

refugees, 39, 77–80; Hall encounters, 14–15, 17, 23, 78, 82, 83, 149. *See also* prisoners of war

Reims, 50, 51, 139, 149, 181, 186, 187, 195; Hall visits, 72–76, 120–121, 168; and damage to Reims Cathedral, 73–74, 101, 182; photographs of, 74, fig. 14, fig. 16

relief organizations, 1–4, 5, 6, 9, 16, 28, 50, 57, 107, 112; Statement on the Coordination of Relief (1917), 1–2; American Relief Administration, 80, 107; and postwar refugees, 80; in Germany, 133–134. *See also* American Red Cross; American Committee for Devastated France; women, and relief work

Reynolds, Annie: Hall mentions, 103; identified, 177

"Richthofen circus" (squadron of German fighter pilot Manfred von Richthofen, the Red Baron): Hall mentions, 62

Romagne-sous-Montfaucon, 187, 195; Hall visits, 143–145, 154–155, 162; photographs of, fig. 31, fig. 32

Saint-Mihiel, 182, 195; Hall visits, 154

Saint-Mihiel offensive, xvii, 13, 18, 20, 45–46, 187

Saint-Quentin, 106, 181, 196; Hall visits, 164–165, 167

Salonica (Thessaloniki), Greece, 150

salvage work. *See* reconstruction

Schenk, Louisa: Hall mentions, 133; identified, 178

scorched-earth policies, 105–107. *See also* battle sites, devastation of

search work, 4; Hall mentions, 16, 19

Sedan, 181, 188, 196; Hall visits, 99–101

Selective Service Act (1917), 1

Senon. *See* Cenon

ships: *Mount Vernon*, xxii, 20; *Chicago*, 1, 5–10; *Lorraine*, 9, 10; *Brussels*, 169; *La France*, 169

Smiles (film), 109

Smith College Relief Unit, 3–4, 78, 107; Hall mentions, 6, 15, 17, 18, 22–23, 25

Soissons, 19, 24–25, 45, 98, 150, 181, 186, 187, 196; Hall visits, 166

soldiers, xxiv–xxvi; casualty rates of, 12, 44, 47, 136–137, 160; Hall describes, 32, 51, 57, 58, 59, 63, 64, 65, 76, 84, 86, 87, 110, 116, 119–120, 121, 146–147, 149, 162, 163. *See also* Cantine des Deux Drapeaux, Hall describes work at; illnesses; injuries; military transport; prisoners of war

Somme, Battle of the, 106, 184. *See also specific battle sites*

Somme Py, 196; Hall visits, 100, 152–153, 162

Souain, 196; Hall visits, 162

Souilly, 196; Hall visits, 142

souvenirs of war, 100, 139, 140; collecting, 74, 92–94, 98, 99, 107–108, 138, 144; soldier gives to Hall, 76, 87, 156

Steiner, Amy: Hall mentions, 167; identified, 178

Stenay, 181, 187, 197; Hall visits, 111–112

Strasbourg, 116, 197; Hall visits, 128, 129–130

strikes, 12, 123–124, 185

St. Wendel (Saarland), 197; Hall visits, 131, 132

submarine chasers, 121

Taft, Helen: Hall mentions, 168; identified, 178

Tahure, 196, 197; Hall visits, 162; photograph of, fig. 33

Thomas, M. Carey, 92; Hall mentions, 168; identified, 178

Tissier, Joseph-Marie (bishop of Châlons): Hall mentions, 41, 50, 64; identified, 178

Tours, canteen at, 134

trains. *See* hospital trains; military transport

Treaty of Versailles. *See* Versailles Treaty

Treves (Germany), 197; canteen at, 133–134

Trier. *See* Treves

Turkey, 66; Hall hears rumors of peace request, 63–64

Vanderbilt, Anne, 27, 28; Hall mentions, 16, 17; identified, 178

Varennes-en-Argonne, 187, 197; Hall visits, 142–143; photograph of Mme. Oblin at, fig. 20

Verdun, 84, 103, 106, 122, 136, 138, 139, 149, 181, 185, 197; Hall visits, 109–111, 112–115, 141, 142, 153,

154, 162; photographs of, 105, 110, fig. 28
Verdun, Battle of, 106, 136, 183, 184; Hall comments on, 142, 147, 153
Versailles Treaty, 124, 125, 127, 157–160; reparations, German, 107, 158, 159, 160; risk of continued conflict before signing, 154, 157–158; signing of, 160, 162
Vimy Ridge, 183, 185, 197; Hall visits, 163–164
Vinton, Warren Jay: Hall mentions, 169; identified, 178
Vouziers, 198; Hall visits, 100, 152

Wallace, Hugh Campbell: Hall mentions, 163; identified, 178
Watriss, Martha: Hall mentions, 133; identified, 178–179
Wharton, Edith, 13; description of Châlons-sur-Marne, 28
White, Amelia Elizabeth: Hall mentions, 64–65; identified, 179
Wiesbaden (Germany), 198; Hall visits, 131–132
Wilhelm (crown prince): Hall mentions, 71, 100, 111, 112, 155; identified, 179
Wilhelm II (kaiser): Hall mentions, 71, 112, 129, 168; identified, 179
Wilson, Edith: Hall mentions, 96, 102
Wilson, Margaret: Hall mentions, 96
Wilson, Woodrow, xxi, xxiv; on women's suffrage, xviii–xix; coordinates relief efforts, 1–2; and peace negotiations, 67–68, 69, 157, 158–159, 160; Hall mentions, 95, 96, 103, 148; identified, 179
women, wartime work of, xxiii, 12, 15, 161, 166; and relief work, 1, 2, 3–4, 6, 27, 29, 30, 50, 57, 107; German, rumors of fighting, 19. *See also* nurses
women's colleges: and American women's relief work, 3. *See also individual graduates*; Smith College Relief Unit
Worthington, Louisa Skinner: Hall mentions, 102, 132–133; identified, 179

Yale Unit: Hall mentions, 118
Young Men's Christian Association, 3, 28; Hall notes presence of, 5, 9, 16, 50, 110, 111, 133, 142–143, 147, 168; accommodations with, 15, 109, 120, 141, 143, 144–145, 162, 167
Young Women's Christian Association: accommodations with, 95

Ypres (Belgium), 198; battles at, 136, 137, 182, 183, 185; Hall visits, 164; photographs of, 164 (Cloth Hall), fig. 22

Zeebrugge (Belgium), 182, 186, 198; Hall visits, 168–169; photograph of, 169